Linux Operations and Administration

Alfred Basta

Dustin A. Finamore

Nadine Basta

Serge Palladino

COURSE TECHNOLOGY
CENGAGE Learning®

Australia • Brazil • Japan • Korea • Mexico • Singapore • Spain • United Kingdom • United States

COURSE TECHNOLOGY
CENGAGE Learning

Linux Operations and Administration
Alfred Basta, Dustin A. Finamore,
Nadine Basta, Serge Palladino

Vice President, Careers & Computing:
Dave Garza

Director of Learning Solutions:
Matthew Kane

Executive Editor: Steve Helba

Acquisitions Editor: Nick Lombardi

Managing Editor: Marah Bellegarde

Product Manager: Natalie Pashoukos

Development Editor: Lisa M. Lord

Editorial Assistant: Sarah Pickering

Vice President, Marketing:
Jennifer Ann Baker

Marketing Director: Deborah Yarnell

Associate Marketing Manager:
Erica Glisson

Production Director: Wendy A. Troeger

Production Manager: Andrew Crouth

Senior Content Project Manager:
Andrea Majot

Senior Art Director: Jack Pendleton

Technology Project Manager: Joe Pliss

Media Editor: William Overocker

For product information and technology assistance, contact us at
Cengage Learning Customer & Sales Support, 1-800-354-9706

For permission to use material from this text or product,
submit all requests online at **cengage.com/permissions**
Further permissions questions can be emailed to
permissionrequest@cengage.com

Library of Congress Control Number: 2012938293

ISBN-13: 978-1-1110-3530-3

ISBN-10: 1-1110-3530-X

Course Technology
20 Channel Center Street
Boston, MA 02210
USA

Cengage Learning is a leading provider of customized learning solutions with office locations around the globe, including Singapore, the United Kingdom, Australia, Mexico, Brazil, and Japan. Locate your local office at: **international.cengage.com/region**

Cengage Learning products are represented in Canada by Nelson Education, Ltd.

For your lifelong learning solutions, visit
www.cengage.com/coursetechnology

Purchase any of our products at your local college store or at our preferred online store **www.cengagebrain.com**

Visit our corporate website at **cengage.com**.

Printed in the United States of America
1 2 3 4 5 6 7 16 15 14 13 12

Brief Contents

Table of Contents

Introduction

Welcome to *Linux Operations and Administration*! This book is a detailed guide to using and administering the Linux operating system. From preinstallation to security auditing, this book gives you a comprehensive, in-depth explanation of Linux administrative skills and techniques as well as best practices in Linux administration. Along the way, you learn essential security strategies that IT professionals need to protect networks.

Linux was developed in 1991 by Linus Torvalds, and this stable, easy-to-use operating system is now available in many different distributions (versions). For this book, openSUSE was chosen because it's one of the most popular Linux distributions and the second largest on the market. It's more stable than many of its counterparts and is well supported by the openSUSE community. Like other Linux distributions, it's bundled with a wide variety of tools and packages and offers a choice of graphical desktop environments.

Intended Audience

This book introduces you to the Linux operating system (OS) by using virtual machines. VMware Player has been used to write all activities and projects to make sure everyone can do them, regardless of hardware differences. In addition, virtual machines enable you to run more than one OS on the same computer without having to set up complicated dual-boot procedures or invest in removable hard drives for separate OSs. No previous knowledge of Linux is assumed, and this book has been written to accommodate readers with varying degrees of technical background.

Chapter Descriptions

Here's a summary of the topics covered in each chapter of this book:

- **Chapter 1**, "Introduction to the Linux Operating System," introduces the functions of an operating system and gives you an overview of openSUSE, the Linux architecture, and Linux components, including the kernel, desktop environment, and file structure. This chapter also summarizes Linux command shells.

- **Chapter 2**, "Installing OpenSUSE," prepares you for the openSUSE installation by explaining installation phases and options. It introduces virtualization software and walks you through the steps for installing VMware Player to use for this book's hands-on activities. This chapter also introduces YaST, a GUI administration utility in openSUSE, and gives you an overview of features in the GNOME and KDE desktop environments.

- **Chapter 3**, "Managing Files and Directories," describes the Linux directory structure and the Filesystem Hierarchy Standard, which specifies requirements for file and directory placement that are used by software developers. You also learn basic commands for navigating the Linux directory structure, viewing documentation (man pages), and creating hard and symbolic links.

- **Chapter 4**, "Creating and Editing Files with Text Editors," covers the GUI text editors in openSUSE Linux—KWrite and gedit—and the command-line text editor vim. You learn about vim's three modes, key combinations for performing certain tasks, and extended mode commands for saving text files and exiting the vim editor.

- **Chapter 5**, "Creating Shell Scripts and Displaying File Contents," walks you through creating shell scripts with the vim text editor. This chapter also explains using Linux file permissions, using variables and conditions in scripts, and displaying the contents of scripts and text files.

- **Chapter 6**, "Managing Data: Backup and Recovery Processes," focuses on system backups and command-line utilities for creating archives and compressing files. You also learn how to schedule backups with user and system cron tables.

- **Chapter 7**, "Managing Users and Groups," explains configuration files used for authentication and database files containing user account information. You also learn how to create and modify user and group accounts at the command line and manage user and group accounts in YaST.

- **Chapter 8**, "Network Communications," explains how to configure a Linux system to communicate on a network. This chapter introduces TCP/IP, explains the important protocols at each layer of the TCP/IP model, and describes how to work with IP addresses. You also learn command-line utilities for checking TCP/IP configuration and network connectivity.

- **Chapter 9**, "Installing Software Packages," covers using the RPM utility to install, query, update, and remove software. You also learn how to work with software packages in YaST.

- **Chapter 10**, "Apache Web Server," introduces you to the most widely used Web server on the Internet. It's the most secure, efficient, and extensible Web server on the market. You learn how to install and configure a Web server with GUI or command-line utilities and create an HTML Web page for the Apache Web server you configure.

- **Chapter 11**, "Domain Name System," explains how to configure a Linux system to be a DNS server. This chapter covers hostname–to–IP address resolution, name servers, forwarders, caching, top-level domains, resource records, and zones. You also learn how to install and configure BIND and check a DNS server's status from the command line.

- **Chapter 12,** "Configuring a Mail Server," explains the modular e-mail architecture in Linux and the role of mail transfer agents and mail user agents. This chapter also walks you through configuring a Linux mail server in YaST.

- **Chapter 13,** "Working with the Network File System," explains how to use NFS, how to export and import directories, and how to control access to the NFS server in YaST. You also learn about Remote Procedure Calls (RPC) and editing NFS configuration files.

- **Chapter 14,** "Planning for a Linux Installation," describes how to analyze system components before installing Linux. It gives you an overview of useful hardware information, including the processor, memory, nonvolatile storage devices, and video cards. You also learn how to create a preinstallation checklist and use an automated method to install openSUSE.

- **Chapter 15,** "Linux File System Management and Administration," explores advanced Linux file system topics and explains how to administer the file system at the command line. You also learn how to perform file system management tasks with command-line utilities and YaST.

- **Chapter 16,** "Managing Resources in Linux," explains how to configure X Window with Linux utilities and use a display manager in GNOME and KDE. You also learn command-line utilities for managing the root account and working with disk quotas.

- **Chapter 17,** "Networking in a Linux Environment," describes features of the Network Information Service (NIS) and installing and configuring an NIS server and client. You also learn how to configure a local printer queue and install and configure a DHCP server.

- **Chapter 18,** "Using Samba for Interoperating Linux and Windows," discusses how to operate in a multi-OS environment with Samba. You learn how to configure a Samba server at the command line, in YaST, and with a Web-based utility.

- **Chapter 19,** "Securing Linux," discusses types of server attacks and describes system security measures, including shutting down nonessential services. You also learn how to secure Web servers, configure Linux-based firewalls, and secure data from the command line.

- **Chapter 20,** "Advanced Linux Administration," explains how to manage kernel modules and how to load and configure the Linux kernel. In addition, you learn procedures for system monitoring, performance tuning, and network problem solving and troubleshooting.

Features

To help you understand Linux operations and administration, this book includes many features designed to enhance your learning experience:

- *Chapter objectives*—Each chapter begins with a comprehensive list of the concepts to be mastered. This list gives you a quick reference to the chapter's contents and serves as a useful study aid.

- *Figures and tables*—Numerous screenshots show you how to use Linux GUI and command-line tools and help you understand common installation and management procedures. In addition, a variety of diagrams aid you in visualizing important concepts. Tables are used throughout the book to organize information and describe command options in an easy-to-grasp manner.

- *Hands-on activities*—One of the best ways to reinforce learning is to practice using the many tools Linux system administrators use. Hands-on activities are interspersed throughout each chapter to give you practice in applying what you have learned.

- *Chapter summary*—Each chapter ends with a summary of the concepts introduced in the chapter. These summaries are a helpful way to review the material covered in each chapter.

- *Key terms*—All terms in the chapter introduced with bold text are gathered together in the key terms list at the end of the chapter, with full definitions for each term. This list is a useful reference.

- *Review questions*—The end-of-chapter assessment begins with review questions that reinforce the main concepts and techniques covered in each chapter. Answering these questions helps ensure that you have mastered the chapter's objectives.

- *Case projects*—Each chapter closes with one or more case projects that help you evaluate and apply the material you have learned. To complete these projects, you must draw on real-world common sense as well as your knowledge of the technical topics covered to that point in the book. These projects often require conducting research or applying your knowledge to a hypothetical company.

- *DVD*—The DVD accompanying this book contains openSUSE Linux 11.2 that you can install on a virtual machine you set up.

Text and Graphic Conventions

Additional information has been added to this book to help you understand what's being discussed in the chapter. Icons throughout the book alert you to these additional materials:

The Note icon draws your attention to additional helpful material related to the subject being covered.

Tips offer extra information on resources and how to solve problems.

Caution icons warn you about potential mistakes or problems and explain how to avoid them.

Each hands-on activity in this book is preceded by the Activity icon.

Case Projects icons mark end-of-chapter case projects, which are scenario-based or research assignments that ask you to apply what you have learned.

Instructor Resources

The following supplemental materials are available when this book is used in a classroom setting. All the supplements are provided to instructors on a single CD, called the Instructor Resources CD (ISBN 9781111035310), or can be downloaded from *www.cengage.com*.

- *Electronic instructor's manual*—The instructor's manual that accompanies this book includes additional instructional material to assist in class preparation, including suggestions for classroom activities, discussion topics, and additional activities.

- *Solutions*—Instructor resources include solutions to all end-of-chapter material, including review questions, hands-on activities, and case projects.

- *ExamView*—This book is accompanied by ExamView, a powerful testing software package that allows instructors to create and administer printed, computer (LAN-based), and Internet exams. ExamView includes hundreds of questions that correspond to the topics covered in this book, enabling students to generate detailed study guides that include page references for further review. The computer-based and Internet testing components allow students to take exams at their computers and save instructors time by grading each exam automatically.

- *PowerPoint presentations*—This book comes with Microsoft PowerPoint slides for each chapter. They're included as a teaching aid for classroom presentation, to make available to students on the network for chapter review, or to be printed for classroom distribution. Instructors, please feel free to add your own slides for additional topics you introduce to the class.

- *Figure and table files*—All figures and tables in the book are reproduced on the Instructor Resources CD. Similar to the PowerPoint presentations, they're included as a teaching aid for classroom presentation, to make available to students for review, or to be printed for classroom distribution.

Lab Requirements

The hands-on activities in this book help you apply what you have learned in each chapter. They're designed for classroom-led or self-paced study. Although this book's DVD includes openSUSE Linux 11.2, most activities will work with later openSUSE versions as well as other Linux distributions, such as Fedora and Ubuntu. Just keep in mind that steps and file locations are likely to vary.

In Chapter 2, you download and install VMware Player so that you can install openSUSE Linux in a virtual machine, which allows you to run Linux separately from the OS running on your desktop. The following list summarizes hardware requirements for running openSUSE 11.2. If your computer meets these requirements, it has the necessary hardware to run VMware Player:

- Processor: Standard x86-compatible or x86-64 with Intel VT or AMD-V compatible PC with a processor speed of 1.3 GHz or faster

- Memory: 1 GB RAM (2 GB recommended)

- Hard disk: At least 3 GB available disk space (with 1 GB free space for each guest OS you run)

About the Authors

Alfred Basta is a professor of mathematics, cryptology, and information security. He's a member of the editorial board for the *Norwich University Journal of Information Assurance* and conducts speaking engagements on Internet security and networking.

Dustin A. Finamore has 14 years of experience with the United States Air Force, where he developed and taught UNIX security and UNIX advanced administration courses. As an airman, he installed, configured, and maintained intelligence computer systems worldwide. He's a graduate of Bellevue University and is currently an instructor at Virginia College, where he teaches Linux courses, among others.

Nadine Basta, MS, is a professor of computer science, information technology, and security. In addition to her academic degrees, Nadine holds many certifications, such as MCSE, MSDBA, CCDP, NCSE, NCTE, and CCA. She is also a security consultant and auditor, and she combines strong in-the-field experience with her academic background.

Acknowledgements

Dustin Finamore: I would like to thank my editor, Lisa Lord, for all the hard work, long hours, and patience she had with me while completing this project. You were amazing to work with—thank you! I would also like to thank my project manager, Natalie Pashoukos, for her wisdom and kindness. In addition, thank you to the copyeditor, Christine Clark; the proofreader, Suzanne Huizenga; and the testing expertise of GreenPen Quality Assurance. Finally, I must thank Serge Palladino, who contributed so much to this book by revising and polishing many chapters and by reviewing page proofs to make sure everything was accurate.

I'd also like to thank the reviewers for their helpful feedback: Dean Farwood, Keith Morneau, James Rust, and L. Ward Ulmer.

I welcome you to e-mail me your comments, questions, and suggestions for the next edition of this book at *dustin.finamore@vconline.edu*.

Dedication

To my wife, Nadine: It is the continuing symphony of your loving thoughts, caring actions, and continuous support that stands out as the song of my life.

To our daughter, Rebecca, and our son, Stavros: Fix your hearts upon God, and love Him with all your strength, for without this no one can be saved or be of any worth. Develop in yourselves an urge for a life of high and noble values. You are like little birds that will soon spread your wings and fly.

To my mother: You are a never-ending melody of goodness and kindness. You are without equal in this world.

And to the memory of my father: If one is weighed by the gifts one gives, your values given are beyond estimation.

—Alfred Basta

To my mom, who always worried about my health and constantly encouraged me; although she despises computers, she eagerly read and commented on all the chapters I sent her. Most important, to my two sons, Isaiah and Elijah, and my two daughters, Jasmine and Chloe: The four of you are a perpetual source of friendship, and I want to thank you for giving me the greatest gift of all—your faith in me.

—Dustin Finamore

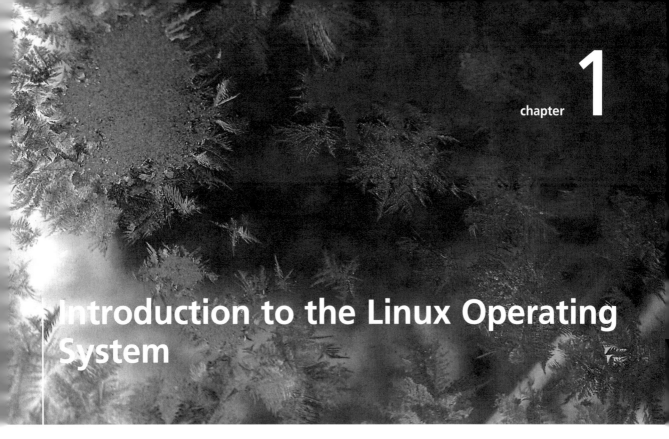

## chapter 1

Introduction to the Linux Operating System

After reading this chapter and completing the exercises, you will be able to:

- Summarize the functions of an operating system
- Identify key historical points in the development of Linux
- Explain the components of the Linux architecture and features of the operating system

Linux is a multitasking, multiuser operating system that's distributed free. In this chapter, you learn about the functions of an operating system before learning about the development of Linux. Next, you get an overview of openSUSE, the Linux version you learn in this book, and examine the Linux architecture and its components, including the kernel, desktop environment, and file structure. This chapter also gives you an overview of the main features of Linux as well as a summary of command shells available in Linux.

Overview of Operating System Functions

Before you install openSUSE and explore its features, you need to know a little more about this operating system. Linux is a practical alternative to the more costly Windows and Macintosh operating systems. Most current Linux versions include a graphical desktop, a Web browser, e-mail, sound, video, and just about any other feature that Windows has to offer. This section gives you an overview of the functions in any operating system so that you can better understand how they work in Linux.

Software Licensing Agreements

To fully grasp the Linux operating system—or any operating system, for that matter—you need a basic understanding of software licensing agreements. When you install software you have purchased, do you actually read the licensing agreement before clicking "I Accept"? Few people do. If you read a software licensing agreement carefully, you'll discover that you don't actually own the software. Instead, you're granted a license to use it. If you buy a single copy of Windows 7, for example, you can't load it on every computer in your house. Table 1-1 explains some licensing terms you should be familiar with.

Table 1-1 Licensing agreement terms

Term	Description
Open source	The main characteristic of open-source software is that its source code is published with the software. For instance, if Coca-Cola were open source, it would post the formula on the Internet (but don't hold your breath waiting for this to happen!). Because the source code is included, users can modify and redistribute open-source software.
Closed source	The source code isn't published with the software, and users can't legally modify it. Windows is an example of closed-source software.
Freeware	This software is free, but the author doesn't have to publish the source code.
Shareware	This software is also free but on a trial basis. Users have access to it for only a limited time before it expires.

All Linux versions are open source. A program is **open source** when it's distributed with its source code so that users can view or modify it. **Source code** is simply the instructions defining how a program works. The Linux kernel was published under the General Public License (GPL), which you learn about later in "The History of Linux."

Activity 1-1: Reviewing Licensing Agreements

Time Required: 90 minutes

Objective: Learn how the General Public License compares with other software licensing agreements.

Description: Most users don't bother to read licensing agreements when they're installing software. In this activity, you examine the licensing agreement of an application of your choice and compare it with the GPL to better understand what's involved in licensing software.

1. Start your Web browser, and go to **www.gnu.org/licenses/gpl.html**.

2. Read through the GPL to get a better understanding of the licensing terms and conditions.

3. Click the **A Quick Guide to GPLv3** link at the top. This guide is a good overview of the GPL's benefits.

4. Choose an application installed on your computer and search for its licensing agreement on the Internet. For instance, if your Web browser is Firefox, type **Firefox licensing agreement** in a search engine, such as Google or Bing.

5. Read the licensing agreement and compare it with the GPL.

6. When you're finished, exit your Web browser and be ready to discuss your findings with the class.

Functions of an Operating System

Turning on your computer is as automatic as switching on a light; you expect it to come on immediately, but you probably don't know exactly how it works. In addition, you know you can perform many tasks at the same time. You can surf the Web, peruse your music library, reminisce over family photos, and join a massive multiplayer online game, even if you don't know the computer's language of binary 1s and 0s. You can do all this because of the **operating system (OS)**, which is essentially software that's designed to control hardware. An OS also provides an interface between computer hardware and the software you use. At the core of an OS is the kernel, which performs the most basic computing functions. You might be familiar with processors, memory, keyboards, and DVD-ROM drives, but without the kernel, you would have no way to communicate with these devices. Every OS is unique in some way. Table 1-2 summarizes some common OSs.

Table 1-2 Features of common operating systems

Operating systems	Description
Windows 7	Offers new features not available with older versions of Windows, such as improved Backup and Restore, and new security features, such as Clean System for eliminating suspicious software. Windows 7 was also designed with performance improvements, including better memory use.
Mac OS X	This graphical OS is built on a UNIX foundation and was designed to be easy to learn and use.
Linux	Linux was developed under the GNU General Public License by Linus Torvalds. Developers around the world have helped add to the Linux kernel.
openSUSE	openSUSE is a free Linux version for PCs, laptops, or servers. In this book, you focus on openSUSE.

After you power on your computer, what is the OS doing? Most OSs include the following functions:

- *User interface*—For people to communicate or interact with machines, they need a user interface, and the efficiency of a user interface has an effect on how popular the OS is. For instance, if you had to type a long sequence of random numbers to check your e-mail, you'd find another e-mail interface quickly. Two common interfaces are the graphical user interface (GUI) and the command-line interface (CLI). A GUI enables users to interact with computers by using graphical elements, such as menus and buttons. A command-line interface, on the other hand, is text based, so users communicate with the computer by typing commands.

- *File systems*—What purpose would a computer have if users had no way to access their data? File systems have changed throughout the years, but their purpose remains the same: giving users a way to find and access their files. Chapter 3 covers file systems.

- *Device drivers*—An OS is responsible for communicating with computer devices, such as disk drives and keyboards. For this communication to take place, each hardware device, such as a printer or video card, must have its own driver so that the OS can detect it. Most OSs detect hardware automatically, but sometimes you have to install a specific device driver so that the OS can recognize a device.

- *System services*—Every time you run an application, the OS starts a process, called a "system service," to handle it. The process runs in the background and carries out application-related tasks. Some system services start automatically when a computer is booted, such as the Network Service in Linux, which handles all network interfaces.

History of Linux

Before you learn about Linus Torvalds and the creation of Linux, a little background on American Telephone & Telegraph (AT&T) is helpful to lay the foundation. In the early 1900s, AT&T was the only phone company. According to the AT&T Web site, this monopoly was valid because the communication technology was new, and to operate efficiently, AT&T needed to provide universal service. The government agreed, so for years, AT&T dominated the market. In fact, by 1969, 90% of American homes had AT&T phone service.

AT&T's history is documented on its Web site, along with some fascinating photos illustrating historical moments. If you're interested in learning more, visit *www.corp.att.com/history/history3.html*.

Throughout the 20th century, AT&T testing and research were conducted at Bell Laboratories. In 1969, AT&T expanded beyond phone service when Dennis Ritchie and Ken Thompson, two Bell employees, created the UNIX operating system. It was a huge hit in the computer world, but because the government had started investigating AT&T's powerful monopoly, AT&T decided not to sell UNIX. Because UNIX was available free, many professors began using it for testing and research in university labs.

However, by the early 1980s, AT&T realized UNIX's moneymaking potential and decided to license it and charge institutions a hefty price to use it. It didn't take long for people to protest this licensing. For example, Richard Stallman created the GNU Project and developed the GPL. The main idea behind the license stems from Stallman's philosophy that software should be free, by which he meant having the freedom to change the source code. The GPL states the following:

- You can use, view, and change the source code.
- You are able to redistribute the software and sell it for a profit.
- If you decide to sell the software, you must make the source code available.

You can view the GPL at *www.gnu.org/licenses/gpl.html*.

Another example is Andrew Tanenbaum, a professor who used UNIX to teach his students how to use an OS. After UNIX began requiring a license, Tanenbaum had to find a new way to teach this topic, so in 1987, he created his own OS called MINIX. This UNIX-like OS was popular in the computer community, and as with the GNU Project, the source code was made available to everybody. The main difference between the MINIX license and the GPL was that MINIX users could only view the source code; they couldn't change it.

A few years after MINIX's release, Linus Torvalds, a student, stepped up to make his own changes. In 1991, he created his own kernel, called the Linux kernel. He licensed it through the GPL, which made the source code available to the public. Since 1991, Linux has continued development and is currently one of the fastest growing OSs. Many different versions (distributions) of Linux are available, such as the following:

- Red Hat (*www.redhat.com*)
- Ubuntu (*www.ubuntu.com*)
- Debian (*www.debian.org*)
- PCLinuxOS (*http://pclinuxos.com*)
- FreeBSD (*www.freebsd.org*)
- openSUSE (*www.novell.com/linux*)

Table 1-3 gives you a short version of the Linux timeline.

Table 1-3 Linux timeline

Date	Event
1907	AT&T president, Theodore Vail, formulated the principle behind the company's monopoly.
1913	U.S. government agreed to the AT&T monopoly.
1965	MIT, General Electric, and Bell Labs created the OS called Multiplexed Information and Computing Service (MULTICS), a time-sharing OS that used page-segmented storage. Bell Labs abandoned the project in 1969.
1969	Dennis Ritchie and Ken Thompson created UNIX.

Table 1-3 Linux timeline (*continued*)

Date	Event
1980s	AT&T decided to license UNIX and sell it for a profit.
1983	Richard Stallman announced the GNU Project.
1989	Richard Stallman published the GPL.
1991	Linus Torvalds wrote the Linux kernel.

Overview of SUSE

SUSE was developed in Germany in 1992 by Hubert Mantel, Burchard Steinbild, Roland Dyroff, and Thomas Fehr. The name "SUSE" is an acronym for "Software und System Entwicklung" (Software and System Development). It became a top Linux seller in Europe and was eventually sold to Novell for $210 million. Novell is a multinational software and services corporation that provides support to more than 50,000 companies in 43 countries. The pronunciation of SUSE is debatable. Some system engineers pronounce it "Susie"; others pronounce it "Seuss," as in Dr. Seuss. You can hear more variations when viewing YouTube videos on SUSE. However, Ron Hovsepian, Novell's president and CEO, can be heard pronouncing it "Soo-Sa."

OpenSUSE comes with the Linux kernel and the latest versions of two desktop environments: KDE and GNOME. Both desktop environments come with Mozilla Firefox for Web browsing and OpenOffice.org for word-processing, spreadsheet, and presentation software. OpenSUSE also includes Yet another Setup Tool (YaST), a configuration tool that enables administrators to install and manage software. You use YaST in many of this book's activities.

Linux Architecture

Linux is a modular system, which means all its components are separate from one another. This design makes it possible for different teams to develop components that don't affect one another. For instance, one team might update the kernel, and another team might create applications. In fact, you can create applications that meet your own needs or even contribute to the Linux kernel. A Linux distribution, such as openSUSE 11.2, consists of all the Linux components put together and released as one OS. Figure 1-1 shows components of the Linux architecture.

The **kernel**, the core of the OS, manages hardware, such as disk drives and memory. The **shell** is an interface that accepts and translates user input so that the kernel can process it. **Daemons** are programs that run in the background independently of the user, meaning the user doesn't start them. Windows has the same programs, but they're called services.

Daemons are pronouced "dee-mons." Some users are uncomfortable with this term and call them "day-mons" or just services. The http daemon (httpd) is an example of an Apache Web Server daemon that runs in the background waiting to serve Web pages on request. You learn more about Apache Web Server in Chapter 10.

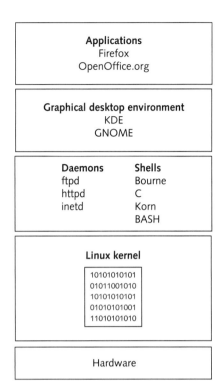

Figure 1-1 Components of the Linux architecture
© Cengage Learning 2013

Applications are programs that require an OS to run and give users a specific function, such as word-processing programs, media players, and so forth. You use a desktop environment to access applications. Now that you know the major components of Linux, you can explore them in more detail in the following sections.

Kernel

The Linux kernel is licensed under the GPL, which allows public access to the source code. You can think of it as a resource manager. Two major resources it manages are processes and memory. Linux, like most current OSs, can perform multiple processes at the same time. In later chapters, you examine some Linux processes, but for now, you just need to know that everything Linux does is considered a process. A **process** is a program the kernel launches into memory for the purpose of performing specific tasks. Because you have more processes running than you have CPUs, the kernel needs a way to assign processes to CPUs. To do this, it uses a scheduling algorithm, but users see it as simultaneous execution of multiple processes.

Another resource the kernel manages is memory. **Random access memory (RAM)** is the storage space where a computer reads and writes data. In this way, the CPU doesn't have to access the hard drive every time it needs to read or write data, which would slow down processes considerably. RAM is considered "volatile" storage because data stored there is erased when the computer shuts down. The Linux kernel also supports **demand paging**, which makes it possible to load only needed sections of a program into RAM. For instance, you might need to run a query with a database, but there's no need to load the entire database into RAM. With demand paging, the Linux kernel is able to load only the database records you need for the query into RAM.

Linux Desktop Environments

Two desktop environments available in openSUSE are K Desktop Environment (KDE) and GNU Network Object Model Environment (GNOME). They're very similar, offering nearly the same functions. They differ mainly in the programming language used to write them. KDE is written in the C++ programming language, and GNOME is written in the C programming language. Figures 1-2 and 1-3 show these two GUI environments.

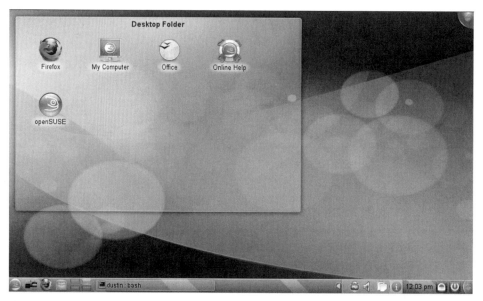

Figure 1-2 The KDE interface in openSUSE
Source: openSUSE

Linux File Structure

Linux has a file system organized in a hierarchical, treelike structure. The highest point in the file structure is the root directory, indicated with the / symbol. Everything in Linux is considered a file. Even the CD/DVD-ROM drive is represented as a file, located under the root directory. Linux has three kinds of files: device files, "regular" files, and directory files. A **device file** is a special file stored in the /dev directory that represents a hardware device on the system, such as a CD-ROM drive or hard drive. Regular files are simply files containing data, such as text files or executable files. A **directory file** is like a folder in Windows, and it can contain files and other directories; a directory inside another directory is sometimes referred to as a "subdirectory."

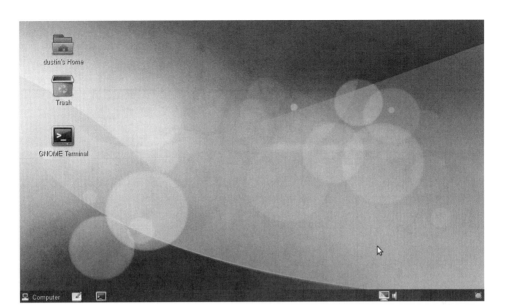

Figure 1-3 The GNOME interface in openSUSE
Source: openSUSE

Features of Linux

Every Linux kernel offers the following features:

- *Multiuser*—The **multiuser** feature enables multiple users to log on to a single computer at the same time. You might be picturing several people hovering over one computer, but that's not how multiuser systems work. Instead, a company might designate a server, locked in a separate room as a security measure, as the multiuser system, and users could log on to it via their desktop computers. One advantage of having a multiuser system is eliminating the need to back up multiple computers. If all data and applications are on a server, for instance, the computer staff needs to secure and back up only that system. The disadvantage of a multiuser system is that it creates a single point of failure. If the multiuser system goes down, users can't do their work. Typical home users rarely need a multiuser system.

- *Multitasking*—A process (or task) is associated with every running program. For example, when you start the Firefox Web browser, a process associated with this program starts running. With **multitasking**, multiple processes can run simultaneously, so you can browse the Web, print a document, and check your e-mail, all at the same time. In **preemptive multitasking**, the scheduler (a component of the Linux kernel) decides when a process stops and another process starts. It assigns a certain amount of time to each process, which is referred to as "timesharing." The scheduler starts high-priority processes sooner, giving them more time. Users don't see this timesharing or notice interruptions in processes because the scheduler resumes stopped processes rapidly.

- *Networking connectivity*—Linux comes with Transmission Control Protocol/Internet Protocol (TCP/IP), an internationally accepted set of rules for connecting computers to the Internet and most other networks. Chapter 8 covers networking features in more detail, but for now, just know that openSUSE includes everything needed to connect to your home network and access the Internet.

- *Security*—You'll hear this saying in almost every office: The only safe computer is one that's disconnected, turned off, and buried. In reality, of course, users need to access files, check their e-mail, and run applications securely over the network. Home users should be able to store personal information, such as photos, e-mails, and financial documents, in a secure environment. The nature of open-source software encourages discovering and reporting security vulnerabilities, often even before an OS is hacked. Linux offers basic security features, such as login and password authentication, file ownership, and permissions and has a firewall for protecting network resources from users outside the network.

You learn about configuring firewalls in Chapter 19.

Command Shells Available in Linux

As mentioned, a shell is the command-line interface between users and the kernel. Like most Linux distributions, openSUSE comes with a GUI, but sometimes administrators need to use a shell for more advanced configuration tasks. Some shells include a history function, which is useful for remembering commands a user typed previously. The number of commands remembered varies from shell to shell, but the default is 1000. Table 1-4 summarizes common Linux shells, all of which are stored in the /bin directory.

This section gives you an overview of the shells available in Linux. Instructions on how to install openSUSE and navigate its file structure are in Chapter 2.

Table 1-4 Common shells in Linux

Shell	Executable filename	Description
Bourne	sh	The original UNIX shell developed in 1977 by Stephen Bourne at Bell Laboratories. This shell, distributed with all UNIX systems, has no history function.
C	csh	Written by Bill Joy at the University of California at Berkeley in 1978 to have an interface similar to the C language. Although it has a history function, it's incompatible with the Bourne shell, so it never really caught on.
Korn	ksh	Written by Dave Korn at Bell Laboratories to combine the best of the C and Bourne shells. It has a history function and enables users to edit the history file while viewing it.
BASH	bash	Bourne Again (BASH) is the default shell in openSUSE and most other Linux distributions. Part of the Free Software Foundation's GNU Projects, it has a history function that can also be used to remember commands entered in previous sessions as well as the current session.

Chapter Summary

- All Linux distributions are open source and licensed under the General Public License (GPL), which gives users the legal right to use, view, and change the source code.

- Linux distributions, such as openSUSE, come with a graphical desktop environment, a Web browser, e-mail, sound, video, networking capability, and many other features that are comparable with rival operating systems, such as Windows and Mac OS.

- An operating system is software designed to control computer hardware so that users and applications can make use of it. All operating systems are responsible for the user interface, file system, device drivers, and system services.

- At the core of the Linux operating system is the kernel, which performs the most basic computing functions.

- The two main user interfaces are the graphical user interface (GUI) and command-line interface.

- The UNIX OS led to the creation of the GNU Project, a protest against licensing UNIX as a for-profit software product.

- The Linux architecture consists of the kernel, shell, applications, GUI, and desktop environment.

- KDE (written in C++) and GNOME (written in C) are the two desktop environments that come with openSUSE.

- The Linux file system is organized in a hierarchical, treelike structure. The highest point in this file system is the root (/) directory.

- Everything in Linux is considered a file, including users, disk drives, and directories.

- The Linux kernel offers features such as multiuser, multitasking, networking connectivity, and security.

- A shell is a command-line interface between users and the kernel. BASH is the default shell in most Linux distributions.

Key Terms

daemons Programs that run in the background independently of the user. Typically, a daemon waits for specific system activity and then acts accordingly.

demand paging A feature that makes it possible to load only the needed sections of a program into RAM. *See also* random access memory (RAM).

device file A file in the /dev directory that represents a hardware device.

directory file A file that can contain regular files and other directory files.

kernel The core of an operating system; performs the most basic computing functions.

multitasking A feature that allows running multiple processes at the same time.

multiuser A feature that enables multiple users to log on to a computer at the same time.

open source   A licensing agreement term describing software that's distributed free with its source code so that users can view or modify it.

operating system (OS)   Software designed to control computer hardware so that users and applications can make use of it.

preemptive multitasking   A method of multitasking in which the scheduler decides when a process stops and another process starts. *See also* multitasking.

process   A program the kernel launches into memory for the purpose of performing specific tasks. *See also* kernel.

random access memory (RAM)   The volatile storage space where a computer can read and write data.

shell   A command-line interface between users and the kernel. *See also* kernel.

source code   A set of instructions defining how a program works.

Review Questions

1. The Linux kernel is part of the operating system. True or False?

2. What do users need to communicate with computers?
    a. A graphics card
    b. A basic knowledge of the computer's language
    c. An interface
    d. All of the above

3. Most Linux distributions have a GUI, so a command-line interface isn't needed. True or False?

4. What type of file does each piece of hardware need for the kernel to communicate with it?
    a. Regular file
    b. Device driver
    c. Directory file
    d. Kernel file

5. Users must install all device drivers manually. True or False?

6. Who created the Linux kernel?
    a. Richard Stallman
    b. Linus Torvalds
    c. Andrew Tanenbaum
    d. Ken Thompson

7. Explain the main difference between the MINIX license and the GPL.

8. What's the main difference between the KDE and GNOME desktop environments?

9. What's the highest point in the Linux file structure?

   a. /dev

   b. /

   c. /etc

   d. /home

10. Which of the following is considered a directory file?

    a. A pointer to a device driver

    b. A file containing other files

    c. An executable file

    d. The CD-ROM drive

11. Which of the following is considered a device file?

    a. A CD-ROM drive

    b. An executable file

    c. A file containing other files

    d. A file pointing to the root directory

12. What OS feature enables you to browse the Web while listening to music on your computer?

    a. Multiuser

    b. Networking connectivity

    c. Kernel

    d. Multitasking

13. What OS feature enables an entire office of employees to log on to a single system?

    a. Multiuser

    b. Networking connectivity

    c. Kernel

    d. Multitasking

14. What's the default shell in openSUSE?

    a. Bourne

    b. C

    c. BASH

    d. Korn

15. Which of the following shells has a history function? (Choose all that apply.)

    a. Bourne

    b. C

    c. BASH

    d. Korn

Case Projects

CASE PROJECTS

Case Project 1-1: East Coast Career College Contemplates Migrating from Windows to Linux

East Coast Career College is a private educational institution offering associate degrees and diploma courses at its campuses along the East Coast. Dr. Pete Thompson, president of the main campus in Virginia Beach, has just received word that a few departments need to cut spending for the school to stay afloat. Currently, the Virginia campus has five computer labs, and each lab has 15 Dell desktop computers. These computers are Pentium 4 1.8 GHz with Windows XP installed. The school had planned to upgrade to Windows 7, but after further research realized all computers would have to be replaced with higher-end models that could handle Windows 7. Dr. Thompson hired you as a computer consultant to come up with a practical alternative to the Windows 7 upgrade. He told you he heard about an open-source operating system called Linux and recommended you start there on your research. He wants to know whether students will still be able to perform all the tasks they need to do (for example, access the file server, write documents, create presentations, and so forth) and whether the learning curve will be too steep for them. Write a one- to two-page memo on the migration from Windows to Linux, making sure you address all Dr. Thompson's concerns.

## chapter 2

Installing OpenSUSE

After reading this chapter and completing the exercises, you will be able to:

- Check your system configuration to determine whether it meets openSUSE installation requirements
- Describe the benefits of installing an OS on a virtual machine
- Summarize the installation phases in openSUSE
- Describe features of the GNOME desktop environment
- Describe features of the KDE desktop environment

The best way to learn the Linux operating system is to get some hands-on experience. This chapter prepares you for installing openSUSE by explaining installation phases and options in YaST, but going through the actual steps is an important foundation for the rest of the book.

First, you review the minimum hardware requirements for installing openSUSE. Virtualization software makes installing Linux on a Windows system easy, and in this chapter, you're introduced to the benefits of virtual machines and see how to install VMware Player as your virtualization software for this book's hands-on activities. Next, you install openSUSE on a virtual machine, and then explore the features of the GNOME and KDE desktop environments to prepare you for upcoming chapters.

Checking Your System Configuration

OpenSUSE includes YaST, a GUI tool that enables you to customize the OS during and after installation. In this chapter, you use YaST to install openSUSE. YaST guides you through the installation process by analyzing your current system components and displaying installation settings based on this analysis. During installation, YaST displays an overview of installation steps with help documents for each step (see Figure 2-1).

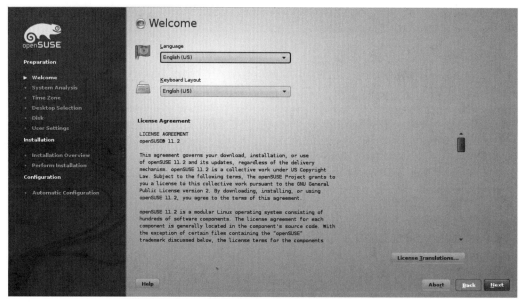

Figure 2-1 An overview of installation steps in YaST
Source: openSUSE

Your system configuration determines how you install openSUSE. For example, you load different software applications during installation if you have a laptop rather than a desktop. You also load server applications if your system is to be used as a server or desktop applications if your system is to be used as a personal computer. To a beginner, these different configurations might sound a bit intimidating, but YaST is an excellent tool designed to help you perform these tasks easily.

Requirements for Installing Linux

The more software you install, the sooner you realize that "minimum requirements" are just that—minimum. In fact, most software installations run more smoothly if your computer exceeds the minimum requirements. The following minimum requirements are from the openSUSE Installation Quick Start Guide:

 You can view the Installation Quick Start Guide at *www.novell.com/documentation/opensuse112/*.

- Pentium III 500 MHz or higher processor
- 512 MB RAM
- 3 GB free disk space
- 800 × 600 display resolution

However, for better performance, the following hardware requirements are recommended:

- Pentium 4 2.4 GHz or higher, any AMD64, or an Intel EM64T processor
- 1 GB RAM
- More than 3 GB free disk space
- 1024 × 768 or higher display resolution

The Unified Installation Method with Virtual Machines

Many large companies have **server farms**, which are groups of servers networked together in a single location. They can contain file servers, Web servers, primary and backup servers, routers, switches, and many other types of servers. However, setting up virtual machines is usually more feasible and economical than installing hundreds of physical servers. A **virtual machine (VM)** is a software container with its own OS, IP address, and applications. A **host** is the physical computer where the virtual machine runs, and a **guest** is the virtual machine using the host's physical hardware resources. Some additional benefits of using virtualization in a network include the following:

- Allows running multiple OSs on one machine
- Gives you the opportunity to test applications before actually installing them on a host machine
- Reduces costs by decreasing the physical hardware that must be purchased for a network
- Offers the chance to experiment with untested programs without infecting host machines with viruses or other malware

You can have Windows running on a physical computer and another OS, such as openSUSE, running on a virtual machine. Imagine the money a school or company could save if, instead of buying two physical machines, two expensive video cards, and two monitors, it bought only one machine and then loaded a VM on it.

You can download many virtualization software packages free. Table 2-1 gives you an overview of some virtualization software packages; you use VMware Player to run openSUSE in this book's activities.

Table 2-1 Virtualization software packages

Name	Host OS	Guest OS	Description	Web site
Cooperative Linux (CoLinux)	Windows 2000, XP, Vista, 7	Linux	Free and open source; allows running a VM in parallel with the host	*www.colinux.org*
Windows Virtual PC	Windows 7 Home Basic, Home Premium, Professional, Ultimate, and Enterprise	Windows XP (SP3) Professional; Windows Vista Enterprise (SP1), Ultimate (SP1), and Business (SP1); Windows 7 Professional, Ultimate, and Enterprise	Free to download; offers the latest Microsoft virtualization technology (at the time of this writing)	*www.microsoft. com* and do a search for "Windows Virtual PC"
Sun Virtual Box	Windows, Linux, Mac, OpenSolaris	Windows, DOS, Linux, Solaris, Open BSD UNIX	Free and open source; a full virtualization package that supports multiple guest OSs	*www.virtualbox. org*
VMware Player	Windows, Linux	Windows, Linux	Free; supports multiple guest OSs	*www.vmware.com/ products/player*

Overview of VMware Player

VMware Player 3.1.5 is a free application that enables you to create, configure, and run virtual machines on a Windows or Linux system. With VMware Player installed, a guest OS can access all the host machine's hardware, including printers, network interface cards (NICs), and USB drives. A major benefit of having VMware Player is being able to create virtual machines to test different OSs and applications without concern about damaging the host. For the purposes of this book, you load VMware Player and install openSUSE as a guest OS. The Getting Started Guide for VMware Player 3.1.5 lists the following requirements for the host machine:

You can download the Getting Started Guide for VMware Player PDF by doing a search for "VMware player getting started guide" at *www.vmware.com*.

- *Architecture*—Standard x86-compatible or x86-64 with Intel VT or AMD-V–compatible PC
- *Processor speed*—1.3 GHz or faster
- *Memory*—Minimum 1 GB, but 2 GB or more recommended
- *Hard disk*—At least 1 GB free disk space recommended for each guest OS

Activity 2-1: Downloading VMware Player

Time Required: 15 minutes

Objective: Register a VMware account and download VMware Player 3.0.

Description: VMware Player is a free virtualization program. You just have to register with a valid e-mail address.

1. Start your Web browser, and go to **http://downloads.vmware.com/d/info/ desktop_downloads/vmware_player/3_0**.

At the time of this writing, the preceding URL was the correct location to download VMware Player. If this URL no longer works, do a search for VMware Player at *www.vmware.com*.

2. Click the **Download** button in the Product Downloads tabs.

3. To register a VMware account, enter your first name, last name, and e-mail address in the registration section on the right, and then click **Continue**. If you already have a VMware account, enter your login information, click **Continue**, and then skip to Step 6.

4. Enter your contact information, and accept the license agreement. If you don't want to be contacted, click to clear the option for getting e-mails about VMware Player, and then click **Register**.

5. Open the e-mail account you used in Step 3. In the validation e-mail from VMware, click the **Activate Now** button.

6. In the list of VMware Player installation files you can download, click **VMware Player 3.1.5** under Version History - VMware Player 3.1.5. When you click the **Download** button, you're prompted to save the file. Click **Save File**, and then exit your Web browser.

7. Leave your system running for the next activity.

Installing VMware Player on a Windows Host

To install VMware Player, you use the VMware-player-*xxxxxx*.exe installation file; *xxxxxx* represents the version and build numbers. Activity 2-2 walks you through installing VMware Player on a Windows host system.

Activity 2-2: Installing VMware Player 3.1.5 on a Windows Host

Time Required: 10 minutes

Objective: Install VMware Player 3.1.5 on a Windows host.

Description: In this activity, you install VMware Player, a free program for creating, configuring, and running virtual machines. You use VMware Player to perform most activities in this book.

1. Locate the VMware-player-*xxxxxx*.exe installation file you downloaded in Activity 2-1, and double-click it to start the installation.

2. If you get a security warning message, click **Run**.

3. In the Welcome window, click **Next**.

4. In the Destination Folder window, you select where you want to install VMware Player. For this activity, leave the default location (C:\Program Files\VMware\VMware Player\), and click **Next**. (To choose another location, you can click **Change** and browse to or enter the new path.)

5. In the Shortcuts window, you have the option to create shortcuts for VMware Player. By default, all three options (Desktop, Start Menu Programs folder, and Quick Launch toolbar) are selected. Leave this default setting (unless your instructor wants you to select another option), and then click **Next**.

6. Click **Continue** to begin the installation or click **Back** to review or change any settings.

7. Click **Restart Now** if you're ready to restart your computer. If you want to restart your computer at another time, click **Restart Later**.

If you select the Restart Later option, you must remember to restart your computer before you can use VMware Player.

Installing OpenSUSE

As mentioned, openSUSE is a free, open-source Linux OS, meaning you can download, install, and use the software at no cost as well as view and change the source code. This book's DVD includes openSUSE, but you can also download the International Organization for Standardization (ISO) image file at *http://software.openSUSE.org/112/en*. An **ISO image** is an archive file containing the contents of a CD or DVD. You can think of an ISO image as a "virtual" CD or DVD because it's a digital replica of a physical CD or DVD. Operating systems can be stored conveniently as ISO images, making it easier to install an OS without needing to have the installation medium.

The openSUSE installation is divided into three main phases: preparation, installation, and configuration. The **preparation phase** is interactive, meaning you select the language, time zone, desktop environment, hard disk setup, and user account and password. The **installation phase** is not interactive, so you don't have to take any action. The software is simply installed by using the options you set during the preparation phase. After the installation phase is finished, your system restarts so that it's ready for the **configuration phase**, where you set up the network, Internet access, and hardware components.

Activity 2-3: Creating a Virtual Machine

Time Required: 15 minutes

Objective: Create a virtual machine that can be used for installing an OS.

Description: In this activity, you create two virtual machines (one for each desktop environment) that you use later for installing openSUSE.

1. Start VMware Player by clicking one of the shortcuts created in Activity 2-2.

2. Click the **Create a New Virtual Machine** link at the right to start the New Virtual Machine Wizard.

3. In the welcome window, click the **I will install the operating system later** option button, and then click **Next**.

4. In the Select a Guest Operating System window, click the **Linux** option button. In the Version drop-down list, click **SUSE Linux 64-bit** or **SUSE Linux** (depending on your system), and then click **Next**.

5. In the Name the Virtual Machine window, type **openSUSE_GNOME** in the Virtual machine name text box, and leave the default location. Click **Next**.

6. You can set the size of the virtual disk anywhere from 0.1 GB to 2 TB. For the pupose of this activity, leave the default size, which is 20 GB. You also have the option to store the virtual disk as a single file or split it into multiple files. You should use multiple files if your file system can support only files no larger than 2 GB. For this activity, click **Store virtual disk as a single file**, if it's not already selected, and then click **Next**.

7. The Ready to Create Virtual Machine window displays the virtual machine settings you have entered. After reviewing the settings, click **Finish**.

8. Repeat the preceding steps to create a second virtual machine, but name it **openSUSE_KDE**.

After clicking Finish, you might see a Software Updates message (see Figure 2-2). If so, click Download to get the updates.

OpenSUSE Boot Options

In Activity 2-4, you install openSUSE on the virtual machine you created in Activity 2-3. The first window displayed when you install openSUSE is the Boot Options window shown in Figure 2-3.

Figure 2-2 The Software Updates message box
Source: VMware Player

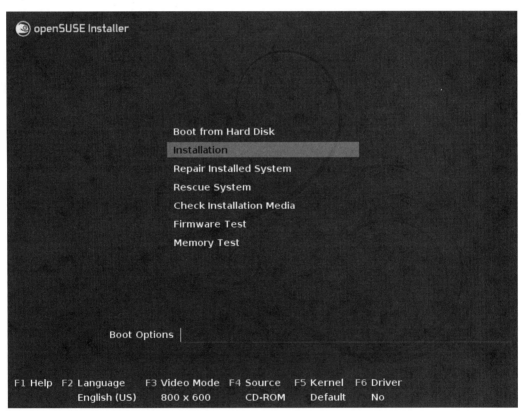

Figure 2-3 The OpenSUSE Boot Options window
Source: openSUSE

The Boot Options window displays options for the installation procedure. Table 2-2 explains the options in the Boot Options window.

Table 2-2 Settings in the Boot Options window

Option	Description
Boot from Hard Disk	This option starts your machine in the OS originally installed on it. If you're using VMware Player to install openSUSE, don't select this option because the virtual disk has no OS installed yet.
Installation	This option is used to start an openSUSE installation and boot the system into the preparation phase (discussed in the next section).
Repair Installed System	This option boots into a graphical repair utility for recovering a corrupted system.
Rescue System	This option boots into a minimal Linux system without a GUI. You use this option if you need to recover or modify important system files.
Check Installation Media	Select this option only if you use an ISO image for installation. It's used to ensure that a DVD created from an ISO image isn't corrupt.
Firmware Test	Select this option to start a utility that checks your system's BIOS.
Memory Test	This option tests your system RAM. The only way to stop the test is to press Esc, which restarts the VM in the Boot Options window.

At the bottom of the window, you see additional options you can access by pressing the corresponding function key:

- *F1 Help*—This help feature is context sensitive, meaning that if the Boot from Hard Disk option, for example, is selected and you press F1, you get information about this option. The following navigation keys are used to move through the Help information windows:

    - Up arrow: Highlight previous link.
    - Down arrow: Highlight next link.
    - Left arrow or Backspace: Return to previous topic.
    - Right arrow, Enter, or Spacebar: Follow link.
    - Page Up: Scroll up one page.
    - Page Down: Scroll down one page.
    - Home: Go to page start.
    - End: Go to page end.
    - Esc: Exit the help window.

- *F2 Language*—The default language is English (US). You can select this option to change the display language and corresponding keyboard layout.
- *F3 Video Mode*—Select a screen resolution, or select Text Mode if the graphical installation causes problems.

- *F4 Source*—Select the installation source medium. CD-ROM is the default setting.
- *F5 Kernel*—Choose this option, which displays a menu of functions you can disable, if you're having problems with the regular installation.
- *F6 Driver*—Select this option if you have an optional driver update for openSUSE.

The Preparation Phase

At the left of the installation window is an overview of all the steps YaST takes to install openSUSE, as shown previously in Figure 2-1. At the top right, you can select a language and keyboard layout. Clicking Next accepts the license agreement. YaST then performs a system analysis to determine whether other OSs are installed on your system (see Figure 2-4).

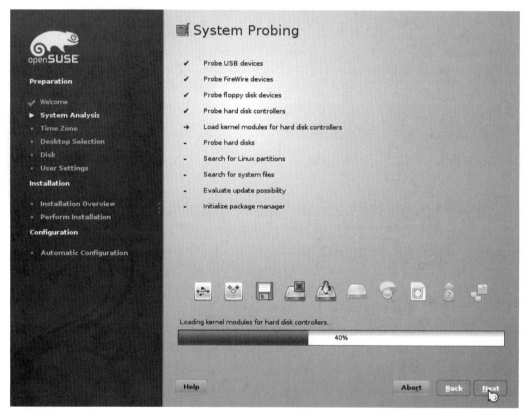

Figure 2-4 The System Probing window

Installation Mode In the Installation Mode window, you have three choices: New Installation, Update, and Repair Installed System. If YaST doesn't find an OS installed during the system probe, you can select only New Installation. The following list describes the three options:

- *New Installation*—Select this option if you want to start a new installation from scratch. This option completely replaces an existing OS and all configuration data.

At times, a clean installation is preferable to updating an existing system, such as when you have misconfigurations or application problems. Before selecting a new installation, however, make sure you back up all your data first.

- *Update*—Select this option only if you already have openSUSE installed and a newer version is available. The advantage of the update option is that configuration settings from your existing system are preserved.
- *Repair Installed System*—Choose this option to repair a damaged system. (It's the same as selecting Repair Installed System in the Boot Options window.)

Two more options are shown at the bottom of the Installation Mode window. The Use Automatic Configuration option is selected by default and is used when performing a new installation. The benefit of this option is that YaST configures your network and hardware automatically, so it's recommend for inexperienced users. You can also select the Include Add-On Products from Separate Media option to install add-ons from software repositories across the network.

Clock and Time Zone The Clock and Time Zone window displays a world map where you can select your region and time zone. You can click to zoom in, and then right-click to zoom back out to the world map. You can also make these selections in the Region and Time Zone drop-down lists.

By default, the hardware clock is set to Universal Time Coordinated (UTC). The benefit of using this setting is that your system can switch from standard time to daylight savings time and back automatically. To modify the clock setting, click the Change button to open the Change Date and Time window.

Instead of entering the date and time manually, you can synchronize your system clock with the openSUSE Network Time Protocol (NTP) server (at *http://0.openSUSE.pool.ntp.org*) by clicking Change, clicking the Synchronize with NTP Server option, entering the NTP server's URL, and then clicking Synchronize now.

Desktop Selection As discussed in Chapter 1, openSUSE offers GNOME and KDE as desktop environments. You use the Desktop Selection window to choose which environment you want. If you select Other, three additional options are displayed: XFCE Desktop, Minimal X Window, and Minimal Server Selection (Text Mode). You might choose one of these options if you don't want a lot of default software packages installed on your computer. For instance, if your Linux system is being used as a server, you don't need many of the graphical functions included with a desktop environment.

Suggested Partitioning One complicated issue that new Linux users face is deciding how to partition the disk. In Windows, most users create two partitions: one for program files and one for data files. The Linux directory structure is more complex and, therefore, requires more planning during the partitioning phase. The good news is that YaST checks your hard disk and displays a proposed partition setup for you. In most cases, the proposed setup can be accepted without making changes. To change the partition setup, you click the Edit Partition Setup button. The kinds of changes you can make are changing the file system type or encrypting the partition. Advanced Linux administrators can create a customized partitioning scheme by clicking the Create Partition Setup button.

The default option is Partition Based, but you can change it by clicking the LVM Based option button. **Logical Volume Management** (**LVM**) is used to create virtual partitions that can span physical hard drives, which means you can resize partitions later, if needed. For instance, if you accept the default Partition Based option and later your /home partition fills up, you would have to delete files to free up space in that partition. With the LVM option, you can increase the size of the /home partition by resizing seldom used partitions, such as /tmp and /share.

Many new Linux users wonder whether they can install Linux on a system already running Windows. A **multiboot** configuration enables you to install multiple OSs on one computer and choose which one to use when you start the computer. If you want to install openSUSE and keep Windows installed, too, in a multiboot configuration, YaST recommends a solution based on shrinking or resizing your existing Windows partition.

Create New User The Create New User window prompts you to create a local user and set the password. After entering the user's full name, openSUSE suggests a username for logging in. You can accept the suggested username or change it. You also enter a password and then retype it to confirm.

Under these text boxes are three check boxes. The first, "Use this password for system administrator," allows using the same password supplied for the user to access the system administrator (root) account. This option is suitable only for a home computer or stand-alone workstation. If more than one person can access this computer, this option shouldn't be selected.

The second check box, Receive System Mail, allows the user to receive system service messages, which are normally sent only to the root user. **Root** is a special user account with full access to all system resources. You can select this option for the most frequently used account. Note that you shouldn't log in as root unless you must have root privileges.

The root user has all permissions needed to change the system, so keep this in mind when you're logged in as root. If you don't know what you're doing, you could accidentally make changes that have undesirable results.

The third check box, Automatic Login, enables you to boot straight to your desktop instead of being prompted for a username and password. Unfortunately, this option allows anyone to have access to all your data. Therefore, you should select this option only if your computer is a home workstation and you're the only one with access to it.

The password encryption in openSUSE is Blowfish, which is a symmetric block cipher that uses a key from 32 bits to 448 bits. In theory, you can create a password between 5 and 72 characters long, but a 5-character password can be guessed too easily, and a 72-character password is much too long to remember. (In fact, you must load special security modules to have a password longer than 8 characters.) Passwords are case sensitive, and you can use numbers and most of the special characters (for example, !, @, #, and $), but you can't use accented characters.

The Installation Phase

After you finish the preparation phase, YaST displays the installation settings. Later in this chapter, you install openSUSE. For now, just be aware that you can alter installation settings by clicking the headers for each section or clicking the Change button. The following list describes options under each heading:

At this point, nothing has been done to your hard disk, so you can safely abort the installation, if needed.

- *Partitioning*—Advanced partitioning mode, where you can make additional changes to partitions.
- *Booting*—Alter the boot configuration, such as the boot loader (which you learn more about in Chapter 22) and its location.
- *Software*—Install or remove software packages.

You can install or remove software packages at any time after an installation is finished. You learn how to do this in Chapter 9.

- *Locale Settings*—Modify the system's language and keyboard layout.
- *Time Zone*—Modify the system clock information.
- *User Settings*—Modify user information, such as user's full name, login name, and password.
- *Default Runlevel*—A **runlevel** is the operating state of the Linux OS. Each runlevel offers different services, and you can change the runlevel your system boots to. For instance, runlevel 5 allows multiple users to log in to the system and enables you to access network and display manager capabilities. Runlevel 5 is the default if you're using a graphical desktop environment, such as KDE or GNOME. Table 2-3 describes openSUSE runlevels.

Some UNIX-like OSs define runlevels differently. For instance, in Solaris 10, runlevel 3 is comparable to runlevel 5 in Linux, in that it boots your system with multiuser and networking capabilities.

Table 2-3 openSUSE Linux runlevels

Runlevel	Description
0	System Halt: At this point, the system can be safely powered down.
1	Single User Mode: You have limited access, and most services are shut down. You use this mode for system maintenance.
2	Text Mode: Multiple users, but there's no network support.
3	Text Mode with Networking: Same as runlevel 2, but you have network support.
4	An expert user mode; openSUSE recommends not using it.
5	Default runlevel: The most common runlevel for workstations, it starts the X display manager for a GUI and is a multiuser mode with networking capabilities.
6	System Reboot: This option is used to restart the machine in the default runlevel.

- *System*—YaST gathers information on your system hardware, such as processor type and amount of memory, and displays the information. You can download this information to a file or removable media, if you like.

- *Installation from Images*—Using an ISO image speeds up installation. Without this option, you would have to install each software package separately. The only time you should disable this feature is when you're having installation problems.

- *Firewall and SSH*—By default, YaST enables SUSEfirewall2 on all configured network interfaces. **Secure Shell (SSH)** is a remote login program used to create a secure encrypted connection to a host on the network. After a firewall is enabled, you can decide to open a port on it for SSH services. You learn more about firewalls in Chapter 19.

Performing the Installation After viewing installation settings and making any necessary changes, you can start the installation. Keep in mind that you perform these steps later in this chapter and will use mostly default settings. The process takes about 15 minutes, depending on your computer and whether you're installing additional software packages. During the process, you can click the Details tab at any time to view the installation log, which contains information such as which software packages are being installed. After the installation is finished, your computer restarts in the configuration phase.

The Configuration Phase

Now that openSUSE has been installed, it's ready to be configured. If you selected the Automatic Configuration option, this process is done automatically. If not, your computer restarts in a manual configuration mode. The following sections describe the steps for manual configuration.

Hostname and Domain Name The **hostname** is a computer's machine name in the network, and the **domain name** is the name of the network the host belongs to. YaST displays a recommended hostname and domain name, but you can change these settings. Keep in mind that for a computer on a network, the hostname must be unique, and the domain name must be the same for all hosts on the network.

You have two additional options for this information: Change Hostname via DHCP and Write Hostname to /etc/hosts. **Dynamic Host Configuration Protocol (DHCP)** is a networking protocol that assigns IP addresses and other network configuration information to hosts automatically. The /etc/hosts file is used to map hostnames to IP addresses, and you learn more about it in Chapters 17 and 18. If this option is selected, your hostname and IP address are written to the /etc/hosts file automatically, and your hostname is always resolved to its IP address. You can disable this option if you have a DNS server on your network that automatically resolves hostnames and IP addresses.

Network Configuration YaST displays network settings based on the information that's been collected about your machine (see Figure 2-5). Because you're using the automatic configuration feature to install openSUSE in this chapter, you don't need to worry about the settings in this window now. Network configuration is covered in more detail in Chapter 8.

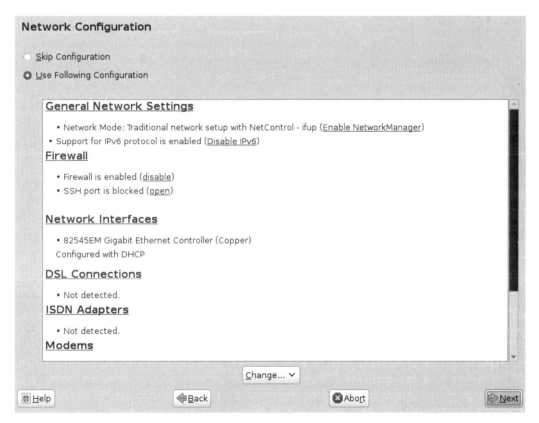

Figure 2-5 The Network Configuration window
Source: openSUSE

Test Internet Connection After configuring the network, you can test it by selecting the "Yes, Test Connection to the Internet" option. A successful test enables you to run YaST Online Update. If the test fails, go back to the Network Configuration window to correct the problem. If the test is successful, the official openSUSE software repository (a local or remote server storing Linux software packages you can download) is configured. You have the option of skipping the test, too.

Online Update YaST can perform online updates as long as an Internet connection is set up. Select Run Update, and then click Next. YaST skips this step if no updates are available or there's no Internet connection. Click Accept to install the patches, and then click Next to continue with the system configuration.

Downloading updates can take some time, depending on the speed of your Internet connection and the file size of updates. Some updates require restarting; if so, YaST prompts you.

In case you don't have enough space on your hard disk for YaST to install openSUSE, you should abort the installation and boot to your Windows OS, where you can delete files you don't need to free up space. Next, clean up your system by running a program such as Windows Disk Defragmenter, and then try restarting your multiboot installation.

Activity 2-4: Installing OpenSUSE as a Guest OS

Time Required: 30 minutes

Objective: Install openSUSE as a guest OS on your Windows computer.

Description: In this activity, you install openSUSE as a guest OS so that you can run it on a virtual machine with VMware Player.

1. Start VMware Player by clicking one of the shortcuts created in Activity 2-2.

2. At the left of the main VMware Player window, click the **openSUSE_GNOME** virtual machine you created in Activity 2-3, and then click the **Edit virtual machine settings** link.

3. Click the **CD/DVD (IDE)** device, and then click the **Use physical drive** option button. Make sure the CD accompanying this book is in the CD-ROM drive, and then click **OK**. Click the **Play virtual machine** link to start the openSUSE installation.

4. In the Boot Options window that's displayed, click the **Installation** option.

5. In the welcome window, accept the default language (English) and keyboard layout by clicking **Next**.

6. In the Installation Mode window, click the **New Installation** option button, and if necessary, click to clear **Include Add-On Products from Separate Media**. Click the **Use Automatic Configuration** check box, and then click **Next**.

7. In the Clock and Time Zone window, click the **Region** list arrow and click **USA**. Click the **Time Zone** list arrow, and select your time zone. Click the **Hardware Clock Set To UTC** check box, and then click **Change** to set the correct time. Finally, click **Accept** to return to the Clock and Time Zone window, and click **Next** to continue the installation.

8. In the Desktop Selection window, click the **GNOME Desktop** option button, and then click **Next**.

9. In the Suggested Partitioning window, click **Next** to accept the default settings.

10. In the Create New User window, type your first and last name in the User's Full Name text box. YaST uses this information to populate the Username text box. Type **Op3n$use** in the Password text box and retype it in the Confirm Password text box. (You use this password for the options at the bottom of the window.) Make sure all three check boxes at the bottom are selected, and then click **Next**.

11. In the Installation Settings window, click **Install**. YaST displays a confirmation message to make sure you don't want to make changes. Click **Install** again to proceed.

12. After the installation is finished, your virtual machine restarts and continues with its auto configuration. When the auto configuration is completed, your system boots into the desktop environment you selected.

13. If time permits, repeat these steps to install openSUSE on your KDE virtual machine, but click **openSUSE_KDE** in Step 2 for the virtual machine and the **KDE Desktop** option button in Step 8.

The GNOME Desktop Environment

GNOME is an easy-to-use graphical desktop environment that gives you quick access to applications you use often, such as a word-processing program, a Web browser, and e-mail software. The following sections describe useful features of GNOME.

If you haven't already created an openSUSE virtual machine with the GNOME desktop environment, you should do so now. You can use it to get some hands-on experience while learning about GNOME.

Features of GNOME

At first glance, the GNOME desktop has two icons: a folder representing your home directory and a trashcan representing deleted files (see Figure 2-6). If you have a CD/DVD in the CD-ROM drive, a third icon representing this drive is displayed. As in Windows, you can double-click icons to open them and right-click icons to display a menu of options. The Panel at the bottom is often compared with the taskbar in Windows. By default, it contains only two items: the Computer menu and the Tomboy Notes applet. The Computer menu is similar to the Windows Start menu. **GNOME applets** are small programs available on the GNOME Panel that are designed to give you quick access to useful applications. (Applications are typically much larger stand-alone programs.) To see a list of GNOME applets, right-click the Panel and click Add to Panel.

User's home directory ——

Trashcan (holds deleted files) ——

CD-ROM drive (icon not shown if a CD/DVD isn't inserted in the drive) ——

Workspace Switcher ——

Panel ——

Tomboy applet ——

Computer menu ——

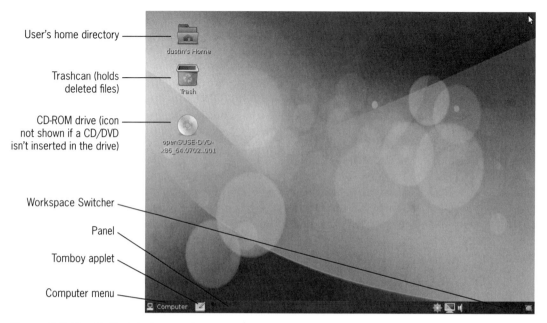

Figure 2-6 The GNOME desktop environment
Source: openSUSE

At the right of the Panel is the Workspace Switcher. A **workspace** is a virtual screen on the Linux desktop for displaying open applications. With the Workspace Switcher, you can change between workspaces easily and open different applications in each workspace. The following sections give you an overview of other helpful features in the GNOME desktop environment.

Web Browser GNOME includes Firefox as the default Web browser. It can be customized with add-ons you download, and you can download personas to modify the look of the Firefox toolbar. To start Firefox, you use the Computer menu; Firefox is listed under Favorite Applications. You can also create a desktop icon for starting Firefox.

To find out more about Firefox features, go to *http://en-us.www. mozilla.com/en-US/firefox/features/*.

File Manager Nautilus, the file manager (sometimes referred to as a "file browser") in GNOME, is used to organize and access folders, files, and applications. You can use Nautilus for a wide variety of tasks, including the following:

- Create and move folders and files.
- Search for, copy, and delete files and folders.
- Create and run scripts (covered in more detail in Chapter 5).

- Start applications.
- Customize the display of files and folders.
- Write files to CDs/DVDs or other removable media.

To start Nautilus, use the Computer menu or double-click the Home directory on your desktop.

The Desktop User Guide includes several sections on how to use Nautilus. To open it, press F1 while you're in Nautilus.

TIP

Word Processing GNOME includes OpenOffice.org Writer, an open-source word-processing program for creating documents and incorporating charts, tables, and graphics. A helpful feature of Writer is that you can save documents in many different formats, such as the default OpenDocument format (.odf) or the Microsoft Word format (.doc or .docx). So when you create a document in Writer, you can view it on your Windows computer with Word.

E-mail Evolution is the e-mail software included with GNOME. It can handle basic e-mail needs, such as composing and storing e-mails, address books, memos, tasks, and calendars, but it can also handle more complicated tasks, such as the following:

- *Junk mail control*—Evolution uses SpamAssassin to scan for and filter junk mail. You can train this filter by right-clicking an e-mail you consider junk and clicking Mark as Junk. If legitimate e-mail ends up in your junk mail folder, right-click the e-mail and click Mark as Not Junk.
- *Search folders*—You can search for specific e-mails with criteria such as date, sender, or subject line, for example. You can also click the Search toolbar icon and set up more advanced search criteria.
- *Security*—You can digitally sign and encrypt e-mails with GNU Privacy Guard (GPG) and S/MIME.
- *Desktop integration*—Other GNOME applications are integrated with Evolution. For instance, a GNOME calendar applet is available; it lists appointments and tasks you have stored in Evolution.
- *Calendars*—You can set up multiple calendars and even have calendars accessible via the Internet to share with a group.
- *Multiple e-mail accounts*—You can set up, manage, and organize multiple e-mail accounts. You might want separate e-mail accounts for work and personal use, for example.

Before starting Activity 2-5, you need to complete Activity 2-4 so that you have a GNOME virtual machine.

NOTE

Activity 2-5: Working with the GNOME Desktop Environment

Time Required: 20 minutes

Objective: Get hands-on practice in working with GNOME.

Description: In this activity, you learn how to change your desktop background and explore features, such as Nautilus. You also get some practice using Writer and Firefox. You need an Internet connection to try some of GNOME's features.

1. Start VMware Player and log in to **openSUSE_GNOME** (the openSUSE virtual machine running the GNOME desktop).

2. When openSUSE starts, right-click the desktop and click **Change Desktop Background**.

3. In the Appearance Preferences window, you can select one of the available backgrounds or click the **Get more backgrounds online** link. (If you select an available background, skip to Step 6.)

4. When you find a background you like, click the **Go** button under the picture to display it full size. Right-click the background and click **Set As Desktop Background**. In the message box, click **Set Desktop Background**.

5. Exit the Web browser by clicking **File, Quit** from the Firefox menu, and close the Appearance Preferences window.

6. Double-click the **Home** directory on your desktop to open the Nautilus file manager.

7. Double-click the **Documents** directory, and then double-click **New Document.ott** to open a blank Writer document.

8. On three separate lines, type your first and last name, today's date, and **Activity 2-4**.

9. Click **File, Save As** from the menu. In the Name text box, type **Activity2-4**, and then click **Save**.

10. Exit Writer by clicking **File, Exit** from the menu. Close Nautilus by clicking **File, Close** from the menu.

11. Click the **Computer** icon at the left of the GNOME panel, and then click **Firefox** to start the Web browser. Take some time to explore the options, and then exit Firefox.

The KDE Desktop Environment

The K Desktop Environment (KDE) is also a graphical interface for communicating with the Linux kernel and gives you quick access to applications, such as word-processing programs, Web browsers, e-mail, a file manager, and so forth. The following sections describe useful features of KDE.

If you haven't already created an openSUSE virtual machine with KDE, you should do so now. You can use it to get some hands-on experience while learning about KDE.

Features of KDE

After you log in to KDE for the first time, you see the desktop interface shown in Figure 2-7. By default, a Folder View widget called Desktop Folder is displayed. It contains the contents of your Desktop directory, a subdirectory of your home directory.

Folder View widget

System tray
KDE Panel
Quick Launch area

Figure 2-7 The KDE deskop environment
Source: openSUSE

Desktop Folder The Desktop Folder widget shows the contents of the ~/Desktop directory. (Recall that the ~ symbol represents your home directory.) The default icons in this folder are Firefox, My Computer, Office, Online Help, and openSUSE, described in the following list:

- *Firefox*—Like GNOME, KDE includes Firefox as the default Web browser. You can click this icon to start Firefox.

- *My Computer*—Click this icon to display important information about your openSUSE system, such as processor type and speed as well as memory and disk information. It also shows OS information, such as the kernel version, the user currently logged in, the OS type and version, and the KDE version number.

- *Office*—You click this icon to start OpenOffice.org, the same office application available in GNOME.

- *Online Help*—You can use this icon to access the openSUSE help Web page (*http:// help.opensuse.org*), where you can find documentation resources and chat with other openSUSE users.

- *openSUSE*—Click this icon to open an openSUSE welcome window containing links to Web resources.

Quick Launch Area The Quick Launch area is part of the KDE Panel reserved for shortcuts to often used applications. By default, it contains Main Menu, Show Dashboard, Firefox, and Dolphin icons. The Main Menu icon opens a window with a search feature at the top and application buttons at the bottom. The Show Dashboard icon is used to give you a preview of your desktop. The Firefox icon, of course, starts Firefox, and the Dolphin icon starts KDE's default file manager.

KDE Panel The KDE Panel (also known as Kicker) is located at the bottom of the desktop by default. It consists of the Quick Launch area, taskbar, and system tray. You can change its location, add or remove icons, and change its appearance.

System Tray The system tray at the far right of the KDE Panel contains the system clock, a volume control icon, and the Lock and Leave icons.

Before starting Activity 2-6, you need to complete Activity 2-4 so that you have a KDE virtual machine.

Activity 2-6: Working with KDE

Time Required: 20 minutes

Objective: Get hands-on practice in working with KDE.

Description: In this activity, you explore KDE features, such as Dolphin. You need an Internet connection to try some of these features.

1. Start VMware Player and log in to **openSUSE_KDE** (the openSUSE virtual machine running KDE).

2. When openSUSE starts, take a look at the icons in the Desktop Folder. Click the **Online Help** icon to view the KDE online resources. When you're finished, click **File, Quit** from the menu to close the Web page.

3. To find and start the Dolphin file manager, click the **Main Menu** icon in the Quick Launch area of the desktop, type **dolphin** in the search text box, and then click the **Dolphin** icon.

4. While Dolphin is open, click the **Show the Plasma Dashboard** icon in the Quick Launch area to see a preview of your desktop background. Click the background anywhere to go back to the Dolphin application.

5. Exit Dolphin by clicking **File, Quit** from the menu, and then shut down your virtual machine.

Chapter Summary

- openSUSE includes YaST, a GUI tool that enables users to customize their OS settings during and after installation.

- With virtualization, you can run multiple OSs on one machine, test applications, decrease the amount of physical hardware in a network, and experiment with untested programs without infecting your computer with possible malware.

- In virtualization terms, a host machine is the physical computer on which a virtual machine runs. A guest is the virtual machine.

- VMware Player is a free virtualization software package that can be used to create, configure, and run virtual machines on Windows or Linux PCs.
- An openSUSE installation is divided into three phases: preparation, installation, and configuration.
- The desktop environments used most often with openSUSE are GNOME and KDE.
- A runlevel is the current operating state of the Linux OS. The default runlevel in openSUSE is 5, which provides full multiuser support and starts the X display manager for a GUI.
- GNOME is an easy-to-use graphical desktop environment. It includes Firefox as the Web browser, Nautilus as the file manager, OpenOffice.org Writer as the word-processing program, and Evolution as the e-mail software.
- KDE is also an easy-to-use graphical desktop environment. It offers Firefox as the Web browser, Dolphin as the file manager, and OpenOffice.org Writer as the word-processing program. To make accessing applications and navigating your system easier, it includes features such as the KDE Panel, the Desktop Folder, and the Quick Launch area.

Key Terms

configuration phase   An openSUSE installation phase in which the network, Internet access, and hardware components are configured.

domain name   The name of the network a host belongs to.

Dynamic Host Configuration Protocol (DHCP)   A networking protocol used to assign IP addresses and other network configuration information to hosts automatically.

GNOME applets   Small programs available on the GNOME Panel for providing quick access to useful applications.

guest   A virtual machine that uses the host's physical hardware resources.

host   The physical computer where a virtual machine is installed.

hostname   A computer's machine name in the network.

installation phase   An openSUSE noninteractive installation phase in which software is installed with the settings configured during the preparation phase.

ISO image   A virtual copy of a CD or DVD.

Logical Volume Management (LVM)   A feature used to create virtual partitions that can span physical hard drives.

multiboot   A configuration that allows you to install more than one OS on a computer.

preparation phase   An openSUSE installation phase in which users can configure settings for language, time zone, desktop environment, hard disk setup, and user account and password.

root   A special user account with full access to all system resources.

runlevel   The operating state of the Linux OS.

Secure Shell (SSH)   A remote login program designed to provide a secure encrypted connection to a host on the network.

server farms A group of servers networked together in a single location.

virtual machine (VM) A software container with its own OS, IP address, and applications.

workspace An area of the desktop that can contain different windows and processes.

Review Questions

1. A virtual machine shares its IP address with the host. True or False?

2. What's the term for a virtual machine using the hardware resources of a physical computer?
   a. Guest
   b. Virtual player
   c. Host
   d. Software container

3. What's the term for the physical computer on which a virtual machine runs?
   a. Guest
   b. Manager
   c. Host
   d. Hardware container

4. With VMware Player installed, a virtual machine can access the host computer's hardware. True or False?

5. Summarize the benefits of using virtualization software.

6. List the three phases of an openSUSE installation.

7. Which setting in the Boot Options window is used to boot to the graphical repair system?
   a. Rescue System
   b. Repair Installed System
   c. Installation
   d. Firmware Test

8. Which setting in the Boot Options window boots into a minimal Linux system without a GUI?
   a. Rescue System
   b. Repair Installed System
   c. Installation
   d. Memory Test

9. Describe the benefit of choosing the update installation mode for openSUSE.

10. Describe a benefit of using the Logical Volume Management (LVM) option instead of a partition-based setup.

11. What user account has full access to all system resources?
    a. The user created during installation
    b. The user created after installation
    c. Root
    d. Administrator

12. The user password for openSUSE must be at least how many characters?
    a. 72
    b. 10
    c. 8
    d. 5

13. What's the default runlevel in openSUSE?
    a. 0
    b. 2
    c. 3
    d. 5

14. Explain how the root password is set during the openSUSE installation.

Case Projects

CASE PROJECTS

Case Project 2-1: East Coast Career College Decides on a Desktop Environment

East Coast Career College is excited to announce the switch from Windows to Linux. Based on your recommendations, Dr. Thompson decided to have openSUSE installed on all 75 computers. After the IT staff finished the installation, they realized that some staff members chose KDE as the desktop environment and others chose GNOME. Dr. Thompson wants the same desktop environment and software packages on all computers. He has asked you to recommend which desktop environment to use. Using the virtual machines created in this chapter as well as research you conduct on the Internet, spend some time exploring both environments. Write a one- to two-page memo to Dr. Thompson explaining the reasons for your recommendation. In addition, if you think employees should have a choice of which environment to use, include your reasons for this opinion.

## chapter 3

Managing Files and Directories

After reading this chapter and completing the exercises, you will be able to:

- Describe the Linux file system and the Filesystem Hierarchy Standard
- Navigate the Linux directory structure
- Manage files and directories in Linux

Now that you've installed openSUSE, it's time to open a terminal window and gain some command-line skills. Most major Linux distributions include a GUI desktop environment, such as GNOME or KDE, but learning the command line is important, especially for server administrators. In business environments, most Linux servers are in a locked room for security reasons and are administered from a remote terminal via the command line.

This chapter begins with the Linux directory structure and describes its major differences from the Windows directory structure. You're introduced to the Filesystem Hierarchy Standard, which specifies requirements and guidelines for file and directory placement. With this standard, software developers can create software that runs on all major Linux distributions.

Next, you learn commands for navigating the Linux directory structure and arguments for adding information to commands. You also learn how to find Linux documentation by using man pages and how to use wildcards to move around the directory structure quickly. You then learn how to manage files and directories and create hard and symbolic links, which are often compared with shortcuts in Windows. Finally, you see why using the root user account judiciously is important.

An Overview of the Linux Directory Structure

A **file system** is the way files are stored and organized to simplify access to data. Learning the Linux file system can be difficult because of its differences from Windows. For example, in Windows (see Figure 3-1), each partition is assigned a drive letter, such as assigning C to the first partition of the hard drive, and is separate from the others. In addition, each partition in

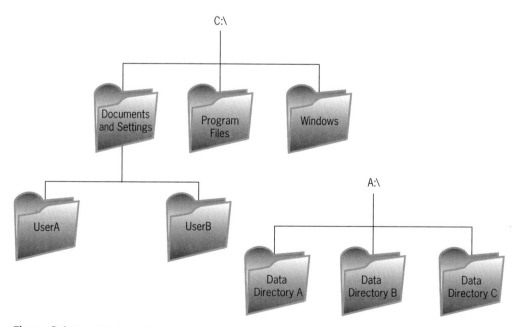

Figure 3-1 The Windows directory structure
© Cengage Learning 2013

Windows has its own root directory. In Linux, however, there's only one root directory, and all files and subdirectories are placed under the root directory in a treelike structure, as shown in Figure 3-2.

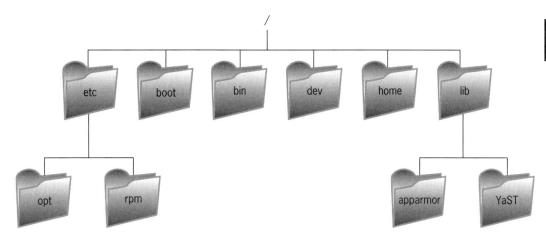

Figure 3-2 The Linux directory structure
© Cengage Learning 2013

As mentioned, Linux distributions vary in their interfaces and features. However, these distributions have nearly identical directory structures because of the **Filesystem Hierarchy Standard (FHS)**. This standard specifies requirements and guidelines for file and directory placement in UNIX-like operating systems (see *www.pathname.com/fhs/pub/fhs-2.3.html*). One benefit of FHS is that users are able to find the correct configuration files regardless of the Linux distribution. For instance, a Red Hat user can find the /etc/hosts file in openSUSE easily because it's in the same location as it is in Red Hat. Another benefit of FHS is that it enables Linux software developers to create software that works in all major Linux distributions.

You can review the Filesystem Hierarchy Standard at
http://proton.pathname.com/fhs/.

A basic understanding of FHS is a valuable tool for Linux administrators and users. Linux distributions closely follow the FHS and place their configuration files accordingly. Being able to find critical configuration files quickly cuts down on troubleshooting time. File systems based on the FHS have two distinctions: shareable versus unshareable files and variable versus static files. These distinctions are important because they indicate the kind of files in each directory. A **shareable file**, such as a user's home directory, can be stored on one machine and used by multiple users on other machines. An **unshareable file**, such as a configuration file in the /etc directory, can't be accessed by multiple users. **Static files,** such as those in the /boot directory, don't change on their own, but **variable files,** which are usually found in the /var directory, can. Table 3-1 lists some Linux directories defined by the FHS.

Table 3-1 Directories defined by the FHS

Directory	Description
/bin	Contains binary commands that can be used by system administrators, users, and scripts; this directory shouldn't contain subdirectories and can be accessed in single user mode
/boot	Contains the Linux kernel and static files needed to boot the computer
/dev	Contains device files, such as the CD/DVD-ROM drive
/etc	Contains static configuration files, which are also unshareable files, meaning they're local to the machine
/home	An optional directory that might not be included in all Linux distributions; in openSUSE, it's the user's home directory
/lib	Contains shared libraries that are loaded when a program starts
/media	Contains the mount point for removable media
/mnt	Empty by default, but administrators can use it to mount other resources, such as CD/DVD-ROM drives
/opt	Contains static shareable add-on software packages
/root	Contains the recommended home directory for the root user; not all Linux distributions use it, but it's used in openSUSE
/sbin	Contains system binaries used by the system administrator
/srv	Contains data files for services
/tmp	Contains temporary files that system administrators should delete whenever the system is booted
/usr	Contains shareable, read-only applications and files
/var	Contains variable data files, such as log files

Navigating the Linux Directory Structure

Imagine getting on a plane and flying to Rome for the first time. A taxi picks you up from the airport and drops you off in front of the Coliseum. Would you know what to do or where to go? How would you navigate the city? This feeling of unfamiliarity with a new setting is similar to what many new Linux users experience. Fortunately, many commands are available to help you navigate the Linux file system. The first commands you learn in this chapter are used to determine your current directory and move in and out of this directory.

When you first log in to a Linux system, you'll probably be in a GUI desktop environment. You can open the file manager and click your way around the Linux directory structure until you find the file or directory you want. The problem is that most Linux servers are installed without a graphical environment, which means you need to learn how to navigate without a GUI.

Here's how to open a terminal window in the KDE and GNOME desktop environments:

- *KDE*—Click the K menu button (the green circle) at the lower left and click Terminal.
- *GNOME*—Click Computer, More Applications to open the Application Browser, and then click the GNOME Terminal icon in the System Groups category.

You can create a desktop shortcut for the terminal window in both environments by dragging the terminal icon to the desktop.

TIP

Changing Directories

Learning the `pwd` (print working directory) command is essential because it displays the directory you're currently working in. It's like looking at a map with an X and the message "You are here!" That's what the `pwd` command does, as shown in this example:

```
~> pwd
/home/dustin
```

Linux is case sensitive, and commands in Linux are lowercase. For example, if you enter `PWD`, you get an error because the shell doesn't recognize the uppercase `PWD` as a command.

NOTE

The **command-line prompt** in the preceding example is `~>`. It simply indicates where to enter commands and varies depending on the shell. For instance, the previous example shows the prompt in the BASH shell, but in the Korn shell, it looks like this:

```
/home/dustin> pwd
/home/dustin
```

To navigate the directory structure, you use the `cd` (change directory) command to switch to other directories. You can add a **command-line argument**, which is information entered after a command to include specific instructions. For instance, you can add a command-line argument specifying which directory to change to, as shown in this example:

```
~> cd /bin
/bin> pwd
/bin
```

If you use the `cd` command without an argument, you return to your home directory, as shown in this example:

The ~ (tilde) symbol represents the user's **home directory**, which is the default directory on the file system where the user has full permission to store files. In the following example, the user's **current directory** is /bin, and the ~ symbol is used to change to the user's home directory:

```
/bin> cd ~
~> pwd
/home/isaiah
```

You can also use the ~ symbol to specify another user's home directory, as in this example:

```
~> cd ~jasmine
```

At this point, you haven't created any users other than the one you created during the openSUSE installation. You create more users in Chapter 7.

Pathnames in Linux So far, the arguments you've used with the cd command have specified the directory by using the **absolute path** method, which states the full pathname starting from root (/), as shown in this example:

```
~> cd /home/jake/Desktop
~/Desktop> cd /etc
~/etc> cd /home
```

You can also use the **relative path** method, which specifies the pathname starting from the current directory, as in this example:

```
~/Desktop> cd ../../../etc
~/etc> cd ..
~> cd home/jake
```

Remember that the absolute method always starts with a / symbol (root), so the command cd/home/jake/Desktop uses the absolute method. The relative method starts with the current directory, as shown in the command cd Desktop. To navigate to a directory above your current directory with the relative method, you use two dots, as shown in this example:

```
~/Desktop> cd ..
/jake> pwd
/home/jake
```

Two dots represent the parent directory, and one dot represents the current directory. The parent directory is one directory above your current directory in the directory structure. The only directory that doesn't have a parent directory is root (/).

The BASH Command Completion Feature You can use the **command completion** feature in the BASH shell to finish commands for you. To enable this feature, press the Tab key. For example, if you're in the /home/daniel directory and want to change to /home/daniel/Desktop, simply type cd De and press Tab. BASH completes the command for you and displays cd Desktop/ at the prompt. Remember to enter enough characters for this feature to work, particularly if you have more than one subdirectory beginning with the same letter. If you're in /home/daniel, and then type cd D and press Tab, you hear a beep: BASH is letting you know that it can't read your mind. If you press Tab again, BASH lists all possible choices, as shown:

```
Desktop/ Documents/ Download/
```

For all activities in this chapter, you can start in the KDE or GNOME desktop environment.

Activity 3-1: Using the `pwd` and `cd` Commands

Time Required: 10 minutes

Objective: Practice navigating the Linux directory structure.

Description: In this activity, you open a terminal window and use the `pwd` command to display your current directory and the `cd` command to change your current directory. You also get practice using the BASH command-completion feature.

1. Use the skills you learned in Chapter 2 to start VMware Player and start an openSUSE virtual machine.

2. Log in to openSUSE as a user other than root, and open a terminal window, using the instructions given earlier in this chapter.

3. Type **pwd** and press **Enter** to view your current directory. What is your current directory?

   _____

4. Type **cd /etc** and press **Enter,** and then type **pwd** and press **Enter.** Is your current directory the same? Why or why not? What method did you use to change to the /etc directory?

   _____

   _____

5. Use the relative method to change to your parent directory by typing **cd ..** and pressing **Enter.** What directory are you in now?

   _____

6. Type **cd** and press **Enter.** What happens when you use the `cd` command without arguments?

   _____

7. Type **cd D** and press **Tab** two times. What's displayed onscreen, and why?

   _____

8. Leave the terminal window open and the virtual machine running for the next activity.

Viewing Files and Directories

So far, you have learned how to determine your current position in the directory structure with the `pwd` command and navigate the directory structure with the `cd` command. To list files and subdirectories in the Linux directory structure, you use the `ls` command. The following example lists the contents of the user's home directory:

```
~> ls
bin Download
Desktop Documents
```

The ls command lists files and subdirectories in the current directory, and you can use arguments to specify other directories. For instance, if you're in your home directory and want a list of all files and directories in the parent directory, you can use an argument to specify this information:

```
~> ls ..
david jasmine lost+found
```

File types are indicated in different colors onscreen. For instance, directories might be blue, and regular files might be green or black. Linux distributions vary in the colors used to represent file types, however, so relying on this method to determine the file type isn't wise.

You can also use **options** to modify the way a command is carried out. Almost all Linux commands follow this syntax:

command -options argument

Notice the hyphen before *options*; you must include it before the first option you use. To view the contents of your current directory in a long list rather than a column format, you use the -1 option, as shown:

Make sure you use a lowercase L for the -1 option, not the number 1. The hyphen used before an option is called different names, such as a dash or a minus sign.

```
~> ls -l
total 548
drwxr-xr-x 2 sarah users 4096 2012-03-06 20:01 bin
drwxr-xr-x 2 sarah users 4096 2012-03-09 09:42 Desktop
drwxr-xr-x 2 sarah users 4096 2012-03-09 12:34 Documents
drwxr-xr-x 2 sarah users 4096 2012-03-07 19:08 Download
-rw-r--r-- 1 sarah users 0 2012-04-15 20:00 file1
```

Another option used often with the ls command is -a, which displays all files, including hidden files. The following example shows using this option to find files in the current directory:

```
~> ls -a
. .cache .local bin Desktop Documents Download .. file1
```

Hidden files in Linux are usually system files that users rarely need. Their names always start with a period, such as .cache and .local in the preceding example, so they're often called "dot files."

You can string options together, too, as shown in this example of specifying a long list of all files and directories in your current directory:

```
~> ls -al
total 9466
drwxr-xr-x 42 alex users 4096 2012-04-15 20:00 .
drwxr-xr-x 5 root root 4096 2012-04-14 13:54 ..
drwxr-xr-x 7 alex users 4096 2012-03-13 11:19 .cache
drwxr-xr-x 3 alex users 4096 2012-03-06 20:02 .local
-rw-r--r-- 1 alex users 0 2012-04-15 20:00 file1
drwxr-xr-x 2 alex users 4096 2012-03-09 09:42 Desktop
drwxr-xr-x 2 alex users 4096 2012-03-09 12:34 Documents
drwxr-xr-x 2 alex users 4096 2012-03-07 19:08 Download
```

The order of options doesn't matter, as long as you add a hyphen in front of the first option, so `ls  -la` is the same as `ls  -al`.

TIP

You can use many options with the `ls` command. Table 3-2 describes some of the most common.

Table 3-2   Options with the `ls` command

Option	Description
-a	Lists all files, including hidden files
-F	Appends a special character to each filename to represent the file type, such as * for an executable file and / for a subdirectory
-h	Stands for "human-readable" format, which shows file sizes in megabytes or gigabytes, for example, instead of in bytes
-i	Displays the inode number (discussed later in "Creating Links") for each file
-l	Changes the display from a column format to a long list
-R	Stands for recursive, meaning the `ls` command is repeated for all subdirectories
--help	Lists all options available with a command

Examining the `ls -l` Command The output of the `ls -l` command contains important information in eight separate columns, discussed in detail in the following list. Figure 3-3 gives you an overview of this output.

Here's an example of information the `ls -l` command returns; refer to this example as you read the explanations in the following list:

```
drwxr-xr-x 2 natalie users 4096 2012-02-06 20:01 Desktop
```

- *File type*—In this example, the file type column displays "d," which stands for a directory. Notice that there's no space after this first column.
- *File permissions*—The second column specifies file permissions. In the previous example, the file permissions are `rwxr-xr-x`. You learn about file permissions in Chapter 5, but for now, just be aware that file permissions are displayed for three

categories: user, group, and other. Each category is assigned a combination of read (r), write (w), and execute (x) permissions.

- *Hard links*—The third column displays the number of hard links associated with the file. You learn more about hard links later in "Creating Links."
- *Owner*—The fourth column shows the user owner of the file (explained in Chapter 7).
- *Group*—The fifth column shows the file's group owner (explained in Chapter 7).
- *File size*—The sixth column displays the file size, which is in bytes by default. You can use the -h option to view file size in a format that's easier to read (such as kilobytes, megabytes, or gigabytes).
- *Modification time*—The seventh column displays a timestamp showing when the file was last modified.
- *Filename*—The eighth column shows the name of the file.

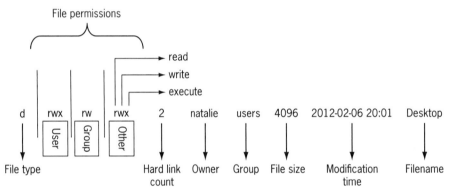

Figure 3-3 A guide to the ls -l command's output
© Cengage Learning 2013

Activity 3-2: Using the ls Command

Time Required: 10 minutes

Objective: Use commands for viewing Linux files and directories.

Description: In this activity, you use the ls command to view files and directories in your current directory and practice using options, including two you choose from Table 3-2.

1. If necessary, start VMware Player and start an openSUSE virtual machine. Log in to openSUSE as a user other than root, and open a terminal window.
2. Type **ls** and press **Enter**, and then type **ls -l** and press **Enter**.
3. Display a long list of the /etc directory by typing **ls -l /etc** and pressing **Enter**.
4. Display a long list of the /etc/hosts file by typing **ls -l /etc/hosts** and pressing **Enter**. What's the timestamp of this file?

_____

5. Display all files in your home directory, including hidden files, by typing **ls -a ~** and pressing **Enter**.

6. Review Table 3-2 and choose two options to use in your current directory. List the options you chose and briefly describe the results of using them:

_____

_____

7. Leave the terminal window open and the virtual machine running for the next activity.

Getting Help

Few administrators, no matter how long they've been working with Linux, have every command memorized. There are thousands of Linux commands, and most have multiple options. The good news is that Linux stores documentation files on all commands. **Man (manual) pages** are documentation files that describe Linux shell commands, executable programs, system calls, special files, and so forth. The following example shows opening the man pages for the `ls` command:

```
man ls
Man: find all matching manual pages
 * ls (1)
   ls (1p)
Man: What manual page do you want?
```

An asterisk to the left of the first entry indicates the default selection. To select the man page for the `ls` command, type `1` (the numeral, in this case) and press Enter, or type `1p` and press Enter to select the POSIX Programmer's Manual page for the `ls` command. Your screen should be similar to Figure 3-4.

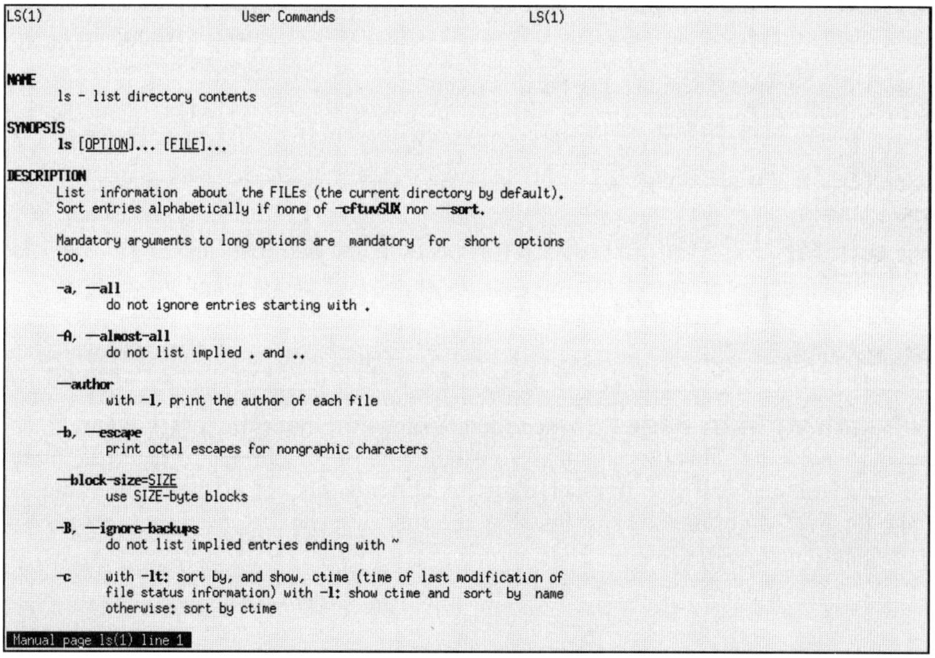

Figure 3-4 Excerpt from the man page for the `ls` command
Source: openSUSE

POSIX (an abbreviation for Portable Operating System Interface) is a set of standards based on UNIX. Many Linux commands have both a Linux man page and a POSIX Programmer's Manual page associated with them.

Man pages are organized into eight sections, described in Table 3-3.

Some UNIX systems offer man pages for section 0 (header files) and section 9 (kernel routines).

Table 3-3 Man page sections

Section	Description	Examples
1	Executable programs or shell commands	man ls, man pwd
2	System calls, which are system requests that programs make to the kernel	man kill, man read
3	Library calls (to access functions in program libraries)	man xcrypt, man stdin
4	Special files, such as the floppy disk, that are usually found in /dev	man fd, man tty
5	File formats and conventions	man passwd, man hosts
6	Games	man tetravex, man AisleRiot
7	Macro packages and conventions	man man (7), man gruff (7)
8	System administration commands	man yast, man suseconfig

You can also find man pages for the man command to get more information on man page sections and other features of this command.

Navigating Man Pages Notice the message at the bottom left in Figure 3-4: "Manual page ls(1) line 1." This message tells you the name of the command (ls), the man page section (1), and the first line number that can be read (line 1), so you're looking at the man page for the ls command, and line 1 is the first line shown onscreen. Table 3-4 lists ways to navigate man pages.

Table 3-4 Methods of navigating man pages

Action	Function
Press f or the spacebar	Move forward one window at a time.
Press b or backspace	Move backward one window at a time.
Press h	Open the help page.
Press / (forward slash)	Enter a string of text to search for in the man page.
Press n	Repeat the previous search.
Press N	Repeat the previous search in the reverse direction.

Activity 3-3: Working with Man Pages

Time Required: 10 minutes

Objective: Find and navigate man pages for any Linux command.

Description: In this activity, you use the man command to open help files on the pwd, cd, and ls commands. You also use the man command to find documentation on another command of your choice and refer to Table 3-4 to navigate the man page.

1. If necessary, start VMware Player and start an openSUSE virtual machine. Log in to openSUSE as a user other than root, and open a terminal window.

2. Display the man page for the pwd command by typing **man pwd** and pressing **Enter**. Press **q** to quit, and then try typing **man 1 pwd** and pressing **Enter**. What's the difference in the output of these two commands?

   _____

3. Display the man page for the cd command by typing **man cd** and pressing **Enter**. Read the information, as time permits.

4. Display the man page for the ls command by typing **man ls** and pressing **Enter**. Read the information, as time permits.

5. Display the man page for a command of your choice. Refer to Table 3-4 to practice navigating it.

6. Leave the terminal window open and the virtual machine running for the next activity.

Using Wildcards

In a card game, a wildcard represents any card the cardholder wants. In Linux, a **wildcard** represents letters and characters used to specify a filename for searches. For instance, you can use a wildcard to get a long list of all files in the current directory starting with "new." Linux administrators use wildcards to navigate to directories faster, move or delete a group of files, and locate files based on a portion of their filenames. You can use them, too, to help you navigate the Linux directory structure and manage files. Table 3-5 describes wildcards used in Linux. The two used most often are * and ?, explained in more detail in the following paragraphs.

Table 3-5 Wildcards

Wildcard	Description
*	Matches zero or more characters in a filename
?	Matches any one character in a filename
[acf]	Matches one of multiple characters in a filename; in this example, a, c, or f
[a-f]	Matches one of a range of characters in a filename; in this example, any character from a through f
[!a-f]	Matches filenames that don't contain a specified range of characters; in this example, filenames that don't contain a through f

The * wildcard is used to represent zero or more characters. Say your current directory contains five files: file1, file2, newfile1, newfile2, and notefile. You want a list of files starting with the letters "fi." You can use this wildcard as shown:

```
ls fi*
file1 file2
```

Note that because this wildcard represents zero or more characters, entering ls file1* would display only file1. You can also specify files ending with a certain character, as in this example:

```
ls *2
file2 newfile2
```

You can use the * wildcard with any command that needs an argument. For example, if you need to switch to a certain directory, but all you remember is that the directory name starts with "new," you can use the following command to list all directories starting with those characters:

```
cd new*
```

The ? wildcard is used to represent only one character, as shown in the following example:

```
~/newdirectory> ls -l
total 20
-rw-r--r-- 1 maria users 0 2012-03-18 22:31 file1
-rw-r--r-- 1 maria users 0 2012-03-18 22:31 file2
-rw-r--r-- 1 maria users 0 2012-03-18 22:31 newfile1
-rw-r--r-- 1 maria users 0 2012-03-18 22:31 newfile2
-rw-r--r-- 1 maria users 0 2012-03-18 22:31 notefile
~/newdirectory> ls file?
file1 file2
```

Activity 3-4: Using Wildcards

Time Required: 10 minutes

Objective: Use wildcards to search for files and directories.

Description: In this activity, you use the common wildcards * and ?. You also see the results of more uncommon wildcards.

1. If necessary, start VMware Player and start an openSUSE virtual machine. Log in to openSUSE as a user other than root, and open a terminal window.

2. Use the absolute method to change to the /etc directory by typing **cd /etc** and pressing **Enter.**

3. Display a long list of files and directories in the /etc directory by typing **ls -l** and pressing **Enter.**

4. Display a long list of files and directories in the /etc directory starting with the letter "h" by typing **ls -l h*** and pressing **Enter.** How are the results different from Step 3?

   _____

5. Display a long list of files and directories in the /etc directory and use two wildcards by typing **ls -l *.?** and pressing **Enter.** How are the results different from Step 3?

   _____

6. Display a long list of files and directories in the /etc directory starting with a, c, or k by typing **ls -l [ack]*** and pressing **Enter.**

7. Display a long list of files and directories in the /etc directory starting with a, b, or c by typing **ls -l [a-c]*** and pressing **Enter.**

8. Display a long list of files and directories in the /etc directory that don't start with the letters a through s by typing **ls -l [!a-s]*** and pressing **Enter.**

9. Change the current directory by typing **cd /h*** and pressing **Enter.** What happened, and why?

   _____

10. Leave the terminal window open and the virtual machine running for the next activity.

Managing Files and Directories

Now that you have explored the Linux directory structure, it's time to learn some important file management tasks. As a Linux administrator, you should know how to use the command line to create files and directories, move files in and out of directories, delete and copy files and directories, and view file and directory contents. The following sections explain how to perform these tasks.

Creating and Deleting Directories and Files

Directories are essential for keeping files organized in the Linux file system. Each directory has its own permissions assigned (as explained in Chapter 5). Remember that your home directory is created to give you full permission to create subdirectories, files, scripts, and so forth; as an administrator, you have the root password, which gives you full access to create directories and files throughout the file system. The commands you learn in this section are mkdir, touch, rm, and rmdir.

Creating Directories The mkdir (make directory) command is used to create directories. The following example shows creating a directory called Studynotes in the home directory:

```
~> mkdir Studynotes
~> ls
bin Documents Music Public Studynotes Videos
Desktop Download Pictures public_html Templates
```

Over time, a home directory usually increases to hundreds of files, which can make managing it difficult. Creating and using subdirectories help you organize files. For instance, in this example, the Studynotes subdirectory was created to contain all the user's study notes. Later, the user might decide to create a subdirectory of Studynotes for each class.

Creating Files There are several ways to create a file in Linux. The simplest is the touch command, used to create a new empty file or update the timestamp of an existing file. The following example shows creating an empty file with this command:

```
~/Studynotes> touch chapter1
~/Studynotes> ls -l
total 4
-rw-r--r-- 1 keith users 0 2012-03-19 13:29 chapter1
```

The timestamp for the new file, chapter1, is 2012-03-19 13:29, which is March 19, 2012 at 1:29 pm. If you use the touch command with this file again, it simply updates the file's date and time to match the current system date and time.

On a Linux file system that's shared across a network, you should update (touch) important files and scripts you have created. Some system administrators create scripts to delete files that haven't been modified in 90 days. This measure clears space in the file system but could delete a file you need. Make sure you use the touch command with important files periodically.

Wildcards are handy when you're updating multiple files at the same time, as shown in the following example with the touch command:

```
~/Studynotes> ls -l
total 16
-rw-r--r-- 1 david users 0 2009-11-03 13:00 chapter1
-rw-r--r-- 1 david users 0 2009-12-19 15:43 chapter2
-rw-r--r-- 1 david users 0 2012-01-12 18:02 chapter3
-rw-r--r-- 1 david users 0 2012-02-10 08:30 chapter4
~/Studynotes> touch *
~/Studynotes> ls -l
total 16
```

```
-rw-r--r-- 1 david users 0 2012-03-19 13:45 chapter1
-rw-r--r-- 1 david users 0 2012-03-19 13:45 chapter2
-rw-r--r-- 1 david users 0 2012-03-19 13:45 chapter3
-rw-r--r-- 1 david users 0 2012-03-19 13:45 chapter4
```

Remember the * represents zero or more characters. In this example, the * used alone instructs the touch command to update every file in the current directory.

Deleting Directories and Files

Depending on the permissions your user account has, deleting directories can be dangerous. If you try to delete a folder in Windows, a message box opens, asking for confirmation that you want to delete it. Typically, there's no confirmation message in Linux. To avoid deleting files accidentally, most Linux users log in with an account that has limited permissions; they switch to the root user only when they need to do administrative tasks. The rm command is used to remove files and directories, and the rmdir command is used to remove empty directories.

You use the su (switch user) command later in "Switching Users and Becoming Root."

The following example shows deleting an empty subdirectory in the current directory:

```
1. ~/Studynotes> cd Math
2. ~/Studynotes/Math> ls
3. ~/Studynotes/Math> cd ..
4. ~/Studynotes> pwd
5. /home/andrea/Studynotes
6. ~/Studynotes> rmdir Math
7. ~/Studynotes> ls -l
8. total 24
drwxr-xr-x 2 andrea users 4096 2012-03-20 09:27 English
drwxr-xr-x 2 andrea users 4096 2012-03-20 09:27 Week1
drwxr-xr-x 2 andrea users 4096 2012-03-20 09:27 Week2
```

The current directory, Studynotes, contains four subdirectories: English, Math, Week1, and Week2. You change to the Math directory (line 1) and use the ls command (line 2) to determine whether this directory is empty. Next, you use the relative method (line 3) to change back to the parent directory and use the pwd command (line 4) to confirm the location. Finally, you use the rmdir command (line 6) to delete the empty directory. If the Math directory had contained files, an error would have been displayed because the rmdir command doesn't remove directories containing content.

If you try to remove a directory that isn't empty, you get an error message similar to the following:

```
rmdir: failed to remove 'Math': Directory not empty
```

Before removing a directory containing files, you must use the rm command to delete the files. Remember that there's no confirmation message in Linux, so be sure you're deleting the correct file. The following example shows using the rm command to delete files in the Math directory:

```
~/Studynotes/Math> ls -l
total 4
-rw-r--r-- 1 andrea users 0 2012-03-20 10:44 file1
~/Studynotes/Math> rm file1
```

You can also use the -r option with the rm command to delete directories and their contents recursively, meaning you don't need to delete files first. In other words, this option enables you to remove directories that aren't empty.

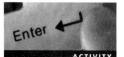

Activity 3-5: Creating and Deleting Directories and Files

Time Required: 15 minutes

Objective: Use Linux commands for creating and deleting directories and files.

Description: In this activity, you create a directory with the mkdir command, create files with the touch command, and update file timestamps by using the touch command with wildcards. Finally, you use the rm command to delete files and the rmdir command to delete a directory.

1. If necessary, start VMware Player and start an openSUSE virtual machine. Log in to openSUSE as a user other than root, and open a terminal window.
2. Change to your home directory by typing **cd** and pressing **Enter**.
3. Create and name a directory by typing **mkdir Activity3-5** and pressing **Enter**.
4. Change to the Activity3-5 directory by typing **cd Activity3-5** and pressing **Enter**.
5. Create three files in the Activity3-5 directory by typing **touch actfile1 actfile2 actfile3** and pressing **Enter**.
6. Display a long list of all files in the Activity3-5 directory by typing **ls -l** and pressing **Enter**.
7. Update the timestamps of these files by typing **touch *[2-3]** and pressing **Enter**. What files are updated?

_____

8. To return to your home directory, type **cd** and press **Enter**.
9. Try to delete the Activity3-5 directory by typing **rmdir Activity3-5** and pressing **Enter**. Were you able to delete the directory? Why or why not?

_____

10. Change to the Activity3-5 directory by typing **cd Activity3-5** and pressing **Enter**. Delete the three files (actfile1, actfile2, and actfile3) by typing **rm *** and pressing **Enter**.
11. Type **ls** and press **Enter**. Is the directory empty?

_____

12. Change to your home directory by typing **cd** and pressing **Enter**.

13. Now that the Activity3-5 directory is empty, delete it by typing **rmdir Activity3-5** and pressing **Enter**.

14. Leave the terminal window open and the virtual machine running for the next activity.

Moving, Renaming, and Copying Files

The command line makes moving or copying multiple files at once easy. Many Linux administrators actually find using the command line for this purpose simpler than using a GUI. In this section, you learn the mv and cp commands. The mv command has a dual purpose: renaming files and moving files from one directory to another. In fact, you can do both at the same time. The syntax for the mv command is as follows:

mv *filename new location*

The following example shows moving the week1notes file from the Math directory to the ~/Studynotes/Week1 directory. The ~ represents the user's home directory:

~/Studynotes/Math> **mv week1notes ~/Studynotes/Week1**

Here's an example of using the mv command to rename a file:

~/Studynotes/Week1> **mv week1notes notes**

The following example shows how to move the notes file to another directory and rename it Newnotes at the same time:

~/Studynotes/Week1> **mv notes ~/Studynotes/Week2/newnotes**

When you move a file to a new location, it no longer exists in the original directory. In other words, the mv command doesn't create new files. To have the same file in two locations, you use the cp (copy) command, which copies files and directories. It has the same syntax as the mv command:

cp *filename new location*

The following example shows creating a copy of the newnotes file in the Week1 directory:

~/Studynotes/Week2> **cp newnotes ~/Studynotes/Week1**

The main difference between the cp command and the mv command is that the cp command creates a new file, and the mv command is used with just one file.

Activity 3-6: Renaming, Moving, and Copying Files

Time Required: 15 minutes

Objective: Use Linux commands for renaming, moving, and copying files.

Description: In this activity, you create a directory called Activity3-6 and create a file in this directory. You use the mv command to rename the file and then move it to the parent directory. You also use the cp command to make a copy of the file in the Activity3-6 directory.

1. If necessary, start VMware Player and start an openSUSE virtual machine. Log in to openSUSE as a user other than root, and open a terminal window.

2. Type **mkdir Activity3-6** and press **Enter**, and then change to this new directory by typing **cd Activity3-6** and pressing **Enter**.

3. Type **touch actfile1** and press **Enter**. Type **ls** and press **Enter**.

4. Type **mv actfile1 actfile2** and press **Enter**, and then type **ls** and press **Enter**. What's the result of this mv command?

   _____

5. Type **mv actfile2 ..** and press **Enter**, and then type **ls** and press **Enter**. What's the result of this command?

   _____

6. Type **cd ..** and press **Enter**. What directory are you in?

   _____

7. Type **cp actfile2 actfile3** and press **Enter**. What's the result of this command?

   _____

8. Type **cp actfile2 Activity3-6** and press **Enter**. What happens? Change to the Activity3-6 directory, and then type **ls** and press **Enter**. What files are in this directory?

   _____

   _____

9. Leave the terminal window open and the virtual machine running for the next activity.

Creating Links

In the previous section, you learned how to create copies of files with the cp command. These copies are separate from the originals, so if you change the original file, the copied file doesn't reflect these changes. In this section, you learn how to create links with the ln command. To understand how links work, however, first you need to know what inodes are and how information is stored on a disk.

Inodes   An inode is a data structure that stores all information (such as file permissions, ownership, and file type) about a file except the actual data and filename. Each inode is identified by an inode number, which can be thought of as an address. The **inode number** references an entry in the **inode table**, which is a list of inodes for all files on a Linux partition. This table entry points to the data's location on the disk. To view a file's inode number, use the ls -il command, as shown:

```
~/Math> ls -il
total 4
3327 -rw-r--r-- 1 dustin users 0 2012-03-21 15:46 algebra
```

The inode number for the algebra file in the preceding example is 3327. To display more inode information (such as file size, permissions, UID, and so forth), you use the stat (status) command. In the following example, it's used with the `algebra` file in the `Math` directory:

```
~/Math> stat algebra
 File: 'algebra'
 Size: 0 Blocks: 8 IO Block: 4096 regular empty file
Device: 803h/2051d Inode: 3327 Links: 1
Access: (0644/-rw-r--r--) Uid: ( 1000/ dustin) Gid: ( 100/ users)
Access: 2012-03-21 15:46:43.740447686 -0500
Modify: 2012-03-21 15:46:43.666449631 -0500
Change: 2012-03-21 15:46:43.761409157 -0500
```

NOTE

Each Linux partition has only one inode table. Every file (including directories) contains a unique inode number, unless you're dealing with hard links, discussed next.

Hard Links Hard links are files that point to data on the hard drive. When you create a file, it's automatically linked to the actual data stored on a partition and assigned an inode number referencing this data. You can then create hard links on the same partition to refer to this data. The following example shows creating a hard link:

```
~/Math/Week1/Calculus> ln notes ~/Math
```

In this example, a hard link is created in the `Calculus` directory to link the `notes` file to a file in the `Math` directory. You could then change to the `Math` directory and use the `ls -il` command to verify that the `notes` hard link was indeed created. The following example shows the results of using `ls -il` in the `Math` and `Calculus` directories. Notice that the link count is 2 and both have the same inode number (522815):

```
~/Math/Week1/Calculus> ls -il
522815 -rw-r--r-- 2 sasha users 0 2012-03-30 20:24 notes
dustin@linux-7cua:~/Math> ls -il
522815 -rw-r--r-- 2 sasha users 0 2012-03-30 20:24 notes
```

When the `ls -il` command is first used in the `Calculus` directory, the link count is 1 (shown in bold in the following line) because it's the only link to the actual data on the hard drive:

```
522815 -rw-r--r-- 1 sasha users 86 2012-03-21 16:29 notes
```

After a hard link to a file in the `Math` directory is created, the link count changes to 2. Notice that the inode number (522815) for the `notes` file in the `Math` directory is the same as for the `notes` file in the `Calculus` directory.

If a file contains three hard links and you delete one, the data isn't affected because two links still exist. For instance, if you delete the `notes` file in the `Calculus` directory in the previous example, the data still exists on the hard drive and can be accessed from the `Math` directory. The data isn't deleted until the last link is deleted.

Symbolic (Soft) Links Symbolic links (also called soft links) are special types of files that point to other files instead of pointing to data on the hard drive. They don't share the same inode number, as hard links do. The benefit of creating a symbolic link is you can link files that are on separate partitions or even different computers. To create a symbolic link, you use the -s option with the ln command, as shown in this example:

```
~/Sports> ln -s football baseball
~/Sports> ls -il
total 4
3935 lrwxrwxrwx 1 edward users 8 2012-03-22 10:11 baseball -> football
3934 -rw-r--r-- 1 edward users 0 2012-03-22 10:10 football
```

The inode number for the symbolic link (3935) is different from the inode number for the target file (3934). The symbolic link (baseball) points to the target file (football), and the target file's inode points to the actual data on the hard drive. If you modify the symbolic link, the target file is also modified. Likewise, if you modify the target file, the symbolic link is modified. If you delete the target file, the symbolic link no longer works.

An advantage of symbolic links is that you can create one to point to a file on a different partition, as shown in this example:

```
~> df -h
Filesystem Size Used Avail Use% Mounted on
/dev/sda2 7.7G 3.5G 3.9G 48% /
udev 372M 312K 371M 1% /dev
/dev/sda3 11G 393M 11G 4% /home
/dev/sda4 20G 10G 10G 50% /data
/data> ln -s cat /home/edward/dog
/data> ls -il
44543 -rw-r--r-- 1 edward users 0 2012-03-22 10:46 cat
/data> cd
~> ls -il
3934 lrwxrwxrwx 1 edward users 3 2012-03-22 10:47 dog -> cat
```

In this example, the df command shows disk space use so that you can see the available partitions. The -h option for output is in human-readable format. Notice that the cat file is on the /dev/sda4 partition, and the symbolic link dog is on the /dev/sda3 partition.

Activity 3-7: Working with Links

Time Required: 20 minutes

Objective: Identify inode numbers and create hard and symbolic links.

Description: In this activity, you identify a file's inode number, and then create a hard link and a symbolic link.

1. If necessary, start VMware Player and start an openSUSE virtual machine. Log in to openSUSE as a user other than root, and open a terminal window.

2. Type **mkdir Activity3-7** and press **Enter**. Change to this new directory by typing **cd Activity3-7** and pressing **Enter**.

3. Create a file in this directory by typing **touch actfile1** and pressing **Enter**. Type **ls -il** and press **Enter**. What's the inode number for `actfile1`?

   _____

4. Display additional inode information for `actfile1` by typing **stat actfile1** and pressing **Enter**.

5. Change to your home directory by typing **cd** and pressing **Enter**.

6. Type **mkdir Linkdir** and press **Enter**. Change to this new directory by typing **cd Linkdir** and pressing **Enter**.

7. Create a hard link by typing **ln ~/Activity3-7/actfile1 .** and pressing **Enter**. Type **ls -il** and press **Enter**. How many links are associated with `actfile1`? Has the number of hard links changed since Step 3?

   _____

8. Type **cd ~/Activity3-7** and press **Enter**. Try to remove `actfile1` by typing **rm actfile1** and pressing **Enter**, and then type **ls -il** and press **Enter**. Is the file removed? Is the data gone? Explain your answers:

   _____

   _____

9. Type **cd ~/Linkdir** and press **Enter**, and then type **ls -il** and press **Enter**. How many links does `actfile1` have, and why?

   _____

10. Type **cd ~/Activity3-7** and press **Enter**. Create a symbolic link by typing **ln -s ~/Linkdir/actfile1 .** and pressing **Enter**, and then type **ls -il** and press **Enter**. What's the link count for `actfile1`?

    _____

11. Type **cd ~/Linkdir** and press **Enter**, and then type **ls -il** and press **Enter**. Is the inode number the same as the inode number for `actfile1` in the `Linkdir` directory? Why or why not?

    _____

12. Leave the terminal window open and the virtual machine running for the next activity.

Switching Users and Becoming Root

You learn about creating users and groups in Chapter 7, but for now, you just need to know that in Linux, every user must have a username and password and belong to a primary group. A benefit of the Linux command line is being able to switch to a different user account while staying in the same terminal window. Remember that the root user has the highest level of permissions, so even if you're a Linux administrator, you should avoid logging in with this account unless you need to perform root administrative tasks, such as editing configuration files. The su (switch user) command enables one user to become another user temporarily. Here's an example of using the su command:

The exit command in lines 5 and 11 is used to switch back to the previous user. For instance, if you're logged in as user1, switch to user2, and then type exit, the command brings you back to user1.

```
1. ~> su jasmine
2. Password:
3. jasmine@client:/home/dustin> pwd
4. /home/dustin
5. jasmine@client:/home/dustin> exit
6. exit
7. ~> su
8. Password:
9. client:/home/dustin # pwd
10. /home/dustin
11. client:/home/dustin # exit
12. exit
13. ~>
```

In this example, the user switches to the jasmine user account, but the current directory doesn't change; it's still the user's home directory. Note that you can't switch to another user if you don't know the account password (unless you're the root user). If you use the su command without an argument, it defaults to the root user, which changes the prompt to a # symbol (as shown in lines 9 and 11).

Another way to switch users is to add - after the su command, as in su - jasmine. This option loads the user's environment variables (discussed in Chapter 5).

Activity 3-8: Switching Users

Time Required: 10 minutes

Objective: Switch users without logging off the computer.

Description: In this activity, you use the su command to switch to the root user and use the - option to load this user's environment variables.

1. If necessary, start VMware Player and start an openSUSE virtual machine. Log in to openSUSE as a user other than root, and open a terminal window.

2. You should be in your home directory. (If necessary, use the pwd command to confirm.) Try to change to the /root directory by typing **cd /root** and then press **Enter**. Were you able to change to this directory? Why or why not?

_____

3. To switch to the root user, type **su** and press **Enter**. When prompted, type the root password you set during installation and press **Enter**.

4. Now that you have switched to the root user, change to the /root directory by typing **cd /root** and then press **Enter**.

5. Type **exit** and press **Enter**. Close the terminal window, and shut down your virtual machine.

Chapter Summary

- Learning to navigate the Linux directory structure at the command line is a useful skill for server administrators because most servers are installed without a GUI.

- In Linux, there's only one root directory, and all files and subdirectories are placed under it in a hierarchical structure.

- Nearly all major Linux distributions follow the Filesystem Hierarchy Standard (FHS), which defines the kind of files that should be in each subdirectory of root.

- The pwd command displays your current directory, and the cd command changes your current directory.

- To change the current directory, you can use the absolute method or the relative method. The absolute method always starts with root (/), and the relative method always starts with the current directory.

- The ls command lists the contents of a directory. The -l option is used with this command to display a long list of files and subdirectories in the directory.

- Linux includes man pages for finding information on commands and other Linux components.

- Wildcards are special characters used to help specify a filename or directory path. The two most common wildcards are * and ?. The * represents zero or more characters, and the ? represents only one character.

- The mkdir command is used to create directories, and the touch command is used to create empty files and update their timestamps.

- The rm command deletes files or directories, and the rmdir command deletes only empty directories.

- The mv command is used to move and rename files, and the cp command is used to create a copy of a file.

- The ln command is used to create hard and symbolic links. Hard links point to data on the hard drive, and soft links point to files that can span multiple partitions.

- The su command enables one user to become another user temporarily.

Key Terms

absolute path The full directory pathname starting from root (/).

command completion A BASH shell feature that finishes a command for you after you enter the first few characters; it's enabled by pressing the Tab key.

command-line argument Information entered after a command to include specific instructions.

command-line prompt An interface that enables users to interact with the OS by typing commands, options, and arguments.

current directory The directory a user is working in.

Filesystem Hierarchy Standard (FHS) A standard specifying requirements and guidelines for file and directory placement in UNIX-like operating systems.

file system The way files and directories are stored and organized to make access to data easier.

hard links Files that point to data on the hard disk and share the same inode number.

home directory A user's default directory on the file system.

inode A data structure that stores information about a file, such as the inode number, file permissions, file owner, and so on; the file's actual data and name aren't stored in the inode.

inode number A unique identification for an inode that references an entry in the inode table. *See also* inode.

inode table A list of inodes for all files on a Linux partition; entries in this table point to where files' actual data is stored. *See also* inode.

man (manual) pages Documentation files that describe Linux shell commands, executable programs, system calls, special files, and so forth.

options Information entered after a command to modify the way it's carried out.

relative path The directory pathname starting from the current directory.

shareable file A file that can be stored on one machine and used by multiple users on other machines.

static files Files that don't change on their own.

symbolic links Special types of files that point to other files (even on separate partitions or different computers) instead of pointing to data on the hard drive; they don't share the same inode number. *See also* hard links.

unshareable file A file that can be used only on the local machine.

variable files Files that can change on their own.

wildcard A character used in searches to specify certain conditions.

Review Questions

1. There can be multiple root directories in Linux. True or False?

2. Describe a benefit of the Filesystem Hierarchy Standard (FHS).

3. What command do you use to display your current directory?

   a. ln

   b. cd

   c. pwd

   d. ls

4. What command do you use to change to a different directory?

   a. ln

   b. cd

   c. pwd

   d. ls

5. What command is used to view the contents of your current directory?

    a. ln

    b. cd

    c. pwd

    d. ls

6. The cd /home/user command uses the relative method. True or False?

7. The -l option affects the ls command by:

    a. Changing the format to a long list

    b. Listing all files and directories

    c. Listing only files

    d. Listing inode numbers

8. After entering ls -a, how can you tell which files are hidden?

    a. Their names are displayed in a different color.

    b. Their names start with a . (dot).

    c. Their names start with an uppercase letter.

    d. Their names end with a . (dot).

9. Describe three options you can use with the ls command.

10. Which of the following is displayed after issuing the ls -l command? (Choose all that apply.)

    a. File permissions

    b. Parent directory

    c. File type

    d. Contents of subdirectories

11. Describe three man page sections.

12. After you use the ls command, the following files are displayed:
    file1 file2 file3 file.a file.b file.c files
    List the files displayed with each of the following options:

    a. ls f*

    b. ls file?

    c. ls file[a-c]

    d. ls file[!1-3]

13. What command creates an empty file?

    a. rm

    b. mkdir

    c. touch

    d. rmdir

14. What command deletes files and directories?

    a. rm

    b. mkdir

    c. touch

    d. rmdir

15. What command deletes empty directories?

    a. rm

    b. mkdir

    c. touch

    d. rmdir

16. What command creates directories?

    a. rm

    b. mkdir

    c. touch

    d. rmdir

17. Explain how the -r option affects the rm command.

18. What command is used to rename or move a file?

    a. rn

    b. cp

    c. mv

    d. Both b and c

19. What command is used to copy a file?

    a. rn

    b. cp

    c. mv

    d. Both b and c

20. Explain the difference between an inode table, an inode, and an inode number.

21. How does the `-i` option affect the `ls` command?

    a. Displays the inode table

    b. Displays the inode

    c. Displays the inode number

    d. None of the above

22. Explain the difference between hard links and symbolic links.

23. How does the `-s` option affect the `ln` command?

    a. Creates a symbolic link

    b. Creates a hard link

    c. Gives special permissions to the link

    d. Removes the link

24. What Linux command can you use to switch users without actually logging off your system?

Case Projects

CASE PROJECTS

Case Project 3-1: Working with Modified Files

You're the system administrator for a major automobile company, and you just found out that the chief financial officer (CFO) has resigned. Your boss asks you to find all files in the CFO's home directory that have been modified in the past 90 days, and then move them to your home directory for continuity purposes. What command should you use to find out which files have been modified in this timeframe, and what command should you use to copy these files to your home directory?

Case Project 3-2: Creating a Link

Four science instructors at East Coast Career College ask you whether they can access a particular log file from their home directories. They explain that they update a log file in the `/workgrp/project` directory weekly, and they don't want to change out of their home directories every time they want to view or edit the file. In addition, they want the log file in their home directories to be called `myjournal`. You need to create a link to the log file so that each instructor can access the file from his or her home directory, using the following criteria:

Scientist 1: Michio
Home directory: /home/michio
Scientist 2: Neil
Home directory: /home/neil
Scientist 3: Marty
Home directory: /home/marty
Scientist 4: Ellen
Home directory: /home/ellen
The log file is called sci.journal, and it's in the /workgrp/project directory.

## chapter 4

Creating and Editing Files with Text Editors

After reading this chapter and completing the exercises, you will be able to:

- Describe key features of GUI and command-line text editors available in Linux
- Use the vim editor to create and edit text files

All major Linux distributions come with a text editor that enables you to create and edit text files, and administrators should have text-editing skills to create and modify scripts and to do advanced configuration tasks. In this chapter, you learn about the GUI text editors available with openSUSE Linux—KWrite and gedit—and the command-line text editor vim.

You spend the most time learning the vim editor in this chapter. You learn about its three modes, key combinations that can be used to perform specific tasks, and extended mode commands for saving text files and exiting the vim editor.

Text Editors in Linux

A **text editor** is a program used to create and edit plain text files. In Chapter 2, you explored OpenOffice.org Writer, a word processor included with the GNOME desktop environment. Word processors and text editors are similar, in that you can insert and edit text with both, but the comparison stops there. Word processors aren't more advanced text editors any more than airplanes are more advanced cars. True, both get you from point A to point B, but your purposes for using them differ. The same is true for word processors and text editors.

The main purpose of a text editor is to create a file that can be used by another program. For instance, text files can contain Hypertext Markup Language (HTML) for a Web browser to display or source code that a compiler can process. Another purpose is to create a **shell script**, a text file containing a sequence of commands. Linux has two types of text editors: command-line editors and GUI editors, discussed in the following sections.

GUI Text Editors in Linux

Linux GUI text editors are similar to Notepad in Windows. They have a main window where you can enter and edit text and are easier to manage than their command-line counterparts. For instance, one advantage of using a GUI text editor is that you can select and edit text quickly with the mouse. The following sections give you an overview of two widely used GUI text editors.

KWrite: A GUI Text Editor for KDE   KWrite is a GUI text editor, also known as the
programmer's editor for the K Desktop Environment (see Figure 4-1).

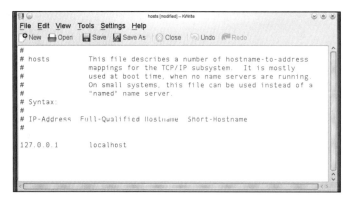

Figure 4-1 KDE's KWrite text editor
Source: openSUSE

Typing `kwrite` at a command prompt opens a new empty file in KWrite, and adding a file-name as an argument opens an existing file for editing. If the file doesn't exist, this argument creates an empty file with the filename you specified. Another way to start KWrite is to use the Kickoff Application Launcher button (known as the K button) at the bottom left. KWrite has some advanced features, including **syntax highlighting** to display text in different colors and fonts for programming languages, such as C, C++, Java, HTML, and Perl. You can select syntax highlighting from the Tools menu after enabling power user mode (which you do in Activity 4-1). Another advanced feature in the Settings menu is **bookmarks**, which are markers placed on certain lines to help navigate through a text file.

4

KWrite comes with KDE but must be installed manually to work in GNOME.

Activity 4-1: Exploring the KWrite Text Editor

Time Required: 20 minutes

Objective: Explore features of the KWrite text editor.

Description: In this activity, you use KWrite to create a simple HTML Web page. You learn how to display line numbers and enable syntax highlighting to improve readability. You also learn how to add bookmarks and navigate to them. Finally, you save the file and open it as an HTML Web page.

1. Start VMware Player, and start an openSUSE virtual machine with the KDE desktop environment.

2. To start KWrite from the command line, open a terminal window, type **kwrite**, and press **Enter**. To start KWrite with the GUI, click the **K** button (green circle at the lower left), point to the **Applications** icon, and click **Utilities**. Next, click the **Editor** utility, and then click the **Text Editor** icon in the list of installed GUI editors.

3. Display line numbers by clicking **View, Show Line Numbers** from the menu.

4. Type **<!--*your first and last name*-->** and press **Enter**. On the second line, type **<!--Activity 4-1-->** and press **Enter**. On the third line, type **<!--*today's date*-->** (substituting the current date in whatever format you like) and press **Enter** two times. The < ! symbol in the first three lines indicates a comment, so the Web browser doesn't read these lines.

5. To enable you to use advanced features, click **Settings, Configure Editor**, and then click the **Enable power user mode** check box. Click **OK**, and then click **OK** again in the Power user mode changed message box. To save the file, click the **Save** button, type **act4.1** for the filename, and click **Save** again. Exit KWrite by clicking **File, Quit** from the menu. Restart KWrite from the command line by opening a terminal window (if necessary), typing **kwrite ~/Documents/act4.1**, and pressing **Enter**. If necessary, display line numbers again.

6. Now that power user mode has been enabled, you can select syntax highlighting for HTML code by clicking **Tools**, pointing to **Highlighting**, pointing to **Markup**, and clicking **HTML**. How did the text in the first three lines change?

7. Start on line 5 and type the following HTML code, pressing **Enter** after each line (twice to create the blank lines shown):

```
<html>
<body>

My little Web page

</body>
</html>
```

8. Click **View** on the menu bar and make sure the **Show Icon Border** option is selected.

9. Put the cursor on line 5, and then click **Bookmarks, Set Bookmark** from the menu. Do the same thing on line 10. What happens?

_____

10. Click **Bookmarks** on the menu bar, and then click **Previous: 5 - "<html>"**. What happens?

_____

11. Save the file by clicking **File, Save As** from the menu, typing **act4-1.html** for the filename, and clicking **Save**. Exit KWrite by clicking **File, Quit** from the menu.

12. Open the Dolphin file manager by clicking the **K** button, and then clicking **File Manager**. Click **Documents**, and then click **act4-1.html**. What results do you see onscreen?

_____

13. Power off the virtual machine, and close any open windows.

Gedit: A GUI Text Editor for GNOME   Gedit, a GUI text editor included with GNOME, is designed to be easy to use, and you can install plug-ins for advanced tasks related to text editing. There are a few ways to start gedit. The simplest way is to open a terminal window, type `gedit`, and press Enter (see Figure 4-2).

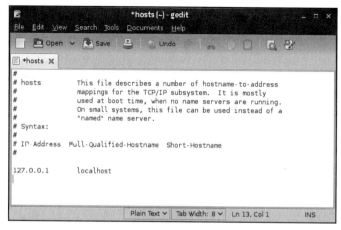

Figure 4-2 GNOME's gedit text editor
Source: openSUSE

One of Gedit's main features is syntax highlighting, which is enabled by clicking View, Highlight Mode from the menu. You see the following options:

- *Plain Text*—The default setting; syntax highlighting isn't displayed.
- *Sources*—Syntax highlighting for source code. This option includes choices for programming languages, such as C++, SQL, and Java.
- *Scripts*—Syntax highlighting for scripts; includes choices for different scripting languages, such as JavaScript or DOS batch scripts.
- *Others*—Syntax highlighting for other types of code, such as CMake, ChangeLog, and CSS.
- *Markup*—Syntax highlighting for markup code, such as HTML and XML.
- *Scientific*—Syntax highlighting for scientific code, such as GAP, Octave, and R.

Another Gedit feature is autosave, which saves text files automatically at regular intervals. Using this feature minimizes the possibility of losing data if there's a power loss.

Activity 4-2: Exploring the Gedit Text Editor

Time Required: 20 minutes

Objective: Learn features of the Gedit text editor.

Description: In this activity, you use the Gedit text editor to write a short Perl script. You learn how to enable the autosave feature, display line numbers, and use syntax highlighting to improve readability.

1. Start VMware Player, and start an openSUSE virtual machine with the GNOME desktop environment.
2. To start Gedit from the command line, open a terminal window, type **gedit act4-2.pl**, and press **Enter**. (To start gedit with the GUI, you can click **Computer**, point to **More Applications**, click **Utilities** (in the Groups section), and then click the **gedit** icon.)
3. To enable the autosave feature, click **Edit, Preferences** from the menu. Click the **Editor** tab, and then click the **Autosave files every ... minutes** check box. Set the minutes to **2**, and then click **Close**.
4. Display line numbers by clicking **Edit, Preferences** from the menu. Click the **Display line numbers** check box, and then click **Close**.
5. Enable syntax highlighting for Perl code by clicking **View**, pointing to **Highlight Mode**, and then pointing to **Scripts**. Notice that the Perl option is already selected. Why do you think it's selected by default?

_____

6. On line 1, type **#!/usr/bin/perl** and press **Enter**. This line tells the kernel to run the script with Perl.
7. On line 2, type **# Activity 4-2** and press **Enter**. On line 3, type **# *today's date*** (substituting the current date in whatever format you like) and press **Enter** two times.

The # symbol in the first three lines tells the Perl interpreter to skip the line because it's a comment.

8. On line 5, type **print "This is a simple Perl script\n";** and press **Enter**.

9. Click **File, Save** from the menu, and then click **File, Quit** from the menu.

10. In the terminal window, type **chmod u+x act4-2.pl** and press **Enter**. This command gives you execute permission for the file so that you can run the script. (You learn more about permissions in Chapter 5.)

11. Type **./act4-2.pl** and press **Enter** to run the Perl script. What do you see?

_____

12. Leave the terminal window open and the virtual machine running for the next activity.

Getting Started with the Vim Editor

The vi command-line text editor is included with most versions of UNIX and Linux. Although learning it takes some effort, most Linux administrators agree that knowing how to use it is crucial. Created by Bill Joy at the University of California at Berkeley in 1976, vi has evolved into many different forms, including vim, which stands for "vi improved." The vi command is now linked to the vim command, so even when you issue the vi command, you're actually starting the vim editor. In the following sections, you learn how to use vim. Practicing the commands until they're familiar is strongly recommended because the best way to learn vim is with hands-on experience. It's a useful tool for editing text files quickly and easily.

Vim is a modular editor, meaning it can run in different operational modes:

- *Command mode*—In **command mode**, you use key combinations as commands instead of typing text. To enter command mode, press Esc.

- *Insert mode*—In **insert mode**, the text you type is what's displayed onscreen. You type a to enter insert mode *after* the cursor and i to enter insert mode *at* the cursor. (You learn other ways to enter this mode in "Insert Mode," later in this chapter)

- *Extended mode*—**Extended mode**, also known as last line mode, is used for more advanced commands, such as saving files, exiting vim, or searching and replacing text. To enter extended mode while in command mode, type the : character.

Starting Vim

There are two ways to start the vim editor: Type vim and press Enter (see Figure 4-3 for the opening window that's displayed), or type vim *filename* (substituting the file you want to edit for *filename*) and press Enter. If the file doesn't exist, vim creates an empty file with this filename.

Figure 4-3 shows the window that's displayed after you start vim. The lines starting with a tilde (~) aren't actually in the file. This symbol represents blank or empty lines in the file. In this example, the user is greeted with information such as the version number and how to access online help. This information isn't displayed when you start vim with a specific filename.

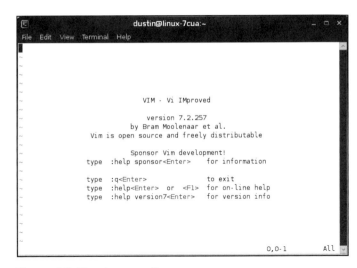

Figure 4-3 The vim text editor
Source: openSUSE

Command Mode

When you start vim, you're in command mode automatically, so text you type isn't displayed onscreen. For instance, if you type the lowercase l, you don't see this letter displayed onscreen. Instead, the cursor moves one place to the right because l is a navigational command. To move the cursor one space to the left, you type h; to move the cursor one space up, type k; and to move the cursor one space down, type j.

NOTE   Navigational keys are programmed as letters on the keyboard because vi was created when keyboards didn't have arrow keys. Assigning the letters h, j, k, and l might seem an odd choice because these letters don't seem related to left, down, up, or right; however, because a typist's right hand is already on the j, k, and l keys, assigning commands to these letters made navigating without arrow keys easier. You can now use the arrow keys to navigate in vim.

Table 4-1 describes advanced navigational commands you should practice in vim.

Table 4-1 Advanced vim navigational commands

Command	Description
Spacebar	Moves the cursor one space to the right.
Enter	Moves the cursor to the beginning of the next line.
^	Moves the cursor to the beginning of the current line.
$	Moves the cursor to the end of the current line.
-	Moves the cursor to the beginning of the current line.
+	Moves the cursor to the beginning of the next line (same as the Enter key).

Table 4-1   Advanced vim navigational commands (*continued*)

Command	Description
H	Moves the cursor to the top of the screen.
M	Moves the cursor to the middle of the screen.
L	Moves the cursor to the last line of the screen.
G	Moves the cursor to the last line of the file.
#G	The # represents a number. For instance, typing 5G moves the cursor to the fifth line of the file.
Ctrl+U	Moves the display up half a screen.
Ctrl+D	Moves the display down half a screen.
Ctrl+F	Moves the display down a full screen.
Ctrl+B	Moves the display up a full screen.
/text	Searches forward for a text string you specify.
?text	Searches backward for a text string you specify.
n	Repeats the search forward.
N	Repeats the search in the opposite direction.

ACTIVITY

Activity 4-3: Using Vim in Command Mode

Time Required: 15 minutes

Objective: Use navigational commands in vim.

Description: In this activity, you navigate a text file in vim and issue commands to move the cursor. You also learn how to search for a text string in a file.

1. If necessary, start VMware Player, start an openSUSE virtual machine with the GNOME desktop environment, and open a terminal window.

2. Type **man vim > act4-3** and press **Enter**. This command opens the vim man page and renames it as "act4-3 file."

3. Type **vim act4-3** and press **Enter**.

4. Press the **spacebar** six times. What happens? Press the **backspace** key until the cursor is at the beginning of the line. Why doesn't the backspace key delete any text?

_____

_____

5. Move the cursor to the first word in the first sentence under the "DESCRIPTION" heading, and type the $ symbol. What happens?

_____

6. Type the / symbol, type **vi,** and then press **Enter.** Type **n.** What happens? Why are instances of "vim" included in the search results, too?

_____

7. Leave the terminal window open and the virtual machine running for the next activity.

Insert Mode

You must be in insert mode to type text. You can switch to insert mode with one of the commands in Table 4-2. The vim editor displays -- INSERT -- at the lower left to indicate insert mode (see Figure 4-4). After you finish entering text, you can press the Esc key to change back to command mode.

4

Table 4-2 Commands for entering insert mode

Command	Description
i	Allows text to be entered at the cursor
I	Allows text to be entered at the beginning of the line
a	Allows text to be entered after the cursor
A	Allows text to be entered at the end of the line
o	Opens a line below the current line
O	Opens a line above the current line

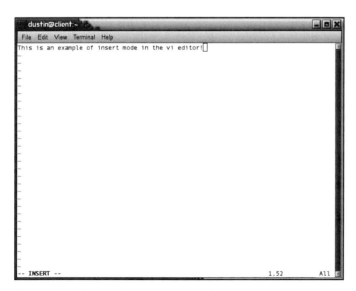

Figure 4-4 The vim editor in insert mode
Source: openSUSE

Modifying Text In vim, you modify text by using the keyboard instead of the mouse. After you get familiar with this technique, you'll be able to modify text files quickly and easily. Table 4-3 lists commands for modifying text in vim. Note that you must be in command mode to use them.

Table 4-3 Commands for modifying text

Command	Description
r	Replaces a single character and returns to command mode automatically
R	Replaces characters until you exit insert mode manually by pressing the Esc key
s	Deletes the character at the cursor and switches to insert mode
S	Deletes the entire line and switches to insert mode
cw	Stands for "change word"; deletes the word the cursor is on and switches to insert mode
~	Changes the case of the character the cursor is on

ACTIVITY

Activity 4-4: Using Vim in Insert Mode

Time Required: 25 minutes

Objective: Change to insert mode and modify text in vim.

Description: In this activity, you switch between command and insert modes in vim. You also learn how to insert text, change words, and change letter case.

1. If necessary, start VMware Player, start an openSUSE virtual machine with the GNOME desktop environment, and open a terminal window.

2. Type **man vim > act4-4** and press **Enter** to populate the act4-4 file with the vim man page.

3. Type **vim act4-4** and press **Enter**.

4. Make sure the cursor is on the "V" in the first line of your text file. Type **O** (uppercase O) to enter insert mode one line above the cursor. Type your first and last name and press **Enter**.

5. Type **Activity 4-4** and press **Enter**, and then type today's date and press **Enter**.

6. Press **Esc** to switch back to command mode. Use the navigational commands you learned in Activity 4-3 to move the cursor to the end of the sentence under the NAME heading. The cursor should be on the "r" in the word "editor."

7. Type **a** to enter insert mode to the right of the cursor. Press the **spacebar**, and then type your last name and press **Enter**. Press **Esc** to switch back to command mode.

8. Move the cursor to the first "S" in the SYNOPSIS heading, and type **i** to enter insert mode at the cursor.

9. Type your first name and press the **spacebar**. Press **Esc** to switch back to command mode.

10. Move the cursor to the first sentence under the DESCRIPTION heading and type **A** to enter insert mode at the end of the line. Press the **spacebar** and type your last name. Press **Esc** to switch back to command mode. Depending on the size of your window, text might wrap to the next line. Maximize the window by clicking the **maximize** button at the upper right to ensure that your name fits on one line.

11. Move the cursor down to the first "O" in the OPTIONS heading and type **cw**. What happened to the text "OPTIONS"? Are you in insert mode? Type **MORE OPTIONS** and press **Esc** to switch back to command mode.

<hr />

12. Move the cursor down to the F in the "FILES" heading and type the ~ symbol five times. What happens? Are you in insert mode?

<hr />

13. Save the file by typing **:** and then **wq!** and pressing **Enter**. (You learn more about saving and quiting the vim editor later in "Extended Mode.")

14. Leave the terminal window open and the virtual machine running for the next activity.

Deleting Text

You can delete text in vim with a variety of commands. For instance, you use x to delete a single character at the cursor and X to delete a single character before the cursor. Table 4-4 lists commands for deleting text in vim.

Recall from Table 4-1 that you can also enter / text to send the cursor to a specific word or string of characters. In files with multiple pages, this command is a time saver.

Table 4-4 **Commands for deleting text**

Command	Description
x	Deletes a single character at the cursor
X	Deletes a single character before the cursor
dd	Deletes the entire line the cursor is on
D	Deletes the remainder of the line to the right of the cursor
dw	Deletes the word the cursor is on
J	Joins two lines

After using the vim deletion commands in Table 4-4, you're still in command mode. For instance, after you type dd, the line is deleted, but you're still in command mode, so you can't enter text.

Cut, Yank, and Paste You can cut, yank (copy), and paste text in vim. The commands you've learned to delete text are the same as those to cut text—that is, store text in a **buffer,** an area of RAM used for temporary storage. For instance, if you enter the dw command while the cursor is on the word "test," this word is deleted and stored in a buffer. You can move the cursor to any point in the text and press P to paste the word "test" after the cursor.

Unlike cut commands, yank commands don't delete text. For instance, if you move the cursor to the word "test" and use the yw command, vim copies the word "test" and stores it in a buffer. Table 4-5 lists commands used to yank and paste text in vim.

Table 4-5 Commands for yanking and pasting text

Command	Description
yw	Yanks (copies) the word the cursor is on. The cursor must be on the first letter of the word because this command copies the word starting from the insertion point.
yy	Yanks the line the cursor is on.
#yw	The # symbol represents the number of words you want to yank. For instance, 3yw yanks the word the cursor is on and the next two words. Again, make sure the cursor is on the first letter of the word.
#yy	The # symbol represents the number of lines you want to yank. For instance, 3yy yanks the line the cursor is on and the next two lines.
p	Pastes buffer text after the cursor.
P	Pastes buffer text before the cursor.

Undo Commands You can undo changes you've made to a file by typing u. In fact, you can keep typing u until you have reached your oldest change. For instance, if you use the dw command to delete the words "test" and "editor" and then type u, "editor" is displayed onscreen again. If you type u again, "test" is displayed again. If you try to type u a third time, you get a message stating that you're already at your oldest change.

Activity 4-5: Modifiying Text in Vim

Time Required: 15 minutes

Objective: Delete, cut, copy, and paste text in vim.

Description: In this activity, you use vim to delete characters and lines in your text file. You also learn how to delete, cut, copy, and paste text.

1. If necessary, start VMware Player, start an openSUSE virtual machine with the GNOME desktop environment, and open a terminal window.

2. Type **man vim > act4-5** and press **Enter**. This command populates the act4-5 file with the vim man page.

3. Type **vim act4-5** and press **Enter**.

4. Move the cursor to the first parenthesis in the VIM(1) heading and type **xxx**. What happens? What mode are you in?

_____

5. Move the cursor to the sentence under the NAME heading and type **dd**. What happens?

_____

6. Move the cursor to the first word under the DESCRIPTION heading and type **dw**. What happens?

4

_____

7. Press **Shift+P**. What happens?

_____

8. Copy the text "DESCRIPTION" by placing the cursor on the letter D and typing **yw**. Did anything change?

_____

9. Move the cursor to the end of the first line of the file, and type **p**. What happens?

_____

10. Save the file by typing **:** and then **wq!** and pressing **Enter**.

11. Leave the terminal window open and the virtual machine running for the next activity.

Extended Mode

Extended mode offers users advanced features, such as save and quit, search and replace, and customization options. To enter extended mode, type the : symbol. You should then see the extended mode prompt (:) at the bottom of the screen.

Typing w at the extended mode prompt saves the file and puts you in command mode. Typing wq at the extended mode prompt saves the file and exits the vim text editor. Table 4-6 describes commands for saving files and exiting vim.

Table 4-6 Extended mode commands for saving and exiting

Command	Description
:w	Writes (saves) the file.
:w newfile	Writes the file; newfile specifies the filename.
:wq	Writes the file and quits (exits) the vim editor.
:w!	Writes the file. The ! symbol forces the save. (You might need to force a save with a read-only file, for example.)
:wq!	Writes the file and quits the vim editor. The ! symbol forces both the save and quit operations.
:q!	Quits vim without saving the file and ignores warnings that changes haven't been saved.

If you try to save a text file with a filename already being used in your current directory, you get a warning message. The ! symbol overwrites the warning and forces the change. You might want to do this if you need to replace an existing file, for example.

The following example is a letter a student entered in vim and saved as `thankyou.txt`:

```
Dear Mr. Garland,

Thank you for taking the time to meet with me at the Ocean Springs
Career Fair today. I appreciate your attention in the midst of so
many students seeking jobs.

You cleared up a lot of questions I had concerning the network
department at WorldNet. Once I understood the job roles and respon-
sibilities, I was positive I was the best person for the job.

Thanks again for your time, and I look forward to hearing from you.

Sincerely
Chloe Grace
~
~
:w thankyou
```

After saving the file, Chloe realizes that the fair was called Ocean Lakes Career Fair instead of Ocean Springs Career Fair. She uses the search and replace command (see Table 4-7) at the extended mode prompt to change the word "Springs" to "Lakes," as shown in this example:

```
:%s/Springs/Lakes
```

Table 4-7 Extended mode commands to search for and replace text

Command	Description
`:s/old/new`	Searches the line the cursor is on for the first occurrence of the string `old` and replaces it with the string `new`.
`:s/old/new/g`	Searches the line the cursor is on for all occurrences of the string `old` and replaces them with the string `new`. The `/g` stands for "global."
`:%s/old/new/g`	Searches all lines for the first occurrence of the string `old` and replaces it with the string `new`.
`:3,15s/old/new/g`	Searches between lines 3 and 15 for all occurrences of the string `old` and replaces them with the string `new`.
`:%s/\<old\>/new/g`	Searches all lines for all occurrences of the word `old` and replaces them with the string `new`.

The difference between a string of text and a word is that a string consists of any consecutive letters. For instance, if you search for the string "the," you find "the," "there," and "then" because the string "the" is found in all these words.

Useful Commands Table 4-8 lists other commands you can use at the extended mode prompt. For instance, you can display line numbers with the command :set nu. You can also create abbreviations; for example, you can set it up so that when you enter an abbreviation, vim displays the full version automatically.

Table 4-8 Additional extended mode commands

Command	Description
:set nu	Shows line numbers; set nu stands for "set number"
:ab usa United States of America	Inserts "United States of America" whenever the user types "usa"; ab stands for "abbreviation"
:una usa	Removes an abbreviation called "usa"

4

Activity 4-6: Using Vim in Extended Mode

Time Required: 15 minutes

Objective: Use vim commands in extended mode.

Description: In this activity, you open a file in vim and issue commands in extended mode. You learn how to save a file with a new name, search and replace text, and display line numbers.

1. If necessary, start VMware Player, start an openSUSE virtual machine with the GNOME desktop environment, and open a terminal window.

2. Type **man vim > act4-6** and press **Enter** to populate the act4-6 file with the vim man page.

3. Type **vim act4-6** and press **Enter**.

4. Enter extended mode by typing :. On the same line, save the file with a new name by typing **w act4-6.new** and pressing **Enter**. Do you notice any changes to the file?

_____

5. Enter extended mode and change every instance of "Vim" to "Vi IMproved" by typing **%s/Vim/Vi IMproved** and pressing **Enter**. How many subsitutions are made?

_____

6. Enter extended mode and display line numbers by typing **:set nu** and pressing **Enter**. How many lines are in your file?

_____

7. Enter extended mode, and then save the file and exit the vim editor by typing **wq!** and pressing **Enter**.

8. Power off the virtual machine, and close all open windows.

Chapter Summary

- Text editors are programs that enable users to create or edit plain text files.

- Linux offers a variety of text editors, such as KWrite, gedit, and vim.

- Linux GUI text editors are easy to use and are comparable with Windows Notepad.

- KWrite is a GUI text editor in the K Desktop Environment. Its main features are syntax highlighting and bookmarking.

- Gedit is a GUI text editor included with the GNOME desktop environment. Its main features are syntax highlighting and autosave.

- The vim text editor, available with every major distribution of UNIX and Linux, operates in several different modes. Insert mode is for entering text in a document, and command mode is used to navigate and modify text in a document. In extended mode, you can save and quit, find and replace, and perform other customizations to a document.

- Unlike the Windows GUI text editor, Notepad, vim is a command-line text editor. Therefore, you can use a variety of keys and key combinations in vim to perform operations.

Key Terms

bookmarks   A feature in KWrite for placing markers on lines of text to help navigate the file.

buffer   An area of RAM used for temporary storage.

command mode   A vim mode in which key combinations instead of text are used to enter commands.

extended mode   A vim mode in which advanced commands, such as saving files and searching and replacing, are available.

insert mode   A vim mode in which text that's typed is displayed onscreen.

shell script   A text file containing a sequence of commands.

syntax highlighting   A text editor feature for displaying text in different colors and fonts for programming languages.

text editor   A program that enables users to create or edit plain text files.

Review Questions

1. What's the main purpose of a text editor?

2. What vim mode are you using if you press keys to perform tasks instead of insert text?

   a. Command mode

   b. Insert mode

   c. Extended mode

3. What vim mode do you enter by typing the : symbol?

    a. Command mode

    b. Insert mode

    c. Extended mode

4. What vim mode are you in if you press Esc?

    a. Command mode

    b. Insert mode

    c. Extended mode

5. What vim mode are you using if the text you type is displayed onscreen?

    a. Command mode

    b. Insert mode

    c. Extended mode

6. What command is used to save and resume editing a file in the vim editor?

    a. :w

    b. :wq

    c. :wq!

    d. :s

7. What command is used to exit vim without saving changes?

    a. :!

    b. :Q

    c. :q!

    d. :wq

8. The yank command performs which of the following operations?

    a. Paste

    b. Copy

    c. Delete

    d. Undo

9. What vim command is used to delete a line the cursor is on?

    a. dd

    b. DD

    c. yw

    d. yy

10. What vim command is used to save a file, exit vim, and force the save?

   a. :w!

   b. :wq!

   c. :q

   d. :s!

Case Projects

CASE PROJECTS

Case Project 4-1: Customizing the Vim Environment

You're the Linux system administrator for a small medical facility in Warrensburg, Missouri. One of your responsibilities is to create and maintain user accounts. You decided to create a log file in vim listing all users and permissions. You changed the vim environment with the :set nu command in extended mode to have line numbers displayed, but every time you start vim, you have to repeat this command to see line numbers. Do some research to find out whether there's a way to display line numbers permanently.

Case Project 4-2: Editing User Text Files

You're a Linux help desk technician and just got a phone call from an employee who was married recently. She tells you her last name changed, but a couple of her files still show her maiden name. She wants to know the quickest way to edit her text files to change her maiden name, Smith, to her new last name, Oliver. The paths to the two files are /home/beth/project/1stqtr and /home/beth/project/2ndqtr. Explain to the employee how to open and edit her text file with the vim editor.

Case Project 4-3: Choosing Vi or Vim?

The company you work for uses Linux software for all its servers and workstations. Your boss, Mr. Weatherington, just hired Aaron to help you administer the network. Mr. Weatherington informs you that Aaron's background is in UNIX, and it's your responsibility to show him the main differences between UNIX and Linux. You decide the best place to start is with the vi editor. Aaron tells you he's an expert at vi but knows nothing about vim. Create a one-page memo summarizing the differences between vi and vim.

## chapter 5

Creating Shell Scripts and Displaying File Contents

After reading this chapter and completing the exercises, you will be able to:

- Identify and change Linux file permissions
- Create and run shell scripts
- Display the contents of a text file

In Chapter 4, you learned about using text editors. In this chapter, you use the vim text editor to create and run shell scripts, which are a useful administrative tool for task automation and troubleshooting. Before you create a shell script, however, you need some background in Linux file permissions because you can't run a script until you have permission to do so. You also learn how to work with variables and conditions in scripts and learn commands for displaying the contents of scripts as well as text files.

An Overview of Linux File Permissions

As you learned in Chapter 3, the `ls` command lists files and directories in your current directory, and the `-l` option displays more detailed information, such as file type and permissions. Figure 5-1 explains the permissions information that the `ls -l` command returns. Notice the three categories of file permissions, **user, group,** and **other:**

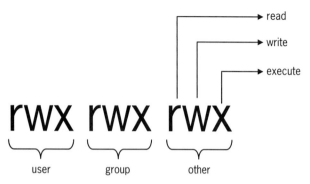

Figure 5-1 File permissions
© Cengage Learning 2013

- *User*—The file owner.
- *Group*—A group of users; users are divided into groups to facilitate administrative tasks. For example, in a corporate environment, you might have an Accounting group or a Human Resources group that includes users from these departments.
- *Other*—Everyone else on the Linux system.

You learn more about creating users and groups in Chapter 7.

Each category has three permission types: **read, write,** and **execute.** The functions of these permissions differ, depending on whether they're applied to files or directories. For instance, execute permission on a directory gives you permission to enter the directory, but execute permission on a file allows you to run the file. Table 5-1 defines permissions for files and directories.

You can't give execute permission for a file that isn't a program or script because the shell can't interpret its contents. Trying to run this type of file results in an error.

Table 5-1 Linux file and directory permissions

Permission	Permission for files	Permission for directories
r (read)	Gives users permission to open a file and view its contents	Allows users to list a directory's contents with commands such as ls
w (write)	Gives users permission to open a file and edit its contents	Allows users to add or remove files and subdirectories
x (execute)	Allows users to run the file (as long as it's a program or script)	Allows users to switch to the directory with the cd command; to read a directory's contents and add or remove files and subdirectories, you must have execute permission

Take a look at the following example:

```
-rw-r--r-- 1 martin users 0 2012-04-11 09:20 file1
```

As you learned in Chapter 4, the first hyphen in the preceding example describes the type of file; it's not a permission category.

For file1, the user category of permissions is set to rw-. The hyphen (-) represents a permission that hasn't been granted. In this example, it means the user doesn't have execute permission. The group category is set to r--, meaning the group has read permission but not write and execute permissions. Similarly, the other category is set to r--, which means every user on the system (other than the file owner and group) has read permission but not write or execute.

Permission Commands

The chmod (change mode) command is used to change permissions on files and directories and has this syntax:

```
chmod permissions file/directory
```

The *permissions* argument is the information used to change permissions, and the *file/directory* argument specifies the file or directory you want to change. You can use the chmod command in two ways to change file permissions: symbolic notation and numeric notation. Symbolic notation uses criteria such as categories and operators (described in Table 5-2) to change file permissions, as shown in this example of adding (the + operator) execute permission (x) on file1 for the user (u, the file owner):

```
chmod u+x file1
```

As another example, if you want to remove write and execute permissions for the other category on `file4`, use this command:

```
chmod o-wx file4
```

Table 5-2 Symbolic notation

Category	Operator	Permission
u (user)	+ (add to existing permissions)	r (read)
g (group)	- (remove from existing permissions)	w (write)
o (other)	= (assign absolute permissions)	x (execute)
a (all)	One of the preceding operators	One or more of the preceding permissions

Numeric notation uses numbers from 0 to 7 (as shown in Table 5-3) to represent file permissions.

Table 5-3 Numeric notation

Permission	Numeric value
- - -	0
- -x	1
-w-	2
-wx	3
r--	4
r-x	5
rw-	6
rwx	7

For example, say that using the `ls  -l` command to view permissions returns these results:

```
-rw-rw-r--  1 dustin users 0 2012-04-11 09:20 file1
-rwxrwxr--  1 dustin users 0 2012-04-11 09:20 file2
-rwxrwxrw-  1 dustin users 0 2012-04-11 09:20 file3
-rwxrwxrwx  1 dustin users 0 2012-04-11 09:20 file4
```

Examine the permissions for `file1`. Both the user and group permissions are `rw-`, which have the numeric value 6. The other permissions are `r--`, which have the numeric value 4. So in the preceding example, `file1`'s permissions (`rw-rw-r--`) are 664 in numeric notation.

5

Trying to memorize eight numeric values can be difficult, so some administrators memorize only the values for r, w, and x, which are 4, 2, and 1. So for a file with the user permission rw-, for example, you can determine the numeric notation with a simple math problem: r(4) + w(2) = 6.

If you want to give the user and group categories read, write, and execute permissions and leave the other category with just read permissions, for example, use this command:

```
chmod 774 file1
```

Each number in the preceding example represents a category (user, group, other) and its permissions, shown in Figure 5-2. The first 7 is the numeric value for the user category, the second 7 is the numeric value for the group category, and the 4 is the numeric value for the other category.

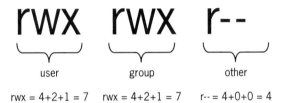

rwx = 4+2+1 = 7   rwx = 4+2+1 = 7   r-- = 4+0+0 = 4

Figure 5-2 File permissions in numeric notation
© Cengage Learning 2013

Creating Shell Scripts

As you've learned, a shell script contains a sequence of commands to execute line by line. Understanding the basics of shell scripting is essential to becoming proficient at system administration because scripts are useful for task automation. When you need to issue several commands to carry out an administrative task, for instance, you can save all the related commands in one executable file. Scripts are also used in troubleshooting. Some scripts run when the Linux system starts, and you need to know how to manage these scripts if problems occur during the boot process.

Before creating your first shell script, you need to know a few programming terms. The source code for scripts is written in a human-readable format known as a **programming language**, a set of rules for instructing a computer how to perform specific tasks. The source code must be converted into machine code so that the computer can process the data. **Machine code** consists of binary 1s and 0s and is the language a computer's CPU understands. Scripts can be considered compiled programs or interpreted programs; the difference is in how source code is converted into machine code. With a **compiled program**, all the source code is converted to machine code and stored in a binary file before the user runs the script. The program used to convert source code into machine code is a compiler. With an **interpreted program**, the source code is converted to machine code, line by line, as the user runs the script; the program for converting source code to machine code in this manner is called an interpreter. The shell scripts you create in this chapter's activities are examples of interpreted programs, and the interpreter you use is the BASH shell.

Creating a shell script is as simple as creating a file and then assigning execute permission for it. By default, files can't be executed; not even root can execute a file unless the file owner adds execute permission manually. This security feature is in place to ensure that only scripts and programs are executed. As mentioned previously, trying to execute a "regular" file causes an error.

After creating a shell script and assigning execute permission, you must enter the absolute or relative path to where it's stored to run it. (As you learned in Chapter 3, the relative path starts at your current directory.) For example, to run a script called `scr1` that's stored in your current directory, you use the command `./scr1`. Activity 5-1 walks you through creating and running a shell script.

NOTE The reason you can't simply type the script name to run it is that when you run a program in this manner, the kernel looks in the directory paths defined by the PATH variable. You learn more about variables in the next section.

TIP In this chapter's activities, line numbers for scripts are included in steps for easy reference, but remember that you don't have to type them.

Activity 5-1: Creating a Shell Script

ACTIVITY

Time Required: 10 minutes

Objective: Create and run a shell script.

Description: In this activity, you use the vim editor to create a shell script, assign the necessary permission, and then run the script.

1. Start VMware Player and start an openSUSE virtual machine.

2. Open a terminal window, and at the command prompt, type **mkdir scripts** and press **Enter**. Recall that the `mkdir` command is used to create directories.

3. To change to the `scripts` directory, type **cd scripts** and press **Enter**.

4. Type **vim scr1** and press **Enter** to open a new empty file in the vim editor.

5. Enter extended mode by typing **:**, and then type **set nu** and press **Enter** to display line numbers.

6. Type **i** to enter insert mode, and then type the following information, pressing **Enter** after each line:

```
1 #!/bin/bash
2 # This is a comment line and can be
3 # recognized by the preceding pound symbol.
4 clear
5 echo Your current directory is...
6 pwd
```

```
 7 echo "You're changing to your parent directory, which is..."
 8 cd ..
 9 pwd
10 echo "You're moving back to the scripts directory."
11 cd ~/scripts
12 pwd
13 echo "Here's a long listing of all your files and
directories."
14 ls -l
```

7. Press **Esc** to exit insert mode. Enter extended mode again by typing **:**, and then save your changes and exit the vim editor by typing **wq!** and pressing **Enter**.

8. Type **ls -l** and press **Enter**. Does the user have execute permission?

9. Give the user (owner) permission to run the script by typing **chmod u+x scr1** and pressing **Enter**. What notation did you use to change permissions: symbolic or numeric?

10. Run the script by typing **./scr1** and pressing **Enter**. What do you see?

11. Leave the virtual machine running and the terminal window open for the next activity.

In line 1 of the `scr1` script, the `#!/bin/bash` command specifies running the script in the BASH shell, which ensures that all users, regardless of the shell they're using, have the same results. Lines 2 and 3 are comments, so the interpreter ignores them. The purpose of a **comment** is to add documentation information for users and anyone else who might need to modify the script. The `clear` command in line 4 clears the screen. The `echo` command in lines 5, 7, 10, and 13 has a dual purpose: to display the text you type or to display the value of a variable, discussed next. Notice the quotation marks used in these lines; they're needed if you want to display an apostrophe.

Variables

An **environment variable** is a placeholder for data that can change; typically, it gets its value automatically from the OS startup or the shell being used. Linux is a multiuser OS, so more than one user can log in at the same time. For this reason, each user has environment variables with different values to define his or her working environment. For instance, the HOME environment variable stores the absolute pathname to a user's home directory, so it varies for each user. Other environment variables are the same for all users logged in to a machine, such as the HOST environment variable that specifies the computer name. Table 5-4 describes a few common environment variables. The env command is used to display a list of all environment variables and their stored values. To see a particular variable's stored value, you can also use the echo command and add a $ symbol before the variable name. For instance, echo $HOME returns the value of the HOME variable.

Using all uppercase letters for variables is common practice because it makes them easier to spot later if they need to be modified.

Table 5-4 Environment variables

Variable name	Stored value
HOME	Home directory
USER	Login name
PATH	Gives the search path, which is the list of directories (separated by : symbols) the shell uses when searching for executable commands
HOST	Computer name

A **shell variable** is similar to an environment variable, but its value is usually assigned in a shell script. These variables are related to a particular script, not necessarily the global environment, as environment variables are. For an example of a shell variable, see the "Direct Assignment" section next.

Variables are also important for specifying how shell scripts run. For instance, you can create a script that greets users by name. There are three ways to store information in a variable: direct assignment, the prompt method, and positional parameters.

Direct Assignment You use the **direct assignment** method when you want to specify the variable's value in the command. For example, COLOR=blue specifies the value of the COLOR variable. In Activity 5-2, you use this method in a shell script.

If you didn't do Activity 5-1, create a directory called scripts in your home directory. You need this directory for the remaining activities.

Activity 5-2: Using the Direct Assignment Method

Time Required: 10 minutes

Objective: Use the direct assignment method to store a value in a variable.

Description: In this activity, you create a shell script that searches for the scr1 file, starting in your home directory. You then use the direct assignment method with two variables and use them as arguments for the find command.

1. If necessary, start VMware Player and start an openSUSE virtual machine. Open a terminal window, type **cd scripts**, and press **Enter**.

2. Type **vim scr2** and press **Enter** to open a new empty file in the vim editor.

3. Enter extended mode and display line numbers. (Refer to Activity 5-1 if you need a reminder of how to do this.)

4. Type **i** to enter insert mode, and then type the following information, pressing **Enter** after each line:

```
1 #!/bin/bash
2 STARTLOCATION=$HOME
3 FILENAME=scr1
4 echo "Searching for the file named $FILENAME"
5 echo "in the $STARTLOCATION directory"
6 find $STARTLOCATION -name $FILENAME
```

5. Press **Esc** to exit insert mode. Enter extended mode by typing **:**, and then save your changes and exit the vim editor by typing **wq!** and pressing **Enter**.

6. Give the user (owner) permission to run the script by typing **chmod 744 scr2** and pressing **Enter**. What method did you use: symbolic or numeric?

    _____

7. Run the script by typing **./scr2** and pressing **Enter**. What do you see?

    _____

8. Leave the virtual machine running and the terminal window open for the next activity.

In the scr2 script, line 2 creates the STARTLOCATION variable and uses the direct assignment method to assign your home directory as the value. Line 3 creates the FILENAME variable and uses direct assignment to assign scr1 as the value. Lines 4 and 5 use the echo command to display the variables you've assigned values to. Line 6 introduces the find command, which searches for files in the directory tree starting from the location specified in the command. In this activity, the -name option is used to specify searching for a file based on its name, which is the value of the FILENAME variable in this example. Line 3 defines this value as scr1. Table 5-5 describes some options used with the find command.

Table 5-5 Options for the find command

Option	Example	Description
-name	find / -name hosts	Starts in the root directory (/) and searches for files named hosts
-type d	find . -type d	Starts in the current directory (indicated by the .) and searches for all subdirectories
-type f	find /home -type f	Starts in the /home directory and searches for all files
-type l	find /etc -type l	Starts in the /etc directory and searches for all symbolic links
-group	find . -group users	Starts in the current directory and searches for all files belonging to the users group
-user	find /home -user jasmine	Starts in the /home directory and searches for all files belonging to the user jasmine
-inum	find / -inum 3911	Starts in the root directory (/) and searches for all files with the inode number 3911
-mmin n	find / -mmin 10	Starts in the root directory (/) and searches for all files that have been modified in the past 10 minutes

5

The `find` command has many more options than the ones listed in Table 5-5. For instance, you can add an option for performing a shell command on files the `find` command encounters. Refer to the man pages for a list of all the options.

The Prompt Method With the **prompt method**, the user is asked to enter a value for the variable. This method is useful when you need information from the user to complete the script, such as a script that asks for the user's first name. In Activity 5-3, you use this method to have the user enter the value of a variable.

Activity 5-3: Using the Prompt Method

Time Required: 10 minutes

Objective: Create a script with the prompt method for storing a value in a variable.

Description: In this activity, you create a shell script that prompts the user for a starting location and filename, and then searches for the filename starting at the location the user chooses.

1. If necessary, start VMware Player and start an openSUSE virtual machine. Open a terminal window, type **cd scripts**, and press **Enter**.

2. Type **vim scr3** to open a new empty file in the vim editor.

3. Enter extended mode and display line numbers.

4. Type **i** to enter insert mode, and then type the following information, pressing **Enter** after each line:

```
1 #!/bin/bash
2 clear
3 echo Welcome to the FIND script
4 echo -n "Enter the location (such as /home) where the search
should start "
5 read STARTLOCATION
6 echo -n "What is the name of the file to search for? "
7 read FILENAME
8 echo "Search starting for the $FILENAME file in the
$STARTLOCATION directory"
9 find $STARTLOCATION -name $FILENAME 2> /dev/null
```

5. Press **Esc** and then **Enter** to exit insert mode. Enter extended mode by typing **:**, and then save your changes and exit the vim editor by typing **wq!** and pressing **Enter**.

6. Give the user (owner) execute permission to run the script by typing **chmod u+x scr3** and pressing **Enter**.

7. Run the script by typing **./scr3** and pressing **Enter**. At the first prompt, type **/** (for the directory where the search should start) and press **Enter**. At the second prompt, type **scr3** (for the filename to search for) and press **Enter**. What do you see?

_____

8. Leave the virtual machine running and the terminal window open for the next activity.

Lines 4 and 6 introduce the -n option for the echo command, which specifies not starting a new line so that the user can respond on the same line. The read command in lines 5 and 7 prompts the user to enter values for the variables STARTLOCATION and FILENAME. At the end of line 9, the 2> /dev/null is used to redirect all error messages (represented by the "2") to the /dev/null directory instead of displaying them onscreen. You learn more about redirection and error messages in Chapter 6, but for now, just know that all data written to the /dev/null directory is deleted. When running this script, the shell tries to examine directories you might not have permission to access. To avoid having to see several "permission denied" errors, you can have error messages redirected to this directory.

You shouldn't always have error messages redirected. They can give you helpful information when you need to know why something isn't working.

CAUTION

Positional Parameters The positional parameter method uses the order of arguments in a command to assign values to variables on the command line. Variables from $0 to $9 are available, and their values are defined by what the user enters. This method is useful in a script when you might want it to run differently each time it's used.

When you issue the command to run a script, for example, its name as well as all arguments following it are stored in positional parameters. For instance, to run the scr1 script, you use this command:

```
./scr1
```

The filename is considered position 0 in the command, and the text ./scr1 becomes the value of the $0 variable. In this example, there are no other arguments, so $1, $2, and so forth have no value. If you want the value of $1 to be /home, the user running the script specifies this argument as follows:

```
./scr1 /home
```

If you create a script that searches for a file the user specifies, you can assign $1 as the value of the first argument and use it as the filename to search for. When a user needs to search for a specific file, he or she enters it on the command line with the name of the script and then runs the script. As an example, say the user is looking for a file called file1 and the scr1 script uses the $1 variable to find a file. Your script would look like the following:

```
#!/bin/bash
clear
echo "Searching for $1"
find $1
```

When the user enters the ./scr1 file1 command, the output is as follows:

```
Searching for file1
file1
test@linux-sdr1:"/scripts>
```

In this example, the first argument is $0, or ./scr1, and the second argument is $1, or file1.

Table 5-6 describes positional parameters. Activity 5-4 walks you through creating a script that uses positional parameters to assign values to variables.

Table 5-6 Positional parameters

Positional parameter	Description	Example
$0	Represents the name of the script	./scr4 (./scr4 is position 0)
$1 to $9	$1 represents the first argument, $2 represents the second argument, and so on	./scr4 /home (./scr4 is position 0 and /home is position 1) ./scr4 /home scr1 (./scr4 is position 0, /home is position 1, and scr1 is position 2)
$*	Represents all the positional parameters except 0	/home scr1 (just /home and scr1)
$#	Represents the number of arguments that have a value	./scr4 /home scr1 echo $# ($* represents positions 1 and 2, which are /home and scr1)

Activity 5-4: Using Positional Parameters

Time Required: 10 minutes

Objective: Create a script that uses positional parameters to assign values to variables.

Description: In this activity, you create a shell script that uses positional parameters to determine where to start a search and which file to search for.

1. If necessary, start VMware Player and start an openSUSE virtual machine. Open a terminal window, type **cd scripts**, and press **Enter**.

2. Type **vim scr4** and press **Enter** to open a new empty file in the vim editor.

3. Enter extended mode and display line numbers.

4. Switch to insert mode and type the following information, pressing **Enter** after each line:

```
1 #!/bin/bash
2 clear
3 echo "Searching for $2 starting in the $1 directory"
4 find $1 -name $2 2> /dev/null
```

5. Exit insert mode and switch to extended mode. Save your changes and exit the vim editor.

6. Give the user (owner) execute permission to run the script by typing **chmod u+x scr4** and pressing **Enter**.

7. Run the script and give position 1 ($1) the value /home and position 2 ($2) the value scr4 by typing **./scr4 /home scr4** and pressing **Enter**. What do you see?

_____

8. Leave the virtual machine running and the terminal window open for the next activity.

Remember to add arguments when using a script that requires positional parameters. For instance, if you use `./scr4` without any parameters on the command line, the script doesn't run correctly because `$1` and `$2` have no value.

Exit Status Codes

Before working with conditions, you need to understand exit status codes. When you quit a program or a command, a numeric code called an **exit status code** is sent to the shell. These codes differ, depending on the Linux distribution or the shell. However, successful commands usually return the code 0, and failures return a value greater than 0. The code isn't actually displayed onscreen, but you can reference it via a script or at the command line with the `$?` variable, as shown in the following example:

```
echo $?
0
cd baddir
bash: cd: baddir: No such file or directory
echo $?
1
```

In this example, the first `echo $?` command is successful and returns the exit status code 0. The second time this command is used, the exit status code 1, indicating failure, is returned because the user tried to change to a directory that doesn't exist.

Conditions

Although commands in shell scripts are often carried out in order, sometimes you need the interpreter to skip commands based on a condition. For instance, you might want a portion of the script to run if the user is in the Marketing Department and have another portion run if the user is in Human Resources. The `if` statement is used to carry out certain commands based on testing a condition, as shown in the flowchart in Figure 5-3.

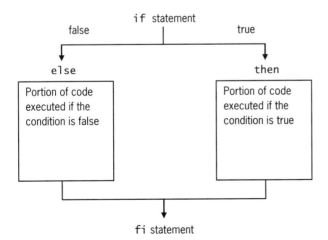

Figure 5-3 A flowchart of the `if` statement
© Cengage Learning 2013

The following list describes common condition statements used in scripts:

- if *statement*—Starts the condition being tested
- then *statement*—Starts the portion of code specifying what to do if the condition evaluates to true
- else *statement*—Starts the portion of code specifying what to do if the condition evaluates to false
- fi *statement*—Indicates the end of the condition being tested

Activity 5-5 walks you through creating a script with if, then, and else condition statements.

Activity 5-5: Using Condition Statements

Time Required: 10 minutes

Objective: Create a script with if, then, and else statements.

Description: In this activity, you create a shell script that tests whether a file the user specifies exists.

1. If necessary, start VMware Player and start an openSUSE virtual machine. Open a terminal window, type **cd scripts**, and press **Enter**.

2. Type **vim scr5** and press **Enter** to open a new empty file in the vim editor.

3. Enter extended mode and display line numbers.

4. Switch to insert mode and type the following information, pressing **Enter** after each line:

```
1 #!/bin/bash
2 clear
3 echo "Enter the name of a file you think is in your current
directory."
4 read FILENAME
5 if [ -a $FILENAME ]
```

When using the if statement, you must use an open bracket ([) followed by a space and then type the condition, followed by another space and a closed bracket (]). In other words, there must be a space before and after the condition.

```
6 then
7 echo "You're right. $FILENAME is in your current directory."
8 else
9 echo "Sorry. $FILENAME isn't in your current directory."
10 fi
11 echo "Hope you enjoyed this script!"
```

5. Exit insert mode and switch to extended mode. Save your changes and exit the vim editor.

6. Give the user (owner) execute permission to run the script. (Refer to previous activities if you need guidance on what command to use.) To run the script, type **./scr5** and press **Enter**. At the prompt, type **scr5** and press **Enter**. What do you see? Rerun the script, but this time, type **badfile** at the prompt and press **Enter**. What do you see?

_____

_____

7. Leave the virtual machine running and the terminal window open for the next activity.

Take a closer look at the `if` statement in line 5. The condition is between brackets, and the `-a` is a file attribute operator that checks whether a file exists. Table 5-7 lists file attribute operators available in the BASH shell. Everything between `then` and `else` (lines 6 through 8) is executed if the condition is true. Everything between `else` and `fi` (lines 8 through 10) is executed if the condition is false. The `fi` statement on line 10 ends the `if` statement and tells the interpreter to go back to running the script line by line in sequential order.

NOTE

`fi` is "if" spelled backward. Other condition statements use backward spelling to indicate the end of the condition, such as `esac` to indicate the end of a `case` statement.

Table 5-7 **File attribute operators in the BASH shell**

File attribute operator	Description
-a	Checks whether the file exists
-d	Checks whether the file is a directory
-f	Checks whether the file is a regular file
-r	Checks whether the user has read permission for the file
-s	Checks whether the file contains data
-w	Checks whether the user has write permission for the file
-x	Checks whether the user has execute permission for the file
-O	Checks whether the user is the owner of the file
-G	Checks whether the user belongs to the group owner of the file
file1 -nt file2	Checks whether file1 is newer than file2
file1 -ot file2	Checks whether file1 is older than file2

Menu Scripts You can also use condition statements to create menu scripts that allow users to choose from a list of options. Activity 5-6 walks you through creating a menu script with `if-then` statements, and in subsequent activities, you see how to use other condition statements to reduce the amount of code needed for the menu script.

Activity 5-6: Creating a Menu Script

Time Required: 10 minutes

Objective: Create a menu script with `if` and `then` statements.

Description: In this activity, you create a menu script with `if` and `then` statements, giving users three menu items to select from.

1. If necessary, start VMware Player and start an openSUSE virtual machine. Open a terminal window, type **cd scripts**, and press **Enter**.

2. Type **vim scr6** and press **Enter** to open a new empty file in the vim editor.

3. Enter extended mode and display line numbers.

4. Switch to insert mode and type the following information, pressing **Enter** after each line:

```
 1 #!/bin/bash
 2 clear
 3 echo Please select a menu item
 4 echo
 5 echo "1) Display your current directory"
 6 echo "2) Display your home directory"
 7 echo "3) List the contents of your current directory"
 8 echo
 9 read CHOICE
10 if [ $CHOICE = 1 ]
11 then
12 pwd
13 fi
14 if [ $CHOICE = 2 ]
15 then
16 echo $HOME
17 fi
18 if [ $CHOICE = 3 ]
19 then
20 ls
21 fi
22 echo
23 echo Have a great day!
```

5. Exit insert mode and switch to extended mode. Save your changes and exit the vim editor.

6. Give the user (owner) execute permission to run the script. Enter the command to run the script, and choose option 1. What do you see?

_____

7. Run the script two more times, selecting options 2 and 3. Finally, run the script and choose an option that doesn't exist (such as 4). What happens?

_____

8. Leave the virtual machine running and the terminal window open for the next activity.

Lines 2 through 8 set up the menu structure; it's what users see when they run the script. Line 9 prompts the user for input. The user's input becomes the value of the CHOICE variable, which is used in lines 10, 14, and 18 as a condition. For instance, if the user types 1 and presses Enter, the condition in line 10 becomes true and the interpreter executes the code between lines 11 and 13. However, the condition in lines 14 and 18 is false, which makes the interpreter skip these lines and execute everything after the fi statement. The if statement can return only a true or false condition; however, sometimes you need to determine the value of a variable that can have one of several values. In Activity 5-6, you used several if-then-else statements for this task, but you can also use an elif (short for "else if") statement when there's another if statement in the else portion of the script. The following example shows how to rewrite the script in Activity 5-6 with elif statements:

```
 1 #!/bin/bash
 2 clear
 3 echo Please select a menu item
 4 echo
 5 echo "1) Display your current directory"
 6 echo "2) Display your home directory"
 7 echo "3) List the contents of your current directory"
 8 echo
 9 read CHOICE
10 if [ $CHOICE = 1 ]
11 then
12 pwd
13 elif [ $CHOICE = 2 ]
14 then
15 echo $HOME
16 elif [ $CHOICE = 3 ]
17 then
18 ls
19 fi
20 echo
21 echo Have a great day!
```

The elif statement combines the else and if statements, which enables you to create multiple conditions without closing each condition. Although using elif reduced the amount of code by only two lines in this script, it can be quite a time saver when used in a script containing thousands of lines.

The case Statement A case statement uses one variable to specify multiple values and matches a portion of the script to each value. This structure enables you to reduce the amount of code needed for a script even more, and the interpreter needs to run only the portion of the script matching the specified value. The syntax of the case statement is as follows:

```
case $VARIABLE in
value1) code for specified value1 ;;
value2) code for specified value2 ;;
```

```
valuen) code for specified valuen ;;
*)code for value not matching any specified choices ;;
esac
```

The double semicolon (;;) marks the end of each code portion matching a specific value. If the value the user enters doesn't match any of the choices specified in the case statement, the *) characters start the code portion that runs in this situation; for example, you could use this code to inform users they've made an invalid selection. As mentioned previously, esac is "case" spelled backward and indicates the end of the case statement. Activity 5-7 walks you through creating a menu script with case statements.

Activity 5-7: Using case Statements in a Menu Script

Time Required: 10 minutes

Objective: Create a menu script with case statements.

Description: In this activity, you create a menu script with case statements to give multiple values to one variable and reduce the amount of code even more. This script also informs the user when an invalid selection is made.

1. If necessary, start VMware Player and start an openSUSE virtual machine. Open a terminal window, type **cd scripts**, and press **Enter**.

2. Type **vim scr7** and press **Enter** to open a new empty file in the vim editor.

3. Enter extended mode and display line numbers.

4. Switch to insert mode and type the following information, pressing **Enter** after each line:

```
 1 #!/bin/bash
 2 clear
 3 echo Please select a menu item
 4 echo
 5 echo "1) Display your current directory"
 6 echo "2) Display your home directory"
 7 echo "3) List the contents of your current directory"
 8 echo
 9 read CHOICE
10 case $CHOICE in
11 1) pwd;;
12 2) echo $HOME;;
13 3) ls;;
14 *) echo You made an invalid selection;;
15 esac
16 echo Have a great day!
```

5. Exit insert mode and switch to extended mode. Save your changes and exit the vim editor.

6. Give the user (owner) execute permission to run the script. Run the script enough times to choose all the options. Finally, run the script and choose an option that doesn't exist (such as 4). How does the result differ from what happened in Activity 5-6 when you selected a nonexistent option?

_____

7. Leave the virtual machine running and the terminal window open for the next activity.

This script has been reduced to only 16 lines of code and informs the user when an invalid selection is made. In lines 10 to 15, the case statement matches one of multiple values to the CHOICE variable, which gets its value from the user in line 9. Line 14 has a special wild-card character (*) to match any value that doesn't equal 1, 2, or 3 so that users can be noti-fied that they made an invalid selection. After the user makes a selection, the script carries out the command and then ends the script.

You can find examples of case statements in the /etc/rc.d directory.

TIP

Looping

Looping is used to perform a set of commands repeatedly. In the menu script, the user is given a list of options to choose from, and after a selection is made, the script ends. With looping, you can enable users to continue running the script until a certain condition is met. For example, in the game of blackjack, you might use a while loop to allow the game to continue as long as a player's points don't go over 21. Three types of loops are often used: while, until, and for. You should be familiar with the following terms before using loops in a script:

*   while *statement*—A loop statement that tests a condition in much the same way as if-then statements. The interpreter continues executing the code in the while loop portion of the script as long as the condition is true.

*   until *statement*—A loop statement that causes the interpreter to continue executing the code in the until loop portion of the script as long as the condition is false.

*   for *statement*—A loop statement that specifies the number of times to execute the portion of code.

*   do *statement*—A loop statement indicating the beginning of the code to be repeated.

*   done *statement*—A loop statement indicating the end of the code to be repeated.

The while Loop A while loop repeats the commands between the do and done statements as long as the tested condition is true (exit status code 0). When the command after the while statement returns an exit status code greater than 0, the while state-ment fails, and the program begins executing the commands after the done statement. Figure 5-4 shows a flowchart of a while loop, and Activity 5-8 walks you through creating one.

5

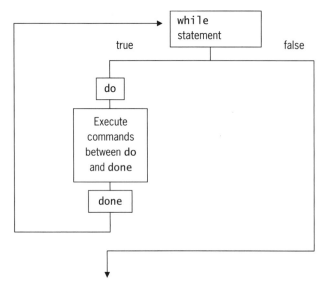

Figure 5-4 A while loop
© Cengage Learning 2013

Activity 5-8: Creating a while Loop

Time Required: 10 minutes

Objective: Create a while loop in a script.

Description: In this activity, you create a file in your scripts directory named testfile. Then you write a script that repeats the commands in the while loop as long as testfile exists. Finally, you delete testfile and watch as your script exits the while loop.

1. If necessary, start VMware Player and start an openSUSE virtual machine. Open a terminal window, type **cd scripts**, and press **Enter.**

2. Next, to create a file used for testing the condition, type **touch testfile** and press **Enter.**

3. Leave this terminal window open, open a second terminal window, and switch to the scripts directory. To open a new empty file, type **vim scr8** in the second terminal window and press **Enter.**

4. Enter extended mode and display line numbers.

5. Switch to insert mode and type the following information, pressing **Enter** after each line:

```
1 #!/bin/bash
2 while cat testfile > /dev/null
3 do
4 echo exit status code is $?
5 sleep 1
6 done
7 echo You deleted the file!
```

6. Exit insert mode and switch to extended mode. Save your changes and exit the vim editor.

7. Give the user (owner) execute permission to run the script, and then run the script. While the exit status code is repeating, go to the other terminal window, and type **rm testfile** and press **Enter**. What happens?

_____

8. Leave the virtual machine running and one terminal window open for the next activity.

The command used to test the condition is cat testfile. The cat command (discussed later in "Displaying the Contents of a Text File") is used to view a file's contents. If testfile exists, the exit status code 0 is returned, and the interpreter executes the commands between do and done. If testfile doesn't exist or is deleted, an exit status code greater than 0 is returned, and the interpreter executes the commands after the done statement. The sleep command in line 5 pauses the program for a specified number of seconds (1 second, in this example). This is done to slow the program down to better illustrate repetition in the while loop.

The until Loop An until loop repeats the commands between do and done as long as the tested condition is false (exit status code is greater than 0)—in other words, *until* the condition is true. When the command following the until statement has the exit status code 0, the until loop fails, and the program begins executing the commands after the done statement. Figure 5-5 shows a flowchart of an until loop.

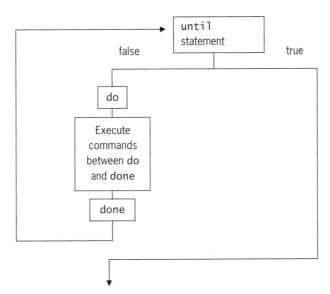

Figure 5-5 An until loop
© Cengage Learning 2013

The following example is similar to the script you created in Activity 5-8, but the loop continues until the condition is true:

```
1 #!/bin/bash
2 until cat untilfile > /dev/null 2> /dev/null
3 do
4 echo exit status code is $?
5 sleep 1
6 done
7 echo exit status code is now $?
8 echo You created the file!
```

The command used to test the condition is cat untilfile. If the exit status code is greater than 0 (meaning the file doesn't exist, so the cat command returns an error), the script stays in the loop, executing the commands between do and done. If the exit status code is 0 (meaning the file exists), the script exits the loop and executes the commands after the done statement.

In Activity 5-7, you created a menu script with the case statement. After the user makes a selection, the script ends. If you want users to be able to continue running the script until they choose to exit, you need to use an until loop, which you add in Activity 5-9.

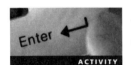

Activity 5-9: Creating an until Loop in a Menu Script

Time Required: 20 minutes

Objective: Create a menu script that continues running until the user decides to exit.

Description: In this activity, you create a menu script with an until loop to give the user the option of deciding when to exit the script.

1. If necessary, start VMware Player and start an openSUSE virtual machine. Open a terminal window, type **cd scripts**, and press **Enter**.

2. Type **vim scr9** and press **Enter** to open a new empty file in the vim editor.

3. Enter extended mode and display line numbers.

4. Switch to insert mode and type the following information, pressing **Enter** after each line:

```
 1 #!/bin/bash
 2 CHOICE=7
 3 until [ $CHOICE -eq 4 ]
 4 do
 5 clear
 6 echo Please select a menu item
 7 echo
 8 echo "1) Display your current directory"
 9 echo "2) Display your home directory"
10 echo "3) List the contents of your current directory"
11 echo "4) Exit the program"
```

```
12 echo
13 read CHOICE
14 case $CHOICE in
15 1) pwd;;
16 2) echo $HOME;;
17 3) ls;;
18 4) echo "Have a good day!";;
19 *) echo You made an invalid selection;;
20 esac
21 echo "Press Enter to continue"
22 read Enter
23 done
```

5. Exit insert mode and switch to extended mode. Save your changes and exit the vim editor.

6. Give the user (owner) execute permission to run the script, and then run the script. Try each option as well as an invalid option, such as 5. Does the script work as expected?

_____

7. Leave the virtual machine running and the terminal window open for the next activity.

Line 2 creates the CHOICE variable and directly assigns its value as 7. Line 3 tells the interpreter to repeat the commands between do and done until the CHOICE variable equals 4. After the user types 4, the script executes line 18 and then exits the loop. No commands follow the done statement, which means the program ends.

The for Loop A for loop repeats the commands between do and done a specified number of times. Each time the script carries out the commands in the loop, a new value is given to a variable. You can assign this value in the command with positional parameters, such as listing the calendar months in a year:

```
for calendar in January February March [code continues]
do
  echo $calendar
done
exit 0
```

The output is as follows:

```
January
February
March
April
[code continues]
```

You can also use the direct assignment method in the for statement, as in the next activity.

Activity 5-10: Creating a `for` Loop

Time Required: 10 minutes

Objective: Create a script that repeats the commands between do and done a specified number of times.

Description: In this activity, you create a script that assigns specific values to the NUMBER variable and then displays each value one line at a time.

1. If necessary, start VMware Player and start an openSUSE virtual machine. Open a terminal window, type **cd scripts**, and press **Enter**.

2. Type **vim scr10** and press **Enter** to open a new empty file in the vim editor.

3. Enter extended mode and display line numbers.

4. Switch to insert mode and type the following information, pressing **Enter** after each line:

```
1 #!/bin/bash
2 clear
3 for NUMBER in 10 9 8 7 6 5 4 3 2 1
4 do
5 echo "$NUMBER"
6 sleep 1
7 done
8 echo Blast off!
```

5. Exit insert mode and switch to extended mode. Save your changes and exit the vim editor.

6. Give the user (owner) execute permission to run the script, and then run the script. What happens?

_____

7. Power off the virtual machine, and close all open windows.

Line 3 starts the for loop and sets the value of the loop variable (NUMBER). Each time the script runs, the commands between do and done (lines 4 to 7), the value of NUMBER changes to equal the number set in line 3. After each value has been entered in the variable, the loop ends, and line 8 is executed.

Displaying the Contents of a Text File

You have learned how to create text files and write shell scripts. In the following sections, you learn commands for displaying a text file's contents. You might want to list a file's contents without actually opening the file in a text editor. There are also commands that allow you to look at the beginning or the end of a file without opening the entire document. The commands discussed in the next sections are quite useful for administrative tasks.

The `cat` and `tac` Commands

Because the cat (concatenation) command displays an entire file's contents at once, it's typically used to display the contents of a small text file. It can also be used to display the contents of multiple files at once (hence the name "concatenation"). The following example uses the cat command to display the contents of your first script:

```
cat scr1
```

The -n option is often used in the following format to display line numbers in a text file:

```
cat -n scr1
```

You can also use the tac command ("cat" spelled backward) to display a text file's contents in reverse order. The main purpose of this command is to display **log files**, which are text files in the /var/log directory containing information gathered about the system. Displaying these files in reverse order means the most recent events are shown first, which is more helpful when troubleshooting.

The head and tail Commands

The head command displays the first 10 lines of a text file, as shown in this example:

```
head scr8
```

You can use the head command to get an idea of the kind of text file you're looking at. For instance, if you have a file in your home directory called project1a, and you can't remember what it contains, the head command is a quick way to check the first few lines to determine whether you should delete the file. If 10 lines are too many lines or not enough, you can specify the number of lines (such as 15) you want to see:

```
head -15 scr8
```

The tail command displays the last 10 lines of a text file, as shown in this example:

```
tail scr8
```

However, you can add an option to display as many lines as you like. For instance, tail - 15 scr8 displays the last 15 lines of the scr8 file. You can also use the + operator to start displaying text at a specified line number all the way to the end of the file. For instance, tail +5 scr8 displays the contents of the scr8 file starting at line 5.

The more and less Commands

The more command displays a file's contents one screen at a time, which is useful with large files that take up multiple screens (see Figure 5-6).

```
#!/bin/bash
until [ $CHOICE -eq 4 ]
do
clear
echo Please select a menu item
echo echo CHOICE is $CHOICE
echo
echo "1)Display your current working directory"
echo "2)Display your home directory"
echo "3)List the contents of your current working directory"
echo "4)Exit the program"
echo
read CHOICE
case $CHOICE in
--More--(67%)
```

Figure 5-6 Output of the `more` command
Source: openSUSE

Notice the "--More--(67%)" message at the bottom, which tells you how much of the file you're viewing. Table 5-8 lists options you can use with the `more` command. Some are preceded by an integer argument (represented by # in the table). For instance, pressing the spacebar displays the next screen; pressing 2 and then the spacebar displays the next two lines.

Table 5-8 Options for the `more` command

Command	Description
Spacebar	Displays the next screen
#+spacebar	Displays the next # lines
Enter	Displays the next line
q	Exits the `more` command
=	Displays the current line number
h	Displays help

The `less` command also displays a file's contents one screen at a time, as shown in Figure 5-7, but allows you to navigate the file by using arrow keys or the mouse wheel. It works the same as the `more` command but offers more flexibility in navigation. The message "scr8 lines 1-16/23 72%" at the bottom tells you that you're viewing lines 1 to 16 of the scr8 file, which has 23 lines, and you're viewing 72% of the file.

```
#!/bin/bash
until [ $CHOICE -eq 4 ]
do
clear
echo Please select a menu item
echo echo CHOICE is $CHOICE
echo
echo "1)Display your current working directory"
echo "2)Display your home directory"
echo "3)List the contents of your current working directory"
echo "4)Exit the program"
echo
read CHOICE
case $CHOICE in
1) pwd;;
2) echo $HOME;;
scr8 lines 1-16/23 72%
```

Figure 5-7 Output of the `less` command
Source: openSUSE

5

Chapter Summary

- Linux file permissions are assigned in the user, group, and other categories. Each category can be assigned read, write, and execute permissions.
- Linux file permissions are changed by using the chmod command with symbolic notation or numeric notation.
- Shell scripts can be run only after the user has been given execute permission for them.
- Values are assigned to variables by direct assignment, positional parameters, or the prompt method.
- Condition statements are used to run specified portions of a script matching the condition.
- An exit status code follows every command execution; for successful commands, the exit status code is 0.
- While loops repeat commands as long as a condition remains true. Until loops repeat commands as long as a condition remains false. For loops repeat commands a specified number of times.
- The cat and tac commands are used to display a text file's contents. The only difference is that tac displays the contents in reverse order.
- The head and tail commands are used to display 10 lines (or another number that you specify) of a file. Use the head command to display the first 10 lines and tail command to display the last 10 lines.
- You use the more and less commands to display a file's contents one screen at a time. The only difference is that with the less command, you can use arrow keys or the mouse wheel for navigation.

Key Terms

comment A piece of information added as documentation to scripts to explain their purpose.

compiled program A program that converts source code to machine code and stores it in a binary file before the user runs the script. *See also* machine code.

direct assignment A method used to assign a value to a variable by entering it explicitly in the command.

environment variable A placeholder for data that can change; typically gets its value automatically at OS startup or from the shell the user is using.

execute A Linux file permission that allows users to run files (scripts or programs) or work in a directory.

exit status code A numeric code indicating success or failure that a program or command sends to the shell when it ends.

group A category of file permissions given to the group of users assigned to a file.

interpreted program A program that converts source code to machine code as it's running. *See also* machine code.

log files Text files that gather information about a system continuously.

looping Performing a set of commands repeatedly.

machine code A language consisting of binary 1s and 0s that a computer's CPU understands.

other A category of file permissions given to all users on a Linux system, as long as they aren't the file owner or don't belong to the group assigned to the file.

positional parameter A method used to assign a value to a variable according to the order of arguments in the command.

programming language A set of rules for instructing a computer how to perform a task.

prompt method A method used to assign a value to a variable, in which the user is asked to enter data.

read A Linux file permission that allows users to view the contents of files or directories.

shell variable A placeholder for data that can change; typically gets its value from the user or shell script.

user A category of file permissions given to the owner of a file.

write A Linux file permission that allows users to edit the contents of files or add files to a directory.

Review Questions

1. Which of the following commands is used to modify permissions on a file?

   a. chmod

   b. admin

   c. chown

   d. su -

2. The notation `rw-r--r--` means the file owner has which of the following permissions?

   a. Read

   b. Read and write

   c. Read, write, and execute

   d. No permissions

3. The notation `rwxrw-r--` means the group has which of the following permissions?

   a. Read

   b. Read and write

   c. Read, write, and execute

   d. No permissions

4. The notation `rw-rw----` means the other category has which of the following permissions?

   a. Read

   b. Read and write

   c. Read, write, and execute

   d. No permissions

5. Execute permission on a directory allows users to switch to it with the `cd` command. True or False?

6. Describe the difference between using symbolic and numeric notation with the `chmod` command.

7. Use numeric notation to give the owner and group read and write permissions for `file1`. Make sure the other category has no permissions.

8. Which numeric notation represents the file permissions `rwxrw-r--`?

   a. 777

   b. 776

   c. 766

   d. 764

9. Explain the three methods that can be used in a script to assign a value to a variable.

10. Explain what the exit status code 0 means.

11. Explain the difference between `if` statements and `case` statements.

12. What type of loop repeats commands between do and done a specified number of times?

    a. while loop

    b. until loop

    c. for loop

    d. unless loop

13. What type of loop repeats commands between do and done as long as the condition is true?

    a. while loop

    b. until loop

    c. for loop

    d. unless loop

14. What type of loop repeats commands between do and done as long as the condition is false?

    a. while loop

    b. until loop

    c. for loop

    d. unless loop

15. Write a command for viewing only the first 15 lines of the scr1 file.

16. Explain why using the more command is a better option than the cat command for viewing large files.

17. Explain the difference between the more and less commands.

Case Projects

CASE PROJECTS

Case Project 5-1: Granting Permissions

You're a Linux help desk technician and just got a phone call from Chris Baxter, a new employee, who is having trouble running shell scripts. He tells you he has replaced the previous employee Aaron Cole, but he can't run any of Aaron's scripts. You check Chris's user account and discover he's a member of the division group. After using the ls -l command in the scripts directory, you see the following information:

```
ls -l
-rwxr--r-- 1 cole division 0 2009-02-10 04:59 bank
-rwxr--r-- 1 cole division 0 2010-01-04 04:59 database
-rwxr--r-- 1 cole division 0 2010-09-17 04:59 project
-rwxr--r-- 1 cole division 0 2011-07-23 04:59 school
```

Why can't Chris run the scripts listed in this output? What command should you use to give Chris the permissions needed to run them?

Case Project 5-2: What's Your Name?

As the Linux system administrator, you're responsible for maintaining all approved scripts. Your manager asks whether you can add a feature to one of the scripts. She wants you to have the script ask users for their names and greet users by name. She asks you to create a test script first and send it to her. Write the commands you'd use to meet these requirements.

Case Project 5-3: Writing a Shell Script

Write a shell script that displays the following menu items. Make sure users can continue running the script until they want to exit.

1. Display a list of files and directories in their current directory
2. Display a long list of files and directories in their current directory
3. Display the last 10 lines of the log file `messages` (`/var/log/messages`)
4. Display the contents of this script
5. Display the contents of this script in reverse order
6. Exit the program

5

## chapter 6

Managing Data: Backup and Recovery Processes

After reading this chapter and completing the exercises, you will be able to:

- Perform system backups at the command line
- Compress and decompress files at the command line
- Explain how to schedule backups with a cron table

Having backups of critical information on your Linux system is like having insurance against drive failures and system crashes. The time to develop a backup plan and the cost of backup media are minor compared with the frustration of losing data because of an unexpected system failure. In this chapter, you focus on system backups, including the difference between full and incremental backups. You learn how to use command-line utilities to create archives and compress files for backup. Finally, you learn how to schedule backups with user and system cron tables.

System Backups

As a responsible Linux administrator, you should have a system backup plan in place. Hard drives don't last forever, and users often delete important files accidentally. Information systems are critical in today's businesses, which means system failures can result in the loss of a hospital's medical records, a bank's financial records, critical military intelligence, and so forth. You must determine the value of your data and know the costs of system failure to help you develop a solid system backup plan. A **system backup** copies files and directories to an archive you can use to restore data in case of a system failure or data loss and corruption. An **archive** is a file containing many other files, each of which is still identified by its filename, owner, permissions, timestamp, and so forth. A system backup can be as simple as copying files to a CD or writing a script that creates backup archives on tape drives automatically. Backups can be done on different types of media, such as tapes, CDs/DVDs, and hard disks. Almost every organization uses disks to some degree to back up its data. However, the most common medium is still tape.

As you've learned, everything in Linux is considered a file. Of the thousands of files on your Linux system, some rarely need to be backed up. For instance, files in the /usr/bin directory rarely change, so you don't need to back them up regularly. However, user files in the /home directory change constantly and, therefore, require diligent backup. You should include the following directories in regular backups:

- /etc—This directory contains core configuration files, including the filesystems table, which mounts file systems automatically when Linux starts. It also includes security files, network configuration files, user and group information, an initialization table that defines the default runlevel, and a "message of the day" file that's displayed after a successful login.

- /home—Because Linux is a multiuser operating system, each user has a /home directory where he or she can create scripts, files, and subdirectories; install programs; and store videos, pictures, e-mail, and so forth.

- /opt—This directory contains software and packages added after the default installation.

- /root—This is the root user's home directory.

- /var—This directory contains system-specific information that changes while the system is running normally. Log files, mailbox files, and printer queues are examples of information in the /var directory.

Creating a backup in Linux is largely about archiving files and directories. You can back up your Linux file system by using existing system utilities, such as tar and cpio.

Organizations must determine which files and directories are essential to back up and which ones can be left out of backups. As a general rule, the /proc directory shouldn't be backed up because it contains data the kernel generates automatically and, as a result, could be very large.

The Tar Utility

The tar (tape archive) utility creates archives by combining files and directories into a single file; it's also used to work with tar archives. For instance, you can use it to extract files from a tar archive. **Extraction** refers to unpacking the members of an archive and making them available. The tar utility was designed to store files conveniently on magnetic tape—hence the name "tape archive." Despite its original purpose, you can use it to store files on a hard disk, CD/DVD, or even on a network.

6

Creating an archive with the tar command doesn't delete or change the original data, and extracting files from a tar archive doesn't delete or change the archive file.

You can use many options with the tar utility to modify how it functions when creating and extracting archives. Table 6-1 describes the most common options.

Table 6-1 Common tar options

Operation	Description
-c or --create	Creates an archive file
-t or --list	Lists an archive's contents
-x or --extract	Extracts an archive's contents
-f or --file	Specifies the archive file's name and location
-v or --verbose	Displays details about copying files to and extracting files from archives
-z or --gzip, --ungzip	Filters an archive through gzip

The following example shows using two options to create a tar archive called files.tar that contains the files file1 and file2:

```
tar -cf files.tar file1 file2
```

When using tar options, you can use the short name, such as -c, or the long name, such as --create.

Activity 6-1 walks you through creating a tar file and then extracting it with the tar utility.

To get help with the tar command, type tar --help and press Enter.

Unless otherwise noted, you can use the KDE or GNOME virtual machine you created in Chapter 2.

Activity 6-1: Using the Tar Utility

Time Required: 10 minutes

Objective: Create, view, and extract tar archives.

Description: In this activity, you use the tar utility to create, view, and extract a tar archive and use its options to name the tar file and view files as they're being archived and extracted.

1. Start VMware Player, and start an openSUSE virtual machine.

2. Open a terminal window. To create a directory, type **mkdir Act6-1** and press **Enter**. Switch to this new directory by typing **cd Act6-1** and pressing **Enter**. To create three empty files, type **touch apple banana orange** and press **Enter**.

3. Type **tar -cvf fruit.tar apple banana orange** and press **Enter** to create a tar file named fruit.tar. (*Note:* Make sure you include a space after fruit.tar.)

The file extension .tar isn't necessary, but it helps you identify the archive file when viewing a directory's contents.

4. To view the contents of your current directory, type **ls -l** and press **Enter**. What's the size of your tar file?

_____

5. To simulate a user deleting files accidentally, type **rm apple banana orange** and press **Enter**. View your current directory again by typing **ls -l** and pressing **Enter**. Are the apple, banana, and orange test files gone?

_____

6. To list the archive file's contents, type **tar -tvf fruit.tar** and press **Enter**.

7. To extract the archive file's contents, type **tar -xvf fruit.tar** and press **Enter**. View your current directory again by typing **ls -l** and pressing **Enter**. Are the three test files back? Is the archive file still there?

_____

8. Remove the tar file by typing **rm fruit.tar** and pressing **Enter**. Leave the virtual machine running and the terminal window open for the next activity.

The archive file's contents you listed in Step 6 are called **members**. The difference between files and members is how they're accessed. For instance, a file is accessed with commands such as ls, cat, more, and so forth, but members can be viewed only with the tar command's -t option.

> **TIP** If the members of a tar archive are the files in your home directory, you shouldn't store the archive in your home directory. If something happened to your home directory, you would lose the data _and_ the backup. It's safer to save the tar file to a disk or move it to another location, such as a network drive.

Sometimes you need to extract only a few members from an archive, as when a user deletes a file accidentally. The following example shows using the tar utility to extract a member from an archive:

```
1. tar -tvf fruit.tar
2. -rw-r--r-- martha/users 0 2012-05-01 11:22 apple
3. -rw-r--r-- martha/users 0 2012-05-01 11:22 banana
4. -rw-r--r-- martha/users 0 2012-05-01 11:22 orange
5. tar -xvf fruit.tar apple
6. apple
```

The command in line 1 lists the members of the fruit.tar archive, displayed in lines 2 through 4. The command in line 5 includes the -x option to specify the member to be extracted (apple, in this case). If you want to extract more than one member, you can use this same option. The following example shows extracting multiple members at once:

```
tar -xvf fruit.tar apple banana orange
```

Advanced Tar Options Now that you have practiced the common tar options, it's time to learn the advanced options, described in Table 6-2.

Table 6-2 Advanced tar options

Option	Description
-r or --append	Adds files to an existing archive.
-u or --update	Compares the date and time of a member with the date and time of the file with the same name. If the file was modified after the archive was created, its newer version is added to the archive.
-A or --concatenate	Similar to the append option but adds one archive to another archive.
--delete	Removes specific members from a tar archive. This option doesn't have a short name.
-d or --compare	Compares specified members with files in the file system having the same name and reports differences in file size, mode, owner, modification date, and contents.

Activity 6-2: Using the Advanced Tar Options

Time Required: 30 minutes

Objective: Use advanced tar options.

Description: In this activity, you use the tar utility to create an archive and view its members, and then use advanced options to add files to an existing archive, update members of an archive, concatenate two archives into one file, delete specific members from an archive, and compare archive members with files of the same name.

1. If necessary, start VMware Player, start an openSUSE virtual machine, and open a terminal window.

2. Type **mkdir Act6-2** and press **Enter**.

3. Type **cd Act6-2** and press **Enter**. Create eight empty files to simulate user files by typing **touch moon sun earth stars tree grass plant flower** and pressing **Enter**.

4. Type **tar -cvf space.tar moon sun earth** and press **Enter**. Type **ls -l** to view the contents of your current directory.

5. Type **tar -tvf space.tar** and press **Enter** to view the members of the tar file.

6. Type **tar -rvf space.tar stars** and press **Enter** to add the stars file to the space.tar archive file. The -r option is used to add files to an existing archive.

7. Type **tar -tvf space.tar** and press **Enter**. Did the archive members change? If so, how?

   _____

8. Type **vim sun** and press **Enter** to open the sun file in the vim editor. Type **i** to enter insert mode, and then type **We need the Sun** and press the **Esc** key to enter command mode. Type **:** to enter extended mode, and then type **wq!** and press **Enter** to save the file and exit the vim editor.

9. Type **tar -uvf space.tar earth moon stars sun** and press **Enter** to compare the members of the space.tar archive with the files earth, moon, stars, and sun. What archive member names were displayed? Why were they displayed?

   _____

10. Type **tar -cvf planet.tar tree grass plant flower** and press **Enter**.

11. Type **tar -Avf planet.tar space.tar** and press **Enter** to add the members of space.tar to the planet.tar archive.

12. Type **tar --delete -vf planet.tar flower moon** and press **Enter** to remove the flower and moon members from the planet.tar archive.

13. Type **tar -cvf new.tar moon flower tree** and press **Enter**.

14. Type **vim tree** and press **Enter**. Type **i** to enter insert mode, and then type **Trees give off oxygen** and press **Esc**. Type **:** and then **wq!**, and then press **Enter**.

15. Type **tar -dvf new.tar moon flower tree** and press **Enter** to compare the members of `new.tar` with the `moon`, `flower`, and `tree` files. The -d option also reports differences in file size, mode, owner, modification date, and contents. Describe briefly what's displayed onscreen:

_____

16. Leave the virtual machine running and the terminal window open for the next activity.

As you've learned, the tar utility retains all file information, such as modification time, permissions, and ownership, when creating an archive. You can use other options, described in Table 6-3, with the -c option to change this file information.

Table 6-3 Modifying tar options

Option	Description
--mode	Changes a member's permissions in an archive with numeric or symbolic notation. For instance, you could use `tar -cvf backup.tar --mode=777 /home` or `tar -cvf backup.tar --mode='a=rwx' /home`.
--mtime	Changes a member's modification date in the tar archive. For instance, `tar -cf backup.tar --mtime='2012-05-02' /home` archives everything in /home, and the members in the archive have 2012-05-02 as the modification date. You can also use terms such as `today` or `yesterday` instead of a specific date.
--owner	Changes the member's owner in the tar archive. For instance, `tar -cf backup.tar --owner=root /home` creates a tar archive of your /home directory and makes root the new owner.
--group	Similar to --owner, except it's used to change the member's group instead of owner.

ACTIVITY

Activity 6-3: Using Tar Options to Modify Archive Members' File Information

Time Required: 20 minutes

Objective: Use advanced tar options to modify file information.

Description: In this activity, you use the tar utility with options to modify archive members' file permissions, change their modification dates, and assign an owner and a group to archive members.

1. If necessary, start VMware Player, start an openSUSE virtual machine, and open a terminal window.

2. Create a new directory by typing **mkdir Act6-3** and pressing **Enter**. To switch to this directory, type **cd Act6-3** and press **Enter**.

3. Create three files in this directory to simulate user files by typing **touch blue red white** and pressing **Enter**.

4. To archive these three new files, type **tar -cvf file1.tar blue red white** and press **Enter**.

5. Type **tar -tvf file1.tar** and press **Enter**. Write down the file permissions for each member in the archive:

_____

6. To set file permissions for all members of the `file2.tar` archive to 777 (numeric notation), type **tar -cvf file2.tar --mode=777 blue red white** and press **Enter**.

7. Type **tar -tvf file2.tar** and press **Enter**. Notice the file permissions for each archive member. How do these file permissions differ from those in the `file1.tar` archive?

_____

8. Type **tar -cvf file3.tar --mtime=yesterday blue red white** and press **Enter** to change the modification date to yesterday's date instead of retaining the file's modification date.

9. Type **tar -tvf file3.tar** and press **Enter**. Notice the modification date for each member in the tar file.

10. Type **tar -cvf file4.tar --owner=root blue red white** and press **Enter** to change the members' owner to root instead of retaining the file's owner.

11. Type **tar -tvf file4.tar** and press **Enter**. Notice who the owner is for each member in the file.

12. Type **tar -cvf file5.tar --group=video blue red white** and press **Enter** to change the members' primary group to video instead of retaining the file's primary group. Next, type **tar -tvf file5.tar** and press **Enter**. Notice who the new group is for each member in the tar file. (This works only if you have a group named video.) If you're not sure what groups you have, you can type **groups** and press **Enter** to list all groups on your system.

13. Leave the virtual machine running and the terminal window open for the next activity.

Using Tar to Perform Full Backups A full backup is an archive of all files on the file system. In a multiuser OS, such as Linux, several users could access the same files at the same time. Therefore, you should never perform a full backup while users are accessing the system because the tar file could be corrupted if files are modified during the backup process. The following example shows using the `tar` command to create a full backup:

```
tar -cvf backup0.tar -V "This is a full backup of the /home directory"
--listed-incremental=/home/backup.snap *
```

This command creates a full backup of the /home directory. The `-cvf` options are used to create an archive called `backup0.tar`, and the `-V` option is used to label the archive with the text between the quotation marks. The `--listed-incremental` option creates a snapshot file named `backup.snap`, which is used during incremental backups to determine which files have changed since the last backup.

Using Tar to Perform Incremental Backups An incremental backup is an archive containing only files modified since the last backup (full or incremental). Organizations have different backup strategies, depending on their needs. For example, some companies find that creating a full backup every Friday night and then creating incremental backups through the week is adequate; other companies might need to do full backups more often. Because incremental backups contain only files changed since the last backup, they take less time to run and require less storage space. The syntax for creating an incremental backup is the same as the command for full backups. If the snapshot file already exists, the tar utility examines it to determine whether any files have changed.

As explained in Table 6-1, you extract files from a tar archive by using the -x option.

Table 6-4 describes important options used with the `tar` command when creating full or incremental backups.

Table 6-4 Full and incremental backup options

Option	Description
-V or --label	Adds a volume header to a tar file. A volume header is simply a digital label used to describe the file. Physically labeling tapes, CDs, and DVDs is important, but you should also digitally label tar files with the --label option. You can view the volume header with the -t option.
-W or --verify	Verifies that files have been included in the archive correctly.
-g or --listed-incremental	Forces tar to archive only files that have been modified since the last backup (full or incremental) by analyzing the **snapshot file**. A snapshot file is created during a full backup and contains the condition of the backed-up directory to determine which files were modified since the last backup. This is a good practice because there's no need to back up files that have already been backed up and haven't changed. The snapshot file is given as an argument to the --listed-incremental option so that the tar utility knows which files have been changed, added, or deleted since the last backup.
--no-check-device	When a device number changes (which can happen when upgrading a kernel version, for example), an incremental backup might back up files that haven't been changed. This option prevents this from happening by forcing the tar utility to not rely on device numbers when preparing for an incremental backup.
--check-device	The default option; necessary only when you want to undo the --no-check-device option.

Activity 6-4: Performing Full and Incremental Backups with the Tar Utility

Time Required: 20 minutes

Objective: Use the tar utility to perform full and incremental backups.

Description: In this activity, you use the tar utility to create a full and an incremental backup, and then use command-line options to verify that files were archived successfully, label your backup, and create a snapshot file.

1. If necessary, start VMware Player, start an openSUSE virtual machine, and open a terminal window.

2. Type **mkdir Act6-4** and press **Enter**, and then type **cd Act6-4** and press **Enter**.

3. Type **touch math english history** and press **Enter**.

4. Type **tar -cvWf $HOME/backup0.tar -V "This is a full backup of the Act6-4 directory" --listed-incremental=$HOME/act6-4.snap * and press Enter**. This command is much longer than commands you've typed previously, so check it carefully to make sure the characters and spaces are correct. In this command, you enter the absolute path ($HOME/backup0.tar) for the archive file. $HOME is an environment variable that specifies the absolute path to your home directory. The --listed-incremental=$HOME/act6-4.snap * option creates a snapshot file, as explained previously. The * at the end is a wildcard that tells the tar utility to archive all files in the directory.

5. Type **cd** and press **Enter**. To list the archive members and display the volume header, type **tar -tvf backup0.tar** and press **Enter**.

6. Type **cd Act6-4** and press **Enter**. To simulate changes to the directory, type **touch science** and press **Enter**.

7. Type **tar -cvWf $HOME/backup1.tar -V "This is an incremental backup of the Act6-4 directory" --listed-incremental=$HOME/act6-4.snap * and press Enter**. This command is similar to the one in Step 4, except the name of the archive file is different. The archive file (backup1.tar) is a backup of everything that has changed since the last backup (which was archived in backup0.tar).

8. Type **tar -tvf backup1.tar** and press **Enter**. What are the members of backup1.tar?

_____

9. Type **cd Act6-4** and press **Enter**.

10. To simulate a system crash, type **rm *** and press **Enter**, which removes all files in the Act6-4 directory.

11. To extract the backup0.tar archive's contents, type **tar -xvf $HOME/backup0.tar** and press **Enter**.

12. To extract the backup1.tar archive's contents, type **tar -xvf $HOME/backup1.tar** and press **Enter**.

13. Type **ls -l** and press **Enter**. Are all the files restored?

_____

14. Leave the virtual machine running and the terminal window open for the next activity.

The Cpio Utility

The cpio (copy in/out) utility uses the results of the ls or find command to generate files to be archived. It operates in three modes: copy-out, copy-in, and copy-pass. In **copy-out mode**, cpio creates an archive from the output of the ls or find commands. In **copy-in mode**, it extracts files from an archive. In **copy-pass mode**, it copies files from one directory to another; in other words, it combines copy-out with copy-in without creating an archive.

Standard Input, Standard Output, and Redirection Before you can learn how to use cpio to create archives, you need to understand the differences between standard input, standard output, and redirection. In Linux, the default **standard input** is the keyboard. For instance, commands such as pwd, cd, and ls are executed by typing them. The < symbol is used to redirect input from the keyboard. Most of the time, input is expected from the keyboard, and for that, you don't see standard input redirection. However, it's useful for commands that don't open files directly, such as the mail command (covered in more detail in Chapter 12). You can use standard input redirection to e-mail the contents of a text file to another user on your system, as shown in the following example; the contents of the letter.txt file become the input for the mail command:

```
mail user1 < letter.txt
```

The default **standard output** is the screen. For instance, the output of the ls command is displayed onscreen. You can use output redirection operators, such as > (the "greater than" symbol) to redirect a command's output to a file or | (the "pipe" symbol) to make one command's output the standard input of another command. The following example shows redirecting the ls command's output to the home_listing file instead of displaying the output onscreen as usual:

```
ls > home_listing
```

The following example shows how to view the home_listing file's contents with the cat command:

cat home_listing
```
Act6-1
Act6-2
Act6-3
Act6-4
act6-4.snap
```

Another redirection operator that you've used before is the pipe symbol (|), used in the following example:

```
ls | more
```

Copy-Out Mode This cpio mode is used with the -o or --create option to create archives by accepting the output of ls or find as the input for an archive. The following example shows using this command to archive all files in your current directory:

```
ls | cpio -o > files.cpio
```

In this example, the results of the ls command are used to determine which files to archive in files.cpio. You can display which files are being archived by adding the -v option, as shown in this example:

```
ls | cpio -ov > files.cpio
```

The following example shows using the find command's results to archive all files in the /home/user1 directory and the -v option to display which files are being archived:

```
find /home/user1 | cpio -ov > home.cpio
```

Copy-In Mode This cpio mode is used to extract archives. Recall that extracting an archive simply refers to unpacking all members of an archive and making them available. The cpio command uses the standard input redirection symbol (<) to extract the archive members. In the following example, the user starts in the /home/student1/Demo directory, which has only the archive file (demo.cpio) in it:

```
cpio -iv < demo.cpio
/home/student1/Demo/file1
/home/student1/Demo/file2
1 block
```

The -i option is used to extract files from a cpio archive, and the -v option lists files as they're being extracted. The < symbol is used to specify the demo.cpio archive as input.

Copy-Pass Mode In copy-pass mode, you can copy files and directories from one directory and paste them in another directory without actually creating an archive. This mode isn't a practical option for backups because you aren't creating an archive, and you can't use this mode to copy the files to a backup medium. The purpose of this mode is simply to copy files from one directory to another. The benefit of using this mode instead of the cp command (covered in Chapter 3) is that the cpio utility preserves modification times and ownership.

The -p option is used to copy files from one directory tree to another. When used to copy files, cpio accepts the output of the find or ls command and "passes" the files to the directory tree, which is specified as an argument. The following example shows passing files from one directory to another:

```
find . | cpio -pv /home/dustin/dir2
/home/dustin/dir2/./juice
/home/dustin/dir2/./water
/home/dustin/dir2/./soda
0 blocks
```

In this example, the find command searches for all files and subdirectories in the current directory. This information is read by the cpio utility, which copies the files and subdirectories to /home/dustin/dir2. Activity 6-5 walks you through using the cpio utility.

Activity 6-5: Using the Cpio Utility

Time Required: 15 minutes

Objective: Use the cpio utility to create and extract an archive.

Description: In this activity, you use the find command to list files and directories for the cpio utility to take as input and create an archive. You also use the cpio utility to extract an archive and copy files from one directory to another.

1. If necessary, start VMware Player, start an openSUSE virtual machine, and open a terminal window.

2. Type **mkdir Act6-5** and press **Enter**, and then type **cd Act6-5** and press **Enter**.

3. Type **touch strong stronger strongest** and press **Enter**.

4. Type **find . | cpio -ov > act6.5.cpio** and press **Enter**. The `find` . command is used to find all files in your current directory, and the cpio utility uses the results to create an archive called `act6.5.cpio`.

5. Type **ls -l** and press **Enter**. What do you see?

_____

6. Type **mkdir dir1** and press **Enter**, and then type **cd dir1** and press **Enter**.

7. Type **cpio -iv < ~/Act6-5/act6.5.cpio** and press **Enter**. The `-i` option is used to extract files from the archive (`act6.5.cpio`). What does the ~ symbol represent?

_____

8. Type **ls -l** and press **Enter** to view the extracted files, and then type **mkdir dir2** and press **Enter**.

9. Type **find . | cpio -pv dir2** and press **Enter**, and then type **cd dir2** and press **Enter**. The `-p` option is used to run in copy-pass mode, and the `-v` option lists the files processed. Type **ls -l** and press **Enter**. What do you see?

_____

10. Leave the virtual machine running and the terminal window open for the next activity.

Compression

Tapes and other backup media can hold only a certain amount of information. For instance, a standard DVD can hold 4.7 GB of data. Often you need to compress data to save storage space, to make it fit on removable media, or to transfer it across the network faster. **Compression** reduces the size of data to store information in less space. Think of it as writing in shorthand. The information stays the same, but you can fit more on a piece of paper. Many compression utilities are available for Linux users. In this chapter, you learn the two most common: gzip and bzip2.

The Gzip Utility

You use the gzip utility to compress files. A file compressed with gzip, which has the extension `.gz`, has the same file permissions, ownership, and modification time as the original file but has a much smaller file size. The compression ratio defines by how much a file is reduced after compressing it. For instance, a 1 MB file with a 60% compression ratio can be reduced to 400 KB. According to the man page for the gzip utility, text files are typically reduced by 60% to 70% with compression. To see a compression ratio for any file, you can use the `-v` option with the gzip utility. Table 6-5 describes this option and others used with the gzip utility.

Table 6-5 Gzip options

Option	Description
-c	Keeps the original files unchanged. For instance, if you type `gzip -c file1 > file1.gz`, you have two files: `file1` and `file1.gz`. The `file1.gz` file is the compressed file. The `-c` option is also used to concatenate files. For instance, if you type `gzip -c file1 file2 > file3.gz`, `file3.gz` is one compressed file, which contains the contents of `file1` and `file2`.
-h	Displays an information page describing the options used with the gzip utility.
-v	Displays information about a file as it's being compressed, such as the compression ratio.

To uncompress a file compressed with the gzip utility, you use the `gunzip` command.

You can combine the `tar` and `gzip` commands to compress an archive as you create it. In the next example, the `tar` command is used twice. The first command (line 1) uses the `-z` option, which filters the tar utility through the gzip utility to compress the archive. The second command (line 2) simply creates an archive without any compression. Lines 4 and 6 compare the two archives and reveal a major difference in file size, shown in bold in the following code lines:

```
1. tar -czf commands.tar.gz cd.man ls.man pwd.man
2. tar -cf commands.tar cd.man ls.man pwd.man
3. ~/dir1> ls -l commands.tar
4. -rw-r--r-- 1 linda users 20480 2012-05-08 21:09 commands.tar
5. ~/dir1> ls -l commands.tar.gz
6. -rw-r--r-- 1 linda users 3802 2012-05-08 21:09 commands.tar.gz
```

Activity 6-6 walks you through compressing and uncompressing files with the gzip utility.

Activity 6-6: Using the Gzip Utility

Time Required: 15 minutes

Objective: Compress and uncompress files with command-line utilities.

Description: In this activity, you create a file containing the man page for the `gzip` command and a file containing the man page for the `tar` command. You then compress these files with the gzip utility, compare the size of the original files with the compressed files, and view the compression ratio.

1. If necessary, start VMware Player, start an openSUSE virtual machine, and open a terminal window.

2. Type **mkdir Act6-6** and press **Enter**, and then type **cd Act6-6** and press **Enter**.

3. To redirect the gzip man page to a file, type **man gzip > gzip.man** and press **Enter**, and then to redirect the tar man page to a file, type **man tar > tar.man** and press **Enter**. Type **ls -l** and press **Enter**. What are the file sizes of gzip.man and tar.man?

_____

4. Type **gzip -h** and press **Enter** to display an information page about options you can use with the gzip command.

5. Type **gzip -v tar.man** and press **Enter** to compress the tar.man file and display the file's compression ratio. What's the compression ratio? Type **ls -l** and press **Enter**. What's the file size of tar.man.gz?

_____

6. To uncompress the tar.man.gz file and display the compression ratio, type **gunzip -v tar.man.gz** and press **Enter**.

7. Type **gzip -cv tar.man gzip.man > gzip.gz** and press **Enter**. The -c option is used to copy the files (tar.man and gzip.man) and compress the copied files but leave the original files unchanged. What's the compression ratio for each file?

_____

8. To check that the uncompressed files (gzip.man and tar.man) are still there, type **ls -l** and press **Enter**.

9. Leave the virtual machine running and the terminal window open for the next activity.

The Bzip2 Utility

The bzip2 utility compresses files and adds the .bz2 extension. The bunzip2 utility is used to uncompress files. Table 6-6 describes options you can use with bzip2.

Table 6-6   Bzip2 options

Option	Description
-c	Use this option to keep the original files unchanged. For instance, if you type bzip2 -c file1 > file1.bz2, you have two files: file1 and file1.bz2 (which is the compressed file). Another use of the -c option is to concatenate files. For example, the command bzip2 -c file1 file2 > file3.bz2 concatenates file1 and file2 into the compressed file file3.bz2.
-v	Displays information, such as compression ratio and filename, about the file as it's being compressed.

Activity 6-7 walks you through compressing and uncompressing files with the bzip2 utility.

Activity 6-7: Using the Bzip2 Utility

Time Required: 15 minutes

Objective: Compress and uncompress files with the bzip2 utility.

Description: In this activity, you use the bzip2 utility to compress a file, view the compression ratio, make a copy of a file, and compress only the copied file.

1. If necessary, start VMware Player, start an openSUSE virtual machine, and open a terminal window.

2. Type **mkdir Act6-7** and press **Enter**, and then type **cd Act6-7** and press **Enter**.

3. Type **man bzip2 > bzip2.man** and press **Enter**. Then type **man gzip > gzip.man** and press **Enter**. Type **ls -l** and press **Enter**. What are the sizes of bzip2.man and gzip.man?

   _____

4. Type **bzip2 -v gzip.man** and press **Enter** to compress the gzip.man file and display the compression ratio. What information is displayed? Type **ls -l** and press **Enter**. What is the size of gzip.man.bz2?

   _____

5. Type **bunzip2 -v gzip.man.bz2** and press **Enter** to uncompress the gzip.man.bz2 file and display the compression ratio.

6. Type **bzip2 -cv gzip.man bzip2.man > bzip2.bz2** and press **Enter**. The -c option is used to copy the gzip.man and bzip2.man files and compress them while leaving the original files unchanged. What information is displayed for each file?

   _____

7. Leave the virtual machine running and the terminal window open for the next activity.

Scheduling Backups

So far, you have created backups at the command line with the tar or cpio command, but often you need to have backups run at night or on weekends. Scheduling system backups during off hours is best because fewer people are logged in to the system and there's less disruption in service.

The **cron daemon (crond)** is a system daemon that uses a configuration file called a **cron table** to schedule commands that run at specified times (see Figure 6-1). The cron table has six fields. Table 6-7 describes the first five fields, and the sixth field contains the command to run.

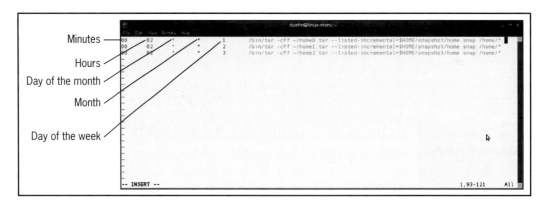

Figure 6-1 A cron table
Source: openSUSE

Table 6-7 The cron table format

Field	Allowed values
1: minutes	0–59
2: hours	0–23 (uses a 24-hour clock)
3: day of the month	1–31
4: month	1–12
5: day of the week	0–6, with 0 representing Sunday and 6 representing Saturday

6

Take a closer look at the first entry in the cron table in Figure 6-1. It specifies running the tar utility every Monday (the 1 in the fifth field) at 2:00 a.m. (the information in the first and second fields). The asterisk in the third and fourth fields can be translated as "first to last," meaning every day of the month (1–31) for the third field and every month (1–12) for the fourth field. To clarify, the number 5 in the third field would mean the tar utility runs on the fifth day of the month and every Monday.

The cron daemon uses two types of cron tables: the user cron table in /var/spool/cron/ tabs and the system cron table in /etc/crontab. Users use the user cron table to schedule tasks, and the system uses the system cron table to schedule system tasks, such as backups. Only the root user can edit the system cron table.

User Cron Tables

Every user (including root) on an openSUSE system has a cron table. The crontab command is used to create, delete, and list cron tables, using the options listed in Table 6-8.

As mentioned in Table 6-8, the -e option opens the user's cron table in the vim editor. However, to make sure you're editing the correct table, you should use the following command to open the vim editor: vim /var/spool/cron/*username*.

Table 6-8 Options used with the crontab **command**

Options	Description
-e	Opens the vim editor to edit the current user's cron table. If the cron table doesn't exist, a blank table is created for you to edit.
-u	Specifies the name of the user whose cron table is to be edited.
-l	Displays the current user's cron table.
-r	Removes the current user's cron table.

Activity 6-8: Editing a User Cron Table

Time Required: 15 minutes

Objective: Edit a user cron table.

Description: In this activity, you edit your user cron table and schedule the Linux system to run the `tar` command every day at 12:30 p.m. This command archives all files in your home directory in a tar archive called `home.tar`. You then view this cron table with the `crontab -l` command.

1. If necessary, start VMware Player, start an openSUSE virtual machine, and open a terminal window.

2. Type **crontab -l** and press **Enter**. What do you see?

_____

3. To use the vim editor, type **crontab -e** and press **Enter**.

4. Type **i** to enter insert mode. To have your system create an archive named `home.tar` that archives all files in your home directory every day at 12:30 p.m., type the following, making sure to press Tab between each field:

The fields shown in this command are separated by spaces.

30 12 * * * tar -cPf ~/home.tar ~/*

Remember that the ~ represents your home directory, and the asterisks represent all files and directories.

5. Press **Esc** and then **:** to enter extended mode. Type **wq!** and press **Enter**.

6. Type **crontab -l** and press **Enter**. What do you see?

_____

7. Now that you've finished this chapter's activities, you can close the terminal window and shut down your openSUSE virtual machine.

System Cron Table

The system cron table is used to schedule tasks, too, but the sixth field is used to specify the user account for issuing commands. Only the root user can edit the system cron table. Typically, the commands scheduled via the system cron table are for backups and system maintenance. You use the following command to start the vim editor so that you can view and edit the system cron table:

```
vim /etc/crontab
```

Here's an example of the system cron table:

```
SHELL=/bin/sh
PATH=/usr/bin:/usr/sbin:/sbin:/bin:/usr/lib/news/bin
MAILTO=root
20 * * * * root mail student1 < /var/log/messages
```

The following list describes each line of this system cron table:

- `SHELL=/bin/sh`—This first entry defines the shell the cron table uses to run the scheduled task. In openSUSE, the system cron table uses the Bourne shell (indicated by `sh`) by default.

- `PATH=/usr/bin:/usr/sbin:/sbin:/bin:/usr/lib/news/bin`—This entry defines the `PATH` variable (explained in Chapter 5). The system cron table uses this entry to search for commands used in the cron table. If `PATH` isn't defined, the absolute path to the command must be used, as in this example:

  ```
  20 * * * * root /bin/mail student1 < /var/log/messages
  ```

- `MAILTO=root`—This entry defines the `MAILTO` variable. The output of a command run from the system cron table is mailed to the user defined by the `MAILTO` variable. The command used in the sample cron table has no output, so nothing is e-mailed to root.

- `20 * * * * root mail student1 < /var/log/messages`—This is the scheduled task, which looks similar to the scheduled tasks in user cron tables. The first five fields of the system cron table are the same as the first five fields of the user cron table. The only difference is in the sixth field. In system cron tables, the sixth field defines the user who's running the command. In the preceding example, it's the root user.

This system cron table is scheduled to e-mail student1 system log messages (which are in the `/var/log` directory) every 20 minutes.

Chapter Summary

- Several directories should be backed up regularly, particularly users' home directories.

- Linux includes backup utilities, such as tar and cpio, to back up files to an archive.

- Archives can be stored on many different types of media, such as tapes, CD-RWs/DVD-RWs, removable media, and hard disks.

- Compression utilities, such as gzip and bzip2, reduce the size of files so that they can fit on backup media or be sent across the network faster.

- The cron table is a configuration file used to specify tasks to run at a certain time; a common task is scheduling backups.

Key Terms

archive   A file containing many other files called members; each of the members are identified by their filename, owner, permissions, and modification time.

compression   The process of reducing the size of data to store information in less space.

copy-in mode   The cpio mode in which files are extracted from an archive.

copy-out mode   The cpio mode in which archives are created from the output of the `ls` or `find` command.

copy-pass mode   The cpio mode in which files from one directory tree are copied to another without creating an archive.

cron daemon (crond)   A system daemon that uses a configuration file called a cron table to schedule commands to run at set intervals. *See also* cron table.

cron table   A configuration file that specifies tasks for the cron daemon to run at specific times.

extraction   The process of unpacking an archive.

full backup   Also known as a level 0 backup; it's an archive of all files in the file system.

incremental backup   An archive that contains only files modified since the last backup.

members   Files stored in an archive. *See also* archive.

snapshot file   A file specified as an argument to the `--listed-incremental` option, which is designed to tell the tar utility which files have been changed, added, or deleted since the last backup.

standard input   A source of input, usually the keyboard.

standard output   A source of output, usually the screen.

system backup   The process of copying files and directories to an archive for the purpose of retrieval in the event of a system failure.

Review Questions

1. Which of the following directories should you back up regularly? (Choose all that apply.)
   a. `/etc`
   b. `/home`
   c. `/bin`
   d. `/usr/bin`

2. An employee named Andrea wants to back up an entire home directory in a file. Which of the following commands should be used?
   a. `tar -cvf home.tar /home/andrea`
   b. `tar -cvf /home/andrea home.tar`
   c. `tar -xvf home.tar /home/andrea`
   d. `tar -xvf /home/andrea home.tar`

3. Which of the following commands should you use to list all members in the `project.tar` archive?

   a. `tar -cvf project.tar`

   b. `tar -lvf project.tar`

   c. `tar -xvf project.tar`

   d. `tar -tvf project.tar`

4. An employee complains that her home directory has disappeared. Which of the following commands should you use to extract the backup archive of her home directory?

   a. `tar -cvf home.tar`

   b. `tar -xvf home.tar`

   c. `tar -tvf home.tar`

   d. `tar -evf /home/backup`

5. Which of the following options is used with the tar utility to add members to an archive?

   a. `-u`

   b. `-r`

   c. `-A`

   d. `-d`

6. Explain the purpose of a snapshot file.

7. Explain the difference between full and incremental backups.

8. Which of the following cpio modes is used when creating an archive?

   a. copy-in

   b. copy-out

   c. copy-pass

   d. copy-from

9. Which of the following cpio modes is used when copying files from one directory tree to another without creating an archive?

   a. copy-in

   b. copy-out

   c. copy-pass

   d. copy-from

10. Your company has a tight budget, and you have been asked to create tar archives to save space on the backup medium. Which of the following commands enables you to archive home directories and compress them at the same time?

   a. `tar -czf home.tar.gz /home`

   b. `gzip -v /home`

   c. `bzip2 -v /home`

   d. `tar -cvf home.tar.gz /home`

11. Describe the first five fields of the cron table.

12. What's the difference between a user cron table and a system cron table?

Case Projects

CASE PROJECTS

Case Project 6-1: Archiving Home Directories

You're the Linux system administrator at East Coast Career College. Ever since Dr. Thompson switched the school's computer infrastructure from Windows to Linux, you have been busy teaching instructors how to use openSUSE. Now that a semester has gone by, you realize that many instructors have important files in their home directories that must be backed up. Write a `tar` command that the administrator can use to archive instructors' home directories. Digitally label the archive "Backup of home directory."

## chapter 7

Managing Users and Groups

After reading this chapter and completing the exercises, you will be able to:

- Identify key user account information in the /etc/passwd and /etc/shadow configuration files
- Describe the default user and group information in the /etc/login.defs and /etc/default/useradd configuration files
- Create and modify user accounts at the command line
- Create and modify groups at the command line
- Manage user and group accounts with the YaST utility

In Chapter 6, you learned how to back up your Linux file system with command-line utilities. In this chapter, you explore working with users and groups. You begin by examining configuration files used for authentication and database files containing user account information. Next, you learn how to create and modify user and group accounts at the command line. Finally, you learn how to manage users and groups with the YaST utility.

Managing Users

For users to log in to a Linux computer, access resources, and perform actions based on their account permissions, their accounts must be confirmed as valid by using authentication. **Authentication** is the process of verifying someone's identity by checking his or her username and password against a central user database. In Linux, the user database consists of two configuration files: /etc/passwd and /etc/shadow.

Linux configuration files vary depending on the Linux distribution. As with all configuration files, you should create a backup before making any changes.

The /etc/passwd File

The /etc/passwd file contains user account information. Each entry has seven fields separated by colons. Everyone has permission to view this file's contents (sometimes referred to as a "world-readable" file because everyone can view it). The following list explains each field in this sample entry in the /etc/passwd file:

amber:x:1000:100:Amber Dawn:/home/amber:/bin/bash

- *Username*—This field contains the name the user enters to log in. Using a combination of uppercase and lowercase letters is possible, but openSUSE recommends using lowercase letters because some mail exchange protocols don't respond to usernames containing uppercase letters.

- *Password*—This field contains the user's encrypted password (represented by x in the preceding example) stored in the /etc/shadow file. If there's no /etc/shadow file, the actual password is stored in the /etc/passwd file.

- *User identifier (UID)*—The **user identifier** (UID) is a unique number representing the username. Regular users typically have a UID greater than 100 because numbers less than 100 are reserved for system accounts (which are nonuser accounts typically used by services, such as www and ftp). The root UID is 0.

- *Group identifier (GID)*—The **group identifier** (GID) is a unique number that corresponds to each group. In the /etc/passwd file, that group is the user's **primary group,** which is the group owner for all new files the user creates. Users can be assigned to multiple groups, but they can have only one primary group. You learn more about group management later in "Managing Groups."

- *GECOS*—This optional field (which stands for General Electric Comprehensive Operating System, an old OS used on mainframes) is used to store additional user information, such as the user's full name.

- *Home directory*—This field lists the absolute path to the user's home directory.

- *Shell*—This field specifies the default shell that starts when the user logs in.

The `/etc/shadow` File

The `/etc/shadow` file is a configuration file containing passwords and password expiration information for all user accounts. It can be read only by the root user. The following list explains each field (separated by the `:` character) in this sample entry in the `/etc/shadow` file:

```
chloe:$2a$05$wa7xVOqOH4lVOrh.qa9ivSX0G0QUCFqbkllYV6:14743:0:99999:7:::
```

- *Username*—This field contains the name the user enters to log in.

- *Encrypted password*—This field stores the user's encrypted password.

- *Last password change*—This field represents the number of days since January 1, 1970 that the password was last changed. In the example, the number 14743 translates to 14,743 days since January 1, 1970.

- *Minimum*—This field specifies the number of days before the password can be changed. The value 0 in this field means the password can be changed any time.

- *Expiration*—This field shows the number of days before the password must be changed. The value 99999 in this field means the user's password never expires.

- *Warning*—This field represents the number of days remaining until the password must be changed. For example, the value 7 in this field means the user gets a warning message a week before his or her password expires.

- *Disabled*—This field contains the number of days after a password has expired until the user account is disabled. No entry in this field, as in the preceding example, means the account is disabled immediately after the password expires.

- *Disabled date*—This field specifies the number of days since January 1, 1970 that the account has been disabled. No entry in this field, as in the preceding example, means the account hasn't been disabled.

- *Reserved*—This field isn't currently in use; it's been reserved for future use.

User Account Information

User information—such as the user's `PATH` variable (explained in Chapter 5), password expiration information, default primary group, location of the home directory, and so forth—is stored in two configuration files: `/etc/default/useradd` and `/etc/login.defs`.

The `/etc/default/useradd` File The `/etc/default/useradd` file is a text file that can be read by all users and contains basic parameters that set certain values for new user accounts. The following list describes each value shown in this example of the `/etc/default/useradd` file:

```
GROUP=100
HOME=/home
INACTIVE=-1
EXPIRE=
```

```
SHELL=/bin/bash
SKEL=/etc/skel
GROUPS=video
CREATE_MAIL_SPOOL=no
```

- GROUP=100—This line lists the primary GID. By default, every new user in openSUSE has the same primary group. To find out which group has a GID of 100, for example, use the command more /etc/group | grep 100.

- HOME=/home—This line shows the location of a new user's home directory. In the example, because the specified value is /home, a new user named john has his home directory in /home/john.

- INACTIVE=-1—This value represents the number of days of inactivity after a password has expired before the account is locked. In the example, the setting -1 disables this feature.

- EXPIRE=—This value specifies the number of days after January 1, 1970 that the account expires. However, you can enter the exact expiration date (in YYYY-MM-DD format) instead of calculating the correct number of days. In the example, omitting a number or date means the account is set to never expire.

- SHELL=/bin/bash—This line indicates the default shell used when the user first logs in. The /bin/bash entry means all new users use BASH as the default shell.

- SKEL=/etc/skel—This line defines the location of the **skeleton directory**, which contains files copied automatically to each new user's home directory. Typically, they're hidden files that affect the user environment, such as .bash_history, which records each command you run and .profile, used to enable different language outputs for applications that use this feature.

- GROUPS=video—This line lists the groups a new user is assigned to by default. When assigning users to multiple groups, separate each group name with a comma and no space.

- CREATE_MAIL_SPOOL=no—This line specifies whether new users have a mail spool, which is in the /etc/var/spool/mail directory. A mail spool is a temporary storage location where mail is first delivered. You learn more about Linux mail servers in Chapter 12.

The /etc/login.defs File The /etc/login.defs file is also a text file that can be read by all users and contains parameters that set certain values for new user accounts, such as default PATH settings, maximum and minimum number of days between password changes, and the range of UIDs and GIDs that can be allocated to user and group accounts.

TIP

You can view the contents of your /etc/login.defs file or /etc/default/useradd file with the less command. For instance, less /etc/login.defs displays the contents of the login.defs configuration file.

Creating User Accounts

You use the `useradd` command to create user accounts and update default information for new users. Table 7-1 describes the options you can use with this command.

Table 7-1 Options used with the `useradd` command

Options	Description
`-c "comment"`	Adds a comment (usually the user's full name) in the GECOS field of the `/etc/passwd` file.
`-d /home/directory`	Specifies the absolute path to a new user's home directory.
`-e YYYY-MM-DD`	Indicates when the user account will be disabled.
`-f number of days`	Indicates the number of days after a password has expired before the account is disabled.
`-g primary group`	Specifies the user's primary group name or GID. In openSUSE, the primary group is "users," which has the GID 100.
`-G group1,group2,group3`	Lists the groups the user will be a member of.
`-m`	By default in openSUSE, a home directory isn't created, so this option must be used to add one for a new user.
`-u UID`	By default, the next available UID in the range listed in the `/etc/login.defs` file is used, but this option can be used to assign a different UID to a new user.
`-s`	Specifies the user's default login shell.
`--help`	Displays a list of valid options with descriptions.

The first thing you must do after creating a user is set the password. The following is an entry in the `/etc/shadow` file for a new user who doesn't have a password yet:

```
user1:!:14745:0:99999:7:::
```

The `!` character in the encrypted password field means no password has been set for this user. Only the root user can set passwords for new users. The following example shows the root user using the `passwd` command to set a password for user1:

```
passwd user1
```

After issuing the `passwd` command, you must enter a new password and then enter it again to confirm. After the password has been set, the user1 entry in the `/etc/shadow` file looks like the following:

```
user1:$2a$10$79rygmrg39tt.nPM5lsLh.wZWEJK3aYWqaqG6p6lLNKYpFMMHNG.
0:14745:0:99999:7:::
```

Users can change their own passwords by typing `passwd` with no argument to specify the username.

Activity 7-1: Creating Users

Time Required: 15 minutes

Objective: Create users with the `useradd` command and user database files.

Description: In this activity, you view your own entry in both user database files and examine the configuration files containing default information for creating users. Finally, you create a user called student1 and set a password for this account.

1. Start VMware Player and start an openSUSE virtual machine.

2. Open a terminal window and display the last 10 lines of your `passwd` file by typing **tail /etc/passwd** and pressing **Enter**. Find the entry for your user account. For instance, for a user logged in as amber, the entry would look like this: `amber:x:1000:100:Amber Dawn:/home/amber:/bin/bash`.

3. Try to view the `/etc/shadow` file by typing **tail /etc/shadow** and pressing **Enter**. Were you able to view this file? Why?

   _____

4. Type **su** and press **Enter**, and then enter the root password. To see the last 10 lines of the `/etc/shadow` file, type **tail /etc/shadow** and press **Enter**. Find the user you're currently logged in as and examine the entry for this user account.

5. View the contents of one of your user account configuration files (`login.defs`) by typing **less /etc/login.defs** and pressing **Enter**. Use the arrow keys (or mouse wheel) to scroll through this file. Find the password aging settings and compare the entries in this file with the information you viewed in Step 4. Which fields in the `/etc/shadow` file show the same password-setting information that's in `/etc/login.defs`? When you're finished examining this file, press **q** to exit the `less` command.

   _____

6. The `useradd` file contains basic user account creation information, such as the location of the skeleton directory. To find your skeleton directory, type **cat /etc/default/useradd** and press **Enter**. In openSUSE, the default skeleton directory is `/etc/skel`. Change to the skeleton directory by typing **cd /etc/skel** and pressing **Enter**.

7. Display a long listing of files and subdirectories in your current directory (`/etc/skel`) by typing **ls -l** and pressing **Enter**. The files and directories you see are the ones copied to a new user's home directory.

8. Review the options for the `useradd` command by typing **useradd --help** and pressing **Enter**. Remember that you must be logged in as root to issue this command.

9. Create a user and add a home directory by typing **useradd -m student1** and pressing **Enter**.

10. Type **tail /etc/shadow** and press **Enter**. Find the student1 entry and notice that the password field has only the ! symbol, which means the password hasn't been set for this user.

11. Set the password for student1 by typing **passwd student1** and pressing **Enter**. Type **Op3nUe** as the new password and press **Enter**, and then enter the password again to confirm.

12. Type **tail /etc/shadow** and press **Enter**. Find the student1 entry, and confirm that the password field now contains a password instead of the ! symbol. (Remember that this password is encrypted.)

13. Display a long listing of files and subdirectories in student1's home directory by typing **ls -l /home/student1** and pressing **Enter**. Compare the results with the results in Step 7.

14. Type **exit** and press **Enter** to exit the root user account. Type **su - student1** and press **Enter** to switch to the student1 user account, and then type **Op3nUe** as the password and press **Enter**.

15. Now that you have logged in as student1, you can exit this user account and return to your regular user account by typing **exit** and pressing **Enter**. Leave the terminal window open and the virtual machine running for the next activity.

Modifying User Accounts

You use the usermod command to change user account information, but you can't change the name, UID, or home directory of a user who's currently logged in. Only the root user can issue this command. Table 7-2 describes common options used with the usermod command.

7

Table 7-2 Options used with the usermod command

Options	Description
-c "comment"	Adds a comment in the GECOS field of the /etc/passwd file. Typical information includes the user's full name or phone number.
-d /home/directory	Changes the absolute path to a user's home directory. You might need to change this path for a number of reasons, such as acquiring a new disk drive and wanting to move all home directories to this new drive.
-e YYYY-MM-DD	Changes the date when the user account will be disabled.
-f number of days	Changes the number of days after a password has expired before the account is disabled.
-g primary group	Changes the user's primary group name or GID.
-G group1,group2,group3	Doesn't change the user's primary group; instead, it specifies a list of groups the user is a member of (discussed more in "Group Management," later in this chapter).
-l name	Changes the user's login name.
-u UID	Changes the user's UID.
-s	Changes the user's default login shell.
-L	Locks a specific user account. After using usermod -L user1, for example, an exclamation point in the encrypted password field in the /etc/shadow file indicates that user1's account is locked. Users can't log in to locked accounts.
-U	Unlocks specific user accounts.
--help	Displays a list of valid options with descriptions.

You can also change user account information by editing the /etc /passwd and /etc/shadow files, but this method isn't recommended because entering a typo in these files might prevent the user from logging in.

To list and modify password expiration information for user accounts, you use the chage command. It allows the root user to modify information such as the number of days between allowed and required password changes and the expiration date. It also enables the root user to change warning information, such as the number of days before the user's account is set to expire. Table 7-3 describes options used with this command.

Make sure you type chage, not "change."

Table 7-3 Options used with the chage command

Options	Description
-l	Displays all password expiration information for the specified user account.
-m	Changes the minimum number of days between password changes. The value 0 indicates that the password can be changed any time.
-M	Changes the number of days the password is valid.
-d	Changes the date the password was last changed; can be set as the number of days since January 1, 1970 or in the format YYYY-MM-DD. You can also set this number to 0 to force the user to change the password at the next login.
-E	Changes the password expiration date; can be specified as the number of days since January 1, 1970 or in the format YYYY-MM-DD.
-I	User accounts are still available even after the password expires. You can use this option to set how many days the user account stays unlocked after the password has expired. For instance, if you set this number to 7, there can be seven days of inactivity after the password has expired before the account is locked. This number is set to -1 by default, which keeps all expired accounts unlocked regardless of the amount of time they're inactive.
-W	Specifies the number of days before a password expires.
--help	Displays a list of valid options with descriptions.

If the chage command is used without options, it's in interactive mode, meaning you're asked questions on password expiration information, and you can enter new information or accept the current values. The current values are placed between brackets, as shown in the following example:

```
chage elijah
Changing aging information for elijah.
Minimum Password Age [0]:
```

Notice that the value for the minimum password age is set to 0. Pressing Enter keeps 0 as the setting.

All users can use the chage command to display their password expiration information, but only the root user can use this command to edit users' expiration information.

Activity 7-2: Modifying User Accounts

Time Required: 25 minutes

Objective: Modify user accounts with the usermod and chage commands.

Requirements: If you didn't complete Activity 7-1, use the commands you've learned in this chapter to create a user called student1.

Description: In this activity, you change a user account's home directory, username, and password expiration information from the command line.

1. If your terminal window is still open, switch to the root user by typing **su**, pressing **Enter**, and then entering the correct root user password. If you don't have a terminal window open or if VMware Player isn't running, follow Step 1 of Activity 7-1.

2. Find the student1 password entry in the /etc/passwd file by typing **cat /etc/passwd | grep student1** and pressing **Enter**. (*Note*: If you didn't complete Activity 7-1, there won't be an entry for student1.) Write down this entry so that you can compare it with the results after you modify the account. The student1 entry should look something like the following:

   ```
   student1:x:1011:100::/home/student1:/bin/bash
   ```

3. Change student1's home directory by typing **usermod -d /home/student1/scripts student1** and pressing **Enter**. Create the new directory by typing **mkdir /home/student1/scripts** and pressing **Enter**. Type **cat /etc/passwd | grep student1** and press **Enter**, and then compare the new student1 entry with what you wrote down in Step 2. The new student1 entry should look something like the following:

   ```
   student1:x:1011:100::/home/student1/scripts:/bin/bash
   ```

4. Change student1's login name by typing **usermod -l student2 student1** and pressing **Enter**.

5. Type **cat /etc/passwd | grep student2** and press **Enter**, and compare the results with those in Step 4. Notice that all the information stayed the same (including the home directory) except the first field, which is the login name. The new student2 entry should look something like the following:

   ```
   student2:x:1011:100::/home/student1/scripts:/bin/bash
   ```

6. Switch to the student2 user by typing **su - student2** and pressing **Enter**. Display the expiration information for the student2 account by typing **chage -l** (the lowercase L, not

the number 1) and pressing **Enter**. Enter student2's password (**Op3nUe**) and press **Enter**. The results should look like the following:

```
Password:
Minimum:    0
Maximum:    99999
Warning:    7
Inactive:   -1
Last Change:        May 14, 2012
Password Expires:          Never
Password Inactive:   Never
Account Expires:          Never
```

7. Switch back to the root user by typing **exit** and pressing **Enter**.

8. Use the `chage` command in interactive mode by typing **chage student2** and pressing **Enter**.

9. To set the minimum password age, type **3** and press **Enter**. To set the maximum password age, type **90** and press **Enter**. Next, you set the password expiration warning. The number 7 in brackets is the default, and if you press Enter, this setting is accepted. Press **Enter** to accept the rest of the defaults. When you're done, you get the message "Aging information changed." Your screen should look like the following:

```
client:/home/dustin # chage student2
Changing aging information for student2.
    Minimum Password Age [0]: 3
    Maximum Password Age [99999]: 90
    Password Expiration Warning [7]:
    Password Inactive [-1]:
    Last Password Change (YYYY-MM-DD) [2012-05-16]:
    Account Expiration Date (YYYY-MM-DD) [1969-12-31]:
Aging information changed.
```

10. To specify that student2 must wait 1 day after getting a new password before changing it and the password expires every 45 days with 3 days of warning before expiration, what command do you use?

   _____

11. Exit the root user account and return to your regular user account by typing **exit** and pressing **Enter**. Leave the terminal window open and the virtual machine running for the next activity.

Deleting User Accounts

You use the `userdel` command to delete user accounts and remove all entries from user database files (`/etc/passwd` and `/etc/shadow`). It doesn't remove the user's home directory; to do this, you need to use the `-r` option. When a user is deleted, all files he or she owned are then owned by the UID. For instance, if student1's UID is 600 and you delete this user, ownership of this user's files are transferred to the UID 600. If you create a new account with the UID 600, this user then owns all files previously owned by student1.

To view the options available with the `userdel` command, type `userdel --help`.

Managing Groups

Groups are helpful for streamlining the process of designating which users can perform certain tasks. For instance, the root user could create a group called ftp and make all users who need to send and receive files via File Transfer Protocol (FTP) a member of this group. Every user is a member of at least one group, called the primary group. The root user can then assign an unlimited number of additional groups called **secondary groups**. In Linux, the group database configuration file is `/etc/group`. You can view all the groups you belong to and their corresponding GIDs by using the `id` command as shown in the following example. The first group listed, users, is the user's primary group. All other groups are secondary groups and are separated by commas.

```
id uid=1000(isaiah) gid=100(users) groups=33(video),1000(ftp)
```

The /etc/group File

The `/etc/group` file is a configuration file that stores group information and can be read by everyone on the system. The following example shows an entry in this file, followed by a description of each field:

```
video:x:33:dustin,student1
```

- *Group name*—This field shows the group's descriptive name rather than the GID.
- *Password*—This field contains the group's encrypted password. Typically, a group password isn't used, but if one is set, other users can join the group by using the `newgrp` command (discussed in the next section).
- *Group identifier (GID)*—This unique number represents the user's primary group.
- *List of members*—A list of group members; each member is separated by a comma.

Creating Groups

You use the `groupadd` command to add a group account. Only the root user has permission to use this command. Table 7-4 describes the options you can use with the `groupadd` command.

Table 7-4 Options used with the `groupadd` command

Options	Description
-g	Forces the GID to what's entered at the command line. It must be a positive number and must be unique. The range of GIDs allowed is defined in the `/etc/login.defs` file.
-o	Allows assigning a duplicate GID.
-p	Allows assigning a group password, which by default is disabled.
--help	Displays a list of valid options for the `groupadd` command.

The `newgrp` command, shown in the following example, is used to change a user's primary group temporarily; it stays in effect until the user logs out. All new files the user creates will have this new group owner.

```
newgrp projects
id
uid=1002(student1) gid=1000(projects) groups=100(users),1000(video)
```

The `newgrp` command opens a new instance of the BASH shell and changes the user's primary group from users to video.

The `newgrp` command opens a new shell even if the command fails. For instance, if you try to use the `newgrp` command to switch to a group that doesn't exist, you get an error, but you're still placed in a new shell.

Modifying Groups

You use the `groupmod` command to modify existing groups, using values specified at the command line. Only the root user has permission to use this command. Table 7-5 describes the options you can use with the `groupmod` command.

Table 7-5 Options used with the `groupmod` command

Options	Description
-g	Forces the GID to be the number specified on the command line. It must be a positive number and must be unique. The range of GIDs is defined in the `/etc/login.defs` file.
-o	Used to assign a duplicate GID.
-p	Used to assign a group password. By default, this feature is disabled.
-A	Adds a specified user to the group account. You can also use the `usermod  -G` command to perform the same task.
-R	Removes a specified member from the group account.
--help	Displays a list of valid options for the `groupmod` command.

Activity 7-3: Working with Groups

Time Required: 15 minutes

Objective: Create and modify groups with the `groupadd`, `groupmod`, and `newgrp` commands.

Description: In this activity, you create a group, examine the group database file, and find the new group's entry. You also add a user to your group, change the user's primary group, and remove a specific user from the group.

1. If your terminal window is still open, switch to the root user by typing **su**, pressing **Enter**, and then entering the correct root user password. If you don't have a terminal window open or if VMware Player isn't running, follow Step 1 of Activity 7-1.

2. View all groups and group members on your system by typing **less /etc/group** and pressing **Enter**. Scroll through the file with the arrow keys or mouse wheel. Press **q** to exit the `less` command.

3. Create a new group by typing **groupadd students** and pressing **Enter**. Display the students group by typing **cat /etc/group | grep students** and pressing **Enter**. The `cat` command used with a pipe (|) to the `grep` command searches for "students" in the `etc/group` file and then displays it. How many users are assigned to this group?

   _____

4. Add your regular user account as a member of the students group by typing **usermod -G students** *login name* and pressing **Enter**. Display the students group again by typing **cat /etc/group | grep students** and pressing **Enter**. Examine the fourth field of the students entry, and notice that your user login name is added.

5. Switch to your regular user account by typing **exit** and pressing **Enter**.

6. Create a new directory by typing **mkdir Act7-3** and pressing **Enter**, and then switch to this directory by typing **cd Act7-3** and pressing **Enter**. Create an empty file by typing **touch file1** and pressing **Enter**. Switch your primary group to students by typing **newgrp students** and pressing **Enter**. Now create a second file by typing **touch file2** and pressing **Enter**.

7. View a long listing of files and directories by typing **ls -l** and pressing **Enter**. What's the difference between `file1` and `file2`?

   _____

8. Switch to the root user by typing **su**, pressing **Enter**, and entering the correct root user password. Remove the user you added in Step 4 from the students group by typing **groupmod -R** *login name* **students** and pressing **Enter**. Type **cat /etc/group | grep students** and press **Enter**. Notice that there are no users in the fourth field.

9. Exit the root user account and return to your regular user account by typing **exit** and pressing **Enter**. Leave the terminal window open and the virtual machine running for the next activity.

Managing User and Group Accounts with YaST

OpenSUSE comes with YaST User and Group Management, a graphical utility for centrally managing users and groups. Its basic features enable administrators to create and remove users and groups as well as assign home directories, passwords, automatic logins, default shells, and password expiration information. You start this utility with the `yast2 users` command. By default, it opens to the Users tab (see Figure 7-1).

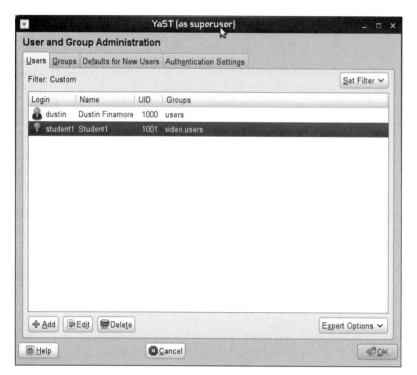

Figure 7-1 The YaST User and Group Management utility
Source: openSUSE

You use the settings in the Users and Groups tabs to add, edit, and delete user and group accounts. By default, YaST filters user accounts so that you see only local users. To filter the type of user accounts you can view, add, edit, or delete, click the Set Filter button to see options. For instance, selecting System Users displays only system users. Another feature is the Expert Options button, which you use to edit advanced settings, such as password encryption type and automatic logins.

Adding or Editing User Accounts

When adding or editing a user account with the YaST User and Group Management utility, you have four tabs in which you can add or change information:

- *User Data*—You use the User Data tab (see Figure 7-2) to enter the user's full name, username, and password. The username should contain only letters, numbers, and special characters (-, ., or _). No other characters are allowed. The encryption scheme currently used for passwords is Blowfish, meaning the password should be between 5 and 72 characters. You must enter your password two times for confirmation.

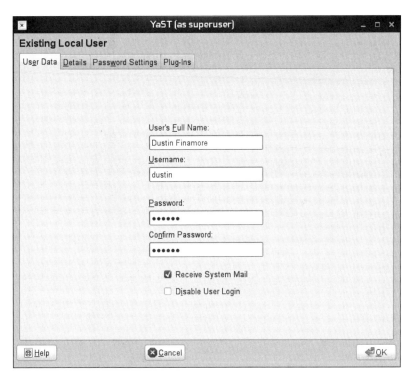

Figure 7-2 The User Data tab
Source: openSUSE

• *Details*—You use the Details tab (see Figure 7-3) to assign a UID, home directory, login shell, default group, and additional user information. There's an option to encrypt the user's home directory, but keep in mind this encryption doesn't provide security from other users on the system. For instance, multiple users should never be allowed to share the same machine if strict security is a requirement (even if home directories are encrypted). You can assign additional secondary groups in this tab by selecting group names in the list box on the right.

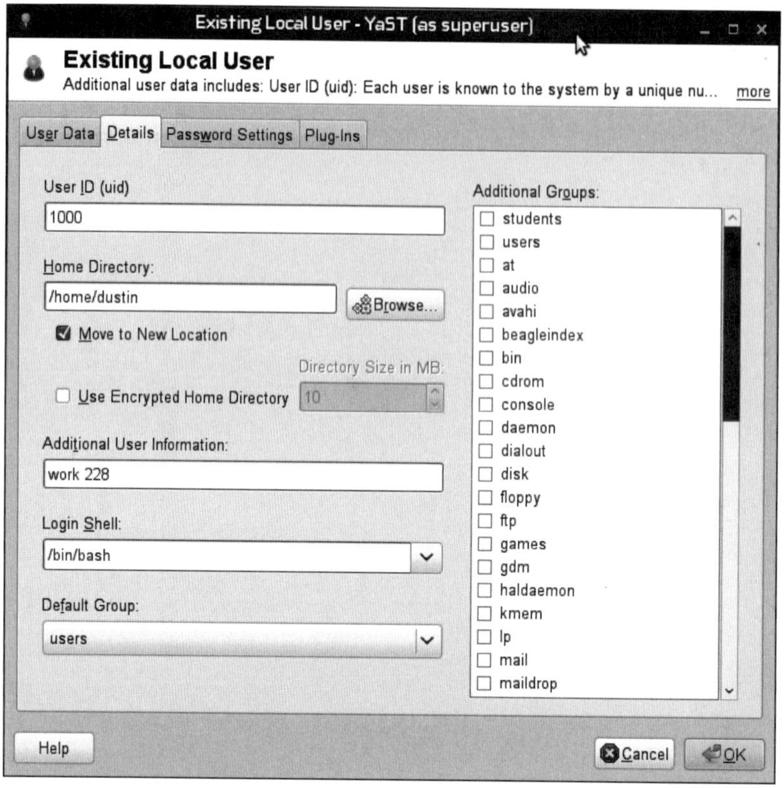

Figure 7-3 The Details tab
Source: openSUSE

- *Password Settings*—This tab (see Figure 7-4) displays password expiration information, just as the /etc/login.defs configuration file does. The last time the password was changed is displayed at the top. By default, new users aren't forced to change their passwords. You can change this setting by clicking the Force Password Change check box.

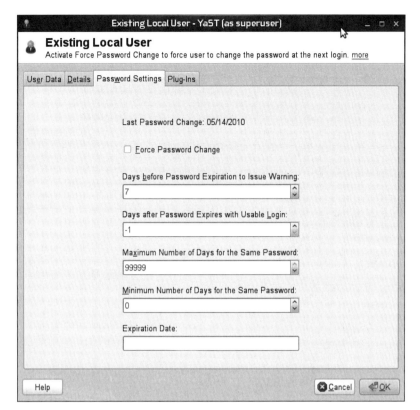

Figure 7-4 The Password Settings tab
Source: openSUSE

- *Plug-Ins*—This tab displays a list of plug-ins for user and group configuration. The default plug-in for openSUSE users is Manage User Quotas, which is used to set limits on how many files a particular user can create, for example. You learn more about disk quotas in Chapter 16. Figure 7-5 shows the Quota Configuration plug-in.

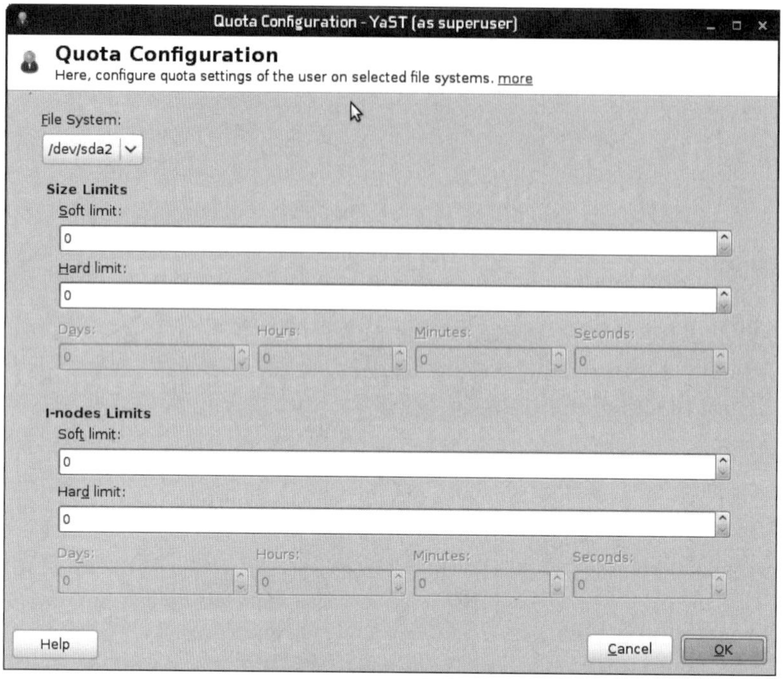

Figure 7-5 The Quota Configuration plug-in
Source: openSUSE

Defaults for New Users

The Defaults for New Users tab, shown in Figure 7-6, is where you assign the user's default group (which is the user's primary group), secondary groups, default login shell, home directory, skeleton directory, umask value (explained later in the section on permissions), expiration date, and number of days after a password expires that the account is still enabled. The information in this tab is similar to information in the /etc/default /useradd file.

Figure 7-6 The Defaults for New Users tab
Source: openSUSE

The user's primary group is chosen from a list of available groups, but secondary groups are entered manually with a comma separating each group name. The home and skeleton directories can be entered or selected by clicking the browse button. The default expiration date must be typed as YYYY-MM-DD or left blank if you want the account to never expire.

Authentication Settings

The Authentication Settings tab, shown in Figure 7-7, displays a summary of modules that can be enabled for login authentication. For instance, you can choose from module types, such as Network Information Service (NIS, discussed in Chapter 17), Lightweight Directory Access Protocol (LDAP), Kerberos, and Samba (covered in Chapter 18). Each module is disabled by default and can be configured by clicking the name or the Configure button at the bottom.

Figure 7-7 The Authentication Settings tab
Source: openSUSE

Activity 7-4: Using the YaST User and Group Management Utility

Time Required: 15 minutes

Objective: Add users and groups in the YaST User and Group Management utility.

Requirements: An openSUSE virtual machine with the GNOME desktop environment

Description: In this activity, you use the YaST User and Group Management utility to create a user, edit the user account information, create a group, and add the new user to the group.

1. If necessary, start VMware Player and start your GNOME openSUSE virtual machine.

2. Open the YaST Control Center by clicking the **Computer** button at the lower left. On the right, click the **YaST** icon in the System section. When prompted, enter your root password.

3. Find the User and Group Management utility by typing **user** in the Filter text box, and then clicking the utility name under Security and Users. (You can also type **yast2 users** and press **Enter** while logged in as the root user.)

4. Create a new user by clicking **Add** and then entering the following information:

   User's Full Name: **Activity 7-4 Student**

   Username: **student3**

   Password: **Op3nUe**

5. View the user account details by clicking the **Details** tab. Write down the user ID, home directory, login shell, and default group:

   _____

6. Force the user to change his or her password by clicking the **Password Settings** tab and clicking the **Force Password Change** check box. How many days before the password expires will the user get a warning? What does the 99999 value for the Maximum Number of Days for the Same Password setting mean?

   _____

7. Create the user account by clicking **OK** at the bottom.

8. Create a new group by clicking the **Groups** tab and clicking **Add**. Enter the following information:

   Group Name: **classroom**

   Group ID (gid): Leave the default information

   Password: Leave blank

9. On the right is the Group Members section. Add student3 as a member of the classroom group by clicking the **student3** check box. Confirm the new group by clicking **OK** at the lower right.

10. Save the user and group information by clicking **OK** at the lower right.

11. You can use the command line to make sure everything was done correctly. To do this, open a terminal window, and then switch to the student3 user by typing **su - student3** and pressing **Enter**. Type the student3 password and press **Enter**.

12. Because the settings changed in Step 6, you must change student3's password. First, enter the old password (**Op3nUe**) and press **Enter**. Type a new password and press **Enter**, and then enter this new password again to confirm.

13. To verify that student3 is a member of the classroom group, type **id** and press **Enter**.

14. Close the terminal window, and shut down your openSUSE virtual machine.

Chapter Summary

- You can verify users through a process called authentication, which involves checking user account information typically stored in two database configuration files: `/etc/passwd` and `/etc/shadow`.

- User account parameters, such as user account expiration, group the user belongs to, and how long it has been since the password was last set, are specified in the `/etc/default/useradd` and `/etc/login.defs` configuration files.

- The useradd command is used to create user accounts, which are stored in the /etc/password file.

- You can set passwords for users with the passwd command. Passwords are then stored in the /etc/shadow file.

- User accounts can be modified with the usermod and chage commands and deleted with the userdel command. If the userdel command is used, all entries are removed from the user database files.

- You can create groups with the groupadd command. The /etc/group file stores group information and can be read by everyone on the system. Group accounts can be modified with the groupmod command.

- OpenSUSE comes with YaST User and Group Management, a GUI utility for adding, editing, and removing users and groups.

Key Terms

authentication   The process of verifying a user's identity by checking for his or her username and password in a system database.

group identifier (GID)   A unique number corresponding to a group.

primary group   The group owner for all new files a user creates (specified in the /etc /passwd file).

secondary groups   Additional groups the root user assigns to other users on the system.

skeleton directory   A directory containing files copied to every new user's home directory by default.

user identifier (UID)   A unique number representing the username.

Review Questions

1. Which Linux configuration file can be read only by root and contains users' encrypted passwords?

   a. /etc/passwd

   b. /etc/shadow

   c. /etc/login.defs

   d. /etc/default/useradd

2. Which Linux configuration file contains users' default information, such as the allowed range of UIDs and GIDs?

   a. /etc/passwd

   b. /etc/shadow

   c. /etc/login.defs

   d. /etc/default/useradd

3. What is the UID in the line from the following /etc/passwd file?

   `joe:x:1003:100:Joe Netti:/home/joe:/bin/bash`

   a. 1003

   b. 100

   c. x

   d. joe

4. Which Linux configuration file contains default user account information, such as the user's default group and skeleton directory?

   a. /etc/passwd

   b. /etc/shadow

   c. /etc/login.defs

   d. /etc/default/useradd

5. Explain the difference between a user's primary and secondary groups.

6. User accounts don't need to have an assigned group. True or False?

7. Which command enables an administrator to add a user account named john with the full name John Smith as a comment?

   a. `useradd -m john`

   b. `useradd john -m "John Smith"`

   c. `useradd -d "John Smith" john`

   d. `useradd -c "John Smith" john`

8. Which of the following user parameters can be set in the /etc/default/useradd configuration file? (Choose all that apply.)

   a. The skeleton directory

   b. Default PATH settings

   c. The home directory

   d. Range of UIDs

9. Which command enables an administrator to change an existing user's home directory to /home/users?

   a. `useradd nicole /home/users`

   b. `usermod -d /home/users nicole`

   c. `useradd -m nicole /home/users`

   d. `usermod /home/users nicole`

10. Which of the following commands displays the groups belonging to the user rob? (Choose all that apply.)

    a. `cat /etc/login.defs`

    b. `cat /etc/group`

    c. `id rob`

    d. `cat /etc/default/useradd`

11. By default, when an administrator deletes a user account in openSUSE, the home directory remains. True or False?

12. Only the root user can view the `/etc/group` file. True or False?

13. Which command does an administrator use to add the user tamie to the projects group?

    a. `groupmod -A tamie projects`

    b. `groupmod -A projects tamie`

    c. `groupmod -g tamie projects`

    d. `groupmod -g projects tamie`

14. Describe the purpose of the skeleton directory.

15. Which of the following is the process of using an account name with a password to log in to a system?

    a. Approval

    b. Authentication

    c. Agreement

    d. Validation

16. UIDs and GIDs should be unique on the system. True or False?

Case Projects

CASE PROJECTS

Case Project 7-1: Assigning UIDs

You have been the system administrator at East Coast Career College for the past year and have created many user and group accounts. Because you know that all users must have unique UIDs, you have always allowed the kernel to assign the next available UID automatically when creating new user accounts. The IT manager thinks it would be beneficial for the network to have a list of UIDs and to track these UIDs with the actual user. The IT manager also wants you to start assigning UIDs manually. Research the benefits of assigning UIDs manually instead of automatically. Decide which method works best for the openSUSE computers at East Coast Career College and explain your reasons in a memo to your IT manager.

## chapter 8

Network Communications

After reading this chapter and completing the exercises, you will be able to:

- Identify the important protocols at each layer of the TCP/IP model
- Describe IP addresses and the difference between the network and host portions of an IP address
- Convert decimal IP addresses into binary numbers
- Describe the five TCP/IP classes
- Configure your Linux network interface card to work with TCP/IP, using the command line
- Interact with network devices by using the ping command

In this chapter, you learn how to configure your Linux system to communicate on a network. This chapter starts with an introduction to TCP/IP and explains the importance of having standard rules to communicate on the Internet. This leads into a discussion of the TCP/IP model and the important protocols at each layer. Next, you learn about IP addresses and how to convert decimal numbers into binary. Finally, you learn how to configure your network interface card with the `ifconfig` command and test your computer's configuration with the `ping` command.

Introduction to TCP/IP

To drive cars safely, everyone must follow certain rules and laws. Imagine the chaos if only a few drivers understood the difference between a green and red light. Just as drivers agree to and follow a set of rules, computers connect and communicate with each other by following rules known as protocols. **Transmission Control Protocol/Internet Protocol (TCP/IP)** is an internationally accepted set of rules for connecting computers to the Internet and most other networks. A network is two or more computers connected with a medium (such as cable or wireless) for the purpose of sharing resources (printers, files, software, and so forth). Although the TCP/IP suite has dozens of protocols, the two most important are Transmission Control Protocol and Internet Protocol. In the following activity, you research several TCP/IP protocols as an introduction to learning more about this protocol suite.

Keep in mind that some network administrators refer to the TCP/IP protocol suite as the Internet Protocol suite.

Activity 8-1: Researching the TCP/IP Protocol Suite

Time Required: 45 minutes

Objective: Learn about several protocols in the TCP/IP suite.

Description: In this activity, you use the Internet or another resource to research several protocols in the TCP/IP suite. You also explore the two most important protocols and explain the differences between them.

1. Use the Internet or another resource to find five protocols in the TCP/IP suite. The only protocols you can't choose are TCP, IP, DNS, and FTP because they're covered in this chapter.

2. Write one to two sentences describing each of the five protocols you researched:

_____

_____

_____

_____

_____

3. Use the Internet or another resource to define TCP and IP and explain the difference between these two protocols.

_____

_____

_____

Working with TCP/IP

The protocols in the TCP/IP suite are organized into these three layers, known as the TCP/IP model:

- Application layer
- Transport layer
- Internet layer

Before you learn how information travels from one computer to the next, you need a brief overview of the two hardware layers that are important in network communication. These layers aren't considered part of the TCP/IP protocol suite because TCP/IP deals with software. The first is the Physical layer, which consists of cables or other connection media and deals with data as bits traveling across a network medium. The second is the Data Link layer, which formats data as **packets**—packages of data to be routed through a network.

TCP/IP was developed to be hardware independent, which means you can use almost any available network architecture.

When a message travels from one computer to the next, it starts out at the Internet layer, where it receives packets and then routes them to the correct destination. The Transport layer is responsible for delivering data from one location to another on the network. The Application layer receives packets from the Transport layer and opens them to convert the message back to its original form.

Internet Layer The TCP/IP model revolves around the Internet layer, which sends packets to their specified destinations. This layer gets its name from its capability to interconnect networks through the use of IP information. When you send information from your computer to another computer on the network, the Internet layer adds an IP-specific header to the packet as it pushes it through the hardware layers. As shown in Figure 8-1, the header contains information such as the source, destination, version, Internet header length (IHL in the figure), protocol, and other information about the data.

The sequence in which packets are received at the destination can be different from the sequence in which they're sent, depending on the higher-level layers at the destination.

0		4		8		16	19			31
Version		IHL		Type of service			Total length			
Identification						Flags		Fragment offset		
Time to live				Protocol			Header checksum			
Source IP address										
Destination IP address										
Options							Padding			

Figure 8-1 Information traveling through a network
© Cengage Learning 2013

The most important protocol at the Internet layer is **Internet Protocol (IP)**. It's the main protocol in the TCP/IP suite and contains addressing information that enables packets to be routed. The two basic functions of IP are addressing and **fragmentation,** the process of dividing packets into smaller packets to transmit them through networks. A packet sent from one network might be too big for another network to receive, so IP splits the packet so that it can be transferred.

Another important protocol in this layer is **Internet Control Message Protocol (ICMP)**, used to generate IP error messages, as when a packet is lost, service is unavailable, or the network is congested.

Transport Layer The Transport layer is placed above the Internet layer in the TCP/IP model. The two essential protocols at this layer are **Transmission Control Protocol (TCP)** and **User Datagram Protocol (UDP)**. IP handles the delivery of data (as packets), whereas TCP is a connection-oriented protocol responsible for keeping track of packets and reassembling them into a single file after they've all arrived. Similar to IP, TCP also controls the flow of messages and makes sure a source network doesn't send data packets faster than the destination network's receiving capacity by ensuring that the sender's transmission rate matches the receiver's. TCP is considered a connection-oriented protocol because it establishes communication between sender and receiver.

UDP is similar to TCP, in that it uses IP to get packets from one computer to another; however, UDP is a connectionless protocol because it doesn't perform error checking or acknowledge that messages were sent successfully. When a fast transfer rate of data packets is more important than an error-free and accurate transfer, UDP can be used. TCP focuses on accuracy rather than transfer time for data packets. Table 8-1 summarizes the differences between TCP and UDP.

Table 8-1 Differences between TCP and UDP

TCP	UDP
Reliable	Unreliable
Connection-oriented protocol	Connectionless protocol
Ordered packet delivery	Unordered packet delivery
Slow	Fast

Application Layer The Application layer, which sits at the top of the TCP/IP model, contains the higher-level protocols used for network communication in the Transport layer. Table 8-2 describes some important protocols in this layer.

Table 8-2 Important protocols in the Application layer

Protocol	Description
Telnet	A virtual terminal protocol for connecting to a remote computer. It's no longer recommended because data (including passwords) isn't encrypted and can be compromised easily.
File Transfer Protocol (FTP)	Protocol used to move files from one computer to another efficiently and accurately. It's not a secure protocol, however, and transmitted data isn't encrypted. You log on to an FTP site with a username and password. Some FTP sites allow anonymous login; these sites are commonly set up to provide software updates.
Simple Mail Transfer Protocol (SMTP)	Protocol used to send e-mail in user-level client applications.
Domain Name System (DNS)	Network resources, such as computers and printers, are recognized by their numeric IP addresses. DNS is used to map a fully qualified domain name with an IP address. For example, DNS maps a Web site, such as *www.cengage.com*, to its corresponding IP address so that names instead of IP addresses can be used to navigate the Internet.
Hypertext Transfer Protocol (HTTP)	Connectionless protocol used for sending and receiving requests between the client and server on a network; one of the most common and widely used protocols.
Secure Shell (SSH)	Used for secure, authenticated communication when connecting to a remote computer over a network. It's more secure than Telnet because data is transmitted in an encrypted format. Can also be used to copy files from a remote computer to a client.

Table 8-2 doesn't list all the protocols at the Application layer. Other protocols, such as Network News Transfer Protocol (NNTP), Simple Network Management Protocol (SNMP), and Routing Information Protocol (RIP), reside at the Application layer. Figure 8-2 shows the TCP/IP model with the associated protocols at each layer.

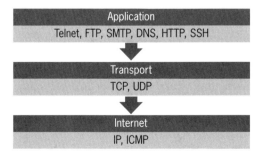

Figure 8-2 Placement of protocols in the TCP/IP model
© Cengage Learning 2013

Working with IP Addresses

An **IP address** is a unique number that identifies a computer or device on a TCP/IP network. To understand the importance of having a unique identifier for each computer and device on the same network, think of an IP address as being like a home address. If two people have the same mailing address yet don't live in the same house, how would they get their mail? Similarly, if two computers on a network have the same IP address, they have problems receiving messages.

The format of an IP address is four numbers separated by periods. In the following example, the ifconfig command is used to view a computer's IP address and the current state of all its active network interfaces. The IP address shown in the output (listed as "inet addr") is 192.168.75.136.

ifconfig
```
eth0  Link encap:Ethernet  HWaddr 00:0C:29:76:77:63
      inet addr:192.168.75.136 Bcast:192.168.75.255 Mask:255.255.255.0
      inet6 addr:fe80::20c:29ff:fe76:7763/64 Scope:Link
      UP BROADCAST RUNNING MULTICAST  MTU:1500 Metric:1
      RX packets:893 errors:0 dropped:0 overruns:0 frame:0
      TX packets:735 errors:0 dropped:0 overruns:0 carrier:0
      collisions:0 txqueuelen:1000
      RX bytes:867477 (847.1 Kb)  TX bytes:60226 (58.8 Kb)
      Interrupt:19 Base address:0x2024
```

The ifconfig command is also used to assign TCP/IP configuration to a NIC (covered in "Configuring Network Interface Cards" later in this chapter).

The ifconfig command is an administrative utility, so you must have root privileges to use it.

Binary and Decimal Numbering Systems

Each of the four numbers in an IP address is called an **octet** because it represents an 8-bit binary number. Decimal numbers, used in IP addresses, have 10 possible digits (0 to 9). The **binary numbering system** uses only two digits (1 and 0), so it's used in computers. Computers, along with all electronic circuits, understand only two possible states: on and off. As far as computers are concerned, the number 1 represents on, and the number 0 represents off. Therefore, the computer converts decimal IP addresses into binary numbers. Understanding how to convert decimal numbers to binary numbers is important because this knowledge comes in handy when you're working with IP addresses on a network, particularly when working with subnet masks to determine an IP address's network and host portions.

A **bit** (also known as a binary digit) represents a single binary value. For instance, the binary number 01110000 has 8 bits. IP addresses are decimal numbers divided into four octets, and because each octet is 8 bits, an IP address has 32 bits.

The 32-bit IP address is used in the first version of Internet Protocol, often called IPv4. The upgraded version of Internet Protocol is IPv6, and IPv6 addresses have 128 bits.

NOTE

To understand the binary numbering system, you need to review the powers of two: the number 2 multiplied by itself a certain number of times. For instance, 2 to the power of 2 equals 4, or $2^2 = 4$. Table 8-3 lists the powers of two from 0 to 7. You're focusing on these eight powers because an octet is made up of 8 bits, each of which is represented by a combination of these numbers. You can use these powers of two to find the binary equivalent of an octet in an IP address. The example after the table shows how to convert the decimal number 112 to its binary equivalent.

Table 8-3 The powers of two

Equation	Answer
2 to the power of 0 (2^0)	1
2 to the power of 1 (2^1)	2
2 to the power of 2 (2^2)	4
2 to the power of 3 (2^3)	8
2 to the power of 4 (2^4)	16
2 to the power of 5 (2^5)	32
2 to the power of 6 (2^6)	64
2 to the power of 7 (2^7)	128

1. Write down the eight powers of two, starting with the number 128:

    ```
    128    64    32    16    8    4    2    1
    ```

2. Determine whether 128 is smaller than or equal to the decimal number you're converting. For the number 112, the answer is no, so enter a 0 under the 128 column:

    ```
    128    64    32    16    8    4    2    1
    0
    ```

3. Now move on to the next power of two (64) and determine whether it's smaller than or equal to the decimal number. In this example, the answer is yes, so enter a 1 under the 64 column and subtract 64 from the decimal number: 112 - 64 = 48.

    ```
    128    64    32    16    8    4    2    1
    0      1
    ```

4. Move on to the next power of two (32), and determine whether it's smaller than or equal to the new decimal number, 48. In this example, the answer is yes, so enter a 1 under the 32 column, and subtract 32 from the decimal number: 48 - 32 = 16.

128	64	32	16	8	4	2	1
0	1	1					

5. Move on to the next power of two (16), and determine whether it's smaller than or equal to the new decimal number, 16. The answer is yes, so enter a 1 under the 16 column, and subtract 16 from the decimal number: 16 - 16 = 0.

128	64	32	16	8	4	2	1
0	1	1	1				

6. Now that the new decimal number is 0, you can enter a 0 under each remaining power of two, as shown:

128	64	32	16	8	4	2	1
0	1	1	1	0	0	0	0

As you can see, the decimal number 112 converts to the binary number 01110000.

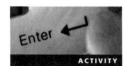

You can test your work by adding each power of two that has a 1 entered in its column. For instance, in the previous example, the only powers of two with a 1 under them are 64, 32, and 16. If you add these numbers, you get the original decimal number: 112.

Activity 8-2: Converting from Decimal to Binary

Time Required: 30 minutes

Objective: Convert a 32-bit IP address into four 8-bit binary octets.

Description: In this activity, you start with the IP address 192.168.75.136 and convert the four octets into their binary equivalents.

1. Use a pen and paper to write down the powers of two, starting with 128:

128	64	32	16	8	4	2	1

2. Start with the first octet in your IP address (192) and convert it to binary, using the steps you learned previously. When you finish, your results should look like the following:

128	64	32	16	8	4	2	1
1	1	0	0	0	0	0	0

3. The second octet in the IP address is 168. Again, use the steps you've learned to convert 168 to its binary equivalent. Your results should look like the following:

128	64	32	16	8	4	2	1
1	0	1	0	1	0	0	0

4. The third octet in the IP address is 75. Follow the same steps to convert 75 to its binary equivalent, and your results should look like the following:

    ```
    128   64   32   16   8   4   2   1
    0     1    0    0    1   0   1   1
    ```

5. The fourth octet in the IP address is 136. Using the same steps, your results should look like the following:

    ```
    128   64   32   16   8   4   2   1
    1     0    0    0    1   0   0   0
    ```

6. The IP address 192.168.75.136 is the following in binary:

    ```
    11000000.10101000.01001011.10001000
    ```

Network and Host Identifiers

An IP address is composed of two parts: a network ID and a host ID. The **network ID** identifies the network where the host is located. The **host ID** identifies a computer or device on a network. This structure is much like phone numbers, with an area code shared by everybody in a certain area and a local number specific to each person with a phone account.

Computers can communicate only with other computers on the same network, so they must have the same network ID to exchange information. To communicate with computers having different network IDs, you need a router, which is used to connect networks and forward packets to their destinations.

Subnet Masks

A **subnet mask** is used to determine which part of an IP address is the network ID and which part is the host ID. Like an IP address, a subnet mask is 32 bits. When a computer reads the IP address 255.255.255.0, for example, it converts the decimal 255 to the binary 11111111. All 8 bits of this octet are 1s. For example, 255.255.255.0 is 11111111.11111111.11111111.00000000 in binary. The 1s in the subnet mask out the network portion of an IP address. Figure 8-3 lines up the binary version of 192.168.75.136 with the binary version of 255.255.255.0 so that you can see how the subnet mask determines which part of the IP address is the network portion and which part is the host portion.

```
11000000.11010000.01001011.10001000   IP address 192.168.75.136

11111111.11111111.11111111.00000000   Subnet mask 255.255.255.0
```

Figure 8-3 A subnet mask
© Cengage Learning 2013

The 1s in the first three octets represent the network ID, and the 0s represent the host ID. The IP address has a network ID of 192.168.75.0 and a host ID of 136 (see Figure 8-4). All the IP addresses on this network have the same network ID, so the first three octets are the same for all computers and devices.

11111111.11111111.11111111.00000000 Network ID 192.168.75.0

00000000.00000000.00000000.10001000 Host ID 0.0.0.136

Figure 8-4 Network and host IDs in an IP address
© Cengage Learning 2013

IP Address Classes

Because the number of IP addresses in IPv4 is limited, they're divided into classes to accommodate varying network sizes. Some are reserved for very large organizations, others for large organizations, and some for small organizations. IP addresses are divided into five classes. The most common are Class A, Class B, and Class C. Class D and E networks are for multicasting—transmitting to multiple destinations from a single source—and experimentation. Table 8-4 describes the different IP address classes.

The IP address 127.0.0.1 is the localhost address for every computer and isn't eligible to be assigned.

Table 8-4 IP address classes

Class	First octet (decimal)	First octet (binary)	Possible networks	Possible hosts
A	1 to 127	00000001 to 01111111	127	16,777,214
B	128 to 191	10000000 to 10111111	16,384	65,534
C	192 to 223	11000000 to 11011111	2,097,152	254

Class A Networks Class A networks can be identified by their subnet mask, which is 255.0.0.0. The first bit of a Class A network is always 0. There can be only 127 Class A networks on the entire Internet, which allows 16,777,214 hosts per network. A typical company needs no more than 16 million unique IP addresses; therefore, Class A networks are assigned to ISPs or very large companies.

Class B Networks In Class B networks, the subnet mask is 255.255.0.0. The first two bits of a Class B network are always 10. Class B networks are assigned to large organizations, such as government agencies, universities, and typical companies.

Class C Networks Class C networks have the subnet mask 255.255.255.0. The first three bits of a Class C network are always 110. More than 2 million possible Class C networks are possible, but each network can have only 254 hosts, so Class C networks are assigned to small organizations.

The Internet Corporation for Assigned Names and Numbers (ICANN, *www.icann.org*) coordinates the unique IP addresses used on the Internet.

Configuring Network Interface Cards

OpenSUSE includes tools and utilities to configure many hardware devices, such as printers, network cards, modems, and others. This section describes the procedures for configuring a network interface card (NIC) and connecting to a network. Linux provides commands such as `ifconfig` for configuring a NIC.

Using the `ifconfig` Command

As mentioned, you use the `ifconfig` command to view a computer's IP address and the current state of all active network interfaces on it. The `ifconfig` command is also used to configure NICs. A NIC is usually detected during an OS installation, and openSUSE configures the correct driver for the NIC automatically. However, as a Linux system administrator, you need to know how to configure a NIC manually in case a NIC isn't recognized or configured during installation. Using the `ifconfig` command without arguments displays network settings in a format similar to the following output:

```
eth0   Link encap:Ethernet  HWaddr 00:0C:29:76:77:63
       inet addr:192.168.75.136 Bcast:192.168.75.255 Mask:255.255.255.0
       inet6 addr:fe80::20c:29ff:fe76:7763/64 Scope:Link
       UP BROADCAST RUNNING  MULTICAST MTU:1500 Metric:1
       RX packets:86 errors:0 dropped:0 overruns:0 frame:0
       TX packets:46 errors:0 dropped:0 overruns:0 carrier:0
       collisions:0 txqueuelen:1000
       RX bytes:14308 (13.9 Kb)  TX bytes:7403 (7.2 Kb)
       Interrupt:19 Base address:0x2024
lo     Link encap:Local Loopback
       inet addr:127.0.0.1  Mask:255.0.0.0
       inet6 addr: ::1/128 Scope:Host
       UP LOOPBACK RUNNING  MTU:16436 Metric:1
       RX packets:22 errors:0 dropped:0 overruns:0 frame:0
       TX packets:22 errors:0 dropped:0 overruns:0 carrier:0
       collisions:0 txqueuelen:0
       RX bytes:1300 (1.2 Kb)  TX bytes:1300 (1.2 Kb)
```

8

The following list describes this output:

- `Link encap`—Specifies the type of interface. In the example, it's Ethernet.
- `HWaddr`—Specifies the hardware address (also known as the MAC address) of a NIC. In the example, the hardware address is 00:0C:29:76:77:63. The purpose of the MAC address is to uniquely identify a NIC (also called a network adapter) on a network. Each NIC is assigned a unique MAC address by its manufacturer.
- `inet addr`—Specifies the IP address as well as the broadcast address (`Bcast`) and the netmask (`Mask`). The broadcast address is made up of two parts: the network ID and the host ID. The host ID is set to 255 (meaning all the bits are set). In the example, the IP address is 192.168.75.136 and the netmask is 255.255.255.0, which tells you it's a Class C network.

- RX packets—This line specifies the number of packets received (RX). It also shows you the number of errors and dropped packets and how many packets were too long to be received or transmitted (called "overruns").

- TX packets—This line displays packets transmitted from the computer over the network, along with the same error information shown for RX packets.

- Interrupt—This line displays the computer's configuration settings; in this example, the NIC is using the interrupt number 19.

If you have only one NIC, it's labeled eth0; all other NICs are labeled eth1, eth2, and so forth. The lo represents the loopback adapter with an IP address of 127.0.0.1. All devices using TCP/IP require the loopback address. Also called the localhost, it's used to test basic functioning of TCP/IP on your computer.

The ifconfig command can also be used to configure your NIC with the following syntax:

ifconfig *interface IP address netmask options*

In this syntax, *netmask* refers to the subnet mask you want to assign to the interface you're configuring. In addition, you can set options for the interface, such as up to open the interface and down to close the interface. The following example shows setting the IP address and subnet mask for the eth0 interface:

ifconfig eth0 192.168.75.200 netmask 255.255.255.0

This command produces the following output:

```
eth0   Link encap:Ethernet  HWaddr 00:0C:29:76:77:63
        inet addr:192.168.75.200  Bcast:192.168.75.255
Mask:255.255.255.0
        inet6 addr:fe80::20c:29ff:fe76:7763/64 Scope:Link
        UP BROADCAST RUNNING MULTICAST  MTU:1500  Metric:1
        RX packets:105 errors:0 dropped:0 overruns:0 frame:0
        TX packets:274 errors:0 dropped:0 overruns:0 carrier:0
        collisions:0 txqueuelen:1000
        RX bytes:28121 (27.4 Kb)  TX bytes:51512 (50.3 Kb)
        Interrupt:19 Base address:0x2024
```

If you restart your computer after using the ifconfig command to configure a NIC, you lose all the network settings. If you want the settings to be configured permanently, you must add them to the /etc/sysconfig/network/ifcfg-eth0 file.

Activity 8-3: Using the ifconfig Command

Time Required: 15 minutes

Objective: View and configure TCP/IP settings with the ifconfig command.

Description: In this activity, you use the ifconfig command to view your computer's TCP/IP configuration and change your IP address.

1. Start VMware Player and start an openSUSE virtual machine.

2. Open a terminal window. Switch to the root user by typing **su** and pressing **Enter**, and then entering the correct password.

3. Display the TCP/IP configuration information for your NIC by typing **ifconfig** and pressing **Enter**. What are the IP address, netmask, and broadcast address for your computer?

_____

4. Change your IP address to 204.21.112.10 by typing **ifconfig eth0 204.21.112.10** and pressing **Enter**.

5. Check whether the IP address has changed by typing **ifconfig** and pressing **Enter**.

6. Restart your Linux computer by typing **reboot** and pressing **Enter**. After your computer starts, open a terminal window and switch to the root user.

7. To see whether the IP address is still 204.21.112.10, type **ifconfig** (with no arguments) and press **Enter**. Is the IP address the same? Why or why not?

_____

8. Exit the root user account by typing **exit** and pressing **Enter**. Leave the terminal window open for the next activity.

The `ping` Command

The `ping` command uses ICMP to send an Echo Request packet to a specified network device on the network and waits for a reply. Administrators use this command in network testing, measurement, and management. For instance, you can use it to check whether you have configured a NIC correctly. The following example shows the output of the `ping` command:

```
ping 192.168.0.6
PING 192.168.0.6 (192.168.0.6) 56(84) bytes of data.
64 bytes from 192.168.0.6: icmp_seq=1 ttl=128 time=0.602 ms
64 bytes from 192.168.0.6: icmp_seq=2 ttl=128 time=0.355 ms
64 bytes from 192.168.0.6: icmp_seq=3 ttl=128 time=0.318 ms
64 bytes from 192.168.0.6: icmp_seq=4 ttl=128 time=0.241 ms
^C
--- 192.168.0.6 ping statistics ---
4 packets transmitted, 4 received, 0% packet loss, time 6006 ms
rtt min/avg/max/mdev = 0.236/0.348/0.602/0.118 ms
```

A brief explanation of this output is in order: Each ping request produces a result, including `icmp_seq` (the number of ping attempts—four, in this case), the time to live (`ttl`, which prevents an undeliverable packet from remaining in the network—128 hops, in this example), and the packet request's round-trip time, which is 0.602 milliseconds (ms) for the first packet.

By default, the `ping` command sends an Echo Request every second until you press Ctrl+C.

TIP

Table 8-5 describes the options you can use with the `ping` command.

Table 8-5 Options used with the `ping` command

Option	Description
-c n	Forces the `ping` command to stop sending Echo Request packets after the number of times specified by n.
-f	This option is called "flood ping" because a period is displayed for every Echo Request packet that's sent, and a backspace takes place for every Echo Request packet that's received. (The result is that the cursor moves back and forth rapidly.) With this option, packets are sent as fast as they're received. By default, only the root user can use this option.
-q	Forces the `ping` command to send packets without displaying statistics onscreen until after the ping has stopped. It's useful when you're running scripts and don't need to see every detail of the `ping` output.
-w n	Gives the `ping` command a deadline, with n representing the number of seconds the ping should run.

ACTIVITY

Activity 8-4: Using the `ping` Command

Time Required: 15 minutes

Objective: Test your TCP/IP configuration with the `ping` command.

Description: In this activity, you test your computer's TCP/IP configuration and make sure it's set up correctly. Then you ping another computer on your network (your Windows host computer) to test whether TCP/IP communication is working.

1. View the IP address on your Windows host machine by clicking **Start**, **Run**, typing **cmd**, and clicking **OK**. At the DOS prompt, type **ipconfig** and press **Enter**. Write down your IP address:

   _____

2. If your terminal window is still open from Activity 8-3, skip to Step 3; otherwise, open a terminal window on your openSUSE Linux virtual machine.

3. Check to make sure TCP/IP is working correctly on your Linux virtual machine by typing **ping 127.0.0.1** and pressing **Enter**. Did you get a reply? What IP address is 127.0.0.1?

   _____

4. Make sure your TCP/IP configuration is set up correctly by pinging your computer's IP address. To do this, switch to the root user, and then type **ifconfig** and press **Enter** to determine your computer's IP address. Then type **ping IPaddress** (replacing *IPaddress* with your own address) and press **Enter**.

5. Ping your Windows host machine's IP address by typing **ping** *IPaddress* (replacing *IPaddress* with the address you wrote down in Step 1) and pressing **Enter**. Are you getting a reply from your Windows host machine? Press **Ctrl+C** to stop the ping. How many packets did you transmit? How many packets were received, and how many were lost?

---

6. Send only seven ICMP Echo Request packets to your Windows host machine by typing **ping -c 7** *IPaddress* and pressing **Enter**.

7. Send a flood ping to your Windows host machine for 5 seconds by typing **ping -fw 5** *IPaddress* and pressing **Enter**.

8. Close the terminal and command prompt windows by typing **exit** and pressing **Enter** on your Linux and Windows computers, and then log off both machines.

Chapter Summary

- Network devices, such as computers and printers, must follow a set of rules for connecting and communicating with each other.

- TCP/IP is a suite of networking protocols organized into three layers: Application, Transport, and Internet.

- IP and ICMP are the major protocols at the Internet layer, which is the base of the TCP/IP protocol suite. IP contains addressing information that enables packets to be routed and handles fragmentation (used to divide packets for transmission through a network). ICMP is used to generate IP error messages.

- TCP and UDP are the major protocols at the Transport layer. TCP is a connection-oriented protocol responsible for keeping track of packets and reassembling them into a single file after they've arrived. UDP is a connectionless protocol because it doesn't perform error checking or acknowledge that messages were sent successfully.

- FTP and HTTP are two important protocols at the Application layer. FTP is used to move files from one computer to another efficiently and accurately. HTTP is a connectionless protocol used for sending and receiving requests between the client and server on a network.

- An IP address is a two-part (network ID and host ID) unique number that identifies a device on a TCP/IP network.

- The binary numbering system consists of only 1s and 0s and is the language computers use, so the computer converts decimal IP addresses into binary numbers.

- Because the number of available IP addresses is limited, IP addresses are divided into classes based on network IDs.

- The `ifconfig` command is used to view and modify TCP/IP configuration settings. The `ping` command is designed to help administrators in network testing, measurement, and management.

8

Key Terms

binary numbering system A numbering system consisting of only 1s and 0s; it's the language computers use.

bit Also known as a binary digit; a single binary value.

fragmentation The process of packets being broken down into small packets to transmit them through different networks.

host ID The second part of an IP address; identifies the computer or device on the network.

Internet Control Message Protocol (ICMP) A protocol in the Internet layer of the TCP/IP model that generates IP error messages.

Internet Protocol (IP) The main protocol in the TCP/IP suite; contains addressing information that enables packets to be routed.

IP address A unique number that identifies a computer or device on a TCP/IP network.

network ID The first part of an IP address; identifies the network on which the host is located.

octet An 8-bit binary number making up each of the four sets of numbers in an IPv4 address.

packets Packages of data that are routed through the network.

subnet mask A method for determining which part of an IP address is used for the network ID and which part is used for the host ID.

Transmission Control Protocol (TCP) A connection-oriented protocol responsible for keeping track of packets and reassembling them into a single file after they've arrived.

Transmission Control Protocol/Internet Protocol (TCP/IP) Also known as the Internet Protocol suite, it's an internationally accepted set of rules for connecting computers to the Internet and most other networks.

User Datagram Protocol (UDP) A connectionless protocol that uses IP to get packets from one computer to another; used when a faster transfer rate is more important than the accuracy of the data being sent.

Review Questions

1. The TCP/IP protocol suite consists of only two protocols: TCP and IP. True or False?

2. Which of the following layers is part of the TCP/IP model? (Choose all that apply.)

    a. Application

    b. Physical

    c. Transport

    d. Internet

3. Which layer of the TCP/IP model is the starting point for a packet when it travels across a network?

   a. Application

   b. Physical

   c. Transport

   d. Internet

4. Which layer at the top of the TCP/IP model is responsible for higher-level protocols, such as Telnet and FTP?

   a. Application

   b. Physical

   c. Transport

   d. Internet

5. How many bits are in a standard IPv4 address?

   a. 8

   b. 4

   c. 32

   d. 16

6. The format of a standard IPv4 address is four numbers separated by a period. What is each number called?

   a. Binary

   b. Octet

   c. Packet

   d. Bit

7. Which binary number represents the decimal number 225?

   a. 11100011

   b. 11000110

   c. 11111111

   d. 11100001

8. What's a single binary value called?

   a. Bit

   b. Byte

   c. Packet

   d. Octet

8

9. Which part of an IP address identifies the network where the host is located?

   a. Host ID

   b. Subnet mask

   c. Network ID

   d. Broadcast

10. Which part of an IP address identifies a device on the network?

    a. Host ID

    b. Subnet mask

    c. Network ID

    d. Broadcast

11. When two computers aren't on the same network, what's needed for them to communicate with each other?

12. Explain the purpose of a subnet mask.

13. The IP address 204.21.112.2 belongs to which of the following classes?

    a. Class A

    b. Class B

    c. Class C

    d. Class D

14. Which IP address class is used for very large companies and ISPs?

    a. Class A

    b. Class B

    c. Class C

    d. Class D

15. Which Linux command do administrators use to view TCP/IP configuration information?

    a. `ipconfig`

    b. `ping`

    c. `netmask`

    d. `ifconfig`

16. If an administrator needs to change the IP address on the first Ethernet interface to 204.21.112.101 and the netmask to 255.255.255.0, which of the following commands should be used?

    a. `ifconfig eth1 204.21.112.101 netmask 255.255.255.0`

    b. `ifconfig eth0 204.21.112.101 netmask 255.255.255.0`

    c. `ifconfig eth1 255.255.255.255.0 IP 204.21.112.101`

    d. `ifconfig eth0 255.255.255.255.0 IP 204.21.112.101`

17. Which of the following commands should a Linux administrator use to check whether local TCP/IP has been installed correctly? (Choose all that apply.)

    a. `ping localhost`

    b. `ping`

    c. `ping 127.0.0.1`

    d. `ping 255.255.255.0`

18. Which of the following commands should a Linux administrator use to send five Echo Request packets to a computer on the network?

    a. `ping 204.21.112.50`

    b. `ping -c 5 204.21.112.50`

    c. `ping 5 204.21.112.50`

    d. `ping -f 5 204.21.112.50`

Case Projects

CASE PROJECTS

8

Case Project 8-1: Configuring a Subnet Mask

You work for a company with a Class B network of 128.100.0.0 and need to configure a subnet mask on all computers in the network. What would the subnet mask be? What would the network ID be for all network computers? How many devices could you have on the network?

Case Project 8-2: Researching IPv6

Use the Internet or other resources to research IPv6. A good place to start is the Internet Assigned Numbers Authority (*www.iana.org*), which is responsible for IP addressing and other Internet protocols. Why is IPv6 needed? Describe some differences between IPv4 and IPv6.

## chapter 9

Installing Software Packages

After reading this chapter and completing the exercises, you will be able to:

- Manage software packages with the RPM utility
- Handle RPM software dependencies
- Install, upgrade, and remove software at the command line
- Add remote software repositories in openSUSE
- Work with software packages in YaST Software Manager

In this chapter, you learn how to work with software packages and use the RPM utility to install, query, update, and remove software. Learning how to use this utility is important so that you can manage software effectively. Although it was created under Red Hat, RPM can be found in many different Linux distributions, so it's a utility you should know how to use. Finally, you get hands-on experience with using tools available in openSUSE to manage software.

Working with RPM Software Packages

In the past, software packages for Linux and UNIX were available in compressed tar archives called tarballs or in cpio (copy in/out) format, which is another type of archive format. However, these formats had no features for upgrading or uninstalling software, and installation was tedious, requiring users to remember lengthy and complex commands. In addition, there was no standard installation procedure that could be used with all software packages. To address these shortcomings, package management utilities were developed. One of the most powerful is **RPM Package Manager (RPM)**, which is used to install and manage software packages. A **software package** is an archive of related files, such as configuration, data, and documentation files, constituting a software application. Like a package you send in the mail, a software package also has a label containing **metadata**, which is descriptive information, such as name, version, size, and description of its contents.

The RPM utility is open-source software licensed under the GPL, which means many Linux distributions, including openSUSE, have it installed already. Although Red Hat, Inc., developed this utility, it's not specific to Red Hat Linux. You can use it in many OSs, such as OS/2, Solaris, AIX, Sun OS, IRIX, UNIX, and several Linux distributions.

Software packages created with the RPM utility are often called "RPM files" or simply "packages."

RPM is used to build, install, query, verify, update, and uninstall software packages in Linux. You can also use this utility to package a software application in source code or binary form so that it can be installed and used on computers running Linux and certain other OSs, such as Novell NetWare. An RPM package contains an archive of files and package details, such as name, version, and description. Packages built with RPM have the following advantages:

- *Upgrading*—You can upgrade packages to a newer version without losing the previous version's customization settings because configuration files are preserved. In addition, special upgrade files aren't needed because you use the same file to install and upgrade an RPM package.

- *Uninstalling*—You can uninstall packages more quickly because you don't need to worry about the different locations where the application has stored its files. RPM makes all the necessary deletions automatically (but preserves configuration files, as mentioned).

- *Verification*—You can verify a package to make sure you haven't deleted a file that was necessary for it to run correctly. If you have, you can then restore the missing file or reinstall the package. In this case, RPM retains any settings you have changed in the package files.

- *Querying*—The RPM utility has options that enable you to search for packages or just certain files. As mentioned, RPM packages contain files that store metadata. RPM can query these files to discover useful information about the package. For example, if you want to find the version number of a package, you can enter the following command: $rpm -q *package_name*.

The RPM Utility

The rpm command can be used in one of the following modes: querying, which can be done by any user, and installing, upgrading, and removing, which can be done only by the root user. Depending on the options you select, you might have to specify the package name, the source RPM name, or a package file. Table 9-1 describes common options used with this command.

Table 9-1   Common **rpm** options

Options	Description
-i or --install	Installs a software package
-U or --upgrade	Upgrades an existing software package or acts like the install option if a software package isn't installed
-F or --freshen	Like the -U option, upgrades an existing software package on your machine but doesn't install a package if there's no earlier version
-h or --hash	Used with install or upgrade options to show progress by printing hash marks (#) while a software package is unpacked
-v or --verbose	Displays detailed information, including progress messages
-e or --erase	Uninstalls a software package
-q or --query	Used to query the RPM database

9

Querying Packages   Querying with the rpm command gives you package details from the RPM database. The -q option is used to run a query. You use it throughout this chapter to determine version and release information for software packages.

Many more options for the rpm command are available, including ones you can use to query the RPM database on your system. To see a comprehensive list, use the rpm --help command. You can also use the man rpm command to get even more information.

TIP

Installing Packages RPM packages have an .rpm extension as well as other filenaming conventions. Refer to this example while you read the following descriptions:

```
OpenOffice_org-writer-3.1.1.4-1.2.3.i586.rpm
```

- *Name*—The first part of the RPM package filename describes the software, such as "OpenOffice_org-writer" in the preceding example. RPM uses the package contents, not the filename, during installation, which means this name can be changed without affecting the installation.

- *Version*—The second part of the filename indicates the package's version number, which is 3.1.1.4 in the example. The hyphen isn't part of the version number.

- *Release*—The third part of the filename is the software release number, which typically starts with 1 and is incremented by 1 with each new version (although this format isn't required). In the preceding example, the release number is 1.2.3; note that again, the hyphen isn't part of the release number.

- *Architecture*—The final part of the RPM filename specifies the architecture (the type of hardware the package is meant to run on). For instance, i586 indicates the package was designed to run on 586-based machines. First introduced by Intel as the i586 Pentium processor, "586" represents a class of computer processors.

In the following example, the F-Spot package (version 0.6.1.5, release 1.1.1 for i586 hardware) is installed with the -i, -v, and -h options; the second and third lines show some of the command's output:

```
rpm -ivh f-spot-0.6.1.5-1.1.1.i586.rpm
Preparing...                    ################################# [100%]
   1:f-spot                      ################################# [100%]
```

F-Spot is a photo management program for the GNOME environment.

The RPM utility performs the following functions during installation:

- *Dependency checks*—This process determines whether the package has dependency requirements (explained in "RPM Dependencies" later in this chapter) and displays this information to prevent installation problems.

- *Preinstallation tasks*—Some software packages require issuing commands before installation. RPM performs these tasks as directed by the package builder, thereby eliminating problems during installation.

- *Conflicts*—Checks whether the package you're trying to install is already installed on your system and makes sure you're not trying to install a version older than the existing one.

- *Unpacking*—Opens the software package and installs each file in the correct location in your file system.

- *Postinstallation tasks*—As with preinstallation tasks, some software requires using commands after installation, and RPM carries out these tasks for you.

- *Storage*—Keeps track of all installed packages in the RPM database.

Upgrading Packages Upgrading packages with the RPM utility is similar to installing them, but you use the -U option, as shown in this syntax example:

```
rpm -U install-options package-filename
```

In the following example, a software package is upgraded:

```
rpm -q f-spot
f-spot-0.6.1.5-1.1.1.i586
rpm -Uvh f-spot-0.6.1.5-1.2.1.i586.rpm
Preparing...                      ################################### [100%]
   1:f-spot                       ################################### [100%]
rpm -q f-spot
f-spot-0.6.1.5-1.2.1.i586
```

In the first line, a query is issued for information on the F-Spot package, and the version number (0.6.1.5) and release number (1.1.1) of the existing package are displayed in the second line. In the third line, the -U option is used to upgrade to the new version, with progress messages shown in the next two lines. After the upgrade is finished, the -q option is used again to verify that the new version has been installed.

As mentioned, RPM retains the previous version's configuration file, which is called a **smart update**. However, the –U option also works well when no previous version of the package is on your system. In this case, the -U option simply installs the package instead of performing an upgrade.

If you try to upgrade a package and RPM finds a newer version installed on your system, an error results.

As mentioned in Table 9-1, the -F (freshen) option is also used to upgrade software packages. You can use this option with a group of packages. It's especially useful if you have downloaded several packages and want to upgrade only the ones already installed on your system. You don't have to search through the downloaded packages to determine which ones should be installed or upgraded.

The following example shows using the -F option when a previous version doesn't exist:

```
rpm -q f-spot
package f-spot is not installed
rpm -Fvh f-spot-0.6.1.5-1.2.1.i586.rpm
rpm -q f-spot
package f-spot is not installed
```

After the query is issued, a message is displayed stating that F-Spot isn't installed, and no previous versions exist. After the freshen option is issued, a final RPM query shows that the package wasn't installed or upgraded. This example illustrates the difference between the freshen and upgrade options, in that the package wasn't installed because no older version was in place.

The next example shows using the -F option to upgrade an existing package:

```
rpm -q f-spot
f-spot-0.6.1.5-1.1.1.i586
ls
f-spot-0.6.1.5-1.2.1.i586.rpm
rpm -Fvh f-spot-0.6.1.5-1.2.1.i586.rpm
Preparing...                    ################################### [100%]
   1:f-spot                     ################################### [100%]
rpm -q f-spot
f-spot-0.6.1.5-1.2.1.i586
```

You can use the following command to upgrade only the packages for which an older version is already installed:

```
# rpm -Fvh *.rpm
```

Uninstalling Packages RPM makes uninstalling packages fast and easy. You just use the -e option in this format:

```
rpm -e package-name
```

However, you don't have to specify the package's full name, as shown in this example:

```
rpm -q f-spot
f-spot-0.6.1.5-1.2.1.i586
rpm -e f-spot
```

Activity 9-1: Using the RPM Utility

Time Required: 30 minutes

Objective: Download an RPM package and install, delete, and upgrade it.

Description: In this activity, you download an RPM package from the *http://opensuse.org* Web site, and then query the RPM database to determine whether the application has already been installed on your system. Next, you use the -F and -U options to install and upgrade the application, and then use the -e option to delete it.

1. Start VMware Player and start an openSUSE virtual machine. Open a terminal window.

2. Start a Web browser by typing **firefox** and pressing **Enter**. Go to **http://download. opensuse.org/update/11.2/rpm/i586/**, which lists i586 RPM packages.

3. Next, you download the Tiff application, which is used to change file formats to and from TIFF. Click the **tiff-3.8.2-145.4.1.i586.rpm** link to start the download. (Note that this version is the most recent at this writing, but it might have changed by the time of publication.) When you see the message box asking whether you want to open or save the file, click the **Save File** option button, and then click **OK**.

4. Open a new terminal window and switch to the root user with the **su** command. Make sure you enter the correct root password.

5. Switch to the directory containing the downloaded RPM file. (*Tip*: It should be in the Downloads directory, a subdirectory of your home directory.) To do this, type **cd /home/*username*/Download** (or substitute the correct directory name) and press **Enter**.

6. Make sure the RPM file is there by typing **ls -l** and pressing **Enter**.

7. To install the Tiff application, type **rpm -ivh tiff-3.8.2-145.4.1.i586.rpm** and press **Enter**. The -i option is used to install the package, the -v option shows details of the installation, and the -h option shows the installation's progress.

8. Query the RPM database to determine whether Tiff was installed successfully by typing **rpm -q tiff** and pressing **Enter**. What Tiff version has been installed, and what's the release number?

_____

9. Delete the Tiff application by typing **rpm -e tiff** and pressing **Enter**.

10. Use the freshen option to upgrade the Tiff application by typing **rpm -Fvh tiff-3.8.2-145.4.1.i586.rpm** and pressing **Enter**. Explain how you can tell whether this option worked:

_____

11. Next, use the upgrade option by typing **rpm -Uvh tiff-3.8.2-145.4.1.i586.rpm** and pressing **Enter**. Explain why you get different results with this option:

_____

12. Now that you have installed, deleted, and upgraded an RPM package, exit the root user account by typing **exit** and pressing **Enter**. Exit the Web browser, but leave the terminal window open for the next activity.

RPM Dependencies

Another advantage of the RPM utility is the **RPM dependencies** feature, which determines whether a software package depends on another application to run and indicates what capabilities an installed package provides to other applications. For instance, if you try to delete a package that's providing capabilities to another application, you get a message similar to the following:

```
rpm -ev gimp
error: Failed dependencies:
gimp-2.0 is needed by (installed) gimp-help-2.4.2-3.2.noarch
```

In this example, GIMP can't be uninstalled because it provides capabilities to the gimp-help application. This feature is also useful when you're installing a software package that requires the capabilities of another application. As shown in the following example, it displays this dependency information:

```
rpm -ivh vlc-1.0.6-1.13.i586.rpm
error: Failed dependencies:
vlc-noX = 1.0.6-1.13 is needed by vlc-1.0.6-1.13.i586
```

9

RPM dependencies can become a two-edged sword, however. On one hand, they ensure that you can't install an application that won't work, but you might find that the dependent application also depends on another application. For instance, you download Package A and try to install it, only to find out it's dependent on Package B. You download Package B and try to install it but find out it's dependent on Package C. If this continues, you might think you're caught in an RPM "dependency loop." The solution to this problem is a front-end package manager, which provides a user interface to make package management more user friendly. Table 9-2 describes a few widely used front-end package managers.

Table 9-2 Front-end package managers

Front-end package manager	Description
Advanced Package Tool (APT; *http://en. wikipedia.org/wiki/Advanced_Packaging_Tool*)	A package manager originally designed for Debian that's now on the verge of becoming the standard for package management; used to install or upgrade all necessary dependent applications so that an RPM package can be installed
Yellowdog Updater, Modified (YUM; *http://yum. baseurl.org*)	Developed by Yellow Dog Linux and used with the RPM utility to install a package and all its dependencies
YaST Software Manager (*http://en.opensuse.org/ YaST_Software_Management*)	Free from Novell under the GPL; an RPM-based tool for installing software packages and their dependencies with a graphical or command-line interface

Working with Software Packages in OpenSUSE

You have other methods, besides the RPM utility, of working with software packages in openSUSE. After openSUSE is installed, software packages are installed, too, along with repositories used to install or update packages. A **repository** is a storage location for software packages—usually a Web server, but repositories can also be on the local system. For instance, the openSUSE installation CD is considered a local repository.

In addition, software in openSUSE is indexed, meaning you don't have to remember the exact name of software to find it. For instance, you can search for software by using **patterns**, which are collections of packages that define a type of function, such as server packages. In this section, you learn how to install, remove, and update packages with the yast command line and with YaST Software Manager.

The yast Command

You can use the yast command to configure hardware, network connections and clients, services, and general system options, such as language, partitioning, and boot loaders. In this section, you use it to configure software. Table 9-3 describes some common options used with the yast command.

Table 9-3 Common `yast` options

Options	Description
`-i` or `--install`	Installs an RPM package. If you use the absolute path to the package file, just the package is installed if it meets dependency requirements; if you use the short package name, the package is installed along with all dependencies.
`--remove`	Uninstalls an RPM package; the short package name can be used to uninstall the package and all dependencies.
`--update`	Updates an RPM package; the short package name can be used to include all dependencies.
`--qt`	Opens YaST in the QT graphical front-end.
`--gtk`	Opens YaST in the GTK graphical front-end.
`--ncurses`	Opens YaST in text mode, which enables administrators to use the YaST Software Manager if they have no server GUI.

YaST can be used with GUI interfaces, too. QT (*http://qt.nokia.com*) and YaST2-GTK (*http://en.opensuse.org/YaST2-GTK*) are YaST graphical third-party utilities.

9

Activity 9-2: Using the `yast` Command

Time Required: 30 minutes

Objective: Use the `yast` command to install and remove a package.

Description: In this activity, you use the `rpm` and `yast` commands to work with GNU Image Manipulation Package (GIMP) so that you can see the difference in these two commands.

1. If necessary, start VMware Player, start an openSUSE virtual machine, and open a terminal window. Switch to the root user by typing **su**, pressing **Enter**, and then entering the correct root password.

2. Query the RPM database for GIMP by typing **rpm -q gimp** and pressing **Enter**.

3. Use the `yast` command to uninstall GIMP by typing **yast --remove gimp** and pressing **Enter**. What difference do you see in the interface of the `yast` and `rpm` commands? Did you get a package dependencies problem?

_____

_____

4. To remove GIMP, press **Tab** to move to the Possible Solutions section, press the **spacebar** to select the option for removing, press **Tab** two more times to select [OK -- Try Again], and then press **Enter**.

5. Press **Tab** until you move to the Accept option at the lower right, and press **Enter**.

6. Agree to the automatic changes by pressing **Enter** in the Automatic Changes window.

7. After GIMP has been removed from your system, query the RPM database to verify by typing **rpm -q gimp** and pressing **Enter**.

8. Install GIMP with the `yast` command by typing **yast -i gimp** and pressing **Enter**.

9. After the installation is finished, query the RPM database to verify by typing **rpm -q gimp** and pressing **Enter**.

10. Now that you have installed and deleted an RPM package with the `yast` command, exit the root user by typing **exit** and pressing **Enter**. Leave the terminal window open for the next activity.

Software Repositories

The openSUSE Configured Software Repositories tool is another resource for working with software packages. To open it, use the `yast --gtk` command as the root user, and then click the Software Repositories icon. Figure 9-1 shows this tool.

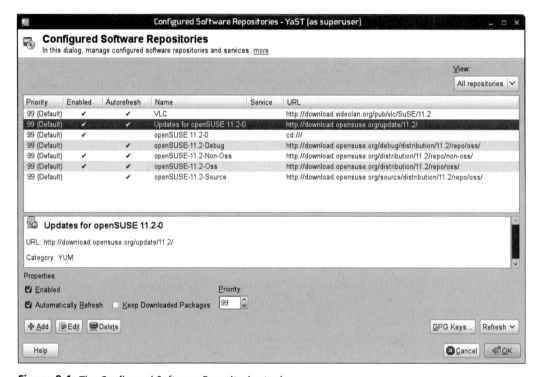

Figure 9-1 The Configured Software Repositories tool
Source: openSUSE

If you use the `yast` command to install software that can't be located in one of your repositories, you get an error similar to the one in Figure 9-2. To prevent this problem, you can use the Configured Software Repositories tool to add software repositories so that YaST has more resources to find the packages you want to install.

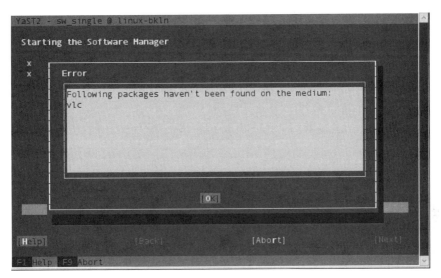

Figure 9-2 An install error
Source: openSUSE

The three types of software repositories for version 11.2 that are available automatically are as follows:

- *OSS (Open Source Software)*—The main openSUSE repository for version 11.2 is *http://download.opensuse.org/distribution/11.2/repo/oss/*.

- *NON-OSS (Not Open Source Software)*—Flash Player and Java are examples of non-open-source software that's available at this repository: *http://download.opensuse.org/distribution/11.2/repo/non-oss/*.

- *Update (official security and bug-fix updates)*—The official 11.2 update repository is *http://download.opensuse.org/update/11.2/*.

Many repositories are available for download. Table 9-4 describes some common ones.

Adding several extra repositories isn't recommended because they can cause dependency issues and conflicts; however, some contain useful software packages, such as VideoLan Client, a free open-source multimedia player.

Table 9-4 Additional software repositories

Repository	Description	Download Web site
Packman (*http://packman.links2linux.de/*)	The largest external repository for openSUSE; offers RPM packages not available with the current distribution or available only in older versions	*http://packman.inode.at/ suse/openSUSE_11.2*
VideoLan Client (VLC; *www.videolan.org*)	Contains binaries and all required libraries not included with the openSUSE installation file	*http://download.videolan. org/pub/vlc/SuSE/11.2*
ATI video drivers (installation guide at *http://en.opensuse.org/ Additional_package_repositories#ATI_ video_drivers*)	Drivers for ATI video cards	*http://linux.ioda.net/ mirror/ati/openSUSE_11.2*
nVidia drivers (installation guide at *http://en.opensuse.org/SDB: NVIDIA_drivers*)	Drivers for nVidia video cards	*ftp://download.nvidia.com/ opensuse/11.2*

Activity 9-3: Using a Third-Party Software Repository

Time Required: 30 minutes

Objective: Add a third-party software repository to your list of trusted repositories.

Description: In this activity, you query the RPM database for a package that isn't included with the openSUSE installation. Next, you add a third-party software repository with the Configured Software Repositories tool, and use the yast command to install a package from the new repository.

1. If necessary, start VMware Player, start an openSUSE virtual machine, and open a terminal window. Switch to the root user by typing **su**, pressing **Enter**, and then entering the correct root password.

2. To query the RPM database for the VideoLan Client package, type **rpm -q vlc** and press **Enter**. Is VLC loaded on your system? Why or why not?

_____

3. Try to install VideoLan Client by typing **yast -i vlc** and pressing **Enter**. Did it work? Why or why not? Press **Enter** at the error message to return to the command prompt.

_____

4. Add the VLC repository by typing **yast --gtk** and pressing **Enter**. Click the **Software Repositories** entry in the right pane to start the Configured Software Repositories tool.

5. Click **Add** to start adding the software repository. If necessary, click the **Specify URL** option button, make sure the **Download repository description files** check box is selected, and then click **Next**.

6. Type **VLC** in the Repository Name text box and **http://download.videolan.org/pub/vlc/ SuSE/11.2/** in the URL text box. Finally, click **Next**. If you get an error message, click **Yes**, and then check the spelling of the URL. Remember that it's case sensitive.

7. Click **OK** at the lower right and click **OK** to any error messages. Click the **Import** button in the Import Untrusted GnuPG Key dialog box. If necessary, click **Yes** to use any unsigned files.

8. When the process is finished, close the YaST Control Center window.

9. Install VideoLan Client by typing **yast -i vlc** and pressing **Enter**. If necessary, click **I Agree** in the Confirm Package License window. Click **OK** to any error messages, and click **Yes** to use any unsigned files.

10. After the installation is finished, query the RPM database for the VideoLan Client by typing **rpm -q vlc** and pressing **Enter**.

11. Exit the root user account by typing **exit** and pressing **Enter**. Leave the terminal window open for the next activity.

YaST Software Manager

So far, you have installed, updated, and removed software by using the command line. OpenSUSE has a graphical utility, however, for performing the same tasks. Like the Configured Software Repositories tool, you can get to the Software Manager in different ways. On a KDE machine, you click the Kickoff Application Launcher button, click the Applications tab, click System, and, finally, click YaST. Another way is issuing the yast --gtk command (logged in as root), and then clicking the Software Management icon (see Figure 9-3).

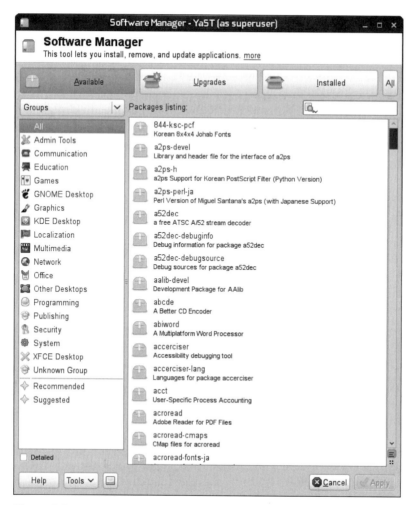

Figure 9-3 YaST Software Manager
Source: openSUSE

The four buttons at the top of the Software Manager window are used for listing software packages:

- *Available*—Displays packages that can be installed based on existing repositories
- *Upgrades*—Displays packages for which newer versions are available
- *Installed*—Displays all packages installed on your system
- *All*—Displays the combined results of the Available, Upgrades, and Installed lists

Under these buttons on the left is the Filter list box, which has the following selections:

- *Groups*—Displays software packages by category, such as Admin Tools or Education
- *Patterns*—Lists packages grouped by function, such as Base Technologies or Graphical Environments

- *Languages*—Contains all language package files
- *Repositories*—Filters packages based on the repository they belong to

Next to the Filter list box is a search field where you can enter the name of a software package to see the RPM name and a summary of its attributes. If you can't remember the package's full name, you can type part of the name to see all matching results. For instance, entering "fox" returns all packages containing this text as part of their name, such as Firefox and fox16.

ACTIVITY

Activity 9-4: Working with the YaST Software Manager

Time Required: 45 minutes

Objective: Use the YaST Software Manager to install, upgrade, and remove packages.

Description: In this activity, you start the YaST Software Manager and explore its functions. Next, you install and remove a package with this tool.

1. If necessary, open a terminal window, start VMware Player, and start an openSUSE virtual machine. Switch to the root user by typing **su**, pressing **Enter**, and then entering the correct root password.

2. Open the YaST Software Manager by typing **yast --gtk**, pressing **Enter**, and then clicking the **Software Management** icon.

3. Click the **Installed** button, and then click **Admin Tools** on the left. Scroll through the Admin Tools packages on the right and try to find some familiar ones, such as the gzip utility. Write a brief description of two packages you recognize:

_____

_____

4. Click the **Upgrades** button. How many upgrades are available for Admin Tools packages?

_____

5. Click the **Filter** list arrow, and then click **Patterns**. Under Server Functions, how many DHCP and DNS Server packages do you have installed, and how many are available?

_____

6. Install bind by clicking **DHCP and DNS Server** at the left and then click **bind** at the right. Click the **Install** button at the lower right, and then click the **Apply** button.

7. After the installation is finished, you're returned to the YaST Control Center window. Open the Software Manager again by clicking the **Software Management** icon.

8. Upgrade the unzip utility by clicking **Admin Tools** in the left pane and then clicking the **Upgrades** button at the top. Click to select **unzip**, click the **Upgrade** button, and then click **Apply**.

9

9. When the installation is finished, you're returned to the YaST Control Center window. Open the Software Manager again by clicking the **Software Management** icon.

10. In a terminal window, query the RPM database for the bind package by typing **rpm -q bind** and pressing **Enter**. What's displayed?

_____

11. Go back to the Software Manager window and remove bind by clicking **Network** in the left pane and then clicking **bind**. Click the **Remove** button at the lower right and then click **Apply**.

12. Next, query the RPM database to ensure that bind has been removed. To do this, go to the terminal window, type **rpm -q bind**, and press **Enter**.

13. Now that you have used the YaST Software Manager to work with packages, close all open windows and power off the virtual machine.

Chapter Summary

- RPM Package Manager (RPM) is a utility used to install and manage software packages.

- A software package is an archive of related files, such as configuration, data, and documentation files, constituting a software application. It contains a label describing the package contents. The label's descriptive information is called metadata.

- RPM packages have several advantages over traditional packages, such as upgrading, uninstalling, verification, and querying capabilities.

- The rpm command is used to query the RPM database and install, remove, and upgrade packages.

- The RPM dependencies feature determines whether a package relies on another application to run. This is important not only when installing packages, but also when uninstalling them.

- Software repositories are storage locations for software packages; they're local on an installation CD or remote on a server.

- YaST Software Manager is an easy-to-use GUI package manager. It makes package management more user friendly because you can install, upgrade, and remove software with a click of a button. YaST Software Manager also makes viewing packages easy with the use of filters.

- The yast command is used to install, update, and uninstall software packages along with their dependencies.

Key Terms

metadata   The contents of a label containing descriptive information about a software package.

patterns   Collections of software packages that relate to a specific function, such as server software.

repository A storage location that's usually a remote Web server; however, it can also be local (CD or DVD).

RPM dependencies A feature of the RPM utility that determines whether a software package requires the capabilities of another application to run and then displays this information.

RPM Package Manager (RPM) A utility for installing and managing software packages.

smart update An RPM feature that retains the previous version's configuration file.

software package An archive of related files, such as configuration, data, and documentation files, constituting a software application.

Review Questions

1. Packages built with RPM have which of the following advantages? (Choose all that apply.)

    a. Upgrading

    b. Querying

    c. Uninstalling

    d. Verification

2. What command should you use if you want to install an RPM package on your Linux system and no previous version has been installed? (Choose all that apply.)

    a. `rpm -i software_package`

    b. `rpm -F software_package`

    c. `rpm -U software_package`

    d. `rpm -v software_package`

3. What command should you use if you want to update an RPM package on your Linux system?

    a. `rpm -i software_package`

    b. `rpm -F software_package`

    c. `rpm -U software_package`

    d. b or c

4. What command should you use if you want to update all RPM packages on your Linux system as long as a previous version has been installed?

    a. `rpm -i *.rpm`

    b. `rpm -F *.rpm`

    c. `rpm -U *.rpm`

    d. a or c

9

5. What command should you use if you want to install an RPM package on your Linux system and see characters to indicate the installation's progress?

   a. `rpm -ih software_package`

   b. `rpm -iv software_package`

   c. `rpm -Uv software_package`

   d. `rpm -Fv software_package`

6. What command should you use if you want to install an RPM package on your Linux system and see detailed information?

   a. `rpm -ih software_package`

   b. `rpm -iv software_package`

   c. `rpm -Uv software_package`

   d. `rpm -Fv software_package`

7. What command should you use if you want to uninstall an RPM package on your Linux system?

   a. `rpm -U software_package`

   b. `rpm -uninstall software_package`

   c. `rpm -E software_package`

   d. `rpm -e software_package`

8. What command should you use if you want to know a package's version and release numbers?

   a. `rpm -U software_package`

   b. `rpm -i software_package`

   c. `rpm -q software_package`

   d. `rpm -e software_package`

9. You must be the root user to use the `rpm` command to install a package. True or False?

10. You must be the root user to use the `rpm` command to query the RPM database. True or False?

11. When querying the RPM database for a specific package, you must supply the full package name. True or False?

12. Describe the four parts of an RPM filename.

13. With the `rpm` command, you can install a package and all its dependencies. True or False?

14. Describe the difference between the `rpm` command's freshen and upgrade options.

15. If you want to install a software package and all its dependencies, what command should you use?

    a. rpm -i *software_package*

    b. rpm -U *software_package*

    c. yast -i *software_package*

    d. yast -U *software_package*

16. Explain the benefit of using a front-end software manager tool.

Case Projects

CASE PROJECTS

Case Project 9-1: Choosing Software Repositories

You're a Linux system administrator, and all employees in your company have openSUSE Linux installed on their computers, but some use the GNOME desktop environment and some use KDE. No employees have permission to add software repositories. A few have complained that they need to install third-party software to do their jobs. A good example of this type of tool is Configured Software Repositories, which can be accessed via YaST in openSUSE. Conduct research online to find two safe software repositories that you can add to their employees' trusted repository lists. Write a one- to two-page report describing the software repositories you chose.

Case Project 9-2: Installing Novell AppArmor

As the Linux system administrator, it's your responsibility to ensure that the company network is secure, and the tool of choice for checking application security is Novell AppArmor. Describe the steps you should take to make sure Novell AppArmor is installed along with all available updates.

9

## chapter 10

Apache Web Server

After reading this chapter and completing the exercises, you will be able to:

- Install Apache Web Server along with additional Apache modules
- Configure an Apache Web server with a GUI utility and by modifying Apache configuration files
- Create a Web page by writing an HTML script

Having a good understanding of Apache Web Server is important because it's the most popular Web server in use on the Internet. In this chapter, you learn how to install Apache Web Server and then see two different approaches to configuring a Web server: with a GUI utility (YaST) and by modifying configuration files manually. Finally, you use your HTML writing skills to create a Web page for your newly configured server.

Installing Apache Web Server

A **Web server** is a network computer with the primary role of serving Web pages to clients on request. It can also host a Web site along with images, style sheets, and other content so that clients (Web browsers) can access Web pages. Although a server is commonly thought of as a network device that provides resources to clients, a Web server differs slightly in that it also receives data from clients. For instance, clients can upload files or submit Web forms to a Web server. One of the most widely used Web servers is Apache. Apache Web Server is open-source, free Web server software developed by the Apache Software Foundation (ASF) that's designed to run on a wide variety of operating systems. The ASF is now a community of software developers who create open-source software. This section explains how to install, configure, and run an Apache Web server.

The Apache Software Foundation's Web site is *www.apache.org*.

Apache version 2.2 is included with openSUSE, but it's not installed by default. It's configured to run "out of the box" with no further modifications needed. The Apache software is mostly modular, meaning it's composed of separate parts that handle different functions. In the first activity, for example, you install the PHP module, which is one of the most popular in use on Web servers today. PHP is a server-side scripting language, commonly used to create dynamic Web pages.

Activity 10-1 walks you through installing Apache Web Server and the PHP5 module. You can install Apache Web Server with the `yast` command you learned previously (specifically, `yast -i apache2`). However, in this activity, you use the YaST Software Management module so that you can install other modules that aren't included automatically with the `yast` command.

PHP is a recursive acronym for PHP Hypertext Preprocessor, an open-source scripting language used for Web development.

Activity 10-1: Installing Apache Web Server

Time Required: 15 minutes

Objective: Install Apache Web Server and other Web-related packages.

Description: In this activity, you use the YaST Software Management module to install packages in the Web and LAMP Server pattern, including Apache Web Server, PHP, and MySQL.

LAMP is an acronym for Linux, Apache, MySQL, and PHP/Perl/Python.

1. Start VMware Player, and start an openSUSE virtual machine that uses the GNOME desktop.

2. Open a terminal window, and switch to the root user by typing **su**, pressing **Enter**, and entering the root password.

3. Open the YaST Control Center by typing **yast --gtk** and pressing **Enter**.

4. Start YaST Software Management by clicking **Software** on the left and then clicking **Software Management**.

5. To set a filter so that the Software Management tool shows all available packages categorized by pattern, click the **Filter** list arrow, and then click **Patterns**.

6. Click the **Web and LAMP Server** check box in the Server Functions section, and then click **Apply** to install Apache Web Server with other packages, such as the database management system MySQL, scripting languages (PHP and Perl, for example), and an Apache configuration module called `yast2-http-server`. Click **Apply** again.

7. When the installation is finished, close Software Management, and then close the YaST Control Center.

8. Query the RPM database for Apache Web Server by typing **rpm -q apache2** and pressing **Enter**.

9. Leave the terminal window open and the virtual machine running for the next activity.

Starting and Stopping Apache

After you have installed Apache, you need to start the apache2 service and make sure it starts automatically when you restart the system. To do this, open YaST and select System Services (Runlevel). In the System Services (Runlevel) window, you simply search for apache2 and enable the service, as you see later in Activity 10-2.

You can also start the apache2 service at the command line. The `rcapache2` command, which can be used only by the root user, is a link to a startup script in the `/etc/init.d` directory; it's used to start, stop, and restart the apache2 service. Table 10-1 describes common options used with this command.

Table 10-1 Common options used with `rcapache2`

Option	Description
status	Checks to see whether Apache is started. If so, you see a message stating that httpd2, the Apache daemon, is running. If not, you see a message stating that httpd2 isn't used.
start	Starts the apache2 service if it isn't already running. If it's already started, the message "Apache is already running (/var/run/httpd2.pid)" is displayed; otherwise, you get the message "Starting httpd2 (prefork)."
stop	Stops the apache2 service (if it's running) by shutting down httpd2 and terminating all child processes.
restart	Stops the apache2 service and then restarts it. If the service is already stopped, this option is the same as using the start option.
reload	Restarts the apache2 service safely because it ensures that all forked processes have finished before shutting down the service. Forked processes refer to child processes that have spawned while the server is running. For instance, a child process might have started to listen for connection requests.
probe	Checks to see whether the Apache configuration has been changed.
server-status	Displays a short status message, such as server uptime or number of connections.
help	Displays rcapache2 options with brief descriptions.

After you have started an Apache Web server, you can test it by starting Firefox and entering `http://localhost` in the address bar. You should see the Apache test page, shown in Figure 10-1.

Figure 10-1 The Apache test page

Source: openSUSE

When you install openSUSE, localhost is automatically set up as an alias in the /etc/hosts file. Localhost resolves to the 127.0.0.1 loopback IP address. So instead of using http://localhost, you can enter http://127.0.0.1.

Activity 10-2: Starting and Testing an Apache Web Server

Time Required: 15 minutes

Objective: Check the status of an Apache Web server, stop and start the apache2 service, and test an Apache Web server at the command line and with a GUI tool.

Description: In this activity, you use the command line to check the status of your Apache Web server and start and stop the apache2 service. You also use YaST to check the status of an Apache Web server, start the service, and assign runlevels 3 and 5. Finally, you use Firefox to view the Apache test Web page.

1. If the terminal window is still open, switch to the root user. If you don't have a terminal window open or if VMware Player isn't running, follow Step 1 in Activity 10-1.

2. Determine whether Apache Web Server is running by typing **rcapache2 status** and pressing **Enter**.

3. Start Apache Web Server by typing **rcapache2 start** and pressing **Enter**.

4. Repeat Step 2 so that you can see how the status message changes when Apache Web Server is running.

5. Stop Apache Web Server by typing **rcapache2 stop** and pressing **Enter**.

6. Use the YaST System Services (Runlevel) tool to check the status of your Apache server by typing **yast --gtk** and pressing **Enter**. When the YaST Control Center opens, click **System** on the left, and then click **System Services (Runlevel)**.

7. Click the **Expert Mode** option button. Find the apache2 service, and check the Running column to see whether it's running (indicated with a "Yes" or "No").

8. Start the apache2 service by clicking to select it, clicking the **Start/Stop/Refresh** button at the bottom, clicking **Start now**, and then clicking **OK**.

9. Ensure that the apache2 service starts automatically when your Linux machine boots by clicking the check boxes for runlevels **3** and **5**. Click **OK** to apply the new settings, and then click **Yes** to save the configuration.

10. Test your Apache server by starting a Web browser and typing **http://localhost** in the address bar. What's displayed in your browser?

_____

11. Exit Firefox, and then exit the root user by typing **exit** and pressing **Enter**. Leave the terminal window open and the virtual machine running for the next activity.

The chkconfig -a apache2 command also ensures that Apache is started automatically when booting in runlevels 3 and 5.

Configuring Apache Web Server

To configure an Apache Web server, you can use the graphical YaST module (yast2-http-server) or modify Apache configuration files. The main configuration file, httpd.conf, contains **directives**, which are instructions that tell Apache how to run. In this section, you learn how to configure an Apache Web server with both methods. The advantage of using configuration files is that you can make more detailed changes; however, the graphical module is convenient and easy to use.

Apache Configuration with HTTP-Server

HTTP-Server is a YaST module for configuring Apache. The package name is yast2-http-server, and it can be installed from YaST Software Management. The installation method you used in Activity 10-1 installs this module, too. If you aren't sure whether it's installed, you can query the RPM database with the rpm -q yast2-http-server command.

To begin the Apache configuration process in HTTP-Server, you use the yast2 http-server command. The first time you start this module, you see the HTTP Server Wizard (see Figure 10-2).

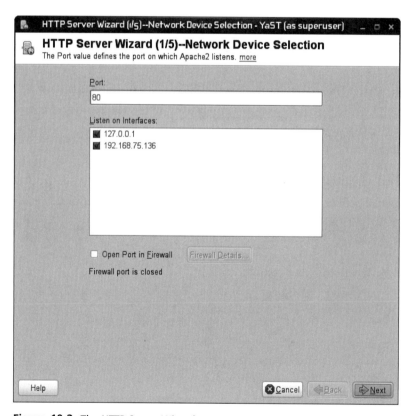

Figure 10-2 The HTTP Server Wizard
Source: openSUSE

The HTTP Server Wizard has five steps, with an option at the end to enter expert configuration mode. You can choose the network interface and ports that Apache listens on. (By default, Apache listens on all network interfaces on port 80.) A **port** is an interface for connecting a hardware device, such as a disk drive or printer, or in networking, it's a data connection established for communication between hosts. The port number identifies the type of function assigned to it. For instance, port 80 is a well-known port used by the Web server (HTTP). The wizard also allows you to enable scripting languages, such as PHP and Perl.

In the wizard's third step (see Figure 10-3), you can configure the Web server's **default host**, which is the first declared virtual host in the configuration file. A **virtual host** makes it possible to run multiple domains on one physical machine, and you can add virtual hosts as needed with this wizard.

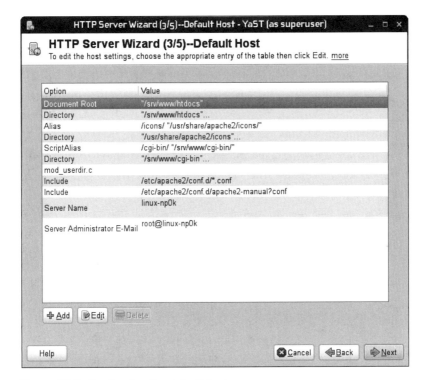

Figure 10-3 Configuring the default host
Source: openSUSE

The following are the default settings for a Web server in Apache:

- *DocumentRoot*—The **DocumentRoot directive** defines the directory path Apache uses to serve files for this host. For instance, entering "localhost" in the preceding activity displayed the index.html file in the directory defined by the DocumentRoot directive (`/srv/www/htdocs`).

- *Alias*—You can add an unlimited number of aliases. An alias maps URLs to file system locations other than DocumentRoot. The format is Alias *URL-path file/directory-path*. The *file*/directory path contains documents that are sent to the client. For example, if you have the alias Alias/sitepages/ftp/pub/sitepages, a request for *http://mysite/sitepages/about.html* results in the server returning the file /ftp/pub/sitepages/about.html.

- *ScriptAlias*—This setting is the same as Alias, but the files in the *file/* directory path are treated as applications that run on the server instead of documents sent to the client. In other words, instead of serving the about.html Web page, as in the previous example, you can run a script from the specified directory.

- *Include*—By default, there are two include directives that allow including other configuration files: /etc/apache2/conf.d/*.conf, which contains external modules, and /etc/apache2/conf.d/apache2-manual?conf, which contains manual configuration files.

- *Server Name*—It's the URL that users enter to reach your Web page.

- *Server Administrator E-Mail*—This setting specifies the Web server administrator's e-mail address.

Activity 10-3: Using the HTTP Server Wizard

Time Required: 15 minutes

Objective: Configure an Apache Web server with the HTTP Server Wizard.

Description: In this activity, you use the HTTP Server Wizard to configure an Apache Web server.

1. If the terminal window is still open, switch to the root user. If you don't have a terminal window open or if VMware Player isn't running, follow Step 1 in Activity 10-1.

2. Open the HTTP-Server module by typing **yast2 http-server** and pressing **Enter**. The HTTP Server Wizard starts, unless you've used this module before.

3. In the HTTP Server Wizard (1/5)--Network Device Selection window, the default HTTP port is 80, and there's no reason to change this setting. This window also contains firewall settings. The only way other computers can access your Web server is to have port 80 open in the server's firewall. Click the **Open Port in Firewall** check box, and then click **Next**.

4. In the HTTP Server Wizard (2/5)--Modules window, click the check boxes next to all the scripting languages, and then click **Next**.

5. In the HTTP Server Wizard (3/5)--Default Host window, compare the default settings with the list preceding this activity. Leave the default settings and click **Next**.

6. In the HTTP Server Wizard (4/5)--Virtual Hosts window, you can add virtual hosts, but you must make sure the hostname can be resolved on the network. If you're using the IP-based method, make sure only one host can be assigned to an IP address. Unless you have created a virtual host manually before starting this wizard, no virtual host will be listed. Leave the default settings, and click **Next**.

7. In the HTTP Server Wizard (5/5)--Summary window, you have the option to force Apache to start automatically when you boot your Linux machine or start the Apache

server manually each time your Linux machine boots. Click the **Start Apache2 Server When Booting** option button, and then click **Finish**.

8. Exit the root user by typing **exit** and pressing **Enter**. Leave the terminal window open and the virtual machine running for the next activity.

The next time you configure Apache Web Server with this wizard, you'll be in expert mode (see Figure 10-4), which enables you to adjust more settings than in the wizard. For instance, you can enable, disable, add, or remove Apache2 modules by clicking the Server Modules tab. You use the Main Host tab for configuring the default host and the Host tab for any virtual hosts.

Figure 10-4 Expert mode in the HTTP Server Wizard
Source: openSUSE

Manual Apache Configuration

You can configure an Apache Web server manually by editing configuration files in the /etc/apache2/ directory. Table 10-2 describes common configuration files stored in this directory.

After editing Apache configuration files, you must restart the apache2 service with the `rcapache2 reload` command.

Table 10-2 Apache configuration files

Configuration file	Description
charset.conv	Defines the character sets for each language. This file should not be changed.
default-server.conf	This global configurations file applies to all virtual hosts, but its information can be overwritten by editing virtual host configuration files. You can change the DocumentRoot directory, alias, include directives, and more.
errors.conf	Contains error response messages that can be modified for all virtual hosts.
httpd.conf	The main Apache configuration file is well documented and contains instructions for configuring an Apache Web server. It also contains many include statements for specifying on which IP addresses and ports Apache should listen and for loading certain modules.
listen.conf	Used to associate Apache with IP addresses and ports. For instance, you can use this file to define multiple virtual hosts that use only one NIC.
server-tuning.conf	Contains general configuration options for controlling Apache's performance. For instance, you can set directives that allow multiple requests per connection.
ssl-global.conf	This file contains instructions for serving Web pages over an HTTPS connection.
sysconfig.d/	This directory contains configuration files that are created automatically during startup when the /usr/sbin/rcapache2 start command is issued.
uid.conf	Defines which user and group ID Apache runs.
vhosts.d/	This directory contains virtual host configuration settings and template files that make creating virtual hosts easy.

Each configuration file contains well-documented directives that can be edited to fit your Web server needs.

Apache configuration files follow the same syntax: one directive per line and # symbols to indicate comments (see Figure 10-5), which are used to document configuration files. The apache2ctl -t command verifies that configuration files have no syntax errors, and it can be used only by the root user.

Activity 10-4: Using Apache Configuration Files

Time Required: 30 minutes

Objective: Explore common Apache configuration files.

Description: In this activity, you view Apache configuration files to find information such as the DocumentRoot directory and the contents of a virtual host template.

1. If the terminal window is still open, switch to the root user. If you don't have a terminal window open or if VMware Player isn't running, follow Step 1 in Activity 10-1.

```
#
# Global configuration that will be applicable for all virtual hosts, unless
# deleted here, or overriden elswhere.
#

DocumentRoot "/srv/www/htdocs"

#
# Configure the DocumentRoot
#
<Directory "/srv/www/htdocs/">
                                    # Possible values for the Options directive are "None", "All",
        # or any combination of:
        #   Indexes Includes FollowSymLinks SymLinksifOwnerMatch ExecCGI MultiViews
        #
        # Note that "MultiViews" must be named *explicitly* --- "Options All"
        # doesn't give it to you.
        #
        # The Options directive is both complicated and important.  Please see
        # http://httpd.apache.org/docs-2.2/mod/core.html#options
        # for more information.
Options None
                                    # AllowOverride controls what directives may be placed in .htaccess files.
        # It can be "All", "None", or any combination of the keywords:
        #   Options FileInfo AuthConfig Limit
AllowOverride None
                                    # Controls who can get stuff from this server.
Order allow,deny
 Allow from all
</Directory>
default-server.conf lines 1-31/104 27%
```

Figure 10-5 Contents of an Apache configuration file

Source: openSUSE

2. Display a long list of all Apache configuration files by typing **cd /etc/apache2; ls -l** and pressing **Enter**. You can enter these two commands on the same line by separating them with a semicolon.

3. View the `default-server.conf` file's contents by typing **less default-server.conf** and pressing **Enter**. Read the comments and directives, and write down the following information. When you're finished, type **q**.

   - DocumentRoot: _____

   - Alias: _____

   - ScriptAlias: _____

4. View the virtual host template's contents by typing **cd vhosts.d;less vhost.template** and pressing **Enter**. The first few comments explain the purpose of the virtual host template. When naming virtual host configuration files, what suffix must you add to the filename for it to load successfully? Type **q** to return to the command prompt when you're finished.

   _____

5. Change back to the `/etc/apache2` directory by typing **cd ..** and pressing **Enter**. Choose two other configuration files to examine. Configuration files have a lot of information that explains the purpose of directives. Make sure to read these comments to understand how configuration files affect an Apache Web server.

6. Leave the terminal window open and the virtual machine running for the next activity.

10

Virtual Hosts

As you've learned, you can use virtual hosts to support multiple Web sites on one physical server. This section explains virtual hosts in more detail and includes an activity for creating your own virtual host. By default, Apache is configured with a default host and no virtual host.

Apache supports **name-based virtual hosts** and **IP-based virtual hosts**. With name-based hosts, multiple Web sites share the same IP address, much like all members of a family sharing the same home phone number. To reach one member of a family, you'd call the home phone number and ask for a specific person by name. IP-based hosts have multiple IP addresses for a single machine. You can think of this setup as similar to running a business from your home. You might have one phone number designated for business and another number designated for personal use. You answer both phones but respond differently depending on which phone is ringing.

Name-Based Virtual Hosts You can create name-based virtual hosts by editing the `httpd.conf` file or with virtual host configuration files, which are included in the Apache configuration after you reboot the Apache server. In both methods, you must define the **NameVirtualHost directive**, which specifies the IP address to use for name-based virtual hosts. The following output shows an `httpd.conf` file that has been modified to support two virtual hosts:

```
NameVirtualHost 192.168.75.128

<VirtualHost 192.168.75.128>
    ServerName vhost1
    ServerAlias www.vhost1.com
    DocumentRoot /srv/www/htdocs
</VirtualHost>

<VirtualHost 192.168.75.128>
    ServerName manual
    DocumentRoot /usr/share/doc/manual/opensuse-manuals_en/manual
        <Directory "/usr/share/doc/manual/opensuse-manuals_en/manual">
        AllowOverride None
        Order allow,deny
        Allow from all
        </Directory>
    ServerAlias www.manual.com
</VirtualHost>
```

The **ServerName directive** specifies the name of the server, and Apache uses it to determine which virtual host is displayed. In the preceding example, the server name for the first virtual host is `vhost1`. All virtual hosts you create must have their server name resolved on the network. For instance, for the preceding example to work, there must be a Domain Name Service (DNS) entry stating that `vhost1` resolves to the 192.168.75.128 IP address. For testing purposes, you can add this entry in the `/etc/hosts` file (see Figure 10-6).

```
#
# hosts        This file describes a number of hostname-to-address
#              mappings for the TCP/IP subsystem.  It is mostly
#              used at boot time, when no name servers are running.
#              On small systems, this file can be used instead of a
#              "named" name server.
# Syntax:
#
# IP-Address  Full-Qualified-Hostname  Short-Hostname
#

127.0.0.1       localhost

192.168.75.128 vhost1 www.vhost1.com manual www.manual.com
~
                                                1,1          All
```

Figure 10-6 The `/etc/hosts` file
Source: openSUSE

You can use the **ServerAlias directive** to define multiple names for a virtual host. In the preceding example, the server name `vhost1` has the alias `www.vhost1.com`, and clients can enter this alias to access the Web page.

Most people type "www" before the Web address they're trying to reach, but usually all you have to type is the server name (such as google.com) to reach the Web page.

TIP

The **Order, Allow, and Deny directives** enable you to define which hosts can access files in a particular directory and which hosts can't. The Order directive tells Apache which filter (allow or deny) should be run first. In the preceding example, everyone is allowed access to the `/usr/share/doc/manual/opensuse-manuals_en/manual` directory.

Sometimes you need to restrict access to your Web site if attackers are trying to spam the Web server, for example. For more information on the Order, Allow, and Deny directives, go to *http://httpd. apache.org/docs/2.2/howto/access.html*.

NOTE

Another way to create virtual hosts is to create a virtual host configuration file in the `/etc/apache2/vhosts.d` directory. This file already contains a virtual host template (`vhost.template`) that you can copy and rename. A virtual host configuration file must have a `.conf` extension. For instance, a virtual host called `vhost1` must have `vhost1.conf` as the name of the configuration file. The advantage of using the `vhost.template` file is it contains a lot of directives you might not have thought about adding. For instance, it has the **ServerAdmin directive**, which lists the Apache administrator's e-mail account. The only directives you must change are ServerName, DocumentRoot, and Directory. The Directory directive applies only to the named file system directory and subdirectories and their contents; the DocumentRoot directory defines the directory path Apache uses to serve files for this host. After creating a virtual host configuration file, you must define the NameVirtualHost directive in the `/etc/apache2/listen.conf` file, as shown in Figure 10-7.

```
# Use name-based virtual hosting
#
# - on a specified address / port:
#
#NameVirtualHost 12.34.56.78:80
#
# - name-based virtual hosting:
#
#NameVirtualHost *:80
#
# - on all addresses and ports. This is your best bet when you are on
#   dynamically assigned IP addresses:
#
#NameVirtualHost *
```
`listen.conf lines 32-47/48 96%`

Figure 10-7 Defining the NameVirtualHost directive in the `listen.conf` file
Source: openSUSE

Activity 10-5: Creating Virtual Hosts

Time Required: 30 minutes

Objective: Use a template to create virtual Apache Web servers.

Description: In this activity, you define the NameVirtualHost directive in the `/etc/apache2/listen.conf` file, and then create two virtual Apache servers. The first virtual server will point to the default document root directory, and the second server will point to the openSUSE documentation files.

1. If the terminal window is still open, switch to the root user. If you don't have a terminal window open or if VMware Player isn't running, follow Step 1 in Activity 10-1.

2. Change to the directory holding Apache configuration files by typing **cd /etc/apache2** and pressing **Enter**.

3. Add the NameVirtualHost directive in the `listen.conf` file by opening this file in the vim editor, and then pressing **Shift+G** to move the cursor to the last line.

4. Enter insert mode, and then create a new line below the cursor by typing **o**. Type **NameVirtualHost *:80**, and then save and close the `listen.conf` file. The * symbol tells Apache that all your IP addresses are to be used for virtual hosts. The :80 tells Apache which port to listen on.

5. In the terminal window, change to the directory containing the Apache virtual host configuration files by typing **cd vhosts.d** and pressing **Enter**.

6. Copy the `vhost.template` file and rename it by typing **cp vhost.template vhost1.conf** and pressing **Enter**.

7. Change the ServerName, DocumentRoot, and Directory directives by opening `vhost1.conf` in the vim editor. Display line numbers so that you can find the correct directives easily. Find the ServerName directive (line 17), and replace **dummy-host.example.com** with **vhost1**. Find the DocumentRoot directive (line 22), and replace **/srv/www/vhosts/dummy-host.example.com** with **/srv/www/htdocs**.

Finally, find the Directory directive (line 93), and replace **/srv/www/vhosts/dummy-host.example.com** with **/srv/www/htdocs**. Save the file, and exit the vim editor.

8. Create another virtual host by using the procedure in Step 6 to copy `vhost.template` to a file called **manual.conf**.

9. In this step, you create a virtual host that serves the openSUSE documentation files when a client requests the server named "manual." Use the procedures in Step 7 to change the ServerName to **manual**, the DocumentRoot to **/usr/share/doc/manual/opensuse-manuals_en/manual**, and the Directory to **/usr/share/doc/manual/opensuse-manuals_en/manual**. When you're done, save the file, and exit the vim editor.

10. Add the two server names to the `/etc/hosts` file by opening this file in the vim editor. Find the loopback file IP address (127.0.0.1); next to it is the alias localhost. Add two more aliases to the right of localhost: **vhost1** and **manual**. The `/etc/hosts` entry should look like this:

        127.0.0.1   localhost vhost1 manual

11. Save and close the `/etc/hosts` file. Restart the Apache server by typing **rcapache2 reload** and pressing **Enter**.

12. Start Firefox, type **vhost1** in the address bar, and press **Enter**. What's displayed? Next, type **manual** in the address bar and press **Enter**. Now what's displayed?

_____

13. Exit Firefox. Exit the root user by typing **exit** and pressing **Enter**. Leave the terminal window open and the virtual machine running for the next activity.

10

Creating a Web Page

As mentioned, the DocumentRoot directive defines the directory Apache uses to serve Web pages to clients. If a client (typically a Web browser) requests a directory, Apache serves the `index.html` file in the directory defined by the DocumentRoot directive. You can tell that a directory rather than a file has been requested because the **Uniform Resource Locator (URL)**, which is an address to a resource on the Internet, ends with a forward slash (/), as shown in Figure 10-8.

Figure 10-8 A URL requesting a directory
Source: openSUSE

The `index.html` file is the main Web page that's served. In Apache, it has the following default content in HTML markup:

```
<html><body><h1>It works!</h1></body></html>
```

Before you create a Web page, you need to understand Hypertext Markup Language (HTML). **Hypertext** contains references or links to access other files or text. A **markup language** consists of instructions called **tags** that define how text is displayed. In the default index.html file, notice the tags <html>, </html>, <body>, </body>, <h1>, and </h1>. Like most tags, they're in pairs to indicate the start and end of text formatted with these instructions. The forward slash (/) indicates the ending tag. The index.html file is usually a simple one that contains only these three tags. Table 10-3 describes these tags and other common ones used in HTML.

 You don't have to place all HTML markup on one line. To make it easier to read, you can put each tag on a separate line, as shown in Figure 10-9.

```
<html>
<body>
<h1>It works!</h1>
</body>
</html>
~
~
:
```

Figure 10-9 Placing HTML tags on separate lines
Source: openSUSE

Table 10-3 Common HTML tags

HTML tag	Description
<html> </html>	Begins the HTML page. The <html> and </html> tags are considered the container holding all your HTML code.
<body> </body>	Contains the main content of an HTML page. Typically, these tags are placed between the <html> </html> tags.
<head> </head>	Encloses information about the HTML page, such as the page title.
<title> </title>	Defines the page title and is typically displayed in a Web browser's title bar, but it's not mandatory. For instance, the default index.html file doesn't have a <title> tag. Firefox displays "Mozilla Firefox" if there's no <title> tag.
<h1> </h1>	Specifies the content formatted as a level 1 heading, which is usually the heading in the largest size. There are six heading levels, with h6 being the smallest.
<b> </b>	Specifies content to be bolded.
<i> </i>	Specifies content to be italicized.
<u> </u>	Specifies content to be underlined.
<a> </a>	Specifies an anchor for creating a link to another document or creating a bookmark in a document. In other words, it's used to create a hyperlink to a URL.
 	Specifies a line break.

To create a Web page in openSUSE Linux, you must use a text editor. In this chapter, you use the vim editor to create a Web page and access it by clicking a link in `index.html`.

Activity 10-6: Creating Web Pages with HTML

Time Required: 30 minutes

Objective: Create a basic HTML Web page.

Description: In this activity, you use the vim editor to create an HTML Web page containing hyperlinks.

1. If the terminal window is still open, switch to the root user. If you don't have a terminal window open or if VMware Player isn't running, follow Step 1 in Activity 10-1.

2. Change to the directory designated to hold Web pages (DocumentRoot) by typing **cd /srv/www/htdocs** and pressing **Enter**. This is the default DocumentRoot directory. Explain how you can change the DocumentRoot directory:

_____

3. To create and edit a new HTML file, type **vim homepage.html** and press **Enter**.

4. Switch to insert mode by typing **i**. Type **<html>** and press **Enter**.

If you need a refresher on the vim editor, refer to Chapter 4.

5. Type **<head>** and press **Enter**.

6. Specify your name as the Web page title by typing **<title>***First_Name Last_Name***</title>** (substituting your own first and last names). When you're done, press **Enter**, and then type **</head>** and press **Enter**.

7. To start the body section, type **<body>** and press **Enter**.

8. Type **This is my Web page** and press **Enter**.

9. To allow users to click a link to get back to the `index.html` page, type **
Click <a href="index.html">here</a> to go back to the main page!** and press **Enter**. What would have happened if you had omitted the <br> tag?

_____

10. To end the body section, type **</body>** and press **Enter**.

11. Type **</html>**. Your HTML code should look like the following:

```
<html>
<head>
<title>your name</title>
</head>
```

```
<body>
This is my Web page
<br>Click <a href="index.html">here</a> to go back to the main page!
</body>
 </html>
```

12. Save the script by entering last line mode and typing **wq!**.

13. To edit the `index.html` file so that you can click a link to access the `homepage.html` file, type **vim index.html** and press **Enter**.

14. When the `index.html` file opens in vim, clean up the display to make it look like Figure 10-9, shown previously.

15. Display line numbers by typing **set nu** and pressing **Enter**.

16. Move the cursor to line 4, type **i** to switch to insert mode, and press **Enter**.

17. Move the cursor to line 4 and type **
Click <a href="homepage.html">here</a> to go to your Web page!** Now save the file, which should look like the following:

```
<html>
<body>
<h1>It works!</h1>
<br>Click <a href="homepage.html">here</a> to go to your Web page!
</body>
</html>
```

18. Test your Web page by starting Firefox and entering **localhost** in the address bar. You have two HTML files in the DocumentRoot directory. How does Apache know which HTML file to serve when you enter the URL?

_____

19. Exit the browser, close the terminal window, and power off your virtual machine.

Chapter Summary

- Apache Web Server is Web server software that can be downloaded free. It's also available with the latest version of openSUSE.

- The Apache software needs little to no configuration after installation.

- You can use the rcapache2 command to check the status of your Apache Web server as well as start, stop, and restart the server.

- HTTP-Server is a YaST application module for configuring Apache.

- Manual Apache configuration consists of modifying directives (instructions) in Apache configuration files.

- With virtual hosts in Apache Web Server, you can run multiple Web sites on one physical machine.

- Apache Web Server supports two types of virtual hosts: name-based virtual hosts and IP-based virtual hosts.

- A number of directives can be configured on an Apache Web server, including the mandatory DocumentRoot, Directory, and ServerName. DocumentRoot specifies the directory your Web pages are served from, Directory encloses a group of directives that apply to a specific directory, and ServerName sets the Web server's hostname.

Key Terms

default host The first declared virtual host in the Apache configuration file. *See also* virtual host.

directives Instructions embedded in Apache configuration files that tell Apache how to run.

DocumentRoot directive An Apache instruction that defines the directory path Apache uses to serve files for the host.

hypertext Text with references or links embedded that take users to other files or text.

IP-based virtual hosts Multiple IP addresses for a single machine.

markup language Consists of instructions called tags that define how text is displayed.

name-based virtual hosts Multiple Web sites sharing the same IP address.

NameVirtualHost directive An Apache instruction that specifies the IP address to use for name-based virtual hosts.

Order, Allow, and Deny directives An Apache instruction that defines which hosts can and can't access the files in a particular directory.

port An interface for connecting a hardware device, such as a disk drive or printer; in networking, a data connection established for communication between hosts.

ServerAdmin directive An Apache instruction that specifies the Apache administrator's e-mail account.

ServerAlias directive An Apache instruction that associates multiple names with a virtual host.

ServerName directive An Apache instruction that defines the server name and tells Apache which virtual host to display.

tags Instructions for formatting text in HTML. They come in pairs to indicate the start and end of text formatted with these instructions.

Uniform Resource Locator (URL) An address to a resource on the Internet.

virtual host An Apache feature that makes it possible to run multiple domains on one physical machine.

Web server A computer on the network with the primary role of serving Web pages to clients on request.

Review Questions

1. Apache Web Server is proprietary software, so you're prohibited from viewing or changing the source code. True or False?

2. Apache is packaged with openSUSE but isn't installed by default. True or False?

3. Which YaST application is used to install Apache?

   a. HTTP Server

   b. Software Repositories

   c. Software Management

   d. Network Services

4. Which software pattern installs Apache and other related modules?

   a. File and Web Server

   b. Miscellaneous Server

   c. Mail and News Server

   d. Web and LAMP Server

5. Which command do you use to restart an Apache Web server safely?

   a. `rcapache2 reload`

   b. `rcapache2 reboot`

   c. `rcapache2 start`

   d. Both a and b

6. Which command do you use to check the status of an Apache Web server?

   a. `rcapache2 help`

   b. `rcapache2 status`

   c. `rcapache2 reload`

   d. `rcapache2 probe`

7. Which YaST application can you use to configure an Apache Web server?

   a. HTTP Server

   b. Software Repositories

   c. Software Management

   d. Network Services

8. After configuring an Apache Web server with the HTTP Server application, you must restart the server with the `rcapache2` command. True or False?

9. Running more than one domain on a physical machine isn't possible. True or False?

10. Which directive defines the directory path that Apache uses to serve files?

   a. ServerName

   b. DocumentRoot

   c. Alias

   d. NameVirtualHost

11. Which directive specifies the IP address for name-based virtual hosts?

    a. ServerName

    b. DocumentRoot

    c. Alias

    d. NameVirtualHost

12. Which directive defines the URL users can use to reach a Web page?

    a. ServerName

    b. DocumentRoot

    c. Alias

    d. NameVirtualHost

13. The `httpd.conf` Apache Web server configuration file contains which of the following directives? (Choose all that apply.)

    a. DocumentRoot

    b. Alias

    c. Hosts

    d. Include

14. Which Apache configuration file is a global configuration file that applies to all virtual hosts?

    a. `default-server.conf`

    b. `listen.conf`

    c. `httpd.conf`

    d. `vhosts.d`

15. Which Apache configuration file do you use to associate an Apache Web server with specific IP addresses and ports?

    a. `default-server.conf`

    b. `listen.conf`

    c. `httpd.conf`

    d. `vhosts.d`

16. What command do you use to verify that configuration files have no syntax errors?

17. Explain the difference between name-based virtual hosts and IP-based virtual hosts.

18. What type of language is HTML?

    a. Scripting

    b. Markup

    c. Interpreted

    d. Compiled

10

19. Which of the following is a tag commonly found in an HTML file? (Choose all that apply.)

    a. <HTML>

    b. <BODY>

    c. <HEAD>

    d. <URL>

20. What are instructions that define how text is displayed in a Web browser?

    a. Tags

    b. XML

    c. HTML

    d. Hypertext

Case Projects

CASE PROJECTS

Case Project 10-1: Creating an Apache Web Server Alias

Joey Grizzle is an IT supervisor responsible for the corporate network and the Apache Web server. The company's main office is in Toccoa, Georgia. After reviewing log files and reports from the help desk, he realizes that a few employees can't access the Web server because they're entering the wrong URL. It's a local intranet site, and the only server name that resolves on the network is ToccoaSales. Joey speaks with the IT technician responsible for the DNS server and asks her to create an entry that allows resolving the name *www.toccoasales.com* to the Apache Web server's IP address. He then asks whether you can make sure both *www.toccoasales.com* and ToccoaSales can be used to display the same intranet Web page. Write a brief report explaining how to configure Apache so that the two server names respond by serving the same Web page.

Case Project 10-2: Creating Virtual Hosts

You're a help desk technician assigned to a corporate network. You arrive at work early and decide to review all the open tickets to see whether you can close any jobs quickly. You find a ticket from a shift supervisor, Ivan Smith, who has requested a new server capable of hosting a small office Web site. Another help desk technician had written on the ticket "Waiting for the budget office to approve purchase of a new server." You know the corporate Web site is hosted on an Apache Web server. Explain how Ivan Smith can get a Web site for his office without buying a new server.

## chapter 11

Domain Name System

After reading this chapter and completing the exercises, you will be able to:

- Describe Domain Name System and how it relates to the Internet
- Install and configure Berkeley Internet Name Daemon (BIND)
- Check the status of a DNS server via the command line
- Identify zones and describe the elements in a zone file
- Explain how the different types of resource records affect zones

In this chapter, you learn how to turn your openSUSE Linux system into a DNS server. First, you see how networks managed resolving hostnames to IP addresses before Domain Name System was introduced. You also learn basic DNS concepts, such as name servers, forwarders, and caching, as well as top-level domains, nodes, and domain names. Next, you install BIND, which is the DNS server software, and configure a DNS server with the YaST DNS module. You also see how to use the command line to check the status of a DNS server.

Introduction to Domain Name System

In the past, computers on the Internet relied on an address book containing host tables. These tables were text files that stored all the names and IP addresses of hosts on the Internet. Whenever a new computer was added to the Internet, the host table had to be updated for all computers.

You can imagine the results when multiple computers were added to the Internet daily. For this reason, name servers were created. A **name server** is a central database that translates names to IP addresses (or IP addresses to names). It simplified network management dramatically because network administrators had to update only one server instead of updating the host table on every resource on the Internet. With a name server on your network, all you needed to know to communicate with a resource was the name server's IP address and the resource name. This method worked for local networks, but new problems emerged when dealing with resources on the Internet. For instance, if every computer on the Internet had resource information (also known as a **resource record**) stored on one name server, you can imagine how difficult it would be to sift through these records to find the one resource you're looking for. Management also becomes a problem. To manage the Internet, it's important to know which entity is responsible for which information. To address these problems, Domain Name System was developed.

DNS on the Internet

The Internet's **Domain Name System (DNS)** follows the name server concept but on a much larger scale. DNS associates an IP address, such as 204.21.112.110, with an actual name, such as server1, so that network resources can be accessed by easy-to-remember names instead of a string of numbers, which isn't as easy to remember. In Linux, a name server known as **Berkeley Internet Name Daemon (BIND)** usually carries out this translation. BIND is open-source software containing the DNS protocols needed to resolve hostnames to IP addresses.

The goal of DNS is to decentralize administration, so DNS is a distributed and hierarchical database that allows controlling DNS management locally. The local DNS server can handle cached hostname requests but doesn't contain information on every hostname on the Internet; instead, it forwards requests for unknown hostnames to a **forwarder**, which is a type of DNS server. The forwarder's job is to handle off-site requests generated at the system known as "localhost." For instance, if you're trying to access *google.com* for the first time, the DNS server on your localhost doesn't know the IP address of *google.com*, so it can't request the Web page from that server. Instead, your local DNS server queries the forwarder, which sends your request to a public DNS server and then caches the information (*google.com*'s IP address) at the localhost for a specified period, known as time to live (TTL, discussed later in "DNS Zones"). The TTL varies, but the default value is typically 86400 seconds, or 1 day. **Caching** is a feature that stores DNS queries on the local site for fast hostname–to–IP address resolution. The idea is to cache IP information locally to save query time when a particular site is accessed regularly.

The Internet Engineering Task Force (IETF) published RFC 1034 on DNS. It's available at *www.ietf.org/rfc/rfc1034.txt.*

Although local administrators can manage local DNS servers, centrally controlled public DNS servers known as root DNS servers are still in use. **Root DNS servers** control the Internet's top-level domains (TLDs). This type of distributed authority over parts of DNS is what makes the huge DNS database a possibility. Table 11-1 describes some of the most recognizable top-level domains.

Table 11-1 **Common top-level domains**

Top-level domain	Description
.com	Commercial organizations, such as *Google.com* and *Apple.com.*
.edu	Educational organizations, such as Virginia College (*vc.edu*) or Bellevue University (*bellevue.edu*).
.gov	Government organizations, such as the FBI (*fbi.gov*) or the CIA (*cia.gov*).
.mil	Military organizations, such as the Air Force (*af.mil*) and the Army (*army.mil*).
.net	Networking organizations, such as Internet providers (for example, AT&T at *att.net*). No real governing body controls how this domain is used, so you see a lot of Web sites under the .net domain that should be .com.
.org	Noncommercial or nonprofit organizations, such as the California Republican Party (*cagop.org*) or the Democratic Party (*democrats.org*).

In addition to the top-level domains shown in Table 11-1, the International Organization for Standardization (ISO) defines another set of TLDs consisting of two-letter codes for countries—for example, .us for the United States and .fr for France.

The DNS database (shown in Figure 11-1) is structured as an inverted tree (also known as the domain namespace), with root at the top of the tree and TLDs beneath it. The nodes (leaves) of the tree are called domains and have labels, such as .gov for the U.S. government domain. Although you can't manage or control the entire DNS database, you can have control over (manage) your domain.

A person or an organization manages each node in the domain name tree. The Internet Corporation for Assigned Names and Numbers (ICANN, *www.icann.org*) controls the root domain at the top of the tree.

Domain names are derived from the node labels, and each level of the hierarchy is separated by dots in the domain name. For instance, the domain name for a host computer at a particular school might be computer1.university.edu. The hostname is computer1, and it belongs to the university domain. The university domain is a subdomain of .edu, which is a TLD.

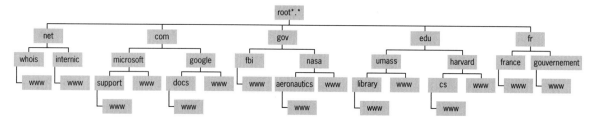

Figure 11-1 The DNS structure
© Cengage Learning 2013

Installing BIND

Installing BIND is similar to installing Apache Web Server. You use YaST Software Management to install the DHCP and DNS Server pattern, which installs all the necessary DNS modules, such as BIND, BIND documentation files, and the DNS Server Configuration utility.

 The DHCP and DNS Server Pattern also installs important Dynamic Host Configuration Protocol (DHCP) modules, which are used to assign network settings automatically instead of configuring them manually on each machine.

The BIND documentation files are in the `/usr/share/doc/packages/bind/arm/` directory and consist of eight chapters. The documentation for DNS administrators provides basic information about BIND version 9, the version included with openSUSE 11.2. In Activity 11-1, you install BIND and access the documentation files.

Activity 11-1: Installing BIND

Time Required: 15 minutes

Objective: Install BIND and other DNS-related packages.

Description: In this activity, you use YaST Software Management to install DNS packages in the DHCP and DNS Server pattern. After installing BIND, you use Firefox to display the BIND 9 Administrator Reference Manual.

1. Start VMware Player and start an openSUSE virtual machine.

2. Open a terminal window. Switch to the root user by typing **su** and pressing **Enter**, and then entering the correct root password.

3. Open the YaST Control Center by typing **yast --gtk** and pressing **Enter**.

4. Open YaST Software Management by clicking **Software** on the left under Groups, and then clicking **Software Management**.

5. To show all available packages categorized by pattern, click the **Filter** list arrow, and then click **Patterns**. Make sure the **Available** option button is selected.

6. Click **DHCP and DNS Server** under Server Functions, and click **Install All** to install BIND with other packages, such as the DNS Server Configuration utility and the BIND documentation files. Finally, click **Apply**.

7. After the installation is finished, close the YaST Control Center.

8. Query the RPM database for BIND by typing **rpm -q bind** and pressing **Enter**.

9. Open the BIND 9 Administrator Reference Manual in Firefox by changing to the `/usr/share/doc/packages/bind/arm` directory, typing **firefox Bv9ARM.html**, and pressing **Enter**. Read the Introduction and Scope of Document sections to get an overview of the content in this manual.

10. Close your Web browser. Stay logged in as root, and leave the terminal window open and the virtual machine running for the next activity.

Configuring BIND

In openSUSE, BIND requires no further configuration after you install it. It runs as a daemon known as named (pronounced "name-dee," not "named"). The main BIND DNS configuration file, `named.conf`, is in the `/etc` directory. To start the named daemon (BIND), you use the `rcnamed start` command. Table 11-2 describes common commands for determining this daemon's status.

11

Table 11-2 Common named commands

Command	Description
rcnamed start	Start the named daemon; can also use /etc/rc.d/named start
rcnamed stop	Stop the named daemon; can also use /etc/rc.d/named stop
rcnamed restart	Restart the named daemon; can also use /etc/rc.d/named restart
rcnamed status	Check the status of the named daemon; can also use /etc/rc.d/named status

You can edit the `named.conf` file with a text editor, such as vim, or use the YaST DNS module, which is available after you install BIND. To start this module, you use the `yast2 dns-server` command, which requires root privileges. The first time you start the module, you're prompted with the setup wizard shown in Figure 11-2, which enables you to add forwarders. After you step through the basic settings, you have access to expert mode for more advanced configuration tasks.

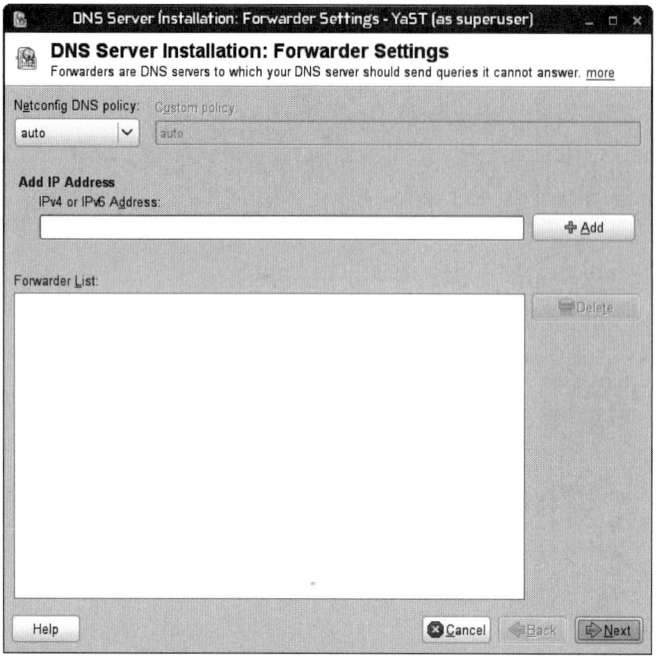

Figure 11-2 The DNS Server Installation Wizard
Source: Domain Name System

Forwarder

You can have up to three forwarders in your DNS configuration. These servers enable you to forward unresolved queries to an off-site DNS server and then cache the results on your local DNS server. The first time you configure a DNS server, the forwarder list is empty because the forwarder declaration in the /etc/named.conf file is, by default, a commented line, as shown:

```
#forwarders { 192.0.2.1; 192.0.2.2; };
```

Deleting the # symbol at the beginning of the line adds the two servers (192.0.2.1 and 192.0.2.2 in the preceding example) to the forwarder list. The DNS administrator must make sure IP addresses in the forwarder list are correct, so the default IP addresses should be removed and replaced with the IP address of your ISP's name server. If you're working with the YaST DNS module, you can use it to add the forwarding server's IP address.

DNS Zones

The DNS namespace is divided into units called **zones** that describe portions of a domain. The data for each zone is stored in a **zone file**, a text file in the /var/lib/named directory on the name server. There are several different types of zones, but the two most common are master name servers and slave name servers. The **master name server** is an authoritative name server that stores the primary copies of zone records. The Linux administrator can modify these records when changes are made to the zone. A **slave name server**, also known as a secondary name server, gets its zone information from the master name server, but it's considered an authoritative server, too. It maintains a copy of the master zone file that's used as a backup and provides redundancy if the master name server is unavailable. In essence, if the master name server becomes unavailable, the slave takes over as the authoritative server. The master name server can be configured to update the slave name server's zone files when changes are made to the master zone file through a zone transfer. The following example displays data for a zone file called `example.com`:

The line numbers are used here to make identifying parts of the zone file easier. They're not actually in the zone file.

```
1. $TTL 2d
2. @     IN SOA server1.example.com.     root.server1.example.com. (
3.       2012021003        ; serial
4.       3h                ; refresh
5.       1h                ; retry
6.       1w                ; expiry
7.       1d )              ; minimum
8. example.com.    IN NS    server1.example.com.
```

The following list explains entries in the zone file:

- *Line 1*—The **time-to-live** (**TTL**) entry is at the start of the zone file. TTL is the amount of time a DNS server caches a resource record. In the example, cached records in the `example.com` zone expire after two days (`2d`). TTL is usually measured in seconds, so you might see two days as `172800 s` (seconds). Other possible time values include `m` for minutes, `h` for hours, and `w` for weeks.

- *Line 2*—The **Start of Authority** (**SOA**) resource record contains basic information about the zone. This mandatory record is considered the most important in the zone file because it defines the zone's global parameters. The "IN" before SOA specifies the address class as Internet. The @ symbol indicates that zone information is extracted from the entry in the `/etc/named.conf` file, and `server1.example.com` is the name server's name. In the preceding example, `example.com` is the master zone because it contains the zone's resource information.

The period at the end of the server name defines the end of the DNS tree; without it, the SOA's domain is appended to the hostname in the record. For instance, `server1.example.com` (without the ending period) is actually `server1.example.com.example.com`.

The last part of Line 2 is the e-mail address of the root user assigned to administer the name server. Most e-mail addresses use the @ symbol, but this symbol already has a use in a zone file, so a period is used instead (`root.server1.example.com.`). The open parenthesis at the end of Line 2 indicates that all lines up to the closed parenthesis in line 7 are included in the SOA record.

- *Line 3*—The serial number is a 10-digit number in the format *YYYYMMDDNN*. The first eight numbers are the date the zone was created; the example's serial number, 2012021003, indicates that the zone file was created February 10, 2012. The last two digits change each time information in the zone file changes. Slave name servers refer to these two digits to determine whether a change has been made.

11

- *Line 4*—The refresh rate specifies how often slave name servers check the serial number to see whether the zone file has changed. In the example, the 3h represents 3 hours.

- *Line 5*—If an error happens, such as a system clock not being synchronized correctly, the retry rate specifies when the slave name server will try to contact the master name server again. In the example, the 1h represents 1 hour.

- *Line 6*—The expiration entry specifies how long the slave name server keeps cached data if it hasn't been able to contact the master name server. In the example, the 1w means the slave name server discards cached data after one week.

- *Line 7*—The negative TTL entry defines how long the DNS server caches the fact that a domain doesn't exist. Storing domain information that doesn't exist is called "negative caching," so the time this information is cached is referred to as "negative TTL." For instance, if you try to reach badhost.example.com and are unsuccessful, the slave name server returns an error until the time specified in this entry has elapsed, and then tries to reach the host again. In the example, the 1d means the negative TTL is set to one day.

- *Line 8*—This entry contains the NS resource record, which defines the name server in charge of the domain. In the example, it's server1.example.com.; however, you could type just server1 because example.com. is added to the end of the name automatically. Other resource records (RRs) can be entered in this line, as described in the following sections.

MX RR The MX RR identifies mail servers (mail exchangers) for a zone. Table 11-3 describes fields in the MX RR, using the following entry as an example:

```
example.com.    IN    MX    2    mailserver1.example.com.
```

Table 11-3 MX resource record fields

Field	Example	Description
Name	example.com.	The name field should be the same as the SOA name field. If you leave this entry blank, example.com. is added to the name field automatically. To make the name a fully qualified domain name, a period must be added at the end of the name. Resource records are organized in the DNS server based on FQDNs, which are domain names that specify all levels in a domain. In the MX record, it specifies the domain name of the e-mail address.
Class	IN	This field identifies the address class, which is Internet (IN) in the example. All resource records using Internet DNS have IN specified in this field.
RR	MX	Identifies the type of resource record (MX for mail server, in this example).
Priority	2	Defines the mail server's preference, meaning the order in which it's tried. The lower the priority number, the higher the server's preference, so the server with the lowest priority number is tried first. If an attempt is unsuccessful, the next server in priority order is tried until delivery of e-mail is successful.
Mail server name	mailserver1.example.com.	Identifies the preferred mail server for the domain. The MX record identifies the mail server for a domain, which means you must also have an A resource record for the IPv4 address to handle the hostname–to–IP address mapping. The A resource record is explained in the next section.

A RR The A (address) RR is the most common resource record. It's used to resolve a hostname to an IPv4 address for locating a resource. Table 11-4 describes fields in the A RR, using the following entry as an example:

```
mailserver1          IN A          192.168.75.150
```

Table 11-4 A resource record

Field	Example	Description
Name	`mailserver1`	Specifies the name of the A resource record. You can write it in FQDN format (`mailserver1.example.com.`), but doing so isn't necessary because all names that aren't fully qualified have `example.com.` appended to the name.
Class	`IN`	This field identifies the address class (Internet, in this example).
RR	`A`	Identifies the type of resource record. In this example, it's an A, which defines the hostname–to–IP address mapping.
IPv4 address	`192.168.75.150`	Specifies that the host mailserver1 has the IPv4 address 192.168.75.150. All NS RRs and MX RRs defined in this domain must have an A RR defining the IPv4 address to the host.

PTR RR The PTR (pointer) RR is used to resolve an IPv4 address to its hostname, so it performs the reverse of what an A RR does. Table 11-5 describes fields in the PTR RR, using the following entry as an example:

```
150.75.168.192.in-addr.arpa.    IN PTR     mailserver1.example.com.
```

Table 11-5 PTR resource record

Field	Example	Description
Name	`150.75.168.192.in-addr.arpa.`	The opposite of an A record; resolves IP addresses to hostnames. In the example, 150 is the host address of this Class C network, so typing 150 in the `named.conf` zone file appends `75.168.192.in-addr.arpa.` automatically. The `in-addr.arpa.` portion is considered a special domain, used when creating reverse DNS lookups.
Class	`IN`	This field identifies the address class (Internet, in this example).
RR	`PTR`	Identifies the type of resource record. In this example, it's a PTR, which defines the IPv4 address for a host.
Name	`mailserver1.example.com.`	Specifies that the IP address 192.168.75.150 resolves to the hostname mailserver1.example.com.

11

CNAME RR The CNAME (canonical name) RR enables you to create an alias for a host. This is important when you're running different services with the same domain name. For example, to access the FTP server at *cengage.com*, the alias is *ftp.cengage.com*. Table 11-6 describes fields in the CNAME RR, using the following entry as an example:

```
mail      IN CNAME          mailserver1.example.com.
```

Table 11-6 CNAME resource record

Field	Example	Description
Name	`mail`	It's the alias for the actual hostname (`mailserver1.example.com.`).
Class	`IN`	This field identifies the address class (Internet, in this example).
RR	`CNAME`	Identifies the type of resource record. In this example, it's a CNAME, which gives an alias for a hostname.
Real-hostname	`mailserver1.example.com.`	Specifies the actual hostname.

Expert Configuration Mode

The final window in the DNS Server Installation Wizard gives you an option to open the DNS port in your firewall and start the DNS server automatically at bootup. After you have completed this wizard, whenever you open the DNS module, you're in expert configuration mode. The following sections describe the options available in each window of the DNS module.

Start-Up Figure 11-3 shows the Start-Up window. The first setting specifies whether DNS starts automatically when the server starts or must be started manually. You can also configure firewall settings, such as opening the firewall port to allow remote computers to access the DNS service. You can use this window to stop, start, and reload the DNS server, too.

Figure 11-3 The Start-Up window

Source: Domain Name System

Forwarders The Forwarders window is used for the same task as in the DNS Server Installation Wizard: adding IP addresses to the list of forwarder servers.

Basic Options The Basic Options window in Figure 11-4 displays the options that have already been defined for the zone. You can use this window or edit the /etc/named.conf file to add options. If you use this window, the information is updated in the /etc/named.conf file automatically. Table 11-7 describes the options that can be added or modified.

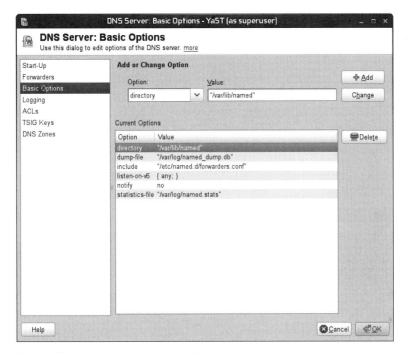

Figure 11-4 The Basic Options window
Source: Domain Name System

11

Table 11-7 Settings in the Basic Options window

Options	Example	Description
directory	directory "/var/lib/named";	This defines the name server's directory (enclosed in quotation marks). By default, openSUSE specifies /var/lib/named as the name server's working directory. This directory holds zone files.
dump-file	dump-file "/var/log/named_dump.db";	This option defines the directory (enclosed in quotation marks) where BIND writes dump and statistics files to the log subdirectory. Dump files store the current DNS cache.
zone-statistics	zone-statistics no;	This option defines whether zone statistics are retained. The default is no. You can view zone statistics with the rndc stats command.

Table 11-7 Settings in the Basic Options window (*continued*)

Options	Example	Description
listen-on-v6	`listen-on-v6 { any; }`	This option tells BIND to listen for IPv6 queries.
statistics-file	`"/var/log/named.stats"`	This option specifies the absolute path (enclosed in quotation marks) to and the filename for the statistics file after the `rndc stats` command is issued.
notify	`no`	Notification messages are sent to other name servers when zone data is changed.
include	`"/etc/named.d/forwarders.conf"`	This option writes the IP address of your ISP's DNS server to the file.

Logging You use the Logging window (see Figure 11-5) to configure logging options for the DNS server. By default, the DNS server sends log data to the systemwide log file /var/log/messages. You can leave the default options by selecting the System Log option button or specify a different file by selecting File. If you specify another file, you must enter a filename, the maximum file size in megabytes, and the maximum number of log file versions to store.

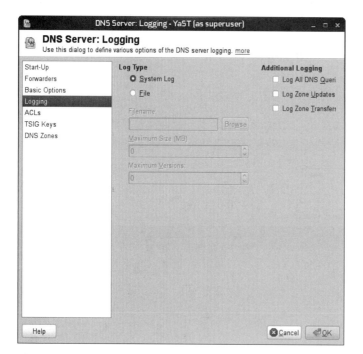

Figure 11-5 The Logging window
Source: Domain Name System

In the Additional Logging section, selecting the Log All DNS Queries option does exactly that: It logs all DNS queries. With this option enabled, the log file grows rapidly, so use this option only for short periods and for debugging purposes. The Log Zone Updates option is used to log data traffic during zone updates between DHCP and DNS. The final option, Log Zone Transfers, is used to log data traffic during a zone transfer from master name server to slave name server.

Access Control List (ACL) BIND administrators use the Access Control List (ACL) window to control who can perform operations on the name server. When creating an ACL, you must give it a unique name and specify an IP address under the Value heading. The IP address must be enclosed by braces and end with a semicolon, as shown:

```
{ 204.21.112.24; }
```

TSIG Keys Transaction signatures are used to secure communication between two servers (usually between DHCP and DNS servers). You can generate keys for this signature in the TSIG Keys window or with the `dnssec-keygen` command.

Review the man pages for the `dnssec-keygen` command to see more information on options you can use.

The DNS Zones window is the final one in the DNS module's expert configuration mode. It's the same as the second window in the DNS Server Installation Wizard.

Activity 11-2: Configuring BIND

11

Time Required: 25 minutes

Objective: Review settings in the `/etc/named.conf` file and configure a BIND server with the DNS Server Installation Wizard.

Description: In this activity, you explore some default settings, and then configure a BIND server with the DNS Server Installation Wizard.

1. If necessary, start VMware Player and start an openSUSE virtual machine. Open a terminal window. Switch to the root user by typing **su** and pressing **Enter**, and then entering the correct root password.

2. To view the `/etc/named.conf` file, type **less /etc/named.conf** and press **Enter**. Write down the values for the directory, dump-file, statistics-file, and listen-on-v6 options:

    _____

    _____

3. Press **q** to quit the file and return to the command prompt. Start the DNS Server Installation Wizard by typing **yast2 dns-server** and pressing **Enter**.

4. In the Forwarder Settings window, click the **Help** button and read the documentation file. When you're finished, close the help file. Don't add a forwarder at this time; instead, click **Next**.

5. In the DNS Zones window, click the **Help** button at the lower left and read the documentation file. Close this file when you're finished reading. Create a master zone by typing **example.com** in the Name text box (if necessary), clicking the **Type** list arrow, and clicking **Master**, if necessary. Click the **Add** button to add this entry to the Configured DNS Zones list box, and then click **Next**.

The IETF has reserved the *example.com* name for testing and documentation purposes.

6. In the Finish Wizard window, click the **Help** button, read the documentation file, and then close this file when you're finished reading. Open the port in the firewall by clicking the **Open Port in Firewall** check box. Make sure the DNS server starts automatically when you start your Linux system by clicking the **On: Start Now and When Booting** option button.

7. Click **Finish**. You're returned to the command prompt. Make sure the BIND service is running by typing **rcnamed status** and pressing **Enter**.

8. Stay logged in as root, and leave the terminal window open and the virtual machine running for the next activity.

Activity 11-3: Creating a Resource Record in YaST

Time Required: 15 minutes

Objective: Use the YaST DNS Server module to create a resource record.

Description: In this activity, you create an A resource record by using the YaST DNS Server module.

1. If necessary, start VMware Player, start an openSUSE virtual machine, and open a terminal window. Switch to the root user by typing **su** and pressing **Enter**, and then entering the correct root password.

2. Start the DNS Server Installation Wizard by typing **yast2 dns-server** and pressing **Enter**.

3. Click **DNS Zones**, the **example.com** master zone, and **Edit**. In the Zone Editor window, click the **Records** tab.

4. Type **mailserver1** in the Record Key text box and the IP address **192.168.75.150** in the Value text box. Leave the default setting **A: IPv4 Domain Name Translation** in the Type text box.

5. Click the **Add** button, and then click **OK** twice to return to the command prompt.

6. Move to the master directory by typing **cd /var/lib/named/master** and pressing **Enter**. To view the master zone file, type **less example.com** and press **Enter**. The A resource record has been added to the bottom of the file, as shown in Figure 11-6.

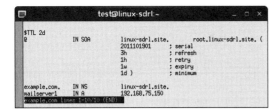

Figure 11-6 An A resource record added to the master zone file
Source: Domain Name System

7. Exit the root user, close the terminal window, and power off the virtual machine.

Chapter Summary

- Domain Name System (DNS) is used to translate domain names and hostnames to IP addresses. The goal of DNS is to decentralize administration.

- BIND is open-source DNS server software that serves as a central database for translating hostnames to IP addresses.

- DNS is a distributed and hierarchical database that allows controlling DNS management locally.

- Local DNS sites can forward DNS queries to a forwarder DNS server, which actually forwards the request to an off-site DNS server.

- The DNS structure is viewed as an inverted tree, with the root DNS server at the top and the top-level domains beneath it.

- The main DNS configuration file is the named.conf file in the /etc directory.

- The YaST DNS module is included with the DNS installation and is used to configure DNS servers.

- A DNS zone file is a text file that stores resource records and other data for a zone.

- In expert configuration mode for the YaST DNS module, you can configure forwarders, assign basic options, configure DNS logging, set up access control lists, and configure transaction signature keys for secure communication.

Key Terms

Berkeley Internet Name Daemon (BIND) Open-source software that contains all DNS protocols needed to resolve hostnames to IP addresses.

caching A DNS feature that stores DNS queries on the local site for fast hostname–to–IP address resolution.

Domain Name System (DNS) A distributed and hierarchical database that allows controlling DNS management on the local site and is used to translate hostnames to IP addresses.

forwarder A type of DNS server that forwards unknown DNS requests generated on the local site to an off-site DNS server.

master name server An authoritative name server that stores primary copies of zone records.

name server A central database that translates hostnames to IP addresses (or IP addresses to hostnames).

resource record A file containing resource information or characteristics about a zone or domain.

root DNS servers DNS servers that control the top-level domains (TLDs) of the Internet.

slave name server An authoritative name server that receives its zone information from the master name server. *See also* master name server.

Start of Authority (SOA) A mandatory resource record in a zone file that contains basic information about the zone. *See also* resource record.

time-to live (TTL) The amount of time a DNS server caches a resource record. *See also* resource record.

zone file A text file that stores DNS zone data.

zones Portions of the domain namespace.

Review Questions

1. Which of the following is the Linux DNS software?

   a. BIND

   b. Apache

   c. Domain Name System

   d. YaST DNS module

2. DNS is managed centrally by a major entity at the root level. True or False?

3. The local DNS server doesn't contain information on every hostname on the Internet. True or False?

4. What type of DNS server sends unknown DNS requests to an off-site DNS server?

   a. Caching server

   b. Forwarder server

   c. Master server

   d. Slave server

5. What DNS feature stores DNS queries on the local site?

   a. TLD (top-level domain)

   b. Forwarder

   c. TTL (time-to-live)

   d. Caching

6. What DNS servers control top-level domains on the Internet?

   a. Master servers

   b. Root DNS servers

   c. Slave servers

   d. Caching servers

7. Describe four top-level domains.

8. Which of the following is the daemon that BIND runs on?

   a. name.d

   b. DNS

   c. named

   d. `named.conf`

9. Which command should you use if you want to stop and start a DNS server? (Choose all that apply.)

   a. `/etc/rc.d/named restart`

   b. `rcnamed stop`

   c. `rcnamed restart`

   d. `/etc/rc.d/named start`

10. Which command should you use if you want to check the status of a DNS server? (Choose all that apply.)

    a. `rcnamed start`

    b. `/etc/rc.d/named status`

    c. `rcnamed restart`

    d. `rcnamed status`

11. What's the main BIND configuration file?

    a. Zone record

    b. YaST DNS module

    c. `name.d`

    d. `named.conf`

12. What command should you use on an openSUSE DNS server if you want to start the YaST DNS module?

    a. `yast2 dns-server`

    b. `yast dns-module`

    c. `yast2 dns-module`

    d. `yast dns-server`

11

13. Which of the following names is used for text files that store the data in each DNS unit?

   a. DNS records

   b. Zone files

   c. Resource records

   d. PTR resource records

14. Explain the purpose of the TTL field.

15. Which resource record is considered mandatory and contains basic information about the zone?

   a. SOA

   b. CNAME

   c. A

   d. PTR

16. Which resource record translates IPv4 addresses to hostnames?

   a. SOA

   b. CNAME

   c. A

   d. PTR

17. Which of the following fields is contained in an A resource record? (Choose all that apply.)

   a. Class

   b. Priority

   c. RR

   d. Real hostname

18. Which resource record enables you to create an alias of an existing host?

   a. SOA

   b. CNAME

   c. A

   d. PTR

19. Describe three basic options you can set when configuring a DNS server.

Case Projects

CASE PROJECTS

Case Project 11-1: Discovering the Domain Name Process

Conduct research to find out how to register a domain on the Internet, and then answer the following questions:

- How much does it cost to register a fully qualified domain name on the Internet?

- How would you go about registering an .edu domain?

- What's the procedure for registering a domain name?

Case Project 11-2: Finding Available Domain Names

In the past couple of years, East Coast Career College has grown quickly and is ready to expand its campus and start an online campus. The president has asked you to come up with four fully qualified domain names that are available on the Internet. He doesn't want an .edu domain name and wants the names to be easy to remember and relevant to the college. He has asked you to have the four names and a brief explanation of why you chose each name on his desk by the end of the week. Research the Web to search for available domain names that meet the president's requirements, and write a memo to the president explaining why you chose these domain names.

11

chapter 12

Configuring a Mail Server

After reading this chapter and completing the exercises, you will be able to:

- Identify key elements in the Linux e-mail architecture
- Describe how MTAs and MUAs are used in the Linux mail system
- Configure a mail server in YaST

249

The most widely used service on the Internet is e-mail, so knowing how to configure an e-mail server is an important part of a Linux administrator's job. In this chapter, you learn about the modular e-mail architecture in Linux and the role of mail transfer agents and mail user agents. You also get hands-on practice using the mailx program to send e-mails via the command line. Finally, you learn how to configure your Linux mail server with the Mail Server Configuration Wizard.

Introduction to the Linux Mail System

E-mail predates the Internet. No one person or organization is responsible for the e-mail technology used today; instead, it has evolved along with the Internet. In the past, research organizations used terminals on a time-sharing computer to exchange real-time text messages. Today, e-mail is the most widely used Internet service. It's based on standard protocols for sending, storing, and receiving electronic messages. OpenSUSE includes sophisticated e-mail programs, such as Evolution and KMail.

The U.S. Postal Service announced in its annual financial report that more than 212 billion pieces of mail were delivered in 2009. Compare these numbers with a recent survey by the Radicati Group (*www.radicati.com*), which reported that 55 billion e-mails (not including spam) are sent every day.

In the Linux environment, e-mail is modular, meaning a separate program is used to manage each function. Figure 12-1 shows the modular architecture of e-mail in Linux.

In this figure, notice the two main types of programs typically used on a Linux e-mail server:

- *Mail transfer agent*—A **mail transfer agent** (MTA) is a program for receiving and delivering messages via Simple Mail Transfer Protocol. In Linux, the MTA is often Postfix or sendmail; in Microsoft, an example is Microsoft Exchange Server.

- *Mail user agent*—A **mail user agent** (MUA) is an e-mail program that enables users to access their mailboxes for reading and sending electronic messages. Evolution, KMail, and the command-line utility mail are examples of MUAs.

Imagine you're an openSUSE Linux user on the example.com domain and want to send an e-mail to a user on the example.net domain. First, you open an e-mail program (the MUA in Figure 12-1), such as Evolution or KMail, draft a message, and specify the recipient's e-mail address in the To line. After you click Send, your message travels via Simple Mail Transfer Protocol to the MTA program on your local mail server. **Simple Mail Transfer Protocol (SMTP)** is the TCP/IP protocol that defines how e-mail is sent across the network.

The default MTA in openSUSE is Postfix. When the MTA receives the message from the MUA, it determines whether the message is intended for a recipient on the local domain or a recipient on another domain. If it's on the local domain (example.com), the MTA saves the message in the local machine's message store until the recipient reads it. For a recipient on another domain, the MTA sends the message via SMTP to a remote MTA.

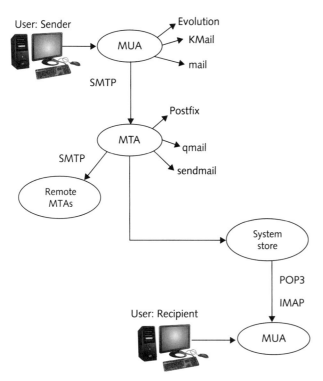

Figure 12-1 The Linux e-mail architecture
© Cengage Learning 2013

Mail Transfer Agents

An MTA is the actual mail server. It's responsible for receiving e-mails from local users and forwarding them to a local message store or a remote MTA. Messages are transferred from the local message store to users via the mail delivery agent (MDA), using Post Office Protocol (POP3) or Internet Message Access Protocol (IMAP). At first glance, the process of sending a message from one user to another seems simple; however, it becomes more complex with messages sent to remote users. For example, the process of an MTA sending messages not belonging to the local domain to a remote MTA isn't automatic. Your domain's DNS settings must be configured correctly so that the MTA can establish a connection with the remote MTA. For instance, the mail server must have an A record pointing to the remote MTA's IP address, an MX record for the local domain that points to the mail server, and a PTR record to support reverse lookups.

To review DNS entries, refer to Chapter 11.

Sendmail Sendmail is the most widely used MTA on UNIX/Linux systems, but it's not the preferred MTA on openSUSE Linux systems. Postfix is the preferred MTA because of its ease of configuration, reliability, and security. If the only function you need is sending e-mails to employees in the same domain, it needs little configuration. However, in most organizations, employees need to send e-mail to many other domains. You can edit the sendmail configuration file to change the MTA behavior to allow multiple domains and to set rules, such as message filters. Because sendmail performs all MTA functions, it's a large program compared with other mail programs.

The source code for sendmail is maintained at *www.sendmail.org*.

Qmail The qmail program, written by Dan Bernstein, is a fast, modular MTA designed to be lightweight, secure, and reliable. Unlike sendmail, qmail was designed with security and ease of use in mind, which makes it easier to configure (such as allowing multiple domains). Multiple modules, each no bigger than 30 KB, handle qmail's MTA functions.

The official Web site for qmail is *http://cr.yp.to/qmail.html*.

Postfix Postfix, developed by Wietse Venema, is the default MTA package on openSUSE Linux systems. Like qmail, it was designed as a modular MTA that's easier to configure as well as more reliable and secure than sendmail. Its modular design enhances security because each module has its own set of permissions to follow the guideline of least privileges.

For more information on Postfix, visit *www.postfix.org*.

Mail User Agents

An MUA is an e-mail program that enables users to send and read messages stored in their mailboxes. In the Linux e-mail system, each user has a local mailbox, and local MTAs send messages to users' mailboxes. The MUA doesn't actually receive messages; instead, it allows users to read messages that have already been placed in mailboxes.

MUAs can store messages in one of two ways. One method is storing them on users' computers instead of on the mail server, which frees up space on the server. For instance, the MTA places e-mails in your mailbox, and you access them by using the MUA. After you access messages, they're stored on your computer, meaning you can't access them on a different computer. With the second method, messages are stored on the mail server, and users can access them from any computer on the local domain. An example is a Web-based MUA, such as Gmail, in which e-mail is accessed from the mail server via a Web client. To free up space on the mail server, users should delete unwanted e-mails or transfer them manually to their computers. Table 12-1 describes four MUA packages included with openSUSE. All these packages can use both methods of storing messages.

Table 12-1 Common openSUSE Linux MUAs

MUA	Description
mailx	A text-based MUA that enables users to access their mailboxes for reading stored messages and sending e-mails to other users.
fetchmail	A text-based MUA that downloads e-mails from an ISP's mail server and places them in users' mailboxes. This program is more suitable for home users or small companies that host e-mail on a server not directly connected to their network. You can set up fetchmail to check the mail server periodically for e-mail by using intervals, which are specified in seconds. It was originally designed for dial-up users.
KMail	A graphical e-mail client for KDE that's compatible with major Internet mail standards.
Evolution	A graphical e-mail client for GNOME designed to help users with office tasks, such as storing, organizing, and retrieving personal information.

Using Mailx The following example shows how to use mailx. The line numbers have been added just for readability:

```
1. mail jeff
2. Subject: Test E-mail
3. This is a test e-mail sent to myself.
4. .
5. EOT
```

The `mail` command is in the `/usr/bin` directory and is linked to the `mailx` command, so you can use other commands to start the mailx program.

In the example, the user sends an e-mail to his own mailbox simply by adding his username after the `mail` command. To send e-mails to users on the same local mail server, you can use this same method; however, if you want to send e-mails to users on another server or network, you must use their full e-mail addresses. In line 2, the mailx program enters interactive mode and prompts you for a subject line and, in line 3, for the content of your message. The period entered in line 4, followed by pressing Enter or Ctrl+D, exits interactive mode and sends the message. The EOT on line 5 stands for "end of transmission."

After you send an e-mail, the message goes to the MTA for processing. The MTA determines whether the message is destined for a mailbox on the local server or should be sent to a remote MTA for delivery.

The following example shows using mailx to read messages in your mailbox:

```
1. mail
2. Heirloom mailx version 12.2 01/07/07. Type ? for help.
3. "/var/spool/mail/jeff": 1 message 1 new
4. >N 1 jeff@server1. Wed Aug 11 19:36   18/623   Test E-mail
5. ? 1
```

12

```
 6. Message  1:
 7. From jeff@server1.site Wed Aug 11 19:36:06 2012
 8. X-Original-To: jeff
 9. Delivered-To: jeff@server1.site
10. Date: Wed, 11 Aug 2012 19:36:06 -0400
11. To: jeff@server1.site
12. Subject: Test E-mail
13. User-Agent: Heirloom mailx 12.2 01/07/07
14. MIME-Version: 1.0
15. Content-Type: text/plain; charset=us-ascii
16. Content-Transfer-Encoding: 7bit
17. From: jeff@server1.site (Jeff Wallace)
18.
19. This is a test e-mail.
20.
21. ?
```

Using the `mail` command with no arguments displays all messages in your mailbox, as shown in line 4; there's only one message in this mailbox. The question mark in line 5 is an interaction prompt, meaning mailx is waiting for you to enter a command. In the example, the user pressed 1 to display the first e-mail. Table 12-2 describes common commands that can be entered at the interactive prompt.

 After you view a message in your mailbox, the message is written to the mbox file in your home directory. You can view messages in this file by using the `mail -f` command.

Table 12-2 Common mailx commands

Command	Description
type	Displays the first available message. You can add a number as an argument at the end to display a specific message. For instance, if you have two e-mails in your mailbox, the command `type 2` displays the second message.
next	Displays the next message in your mailbox.
from	Displays the message header, which contains information such as the sender's name, date and time the message was sent, and subject of the message.
headers	Displays message headers for all messages; the header contains information such as the sender's name, date and time the message was sent, and subject of the message.
r	Allows you to reply to the sender.
delete	Deletes the previously viewed message. You can add a number at the end to delete a specific message.
q	Quits the mailx prompt. Typing `quit` or `exit` works, too.
list	Displays all commands that can be issued at the interactive prompt.

Activity 12-1: Using the Mailx Program

Time Required: 25 minutes

Objective: Send and display e-mails with the mailx program.

Description: In this activity, you create a new user and send this user a test e-mail with the mailx program. You then log in to the new user account, check the mailbox, reply to the test e-mail, and display this message from your original user account.

1. Start VMware Player and start an openSUSE virtual machine.

2. Open a terminal window and switch to the root user by typing **su,** pressing **Enter,** and entering the root password.

3. Use the skills you learned in Chapter 7 to create a user account named **user1.** Make sure user1 has a home directory and a login password set. (*Hint:* If you need help, refer to the man pages for the useradd and passwd commands.)

4. Exit the root user account by typing **exit** and pressing **Enter.**

5. To start the mailx program, type **mail user1** and press **Enter.** When mailx prompts you with "Subject," type **First E-mail** and press **Enter.** On the next line, type **This is the first e-mail message in Activity 12-1.** and press **Enter.**

6. Type a period (.) and press **Enter** or **Ctrl+D** to exit mailx and send your message.

7. Log out of openSUSE by clicking the computer icon at the lower left and then clicking **Logout.** In the Log Out of the Session window, click the **Log Out** option.

8. When the openSUSE user login window opens, click **user1** and enter the password you created in Step 3.

9. Open a terminal window, and check your mailbox by typing **mail** and pressing **Enter.** What do you see?

_____

10. Display the header for all messages by typing **headers** and pressing **Enter.**

11. View the message by typing **type,** adding the correct number of the message, and pressing **Enter.**

12. To reply to the sender, type **r** and press **Enter.**

13. Type a short message, and then exit mailx by typing **.** (a period) and pressing **Enter** or **Ctrl+D.**

14. Log out of user1 and log back in with your own user account. Start mailx, and then display the new message.

15. Exit mailx by typing **q.** Try to view the message again with the mail command. Were you able to view the message? Why or why not?

_____

_____

16. Display saved messages in your mbox file by typing **mail -f** and pressing **Enter.** Exit mailx and power off the virtual machine, but leave the terminal window open and VMware Player running for the next activity.

12

Mail Server Configuration

Understanding how MTAs and MUAs work is useful when you're learning how to configure a Linux mail server. The configuration procedures differ depending on the Linux distribution. With openSUSE Linux, you can use a mail server configuration utility in the YaST Control Center to perform the following configuration tasks, among others:

- Enable virus scanning.
- Define the type of network connection the MTA uses to determine how e-mail is delivered.
- Configure an outbound mail server that's used if you have a dial-up connection or aren't connected to the Internet.
- Define the masquerade name for outgoing e-mail. This setting is useful for companies that prefer using a more professional name than the actual mail server name (which is the default setting).
- Configure incoming mail options, such as firewall settings, the root mailbox account, whether to accept mail from remote servers, local alias accounts, and virtual domains.

The Mail Server Configuration Wizard

The root user can start the Mail Server Configuration Wizard with the `yast2 mail` command. The following sections describe the steps in this wizard.

General Settings The General Settings window (see Figure 12-2) is where you specify the network connection type, which determines how the MTA delivers messages. The default option is "Permanent." Selecting this option allows Postfix (the MTA) to send messages in real time as they're created.

The first time you start this wizard, you're asked what type of configuration to use. You can choose Standard or Advanced. Standard is selected by default and is the option you use in this chapter's activities.

The dial-up option is for Linux machines that connect to the Internet via a dial-up connection. This option forces users to queue the outbound mail server manually when they're ready to send or receive messages. For instance, if you want to e-mail a user on a remote computer, you must use the `sendmail -q` command after sending your message.

The default MTA in openSUSE is Postfix; however, you still use a sendmail command to queue the outbound mail server because the MTA executable is actually called "sendmail."

The "No connection" option is for Linux machines that don't have access to the Internet. Users with this option can e-mail each other only on local machines because Postfix has no means to reach remote MTAs. You can also use this window to enable virus scanning with the AMaViS program (stands for A Mail Virus Scanner). If you don't have AMaViS installed on your machine, it's installed for you automatically when you select this option.

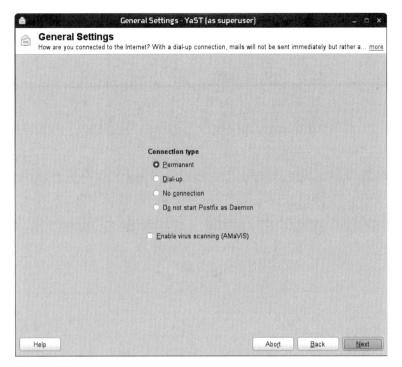

Figure 12-2 The General Settings window
Source: openSUSE

For more information on the open-source AMaViS, see *www.amavis.org*.

Outgoing Mail The Outgoing Mail window shown in Figure 12-3 is used to configure dial-up connections by adding your ISP's SMTP server, such as smtp.provider.com, and then clicking the Authentication button to enter authentication credentials. MTAs can send messages to remote MTAs, so if your mail server is connected to the Internet, you can leave the outgoing mail server entry blank.

When you send e-mails, your full computer name is used in the name field. For instance, if your computer name is linux-001 and your username is John, your e-mails display john@linux-001.example.com as the sender. Most companies prefer to have the organization name displayed, however. To do this, you can click the Masquerading button and set a display name for each user on the network.

Incoming Mail The Incoming Mail window shown in Figure 12-4 is used to set several options. For example, you must specify whether remote SMTP connections should be accepted. If your computer isn't directly connected to the Internet or you have a dial-up connection, this check box is disabled, and you can only send local e-mail or connect to remote MTAs manually when you're online. If you're connected to the Internet directly, select this

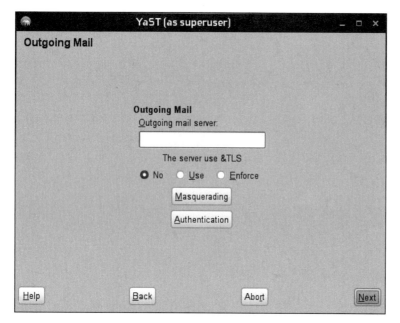

Figure 12-3 The Outgoing Mail window
Source: openSUSE

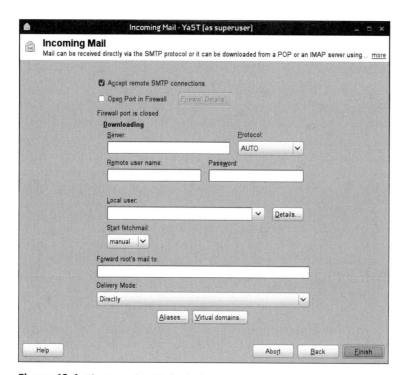

Figure 12-4 The Incoming Mail window
Source: openSUSE

option so that Postfix can listen for remote SMTP connections. If you select this option, you must configure firewall settings. By default, the firewall doesn't allow SMTP connections, so you need to select the Open Port in Firewall check box.

Small companies often host e-mail on a server that isn't connected directly to their networks, such as a mail server provided by an ISP, and use fetchmail to download mail from the remote server. If you're using this method, enter the remote server's credentials in the Downloading section. The following protocols can be used to transfer e-mail from a remote MTA:

- *POP3*—**Post Office Protocol 3 (POP3)** is the standard client/server protocol for receiving e-mail. When you receive e-mail, an Internet server stores it until you or the mail server download it via POP3.

- *IMAP*—**Internet Message Access Protocol (IMAP)** is another standard client/server protocol for receiving e-mail from an Internet server. IMAP has more options than POP3 for storing e-mails on a server and organizing e-mails in folders.

The root user account has full access to all Linux machines on a network. Logging in to the mail server as a regular user with limited permissions is recommended unless you're performing a task that requires root permissions. The problem with logging in as a regular user instead of root is you might miss important system e-mails that are e-mailed to the root user account automatically. However, you can redirect system e-mails to your regular user account by entering your username in the "Forward root's mail to" text box.

Near the bottom of the Incoming Mail window is the Delivery Mode drop-down list containing the following options:

- *Directly*—Postfix uses this default option to deliver e-mail directly to your mailbox.

- *Through procmail*—The Linux utility **procmail** helps you filter and sort incoming e-mail. You can have the MTA transfer inbound e-mail to procmail for delivery.

- *To Cyrus IMAP Server*—**Cyrus** is a type of IMAP server designed to handle increased demands, such as adding thousands of mail accounts. You can learn more about the Cyrus Project at *http://cyrusimap.web.cmu.edu/*.

At the bottom are two buttons: Aliases, used for redirecting e-mail to a different local user or a list of local users, and Virtual domains, used to create an alias for your domain name. If you selected the masquerading option in the Outgoing Mail window, you should configure a domain alias. For instance, if you specified the masqueraded display name john@example.com instead of john@linux-001.example.com, you need to create a virtual domain called example.com.

Activity 12-2: Configuring a Mail Server

Time Required: 90 minutes

Objective: Configure a mail server to send e-mail from a user on one computer to a user on another computer.

Description: In this activity, you create two virtual machines to use as a mail server and a DNS server. You create a domain, an A record for each virtual machine, and an MX record pointing to the mail server. Finally, you configure the mail settings on both servers and send a test message from a user on the DNS server to a user on the mail server.

1. Start VMware Player, if necessary. Create an openSUSE Linux virtual machine with the default settings and name it **openSUSE-Mail Server**. (*Hint*: If necessary, refer to Chapter 2 for the procedure to create virtual machines.)

2. Log in to your new virtual machine. If necessary, open a terminal window, switch to the root user, and start the DNS module by typing **yast2 dns** and pressing **Enter**.

3. Type **mail** in the Hostname text box, **site** in the Domain Name text box, and **site** under the Domain Search text box. Click **Finish** at the lower right.

4. Switch to the root user account, if necessary, and type **ifconfig -a** and press **Enter**. Write down the IP address, and power off the virtual machine.

5. Start VMware Player, if necessary. Create another openSUSE Linux virtual machine with the default settings and name it **openSUSE-DNS Server**. Use the skills you learned in Chapter 11 to install the DHCP and DNS server pattern. Type **rcnamed status** and press **Enter** to verify that the server has started. If the server isn't running, start it by typing **rcnamed start** and pressing **Enter**.

6. Follow the procedure in Steps 2 and 3, but change the hostname to **dns**.

7. To configure the DNS server, switch to the root user account and open a terminal window, if necessary, and then type **yast2 dns-server** and press **Enter**.

8. In the Forwarder Settings window (see Figure 12-5), click **Next**. Type **site** in the Name text box and click the **Add** button. In the Configured DNS Zones section, click **site**, and then click the **Edit** button.

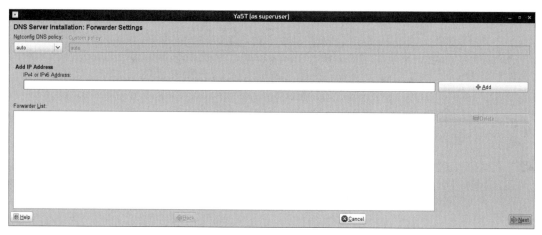

Figure 12-5 The Forwarder Settings window

9. Click the **NS Records** tab, type **dns** in the Name Server to Add text box, and then click **Add**.

10. To add an A record for the DNS server, click the **Records** tab, type **dns** in the Record Key text box, and type the DNS server's IP address in the Value text box. Click **Add**.

11. To create an A record for the mail server, type **mail** in the Record Key text box, and then type the IP address you wrote down in Step 4 in the Value text box. Click **Add**.

12. To create an MX record, type **mail** in the Record Key text box, and then click the **Type** list arrow and click **MX: Mail Relay**. Change the priority to **10**, type **mail** in the Value text box, click **Add**, and then click **OK**.

13. To add a reverse lookup zone, type the first three octets (in reverse order) of your IP address followed by **.in-addr.arpa** in the Name text box. (For example, if your IP address is 192.168.152.130, you enter "152.168.192.in-addr.arpa.") Click **Add**.

14. Select the reverse lookup zone in the Configured DNS Zones text box and click **Edit**.

15. Click the **Automatically Generate Records From** check box, and then click the **NS Records** tab. Type the last octet of your IP address and click **Add**. Click **OK** and then **Next**. Click the **Open Port in Firewall** check box, and then click **Finish**. Make sure your DNS server starts now and when your system boots.

16. Leave the DNS server running. Start VMware Player, if necessary, and then start the openSUSE-Mail Server virtual machine. Open a terminal window and switch to the root user. Next, you add the DNS server's IP address. Start the DNS module by typing **yast2 dns** and pressing **Enter**. Type the DNS server's IP address in the Name Server 1 text box and **site** in the Domain Search text box. Click **Finish**.

17. While both the DNS server and mail server virtual machines are running, make sure DNS is working by typing **nslookup mail** (on the mail server) and **nslookup dns** (on the DNS server) and pressing **Enter**. What results are displayed onscreen?

_____

18. Now that the DNS server is set up, it's time to configure mail settings on both servers. On the mail server virtual machine, switch to the root user account, if necessary. Type **yast2 mail** and press **Enter**.

19. In the welcome window of the Mail Server Configuration Wizard, leave the **Standard** option selected, and then click **Next**.

20. In the General Settings window, click the **Permanent** option button, and then click **Next**.

21. In the Outgoing Mail window, leave the default settings and click **Next**.

22. In the Incoming Mail window, click the **Accept remote SMTP connections** check box, click the **Open Port in Firewall** check box, and then click **Finish**.

23. On both virtual machines, make sure the SMTP firewall ports are open by typing **yast2 firewall** and pressing **Enter**. Back in the wizard, click **Allowed Services** on the left to see whether SMTP with Postfix is an allowed service. If it's not, click the **Service to Allow** list arrow, click **SMTP with Postfix**, and then click **Add**. Click **Next** and then **Finish**.

24. Send a test e-mail from a user on the DNS server to a user on the mail server by typing **mail** *user*@**mail** (replacing *user* with your username) and pressing **Enter**. Type a subject line and a short message. Start the mail server virtual machine, if necessary, and view the message by typing **mail** and pressing **Enter**.

25. Log out and power off both virtual machines.

12

Chapter Summary

- E-mail is based on standard protocols for sending, storing, and receiving electronic messages.

- The mail transfer agent delivers messages between systems via Simple Mail Transfer Protocol, and the mail user agent is the mail application users run to access their mailboxes and send and receive e-mail.

- SMTP is the standard protocol for sending e-mail across a network.

- Although sendmail is the most widely used MTA on Linux systems, Postfix is the preferred MTA in openSUSE because of its ease of configuration, reliability, and security.

- Qmail is a modular MTA designed to be more secure and faster than sendmail.

- KMail and Evolution are the two graphical MUAs included with openSUSE. Mailx is a command-line MUA that enables users on a Linux machine to send and receive e-mails. Fetchmail is another text-based MUA that downloads e-mail from remote mail servers at specified intervals.

- You can configure general settings, outgoing mail, and incoming mail for an openSUSE mail server with the YaST Mail Server Configuration Wizard.

- POP3 is the standard client/server protocol for receiving e-mail.

- IMAP is another client/server protocol for receiving e-mail but includes more options for storing e-mail on a server and organizing e-mail.

- Procmail is a Linux utility that helps you filter and sort incoming e-mail. Cyrus is a type of IMAP server designed to handle increased mail demands.

Key Terms

Cyrus A type of IMAP server designed to handle increased mail demands. *See also* Internet Message Access Protocol (IMAP).

Internet Message Access Protocol (IMAP) An advanced client/server protocol for receiving e-mail from a server; includes options for storing and organizing e-mails on the server.

mail transfer agent (MTA) A program for sending and receiving messages between systems via SMTP. *See also* Simple Mail Transfer Protocol (SMTP).

mail user agent (MUA) An e-mail application that users run to access their mailboxes and send and receive e-mail.

Post Office Protocol 3 (POP3) A standard client/server protocol for receiving e-mail.

procmail A Linux utility used for filtering and sorting incoming e-mail.

Simple Mail Transfer Protocol (SMTP) The TCP/IP protocol that defines how e-mail is sent across a network.

Review Questions

1. Which of the following is the Linux e-mail application for users?

   a. MUA

   b. MTA

   c. MDA

   d. SMTP

2. Which of the following uses SMTP to send and receive e-mail on a network?

   a. MUA

   b. MTA

   c. MDA

   d. POP3

3. Which of the following defines how e-mail is sent across the network?

   a. MUA

   b. MTA

   c. MDA

   d. SMTP

4. Which of the following is an MTA? (Choose all that apply.)

   a. Sendmail

   b. Qmail

   c. KMail

   d. Evolution

5. Which of the following is responsible for receiving e-mails from local users and forwarding them to the local message store or remote MTAs?

   a. MUA

   b. MTA

   c. SMTP

   d. Mailx

6. Which of the following is an MTA package? (Choose all that apply.)

   a. Sendmail

   b. Qmail

   c. Mailx

   d. Postfix

12

7. Sendmail is a modular MTA designed to be secure and fast. True or False?

8. MUAs enable users to read messages that are already in their mailbox. True or False?

9. Describe how fetchmail differs from mailx.

10. What's the difference between KMail and Evolution?

11. Which mailx command option do you use to reply to a message?

    a. from

    b. r

    c. next

    d. q

12. Which option do you use with the `mail` command to view an `mbox` file?

    a. f

    b. r

    c. a

    d. q

13. Which mailx command do you use to quit the mailx prompt? (Choose all that apply.)

    a. q

    b. bye

    c. exit

    d. x

14. Describe the configuration tasks you can perform with the Mail Server Configuration Wizard.

15. What command do you use if you have a dial-up connection and want to e-mail a user on a remote computer?

16. Users who don't have access to the Internet can still send e-mails to other users on their machines. True or False?

17. Which standard client/server protocol is used for receiving mail and has options for storing e-mails on the server and organizing mail in folders?

    a. SMTP

    b. TCP/IP

    c. IMAP

    d. HTTP

18. Which Linux utility is used to filter and sort incoming e-mail?

    a. Procmail

    b. Cyrus

    c. POP3

    d. IMAP

19. Which server is designed to handle increased demands, such as thousands of added mail accounts?

    a. Procmail

    b. Cyrus

    c. POP3

    d. IMAP

Case Projects

CASE PROJECTS

Case Project 12-1: The Fight Against Spam

The speed and ease of e-mail make it possible for anonymous e-mails to shower mail servers with useless junk mail called spam, which is estimated to cost companies more than $700 per employee each year. As a Linux administrator, it's your job to prevent spam from showing up in your users' mailboxes. As a first step, research three open-source antispam programs that are compatible with Linux. Write a report describing these programs, and explain why you chose the one you did for your company.

12

## chapter 13

Working with the Network File System

After reading this chapter and completing the exercises, you will be able to:

- Describe the Network File System
- Export and import file systems with YaST system modules
- Identify key NFS services
- Edit NFS configuration files to export and import network file systems manually

In this chapter, you learn about the Linux Network File System (NFS), which is used to give client machines access to files on a remote machine over the network. You learn how to export directories by using the YaST NFS Server Configuration module and how to control access to the NFS server. You also learn about the NFS client role and how to import directories in YaST. Next, you learn about Remote Procedure Calls (RPC) and the importance of key RPC services. Finally, you see how to export and import file systems manually by editing NFS configuration files.

An Overview of the Network File System

The purpose of a network is to share resources, which is more cost effective than having to install resources on every computer in an organization. By sharing resources, several employees can connect to one printer, for example, and commonly accessed files can be stored centrally on a **file server**, which is a network system where files are stored and shared.

The Linux OS manages the tasks of sharing resources centrally quite effectively. The **Network File System (NFS)** is a distributed file system protocol for allowing remote access to shared resources across networks. With NFS, you can mount shared file systems on remote machines. **Mount** is the term for making files appear as though they're on a local machine instead of on a remote machine, which is similar to drive mapping in Windows.

The original version of NFS, created by Sun Microsystems, was used for experimental purposes. NFSv4 is the version used in openSUSE Linux.

For more information on NFS, read RFC 3530 at *http://tools.ietf.org/html/rfc3530*.

Setting up a file server in openSUSE Linux has the following advantages:

- *Central location*—Files are placed in a single location, so multiple people can access and collaborate on the same files. Another benefit of files being centrally located is that you have to back up only one system instead of backing up data on every computer in the network. In addition, files can be accessed from any computer on the network.

- *Increased security*—Instead of distributing data to all computers and then controlling access, you can define who is allowed to access data from the file server. Users can also be given different levels of permissions as needed, which helps maintain data security. NFSv4 has added security features that require clients and servers to support certain security standards.

- *Remote access*—All clients, Windows and Linux, can access files mounted on the file server without needing to know where they're stored or the method by which they're made available. Files appear to users as though they're on their local machines.

Exporting and Importing File Systems

Exporting and importing file systems are important components of Linux file sharing. Exporting a file system enables users to distribute file systems over the network, and importing a file system makes it possible for users to mount file systems on other hosts. The following sections cover both these tasks in detail.

Exporting File Systems in YaST

An **NFS server** is a Linux network computer that exports directories to all networked hosts that have access to it. The software for configuring a host as an NFS server isn't installed in openSUSE by default. Like the Apache Web Server and DNS Server packages, you must install it manually. To do this, you start YaST and select Software Management. When the Software Management module opens, type `nfs server` for the search term and then click Apply. Activity 13-1 walks you through installing the NFS Server software on an openSUSE Linux machine. After this installation, you can configure the NFS server by using the YaST NFS Server module, which you open with the `yast2 nfs-server` command. The first window you see is the NFS Server Configuration window, shown in Figure 13-1.

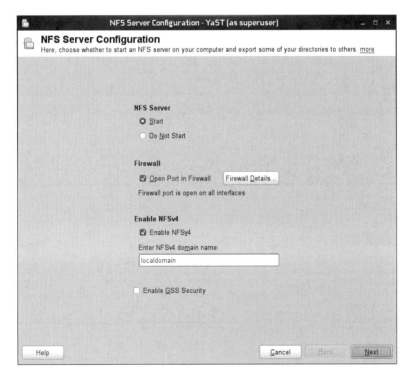

Figure 13-1 The NFS Server Configuration window
Source: openSUSE

If you decide not to start the NFS server at this time, the wizard ends with this window. You can also use this window to open the necessary port in the firewall (port 2049 for NFS) so that remote computers can use NFS services. If the NFS server needs to handle NFSv4 clients, you should select the Enable NFSv4 option. If you don't know the domain name, you can leave the default "localdomain" entry.

Clicking Next takes you to the Directories to Export window (see Figure 13-2). The section at the top lists directories to export and bindmount targets (used to mount a file system in another location and have it accessible from both locations), and the section at the bottom lists the hosts allowed to mount the directory selected at the top.

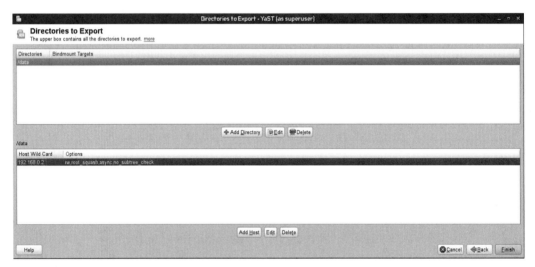

Figure 13-2 The Directories to Export window
Source: openSUSE

When you click Add Directory in this window, you're prompted to enter information for the host wildcard and other options (see Figure 13-3). You can enter the information in the following list in the Host Wild Card text box.

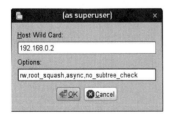

Figure 13-3 Entering options for the added directory
Source: openSUSE

For more information on these options, review the man pages for the `exports` command.

- *Asterisk (*)*—An asterisk represents all hosts on a network, so enter this character if you want every computer on your network to have access to the NFS directory.

- *Single host*—Entering a single hostname allows users on the specified host to have access to the NFS directory.

- *Netgroups*—You can enter a Network Information Service (NIS) netgroup name to control access to the NFS directory. You must have an NIS server set up to use this option.

- *IP networks*—Entering an IP address and netmask pair enables you to export directories to all hosts on an IP network. For instance, if you want every host on the 192.168.152 network to have access, you can enter 192.168.152.0/255.255.255.0 (which can also be written as 192.168.152.0/24 because 24 bits are used in the network address).

The Options text box contains the following options by default:

- ro—This option specifies that all hosts with access to the NFS directory have just read-only permission to view files and directories.

- root_squash—This option maps the root user to the "nobody" user, which means the root user on the client machine doesn't have root privileges on the NFS server.

- sync—This option ensures that data is written to the disk before the server replies to requests.

- no_subtree_check—This option disables **subtree checking**, which is the process the NFS server uses to check whether a requested file is in the exported subdirectory. For instance, if you export a subdirectory but don't export the entire file system, the NFS server performs a subtree check. Disabling subtree checking speeds up transfers if the entire volume is exported.

Table 13-1 describes some common options that aren't included in the default configuration.

Table 13-1 Common NFS options

Option	Description
rw	Used to grant read and write permissions, which allows NFS clients to add, delete, or change information in the NFS directory.
no_root_squash	This option doesn't map the root user to the nobody user, so the root user on the client has root privileges on the NFS server, too.
async	Allows the server to reply to requests before changes have been made. This option improves performance but at the cost of stability; if data isn't committed to storage, a server crash could lead to data loss or corruption.

13

Importing File Systems in YaST

The YaST NFS Client module is installed by default in openSUSE. Authorized users can mount NFS directories in their local file structure and access the resources as though they're local. To open the NFS Client module, you issue the yast2 nfs-client command as the root user. The NFS Client Configuration window shown in Figure 13-4 is displayed.

Figure 13-4 The NFS Client Configuration window
Source: openSUSE

This window has two tabs: NFS Shares and NFS Settings. The NFS Shares tab displays all directories that have been exported from a remote NFS server and mounted locally. The NFS Client module uses the `/etc/fstab` configuration file to fill in information in the NFS Settings tab. (You learn more about the `/etc/fstab` file later in "Importing File Systems Manually.") After you click the Add button, the window shown in Figure 13-5 is displayed, where you enter the information in the following list.

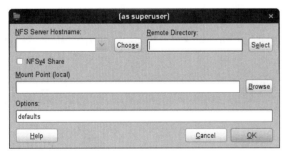

Figure 13-5 Configuring additional settings for the NFS client
Source: openSUSE

- *NFS Server Hostname*—Type the NFS server's hostname, or click the Choose button to browse through a list of servers on the network.

- *Remote Directory*—Enter the absolute path to the exported directory configured on the NFS server, or click the Select button to choose from a list of exported directories.

- *Mount Point (local)*—A **mount point** is typically an empty directory on a local file system that's used as a logical space to mount another file system. Enter a local directory as the mount point, or click the Browse button to select a directory. Directories in the /mnt directory are typically used as mount points.

- *Options*—Notice in Figure 13-5 that the Options text box contains "defaults." Table 13-2 describes these options.

Table 13-2 Default NFS client options

Option	Description
rw	Stands for "read/write" permission; used to mount a file system with read/write permissions.
suid	Stands for "set user ID"; causes programs to run with program owner permissions instead of user permissions.
dev	This default option allows the NFS client to interpret block special devices on the mounted file system. Block special devices are character devices, not hardware devices. For example, dev/random is a character device used for access to the Linux random number generator.
exec	This option allows running binary files on the mounted file system.
nouser	This option prohibits non-root users from mounting a file system.
async	This option means that all input/output to the mounted file system is done asynchronously, which allows other processing to continue before the transmission is finished.
auto	This option allows automatic mounting at startup or when the mount -a command is issued.

The man page for the mount command describes all NFS client options.

TIP

You use the NFS Settings tab to enable NFSv4 and supply an NFSv4 domain name. You can also open a port in the firewall to give remote computers access to NFS services.

Activity 13-1: Creating and Configuring an NFS Server and Client with YaST Modules

ACTIVITY

Time Required: 40 minutes

Objective: Use the YaST NFS Server and Client modules to export and import a file system.

13

Description: In this activity, you team up with a partner and use YaST modules to export and import a file system. Student A installs the NFS Server module and configures the NFS server to export the /data directory. Student B uses the NFS Client module to mount the NFS directory in his or her local mount point.

1. Partner with another student, or start two openSUSE virtual machines in VMware Player. If you don't have a partner, follow the steps for both Student A and Student B. Decide who will be Student A and who will be Student B, and then write down the following information for both students:

   - NFS server hostname: _____

   - Exported directory: _____

   - NFS client mount point: _____

   - NFS client IP address: _____

2. Both Student A and Student B should start VMware Player and log in to an openSUSE virtual machine.

3. Student A performs the NFS server role and should install the NFS Server module in YaST (Steps 4 through 6) and configure the NFS server (Steps 8 through 11). Student B should start with Step 12.

4. Open a terminal window and switch to the root user. To open the YaST Control Center, type **yast2** and press **Enter**.

5. Click **Software** under Groups on the left, and then click **Software Management** to open the YaST Software Manager. If the Summary of changes window opens, close it.

6. Type **nfs-server** in the search text box. Click **yast2-nfs-server**, and then click **Install** at the lower right. Click the **Apply** button under Changes in the right pane, and, if necessary, click the **I Agree** button in all Package License Confirmation windows.

7. Does the NFS client need to install the NFS Client module on his or her openSUSE Linux machine? Why or why not?

   _____

8. After finishing the installation, switch to the terminal window and make sure you're logged in as the root user. Start the NFS Server module by typing **yast2 nfs-server** and pressing **Enter**.

9. Click the **Start** option button in the NFS Server section. Click the **Open Port in Firewall** check box, and then click **Next**.

10. In the Directories to Export window, click the **Add Directory** button. Type **/data** in the Directory to Export text box, and then click **OK**. When you see a message asking whether to create the directory, click **Yes**. Enter your partner's IP address in the Host Wild Card text box, and then set the options shown previously in Figure 13-3: **rw, root_squash,async,no_subtree_check**. Click **OK** and then **Finish**.

11. Open a terminal window, switch to the root user, and change to the **/data** directory. Create a file in the /data directory and name it **report**. Add your name and today's date in the file.

12. Student B: Switch to the root user, and open the `/etc/hosts` file in the vim editor. Move the cursor to the last line, and press **o** to start a new line under the cursor. Type Student A's IP address, press **Tab**, and type Student A's hostname. Save the file, and then exit the vim editor.

13. Start the NFS Client module by typing **yast2 nfs-client** and pressing **Enter**.

14. Click the **Add** button. Type Student A's NFS server hostname in the NFS Server Hostname text box, **/data** in the Remote Directory text box, and **/mnt** in the Mount Point text box, and then click **OK**.

15. Click the **NFS Settings** tab, make sure the port in the firewall is open, and then click **OK**.

16. Student B: Switch to the root user and change to the `/mnt` directory. Display a long listing of all files and directories in this directory, and then view the contents of the `report` file in this directory. What's displayed onscreen?

Student B might not be able to write to the `reports` file even though the `rw` option was set in the NFS Directories to Export window. It depends on what file permissions are set on the `/data/` `report` file for all, as Student B isn't root on Student A's machine because of the `root_squash` option.

17. If you have time, do this activity again, with Student A and Student B switching roles.

18. When you're finished, exit the root user and leave your virtual machine running for Activity 13-2.

Remote Procedure Calls

Remote Procedure Calls (RPC) is a protocol that allows one network computer to request a service from a program on another network computer. You can think of it in terms of the client/server model. For instance, the client is the machine requesting the service, and the server is the machine providing the service. NFS relies on RPC to route requests between the NFS server and client. To function correctly, NFS needs the following RPC services:

- *rpc.mountd*—This service receives mount requests from the NFS client and checks them against the list of exported file systems. It's also known as the mount daemon.

- *rpc.nfsd*—This service specifies how many kernel threads the NFS service should use and the NFS version it should support. It's also known as the nfs daemon.

- *portmapper*—This service provides coordination between the client and the correct port number to communicate with the requested RPC service. The portmapper service must be enabled before the other services in this list can start.

13

The `rpcinfo` command is an excellent troubleshooting tool, used to check the status of current RPC services. The `-p` option probes the portmapper service and lists all active RPC services. The following output is an example of what you might see after using this option:

```
program   vers   proto   port   service
100000     4      tcp     111   portmapper
100005     1      udp    41254  mountd
100021     1      udp    46505  nlockmgr
100003     2      tcp     2049   nfs
100227     3      tcp     2049   nfs_acl
100024     1      tcp    47205  status
```

Output is usually much longer than in this example. For instance, numerous versions of the port-mapper or nfs service might be listed. The following list describes the columns in this output:

- `program`—The RPC program number that identifies an RPC service
- `vers`—The program version number (version of the RPC service)
- `proto`—Defines the protocol that uses the RPC service
- `port`—Defines the port the RPC service uses
- `service`—The RPC service corresponding with the listed program number

For more information on RPC, see RFC 1050 at *www.ietf.org/rfc/rfc1057.txt*.

Exporting File Systems Manually

The NFS server configuration file that lists directories to be made available to NFS clients is `/etc/exports`. The following is an example of an entry in this file:

```
/data    192.168.152.133(rw,root_squash,sync,no_subtree_check)
```

This entry exports the `/data` directory to a network host with the IP address 192.168.152.133. The options in parentheses are delimited by commas and are the same options you learned to configure earlier in "Exporting File Systems in YaST." After making changes in the `/etc/exports` file, you must start or restart the NFS server with the `rcnfsserver` command (also used to stop, reload, and check the status of the NFS server).

In openSUSE, there's no man page for the `rcnfsserver` command; however, you can enter the command by itself to see a list of arguments to use with it.

The NFS Server service (nfsserver) is responsible for exporting the file systems specified in the `/etc/exports` file. By default, it starts every time the machine boots. You can check to make sure the NFS Server service is set to run in its default runlevels with the following command:

```
chkconfig nfsserver on
```

This command enables administrators to change runlevel links at boot time. Runlevels define the mode a machine is in after it boots, and runlevel links simply point to these runlevels in the startup scripts in the /etc/init.d file. As mentioned, restarting the Linux machine starts the NFS Server service and exports directories listed in the /etc/exports file; however, you can also use the rcnfsserver reload command after updating the /etc/exports file instead of restarting the Linux machine.

The exportfs command is used to store a list of exported file systems for NFS in a separate file, /var/lib/nfs/etab. The exportfs command initializes the etab file with directory information from the /etc/exports configuration file, which lists file systems to be exported. The etab file, which the NFS mount daemon reads when a client request is initiated, lists actively exported file systems. As an administrator, you can sync all file systems in etab with the file systems in /etc/exports, or you can add and delete file systems without modifying the /etc/exports file by using the exportfs command; however, note that the etab file is never edited directly. Table 13-3 describes common options used with this command.

For a complete list of options, see the man page for the exportfs command.

Table 13-3 Common exportfs options

Option	Description
-r	Stands for "reexport"; used to synchronize the /var/lib/nfs/etab file with the /etc/exports file. If /var/lib/nfs/etab contains entries that aren't in /etc/exports, this option removes those entries from /var/lib/nfs/etab.
-a	Stands for "all"; used to export all directories listed in the /etc/exports file.
-i	Stands for "ignore"; used to export file systems from the command line without using entries in the /etc/exports file.
-v	Stands for "verbose"; used to display important data while exporting or unexporting file systems. ("Unexporting" a file system makes it unavailable to NFS clients.)
-u	Stands for "unexport"; used to make directories unavailable to NFS clients.

13

Importing File Systems Manually

The /etc/fstab file is a system configuration file that contains information on how file systems and partitions are to be integrated into the overall file structure. To mount an exported directory, you must add an NFS entry in the /etc/fstab file. The rcnfs command is used to start and stop the NFS Client service. However, you can't start this service without an NFS entry in /etc/fstab. A typical NFS entry in this file looks like the following:

```
server:/data        /mnt    nfs     defaults 0 0
```

The following list describes the fields of an NFS entry:

- *File system*—This field defines the storage device; in the example, it's `server:/data`.
- *Directory*—This field specifies where the file system should be mounted. In the example, `server:/data` is being mounted in the `/mnt` directory.
- *Type*—This field defines the type of file system or partition to be mounted. In the example, it's NFS.
- *Options*—Defines options for the file system. In the example, it's set to `defaults`, which gives the file system the default mount settings. Table 13-4 describes some common options used in `/etc/fstab`.

Table 13-4 Common `/etc/fstab` options

Option	Description
auto noauto	Mount the device automatically when the system starts. Mount the device manually after system startup.
user nouser	Allow any user to mount the device. Allow only the root user to mount the device.
exec noexec	Allow running binary files on the partition. Disallow running binary files on the partition.
ro	Mount the file system as read only.
rw	Mount the file system as read/write.
sync async	Input/output should be done synchronously. Input/output should be done asynchronously.

- *Dump*—The dump utility uses this number (0 or 1) to decide whether the file system should be backed up. A 0 means dump ignores the file system, and a 1 means dump backs it up. This utility isn't installed by default, so make sure it's installed before entering a 1 in this field.
- *Pass*—The fsck utility uses this field (0, 1, or 2) to determine the priority in which the file system should be checked. A 0 means fsck doesn't check the file system. A 1, reserved for the root file system, means the highest priority, and a 2 is reserved for all other file systems.

Before you can import a file system from the NFS server manually, you must use the `rcrpcbind start` command to restart the portmapper service, and then you can mount a remote file system with the `mount` command. The `mount` command, used to attach a file system from an NFS server to the local file structure, has the following syntax:

```
mount NFS_Server_Hostname:exported_directory local_directory
```

Here's an example of the `mount` command:

```
mount server:/data /mnt
```

In this example, the NFS client is mounting an exported file system (/data) on an NFS server named server in a local directory named /mnt. After issuing this command, you have access to the exported file system as though it were on your local machine.

The showmount command is used to query the mount daemon (rpc.mountd) on the remote NFS server for information on the server's state. For instance, using this command with the -e option lists all exports from a specific NFS server, as shown in this example:

```
server:~ # showmount -e
Export list for server:
/data 192.168.152.133
```

The output shows that the /data directory is exported to a host with the IP address 192.168.152.133. Table 13-5 describes some options used with the showmount command.

Table 13-5 **Common** showmount **options**

Option	Description
no options	Lists clients being mounted from that host
-a	Stands for "all"; used to list both the client hostname (or IP address) and the mounted directory
-d	Stands for "directory"; used to list only the mounted directories
-h	Stands for "help"; displays a brief summary of help information
-v	Stands for "version"; displays the current version number of the showmount utility
--no-headers	Used to omit descriptive headings in the output

Activity 13-2: Creating and Configuring an NFS Server and Client Manually

Time Required: 40 minutes

Objective: Configure an NFS server and client manually to export and import a file system.

Description: In this activity, you team up with a partner and export and import a file system. Student A configures the NFS server manually to export the /data directory. Student B edits the /etc/fstab configuration file to mount the NFS directory in his or her local mount point.

1. You need to partner with another student or start two openSUSE virtual machines in VMware Player. If you don't have a partner, follow the steps for both Student A and Student B. Decide who will be Student A and who will be Student B, and then write down the following information for both students:

- NFS server hostname: _____
- Exported directory: _____
- NFS client mount point: _____
- NFS client IP address: _____

2. If necessary, both Student A and Student B should start VMware Player and log in to an openSUSE virtual machine.

3. Student A is going to be the NFS server. Student A: Complete Steps 4 through 6 in Activity 13-1 to install the NFS Server module, and then do Steps 4 through 8 in this activity.

4. View the contents of the /etc/exports file by using the **more** command. What's displayed onscreen?

_____

5. To open the NFS Server port in the firewall, type **yast2 firewall** and press **Enter**. After the firewall module opens, click **Allowed Services** at the left if "NFS Server Service" isn't already displayed. Click the **Service to Allow** list arrow, click to select **NFS Server Service**, and then click the **Add** button. Finally, click **Next** and then **Finish**.

6. Open the /etc/exports configuration file in the vim editor. Move the cursor to the last line and press **i** to enter input mode. Then type this NFS entry (using Student B's IP address): **/data *IP_address*(ro,root_squash,sync,no_subtree_check)**. Save the file, and then exit the vim editor.

7. If necessary, create a directory called **data** in the root directory, and then create a file named **data1** in this directory. Type your name and today's date in the file.

8. Reload the NFS Server service by typing **rcnfsserver reload** and pressing **Enter**.

9. Student B: If necessary, follow the procedure in Step 5 to open a port in the firewall, but open the **NFS Client** port. Now try to mount Student A's exported directory by typing **mount *hostname*:/data /mnt** (substituting Student A's hostname for *hostname*) and pressing **Enter**. Were you able to mount the NFS server's exported directory? Why or why not?

_____

10. You can wait for the mount command to time out or press **Ctrl+C** to exit the command. Now start the portmapper service by typing **rcrpcbind start** and pressing **Enter**.

11. Next, try the mount command used in Step 9 again. Did it work this time? What will happen if you restart the NFS client machine? Can you still access the exported directory? Why or why not?

_____

12. Add an NFS entry in the `/etc/fstab` configuration file by using the vim editor. The entry should look like this: **Student A's** *hostname:***/data /mnt nfs defaults 0 0.** Make sure you press **Tab** between each field. For instance, after typing `hostname:/data`, press **Tab** and then type **/mnt**.

13. To mount the file system in the `/etc/fstab` file, type **mount -a** and press **Enter** to restart the computer to check whether you can still access the exported directory. (*Note*: It might take a minute or two until you can see files in the exported directory.)

14. If you have time, do the activity again, with Student A and Student B switching roles.

15. Exit the root user and power off your virtual machine.

Chapter Summary

- The purpose of a Linux file server is to maintain files so that users can access them from any network computer and share them with other users. File servers on openSUSE Linux machines have advantages such as central location, security, and remote access that appears local to users.

- The Network File System (NFS) is a distributed file system protocol that allows remote access to shared resources across networks. NFS makes it possible for users to mount shared file systems on remote machines, which is similar to drive mapping in Windows.

- An NFS server is a Linux machine on the network that exports directories to all networked hosts that have access to it. Administrators can use the YaST NFS Server Configuration module to configure NFS servers. The YaST NFS Client module is included with an openSUSE installation by default and enables administrators to configure NFS clients.

- Remote Procedure Calls (RPC) allows one computer on a network to request a service from a program on another computer on the same network. The three RPC services required for the NFS service are rpc.mountd, rpc.nfsd, and portmapper. The `rpcinfo` command is used to check the status of current RPC services.

- You can configure an NFS server manually by adding NFS entries in the `/etc/exports` directory and restarting the NFS Server service with the `rcnfsserver` command. This service is responsible for exporting file systems specified in the `/etc/exports` file.

- You can configure an NFS client manually by adding NFS mounts in the `/etc/fstab` file and starting the rcnfs service.

- The `showmount` command is used to query the mount daemon on the remote NFS server for information about the server's state.

13

Key Terms

file server A network system where users can store and share files.

mount Making a file system appear as though it's on a local machine.

mount point Typically an empty directory on the local file system that's used as a logical space to mount another file system.

Network File System (NFS) A distributed file system protocol that allows remote access to shared resources across networks.

NFS server A Linux machine on the network that exports directories to all network hosts that have access to it.

Remote Procedure Calls (RPC) A protocol that allows one computer on a network to request a service from a program on another computer on the network.

subtree checking A process the NFS server uses to check whether a requested file is in the exported subdirectory.

Review Questions

1. Describe three advantages of the Network File System.

2. Both the YaST NFS Server and Client modules are included with an openSUSE Linux installation. True or False?

3. In the NFS Server Configuration module, which of the following options do you use to export a file system to a specific host on the network?

   a. Hostname or IP address

   b. An asterisk

   c. IP network address

   d. None of the above

4. In the NFS Server Configuration module, which option do you use to export a file system to all hosts on the network?

   a. Hostname or IP address

   b. An asterisk

   c. IP network address

   d. None of the above

5. When configuring an NFS server, which option do you use to give users on an NFS client machine read access to the NFS directory?

   a. `async`

   b. `root_squash`

   c. `ro`

   d. `sync`

6. When configuring an NFS server, which option do you use to have data written to the disk before the server replies to requests?

    a. `async`

    b. `root_squash`

    c. `ro`

    d. `sync`

7. When configuring an NFS server, which option do you use to make sure the root user on the NFS client doesn't have root privileges on the NFS server?

    a. `async`

    b. `root_squash`

    c. `ro`

    d. `sync`

8. What three RPC services are required for the NFS service to function correctly?

9. What command do you use to check the status of current RPC services?

    a. `rcnfsserver`

    b. `chkconfig`

    c. `rpcinfo`

    d. `exportfs`

10. What command do you use to add or delete file systems without modifying the `/etc/exports` file?

    a. `rcnfsserver`

    b. `chkconfig`

    c. `rpcinfo`

    d. `exportfs`

13

11. What command do you use to start, stop, reload, or check the status of the NFS server?

    a. `rcnfsserver`

    b. `chkconfig`

    c. `rpcinfo`

    d. `exportfs`

12. What command do you use to change runlevel links at boot time?

    a. `rcnfsserver`

    b. `chkconfig`

    c. `rpcinfo`

    d. `exportfs`

13. What NFS configuration file do you edit to add directories to be shared on the NFS server?

    a. `/etc`

    b. `/etc/exports`

    c. `/etc/hosts`

    d. `/etc/fstab`

14. What NFS configuration file do you edit to add NFS entries to be mounted on the NFS client machine?

    a. `/etc/fstab`

    b. `/etc/exports`

    c. `/etc/hosts`

    d. `/etc`

15. You decide to export the `/office` directory to all hosts on the network. You want users to be able only to read the exported directory, not change the information. You don't want the client root user to have root access to the server, and you want to make sure the server replies to requests even before changes have been made. Which of the following is the correct entry in the `/etc/exports` configuration file?

    a. `/office      *(rw,root_squash,async)`

    b. `/office      *(ro,root_squash,sync)`

    c. `/office      *(rw,root_squash,sync)`

    d. `/office      *(ro,root_squash,async)`

16. You want to mount an exported directory named `/office` on an NFS client. The exported directory is on the `server01` server, and you want to mount it in the `/mnt` directory. You don't have the dump utility, and you don't want the fsck utility to check the file system. Which of the following is the correct entry in the `/etc/fstab` configuration file?

    a. `server01:/office    /mnt      nfs    defaults 0 0`

    b. `server01:/office    /mnt      nfs    defaults 0 1`

    c. `server01:/mnt    /office      nfs    defaults 0 0`

    d. `server01:/mnt    /office      nfs    defaults 0 1`

Case Projects

Case Project 13-1: Researching NFS Security Issues

Do research to learn more about security issues NFS servers have and what's been done in openSUSE and other Linux distributions to address these vulnerabilities. A good place to start researching is *http://nfs.sourceforge.net/nfs-howto/*. Write a two- to three-page summary of your findings.

Case Project 13-2: Researching the Benefits of NFSv4

You're a Linux network administrator, and you've been asked to explain the benefits of NFSv4 to upper management personnel, who want to know whether NFSv4 is compatible with openSUSE and whether NFSv3 clients can access directories exported from an NFSv4 server. Conduct research to learn more about NFSv4, and write a one-page memo summarizing NFSv4 benefits and compatibility issues.

13

## chapter 14

Planning for a Linux Installation

After reading this chapter and completing the exercises, you will be able to:

- Identify the hardware components in a Linux computer
- Develop a preinstallation checklist
- Use an automated method to install openSUSE

In Chapter 2, you learned how to perform a standard openSUSE Linux installation. In this chapter, you learn how to analyze system components before actually installing Linux and how to find information on hardware, such as the CPU, RAM, and video cards. You also learn how the processor affects computer speed, how memory is used to improve performance, what nonvolatile storage devices you must have to install openSUSE Linux, and how video cards affect graphics. Finally, you develop a preinstallation checklist and see how to install openSUSE automatically with AutoYaST.

Analyzing Hardware Components

Most computers have operating systems installed when you purchase them, so the only OS configuration that's required is setting the computer name, a time zone, additional user accounts, and so forth. Generally, users don't need to know what type of hard drive or video card they have, nor do they have to understand how communication with the keyboard and mouse takes place.

Installing Linux for personal use doesn't require much planning. You can simply follow the steps you learned in Chapter 2 and have a perfectly functioning Linux machine running in less than an hour. However, as an administrator responsible for installing Linux on multiple computers, understanding hardware's role in the Linux installation process is crucial. Therefore, you should learn how to plan an installation by gathering information on hardware and analyzing it to troubleshoot potential installation problems. Gathering hardware information before you start is also useful when answering installation prompts.

As you learned in Chapter 2, openSUSE (as well as most Linux distributions) detects hardware components during installation. An administrator must determine whether these hardware settings have been detected correctly and whether hardware meets the Linux distribution's installation requirements. For openSUSE, Novell recommends the following hardware:

- Pentium 4 2.4 GHz or higher or any AMD64 for Intel EM64T processor
- 1 GB RAM
- At least 3 GB free disk space
- 1024 × 768 or better display resolution

The following sections go into more detail on hardware components to help you understand these installation requirements.

Microprocessors (CPUs)

The CPU, also known as the microprocessor, is the "brains" of a computer. This core component is an integrated circuit containing millions of transistors that perform arithmetic and logical operations. The CPU consists of the **arithmetic logic unit** (**ALU**), responsible for mathematical and logical (true or false) operations, and the **control unit** (**CU**) that regulates instructions. Typically, the CU loads commands that are sent to the ALU for execution.

Microprocessors operate by using an internal clock. The **clock speed** is the number of pulses per second generated by the motherboard. It doesn't set the time of day; it sets the processor's tempo.

Clock speed is measured in MHz (millions of cycles per second) or GHz (billions of cycles per second). Several factors play a major role in processor speed. A **multiplier** is a component hard-wired into the CPU to determine processor speed. For instance, a computer running at 266 MHz with a multiplier of 2 has a speed of 133 MHz.

Another factor is the **cache,** which is RAM built into the CPU that's used to store frequently accessed data and instructions. There are three types of caches:

- *L1 cache*—A **level 1 (L1) cache** is a small RAM chip built into the CPU. The CPU can load incoming program code into the L1 cache so that it can access information quickly without having to read system RAM or the hard drive.

- *L2 cache*—Microprocessor developers realized the benefits of a cache and created a **level 2 (L2) cache** on a separate chip connected to the CPU. Most processors now incorporate an L2 cache, which is larger and slower than an L1 cache and is capable of reading larger quantities of data from RAM. The L1 cache processes the most frequently used data, and the L2 cache handles recently accessed data to be passed on to the L1 cache when needed. L1 and L2 caches work together for optimum performance.

- *L3 cache*—For L2 caches that have been incorporated into the CPU, developers created a **level 3 (L3) cache,** which is a separate chip connected to the CPU. You can think of this cache as similar to the L2 cache in older computers. It's even larger and slower than an L2 cache but works similarly for even faster CPU performance. With newer multicore processors, an L3 cache is incorporated into the CPU. It's shared across L1 and L2 caches in each core for fast CPU performance. In this arrangement, the L3 cache does the work of reading data from system RAM.

A CPU performs calculations with binary digits (bits). A 32-bit processor can store 32-bit numbers, which correlates with the amount of data a CPU can process per clock cycle. A 64-bit processor can theoretically double the amount of data the CPU can process. You use the uname -m command to determine what type of processor your Linux machine has. For instance, i386/i486/i586/i686 means a 32-bit processor and x86_64 GNU/Linux indicates a 64-bit processor.

With 32-bit processors, you can access up to 4 GB RAM, which is typically more than enough RAM for home users. When using 3-D graphics and software that need more memory, 64-bit processors are usually necessary.

14

Physical Memory: RAM and ROM

Physical memory typically refers to memory chips or hard drives installed on a computer. The two major categories of physical memory are as follows:

- *RAM*—Random access memory, as explained in Chapter 1, is volatile because any data stored in it is lost after you turn the computer off; therefore, it depends on a constant source of power. It's used to store data accessed by the CPU.

- *ROM*—**Read-only memory (ROM)** is nonvolatile memory containing permanent data, such as boot instructions and the system clock. It's considered static and doesn't need a power source to store data.

There are two types of RAM:

- *DRAM*—**Dynamic RAM (DRAM)** is the most common type because it's less expensive. A DRAM chip is made up of millions of transistors and capacitors that store information on a "stick" (chip). DRAM sticks must be dynamically refreshed thousands of times per second to store information. Novell recommends having at least 1 GB DRAM.

- *SRAM*—**Static RAM (SRAM)** doesn't need to be refreshed to store information. As long as the computer has power, SRAM retains the data stored in its memory cells. SRAM is much faster and more expensive than DRAM and is used in L2 and L3 caches as well as other memory chips.

Common types of ROM include the following:

- *Programmable read-only memory (PROM)*—Nonvolatile memory that can be programmed only once; it can't be erased and reprogrammed. A major difference between ROM and PROM is that PROM is manufactured blank, whereas ROM is programmed during manufacturing.

- *Erasable programmable read-only memory (EPROM)*—Nonvolatile memory that can store a small amount of data even after the power is shut off. Data is erased by exposure to UV light, so it must be removed from the device to be erased and reprogrammed. Used to hold the system BIOS in older PCs.

- *Electrically erasable programmable read-only memory (EEPROM)*—Nonvolatile memory that can store a small amount of data even after the power is shut off. This type of ROM can be erased by electricity and then reprogrammed without removing it from the device, which is one of the biggest advantages over EPROM. The act of reprogramming EEPROM is called "flashing." It's commonly used to hold the system BIOS.

- *Flash memory*—Nonvolatile memory that's very similar to EEPROM but is considerably faster because it writes data in larger blocks, typically 512 bytes instead of 1 byte at a time.

Storage Devices

You must have long-term storage devices for a Linux installation. Although you can read and write information to RAM quickly, it must be refreshed constantly for the information to remain intact. RAM works well with processes that can be accessed and manipulated quickly, but it's not suitable for long-term storage. Table 14-1 describes common long-term storage devices.

Table 14-1 Long-term storage devices

Device type	Description
Flash drives	Portable, small, nonvolatile storage devices, such as thumb drives and Secure Digital (SD) cards.
Optical discs	CDs and DVDs use lasers to read and write information. These discs are fairly inexpensive and can be used on a wide array of devices. Performance is slower than hard disks, but CDs and DVDs are more portable.
Hard disks	Typically the largest storage devices in a computer; capable of storing up to a terabyte of data.
Tape drives	Drives that record data on magnetic tape, usually used to archive system data. Tapes are often used to store entire system backups (see Chapter 6).

Almost all computers have a hard drive, also known as a **hard disk drive (HDD)**. It's the main storage device in a computer and typically holds the largest amount of data. You can now buy terabyte (1020 GB) hard drives at a reasonable price (around $125). The two main types of hard drives are **Integrated Drive Electronics (IDE)** and **small computer systems interface (SCSI)**. Hard drives are labeled by how they connect to a computer. For instance, an IDE drive has an IDE interface that connects up to four hard drives via a 40-wire flat parallel cable. **Serial Advanced Technology Attachment (SATA)** is an advanced IDE interface. A SATA cable is much thinner, with only seven-pin connectors, which simplifies cabling and improves air flow. Another advantage of SATA drives is that you don't have to set drive jumpers for master and slave hard drives. A SCSI hard drive is typically used in servers rather than desktops for SOHO use. It's similar to an IDE hard drive but is faster and more expensive and creates more noise and heat. To determine the type of hard disk you have, you can use the `fdisk` command as shown:

```
fdisk -l | grep Disk
Disk /dev/sda: 21.5 GB, 21474836480 bytes
Disk identifier: 0x00063221
```

This output indicates a SCSI hard drive because `sda` is displayed (line 2). For IDE hard drives, `hda` is displayed.

Video Adapter Cards

Video adapter cards (also known as video cards) are expansion devices that plug into a bus on the motherboard and send graphical information to a video device, such as a monitor, TV, or projector. A **bus** is a channel for connecting hardware components to a processor and can be used to swap hardware, such as replacing an existing video card with a faster one. Before buying a video card, make sure the motherboard supports that format. Table 14-2 describes common video card formats.

Table 14-2 Video adapter card formats

Format	Description
Peripheral Component Interconnect (PCI)	Is included in most modern motherboards and has a clock speed of 33 or 66 MHz.
Accelerated Graphics Port (AGP)	Provides a direct connection between the graphics card and the CPU. The biggest difference is that AGP doesn't have to share bandwidth with other devices, as PCI does on a bus.

14

Resolution is the number of horizontal and vertical pixels a monitor is capable of displaying. For example, an 800 × 600 resolution means displaying 800 pixels horizontally and 600 pixels vertically, for a total of 480,000 pixels to display an image onscreen. Most computers now have much higher resolutions.

After deciding on a video card, you need to install the correct driver. This task can be challenging because many vendors use special software that might be closed source. More vendors support Linux now, however, and even offer technical support. Before you choose a video card, make sure the motherboard supports it and a driver is available for the Linux OS. Table 14-3 lists some common video card drivers.

Table 14-3 Video card drivers

Driver	Description	Web site
nVidia	nVidia drivers don't load automatically when installing openSUSE Linux because nVidia is closed source.	For more information on these drivers, go to *http://en.opensuse.org/SDB: NVIDIA_drivers*.
AMD	Acquired ATI Technologies in 2007. AMD has a wide range of video cards, including Radeon and FirePro.	For more information on AMD drivers, refer to *http://en.opensuse.org/SDB: ATI_drivers#1-click_install*.

Developing a Preinstallation Checklist

This book helps you learn the Linux OS by running it on a virtual machine. The nature of virtual machines allows you to skip common hardware problems you might run into if you installed openSUSE on a physical machine. However, as a Linux administrator, you'll probably run into problems caused by Linux not recognizing a hardware component during installation. This section gives you a starting place to look for information in case you do have installation problems.

Before any installation, make sure you have the official manual for the OS. At the time of this writing, openSUSE has several manuals you can download in PDF format and print:

You can download these manuals at *www.novell.com/documentation/ opensuse112/*.

- *openSUSE 11.2 Installation Quick Start*—A brief overview of how to install a default version of openSUSE.
- *openSUSE 11.2 Start-up*—An introduction to openSUSE that explains where to find documentation, how to install the OS, and how to use openSUSE.
- *openSUSE 11.2 GNOME Quick Start*—An overview of using the GNOME desktop environment. It walks you through configuring the OS as well as printers, e-mail, and media files.
- *openSUSE 11.2 KDE Quick Start*—An overview of using the K Desktop Environment.
- *openSUSE 11.2 GNOME User Guide*—A complete manual on using GNOME in openSUSE.
- *openSUSE 11.2 KDE User Guide*—A complete manual on using KDE in openSUSE.
- *openSUSE 11.2 Applications Guide*—Offers information on a variety of applications included with openSUSE, such as the openOffice suite, Kontact, and Evolution.
- *openSUSE 11.2 Reference Guide*—Intended for system administrators, it's a comprehensive guide on advanced installation and configuration.
- *openSUSE 11.2 Security Guide*—This manual introduces system administrators to security measures in openSUSE.
- *AppArmor 2.3.1 Quick Start*—Covers Novell AppArmor, which is security software for the Linux OS.

Novell also has SUSE Linux Enterprise available for purchase; it comes with documentation and unlimited technical support.

After you have all the documentation, you should fill out a hardware and software preinstallation checklist, using the information you learned in Chapter 2. Tables 14-4 and 14-5 help you create this checklist.

Table 14-4 The openSUSE preinstallation checklist for hardware

Hardware	Minimum required hardware	Recommended hardware
CPU	Pentium 4 2.4 GHz or higher or any AMD64 for Intel EM64T processor	Intel Core 2 Duo CPU T7250 running at 2.00 GHz
RAM	1 GB RAM	3.5 GB RAM
CD/DVD drive	No recommendation, but must have a CD/DVD drive to install openSUSE with an ISO image	MATSHITA DVD+-RW
Hard disk drive	3 GB available disk space, which enables you to install and use openSUSE; however, more than this minimum is recommended	Two 300 GB hard disk drives
Video card	1024 × 768 or higher display resolution	GeForce 8400M GS, 1280 × 720 display resolution
Display monitor	No recommendation, but determine whether you'll be working from the command line or in a GUI using a monitor	17-inch screen

Table 14-5 openSUSE preinstallation checklist for software

Software setting	Description
Hostname	Write down the hostnames of all machines. Most hostnames are in the format *hostname.domain*.
Domain name	Determine the registered domain name.
IP address	If you have a DNS and DHCP server, you can use DHCP to set an IP address dynamically; otherwise, you need to write down your IP address before starting the installation.
Netmask	If you have a class C network, your netmask is 255.255.255.0. Refer to Chapter 8 for information on netmasks and determining network classes.
DNS IP address	Write down the DNS server's IP address.
Software packages	To determine which software packages to install, list the purpose of each machine. For example, in Chapter 13, you created an NFS server machine and an NFS client machine. On the server machine, you want to make sure the nfs-server package is installed for this purpose. Although you can install packages after the OS installation, installing them during the OS installation is easier.

14

These checklists are just samples. You should create your own check-list before doing an installation for your organization's network.

Gathering Hardware Information in Windows

Computer manuals are a good source for determining what type of hardware you have. You can use this information for a preinstallation checklist. If you don't have the manual and your computer has Windows installed, you can check the System window (see Figure 14-1). To open it in Windows 7, click Start, and then right-click Computer and click Properties. The System section lists CPU and RAM information.

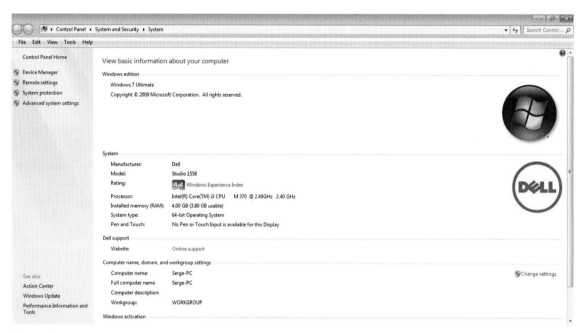

Figure 14-1 The System window
Source: Microsoft

Next, you should check hard drive information to see how many hard drives your computer has and how much free disk space is available. This information is useful during the parti-tioning portion of the openSUSE installation. In the Computer window, right-click the C drive (or the drive letter corresponding to your main drive) and click Properties to open the OS (C:) Properties dialog box (see Figure 14-2).

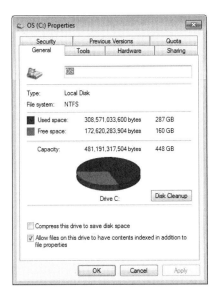

Figure 14-2 Checking disk space
© Cengage Learning 2013

The pie graph shows how much disk space is available, although this information isn't important unless you're installing Linux as a dual-boot system. For the installation's partitioning portion, however, you do need to know the hard drive capacity (448 GB in Figure 14-2).

Finally, to find information on your video card, right-click the desktop and click Screen resolution to open the Screen Resolution dialog box. Figure 14-3 shows a screen resolution of 1366 × 768. For other video card settings, click the Advanced settings link, and then, if necessary, click the Adapter tab, which displays the video card type and memory capacity.

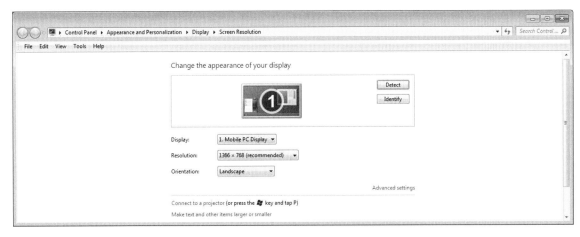

Figure 14-3 The Screen Resolution dialog box
© Cengage Learning 2013

Partitioning

When installing openSUSE, you're prompted to specify partitions for the hard drive. When many files and applications are stored on a hard drive, performance can slow down, and partitioning helps improve performance by reducing the time the OS needs to perform I/O operations, such as opening an application. **Partitioning** divides a hard drive into logical sections; each one is a contiguous section of blocks treated as a separate physical drive. In addition to improving system performance, other reasons for partitioning an HDD are as follows:

- *Installing multiple OSs*—You can install multiple OSs on a single computer or install different OSs on separate partitions to run them more efficiently.

- *Storing different file systems*—You should store file systems of different types on separate partitions so that if a file system becomes corrupted, it's confined to only one partition. Other partitions aren't affected, so the data stored on them is safe.

- *Limiting data growth*—You should assign separate partitions for different areas of openSUSE Linux file systems because some processes consume a large amount of disk space. As a result of a lack of disk space, bookkeeping operations, such as writing to log files, can't be performed. For instance, if you assigned the /home and /var directories to different partitions, and the partition allocated to the /home directory has run out of disk space, logging processes could continue to write data to log files in the /var/log directory because it's on a separate partition from the /home directory.

Primary partitions are installed as part of the Linux boot sector. Linux supports a maximum of four primary partitions on a hard disk. If you need more than four partitions, you can create a **logical partition**. Because there are four primary partitions, logical partitions are numbered beginning with 5. Logical partitions were devised to circumvent the limitation on the number of primary partitions and are created by partitioning a primary partition. An **extended partition** is essentially a container for logical partitions. You can have only one extended partition per primary partition. Linux considers logical partitions to be the same as primary partitions, but logical partitions are set up differently because they're subdivided in the extended partition. You could conceivably boot from a logical partition, but it's normally used to store data.

Swap partitions on an HDD contain the swap space, which the Linux kernel uses to store pages from RAM and, therefore, free up RAM. A page consists of the blocks of RAM allocated to current processes running on a computer. As swap space frees up RAM, it increases the amount of memory available for storing data and information. Linux follows a naming scheme for HDD partitions: /dev/ppdN.

To Windows users, the Linux naming scheme might seem confusing. Windows uses C for the primary hard drive, D for the CD-ROM drive, and so forth. The Linux naming scheme uses a combination of numbers and letters to provide more information about the partition than other OSs do. The /dev indicates the directory where device files are stored. For example, /dev/hda is the primary hard drive located in the /dev directory. The CD-ROM drive might be located at /dev/cdrom.

The pp in the format specifies the type of device on which a partition is created. The most common are hd for IDE disks and sd for SCSI disks. The d in the format specifies the actual device containing a partition with letters such as a, b, and c. For example, the primary hard drive would be indicated with hda, and the secondary hard drive would be indicated with hdb.

Finally, the N in the format specifies the partition number. The first four partitions (primary or extended) are numbered 1 through 4, and logical partitions are numbered starting with 5.

Automating an OpenSUSE Installation

The standard installation procedure is fine for installing openSUSE Linux on only a few machines; however, if you're a Linux administrator responsible for installing Linux on several hundred machines, the standard installation is far too time consuming. AutoYaST is a tool for installing SUSE Linux OSs without user intervention. To use it, you need an **AutoYaST profile**, which is an ASCII XML configuration file used to specify the software being installed, the partitioning scheme, and the root user's password.

You can create an AutoYaST profile manually with an XML file or use the AutoYaST module. This module isn't installed by default, so you have to use YaST Software Manager to add it. You can do this by issuing the yast2 -i autoyast2 command as the root user. After AutoYaST is installed, you can run it with the yast2 autoyast command, which opens the YaST Configuration window shown in Figure 14-4.

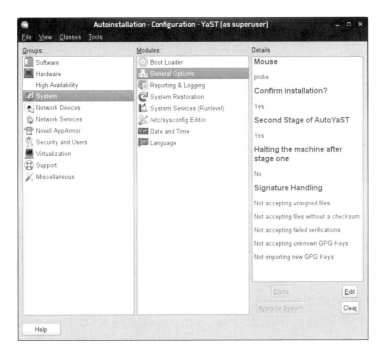

Figure 14-4 The YaST Configuration window
Source: openSUSE

With this tool, you can configure almost all the resources, such as boot loader, partitioning, and software selection, of an AutoYaST profile and collect most of the information available in the YaST Control Center (date and time, language, network services, software packages, and so on).

Creating an AutoYaST Profile Manually

To create an AutoYaST profile manually, use vim or another text editor (even Notepad or WordPad). The following example shows an AutoYaST profile in XML format (with line numbers added for readability):

```
1.  <?xml version="1.0"?>
2.  <!DOCTYPE profile>
3.  <profile xmlns="http://www.suse.com/1.0/yast2ns"
4.          xmlns:config="http://www.suse.com/1.0/configns">
5.  <users config:type="list">
6.  <user>
7.      <encrypted config:type="boolean">false</encrypted>
8.      <user_password>P@$$w0rD</user_password>
9.      <username>root</username>
10.  </user>
11.  </users>
12. </profile>
```

This profile is basic; in fact, the only automated portion is the root user's password, which is set to P@$$w0rD in line 8.

The control file container, or profile, is the configuration description for the system. It looks like the following:

```
1.  <?xml version="1.0"?>
2.  <!DOCTYPE profile>
3.   <profile
4.   xmlns="http://www.suse.com/1.0/yast2ns"
5.   xmlns:config="http://www.suse.com/1.0/configns">
6.
7.  <!-- ADD YOUR RESOURCE CONFIGURATION COMPONENTS HERE -->
8.
9.  </profile>
```

All AutoYaST profiles start with a header (shown in line 1) and end with the footer shown in line 3. Lines 6 to 8 in the preceding example contain the installation information you want to be entered automatically.

Using Auto-Installation

To install openSUSE with an AutoYaST profile, you must decide what boot medium you want to use to store the XML file:

- *NFS server*—You can use an NFS server (discussed in Chapter 13) to host an AutoYaST profile, which can be opened with the autoyast=nfs:///server/path command in the Startup Options window (see Figure 14-5).

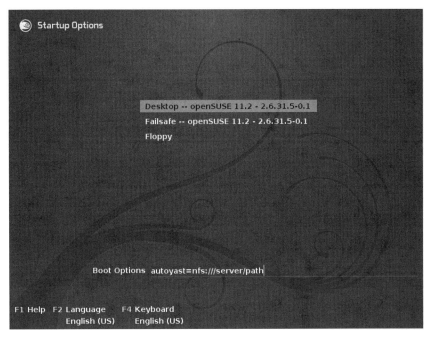

Figure 14-5 Specifying an NFS server in the Startup Options window
Source: openSUSE

- *Web server*—You can use a Web server to host an AutoYaST profile, which can be opened with the `autoyast=http:///[user.password@]server/path` command in the Startup Options window.
- *USB drive*—You can use a USB drive to host an AutoYaST profile and open it with the `autoyast=usb:///path` command in the Startup Options window.

Activity 14-1: Installing openSUSE Automatically

Time Required: 60 minutes

Objective: Use AutoYaST to install openSUSE automatically with a profile.

Description: In this activity, you use AutoYaST to install openSUSE on a new virtual machine and then create a profile and copy it to a USB drive. You then create another virtual machine and use the profile to perform an automatic installation of openSUSE.

1. Start VMware Player and create an openSUSE virtual machine with the default settings. Name your machine **autoyast_install** and select the GNOME desktop environment.

2. Make sure you're logged in to the openSUSE virtual machine you created in Step 1, and switch to the root user, if necessary. Install AutoYaST by typing **yast2 -i autoyast2** and pressing **Enter**. Make sure you agree to all package licenses.

3. After AutoYaST has finished installing, type **yast2 autoyast** and press **Enter** to start it.

14

4. To view the XML file containing the AutoYaST profile, click **View, Source** from the menu. When you're finished, click **View, Configuration Tree** from the menu.

5. To create an AutoYaST profile that's identical to the one for your openSUSE virtual machine, click **Tools, Create Reference Profile** from the menu. Make sure all options except the following are selected: **Mail Server, NFS Client, NIS Client, Printer, Proxy,** and **Samba Server.** Then click the **Create** button at the lower right.

6. View your AutoYaST profile again. Does it look different from what you saw in Step 4?

   _____

7. To ensure that there are no problems with the AutoYaST profile, click **Tools, Check Validity of Profile** from the menu. Were there any errors? Were there any warnings at the end of the validity check? Click **Finish.**

   _____

8. Make sure you add the root username and password so that you have a login account when you finish the installation. To do this, click the **Security and Users** group at the left, click the **User and Group Management** module, and then click the **Edit** button. Click **Set Filter,** and then click **System Users.**

9. Scroll down, click the **root** user, and then click **Edit.** Type **P@$$w0rD** for the password, and then click **OK** twice.

10. Repeat Step 7 to validate the profile. Were there any warnings this time?

   _____

11. Save the profile by clicking **File, Save As** from the menu. Type **my.xml** in the Name text box, click **Save,** and then click **OK** to confirm. Close the AutoYaST Configuration Management System window.

12. Plug a USB drive in the USB port and wait for the File Browser window to open. (If it doesn't open, unplug the USB drive and then plug it back in.) In the File Browser window, click the **File System** icon at the left, and then double-click the **var** folder. Next, double-click **lib** and then **autoinstall.** Finally, double-click the **repository** folder. You should see the my.xml file.

13. Right-click **my.xml** and click **Copy.** Click the USB drive icon at the left under Places. Right-click in the right pane and click **Paste** to copy the my.xml file to your USB drive.

14. Power off the virtual machine. Start VMware Player and click **Create a New Virtual Machine.** Perform the installation steps until you get to the openSUSE Startup Options window. Click **Installation,** type **autoyast=usb:///my.xml** (see Figure 14-6), and then press **Enter.**

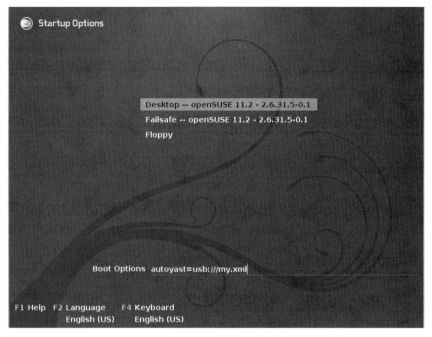

Figure 14-6 The Startup Options window
Source: openSUSE

15. If openSUSE can't mount your USB drive, you get a message that there was an error while fetching the profile. With a virtual machine, Windows might access the USB drive, but your virtual machine might not. If you get this error, unplug the USB drive and plug it back in. Click **OK** and then **Retry**.

16. In the Welcome window, type **root** and press **Enter**. Now type the password you created in Step 9 (P@$$w0rD) and press **Enter**. Power off the virtual machine, and close all open windows.

Chapter Summary

- Planning a Linux installation makes the procedure go more smoothly. You should determine your hardware information and fill out a hardware and software preinstallation checklist before installing Linux.

- A CPU is the microprocessor of a computer. The CPU clock speed and cache play major roles in processor speed. A CPU cache stores frequently accessed data and instructions.

- There are two major types of physical memory: RAM and ROM. RAM is volatile and ROM is nonvolatile. RAM can be dynamic or static. Dynamic RAM is the most common type of RAM. It must be refreshed thousands of times per second to store information, whereas static RAM doesn't need to be refreshed to store its data. The extra circuitry for refreshing DRAM makes it more expensive than SRAM.

- You must have long-term storage devices to install openSUSE Linux. The two main types of hard drives are IDE and SCSI. You use the `fdisk` command on a Linux machine to determine the type of hard drive that's installed.

- Video cards are expansion devices that send graphical information to the monitor. The most common video card formats are PCI and AGP.

- Resolution is the number of horizontal and vertical pixels a monitor is capable of displaying.

- Partitioning a hard drive improves system performance and makes it possible to install multiple OSs and use different file systems. Linux supports a maximum of four primary partitions. Logical partitions are used to bypass the limitation of having only four primary partitions.

- AutoYaST enables administrators to install openSUSE on multiple machines without user intervention. To use it, an AutoYaST profile must be created, which is an ASCII XML configuration file for specifying installation settings.

Key Terms

arithmetic logic unit (ALU)   A component of the CPU responsible for mathematical and logical operations.

AutoYaST profile   An ASCII XML configuration file used to configure an automatic openSUSE installation.

bus   A channel that allows you to connect components such as a video card to your computer's processor.

cache   A place where the CPU can store frequently accessed data and instructions.

clock speed   The number of pulses per second generated by the oscillator on the motherboard.

control unit (CU)   A component of the CPU that regulates instructions.

dynamic RAM (DRAM)   The most common type of memory used in computers; stores information by refreshing the capacitors thousands of times per second.

extended partition   A primary partition that contains a logical partition.

hard disk drive (HDD)   The main storage device; typically holds the largest amount of data in your computer.

Integrated Drive Electronics (IDE)   A type of interface that connects up to four hard drives via a flat 40-wire parallel cable or a seven-pin connector.

level 1 (L1) cache   The small RAM chip built into the CPU.

level 2 (L2) cache   A small RAM chip that's connected directly to the CPU or incorporated into processors. It's larger and slower than an L1 cache and is capable of reading larger quantities of data from RAM.

level 3 (L3) cache   A small RAM chip that's connected directly to the CPU when an L2 cache is used and is incorporated directly into the CPU in multicore processors. Similar functionality as an L2 cache but is even larger and slower.

logical partition   A partition that's created in one of the four primary partitions; begins with the drive number 5.

multiplier A number hard-wired into the CPU for determining processor speed.

partitioning The process of dividing a hard drive into logical sections; each one is a contiguous section of blocks treated as a separate physical drive.

primary partitions Partitions installed as part of the Linux boot sector. Linux supports only four primary partitions, which can be subdivided further. *See also* logical partition.

read-only memory (ROM) Nonvolatile computer memory used to store data permanently.

resolution The number of horizontal and vertical pixels a monitor is capable of displaying.

Serial Advanced Technology Attachment (SATA) An advanced IDE interface for high performance and better reliability; it uses a much thinner cable, which simplifies cabling and improves airflow in the system.

small computer systems interface (SCSI) An interface typically used to connect hard drives in a server rather than a home desktop; it's faster and more expensive and creates more noise and heat than other types of hard disk interfaces.

static RAM (SRAM) Memory capable of storing information without the need to refresh its capacitors, as long as there is power to the computer.

swap partitions Partitions on the HDD that the Linux kernel uses for storing pages from RAM.

video adapter cards Expansion devices that plug into a bus on the motherboard; used to send graphical information to the monitor.

Review Questions

1. Which of the following core processor components performs mathematical and logical operations?

   a. CPU

   b. ALU

   c. CU

   d. Cache

2. Which of the following plays a major role in processor speed by having built-in RAM?

   a. CPU

   b. ALU

   c. CU

   d. Cache

3. Which of the following core processor components regulates instructions?

   a. CPU

   b. ALU

   c. CU

   d. Cache

14

4. Explain the difference between L1, L2, and L3 caches.

5. Which of the following Linux commands is used to determine the type of processor?

   a. fdisk

   b. uname -m

   c. proc

   d. fdisk -h

6. Which type of physical memory is considered volatile and depends on a constant flow of electricity to store information?

   a. ROM

   b. USB drive

   c. RAM

   d. Hard disk drive

7. Which type of physical memory is considered nonvolatile and contains a computer's startup instructions?

   a. ROM

   b. USB drive

   c. RAM

   d. Hard disk drive

8. Which type of RAM needs to be refreshed to store its information?

   a. SRAM

   b. L3 cache

   c. DRAM

   d. L2 cache

9. Which type of RAM doesn't need to be refreshed to store its information? (Choose all that apply.)

   a. SRAM

   b. L3 cache

   c. DRAM

   d. L2 cache

10. Why isn't RAM a suitable solution for long-term storage?

11. What's the main storage device that typically holds the largest amount of data?

   a. SRAM

   b. ROM

   c. HDD

   d. IDE disk

12. Explain the difference between IDE and SATA.

13. Which of the following items should be part of a preinstallation checklist for hardware? (Choose all that apply.)

    a. CPU

    b. RAM

    c. Keyboard

    d. Video card

14. List two benefits of creating multiple partitions on an HDD.

15. Which type of partition begins with the number 5?

    a. Primary partition

    b. Logical partition

    c. Extended partition

    d. Swap partition

16. Which type of partition does the Linux kernel use for storing pages from RAM?

    a. Primary partition

    b. Logical partition

    c. Extended partition

    d. Swap partition

17. Which type of partition is installed as part of the Linux boot sector and supports a maximum of four partitions?

    a. Primary partition

    b. Logical partition

    c. Extended partition

    d. Swap partition

14

Case Projects

CASE PROJECTS

Case Project 14-1: Locating Hardware Information

You're an IT administrator for a small office with 10 Windows computers; all were purchased at the same time and contain the same type of hardware. Your boss has asked whether installing openSUSE Linux on all 10 computers is possible. You know Linux will probably recognize all hardware devices on these computers, but you want to make sure. How can you use Windows to find hardware information? What information should you look for?

Case Project 14-2: Researching and Creating an AutoYaST Server

Now that you have determined that all computers in the office described in Case Project 14-1 have the correct hardware to install openSUSE, your boss wants you to set up an AutoYaST server on one machine as well as an AutoYaST profile so that openSUSE can be installed on the other machines automatically. Conduct research to figure out how to create an AutoYaST server, and write the commands you use to call the AutoYaST profile.

## chapter 15

Linux File System Management and Administration

After reading this chapter and completing the exercises, you will be able to:

- Describe features of Linux file systems
- Administer the Linux file system at the command line
- Perform file system management tasks

In this chapter, you explore more advanced Linux file system topics. You start with an overview of Linux file systems, particularly the default file system in openSUSE: ext4. You learn the commands for mounting and unmounting Linux file systems as well as how to administer a Linux file system at the command line and use the YaST LVM module to create a logical partition.

Overview of Linux File Systems

As you learned in Chapter 3, a file system is the way files are stored and organized to simplify access to data and help the OS keep track of how files are organized and how available space is managed on a disk. A file system also consists of disk partitions, which allow better organization and productivity, data security, data backup, and more.

The Linux file system has a hierarchical directory structure descending from the root directory (/). All partitions are contained under the root directory. Unlike other OSs, Linux treats all objects, such as devices and directories, as files. Partitions, as described in Chapter 14, are logical divisions of hard drives. A hard drive can have 16 partitions, with a maximum of 4 primary partitions (IDE or SCSI) and an extended partition that can be divided into 12 logical partitions. In Linux, partitions are named according to their location. Linux treats each device, such as a monitor, keyboard, or hard drive, as a single file and stores it in the /dev directory (where all device files are stored).

A file system can be viewed as rectangular blocks containing data. The first block is the master block containing the boot sector, and subsequent blocks contain the OS, applications, and data. The Linux file system structure is divided into the following blocks:

- *Superblock*—Stores information about the file system, such as file system size
- *Inode*—Contains all information about a file (permissions, ownership, and so on), except its name and the actual data
- *Directory block*—Contains the filename and corresponding inode number
- *Data block*—Consists of blocks that store the data in a file

Linux has two main types of file systems: Network File System (NFS) and a disk file system, which is mounted on a local computer. In Linux, disk file systems include ext2, ext3, and ext4. As you learned in Chapter 13, NFS is mounted on a different partition of a local computer or on a remote computer, in which case it appears as though it were on the local computer. It's accessed with the NFS protocol.

Other file systems in Linux include Coda, FAT, and the extended file system. The Coda file system is a distributed file system much like NFS. Coda saves a copy of files in the /coda directory so that the file system can continue operating during partial network failures. The File Allocation Table (FAT) is a disk file system developed by Microsoft. Linux supports access to all versions of FAT using the VFAT kernel module. FAT32 is the most recent version of FAT. The extended file systems (ext2, ext3, and ext4) are discussed in the following sections.

Features of Ext4

Originally, Linux used the MINIX file system, which was easy to use but didn't allow adding new file systems. For this reason, the Virtual File System (VFS) was introduced with the Linux kernel, which led to the development of the Extended (ext) File System. This file system supports disk space of 2 GB and a maximum filename length of 255 characters. However, it didn't support separate access for each user and group, inode modification, and data modification timestamps. It used linked lists to keep track of free blocks and inodes, which affected performance negatively; as the file system was used, linked lists became unsorted, and the file system became fragmented. As a solution to these problems, the **Second Extended (ext2) File System** was developed; it included the following features:

- Standard UNIX file types, such as regular files, directories, device special files, and symbolic links

- File systems created on much larger partitions than the previous 2 GB limitation

- Variable-length filenames with a maximum size of 255 characters

- Reservation of blocks for the super user (root) that enables administrators to recover from user processes filling up file systems

The **Third Extended (ext3) File System** is an updated version of ext2 that supports file sizes up to 2 TB and filenames up to 255 characters. In addition, it supports a file system up to 16 TB with up to 32,000 subdirectories, and deleted data can be retrieved by the use of journaling (described in the following section).

The **Fourth Extended (ext4) File System,** now included with openSUSE and most current Linux distributions, is an improvement over ext3; it has better performance, increased reliability, and features such as the following:

- *Compatibility*—You can migrate from ext3 to ext4 without reformatting the hard drive. However, going back to ext3 does require reformatting the hard drive.

- *Larger file sizes*—Ext4 supports files as large as 16 TB and a file system up to 1 exabyte (EB, which is 1 billion gigabytes).

- *Unlimited subdirectories*—Ext4 supports an unlimited number of subdirectories.

- *Extents*—To divide large files, ext4 uses **extents,** which is a set of contiguous physical blocks used to reduce fragmentation and improve performance. There's no need for a defragmentation utility in this file system. FAT, discussed earlier, stores files contiguously, one after the other. When changes are made to files, they become fragmented because there's no room to expand. In ext4, files are stored in blocks with blank spaces between them to allow for expansion and prevent fragmentation. If there's not enough room on the drive to keep the file as one unit, it becomes fragmented. That's not to say fragmentation doesn't occur in ext4, but the drive would have to be nearly maxed out before it would begin to happen.

- *Multiblock allocation*—Block allocators decide which free blocks on a hard drive are used to write data. In ext3, only one 4-KB block could be allocated at a time, so the block allocator had to be called thousands of times just to write a small block of data. Ext4 can allocate multiple larger blocks in a single call.

15

- *Faster performance of the* `fsck` *command*—The `fsck` command is used to check and repair Linux file systems. In ext3, it works slowly because it has to check all inodes in the file system. In ext4, however, it doesn't check unused inodes, which speeds up performance. Of course, `fsck` must be used first to determine the used and unused inodes, so it always runs slowly the first time it's issued.

- *Journal checksumming*—Ext4 uses checksums to make sure blocks on a disk aren't corrupted, which can happen if the system crashes. A checksum is a calculated number that's sent with data to check its validity after it has been transmitted.

Journaling

When the kernel is writing data to a storage device, it might cache the data until it decides where to place it. If the system fails during this process, the cached data is lost. With **journaling**, the file system caches the data in a hidden file until the kernel has finished writing the data to a drive. If there's a system failure, the fsck utility keeps track of the location where data is to be placed to prevent data loss. Journaling was added in ext3, which supports three journaling modes:

- *Writeback*—Only metadata (descriptive information about file contents, such as file owner, last modified date, and so on) is stored in **writeback mode**. The journaled data blocks are stored in their location on the disk, which preserves the file system structure.

- *Ordered*—**Ordered mode** is the default. It also stores metadata, but it writes data first. This is important because if the system crashes before data blocks are written, the data can be corrupted (even if it was journaled).

- *Data*—**Data mode** is the slowest mode because it requires the file system to write every change twice: first to the journal and then to the file system. It logs all file system data and metadata changes, so it reduces the chance of losing any changes to files.

Verifying File System Integrity with the Fsck Utility

File systems write every metadata change on disk simultaneously. These changes are written to the disk by separate writes, and if there's a system failure during the writing process, metadata might be in an inconsistent state, leading to inconsistencies in the file system. To ensure file system integrity, you use the fsck utility, which performs a sequential investigation of the file system. If it finds a misplaced directory or a file with no inode number, it places these directories and files in the `/lost+found` directory, which is created on each partition.

The fsck utility takes the name of the file system as an argument to monitor its status. The superblock contains a flag that informs the kernel whether the file system has been mounted correctly. If it is, it's flagged as clean; if it's not, it's flagged as not clean. When the system is started, the flag is read, and if it's not clean, the fsck utility runs. Table 15-1 describes options you can use with the `fsck` command.

You shouldn't use the `fsck` command on a mounted file system because it could corrupt the file system.

Table 15-1 Options for the `fsck` command

Option	Description
N	Displays what would be checked but doesn't allow the fsck utility to actually perform the check. If there are certain changes you don't want to make to the file system, this option is useful to see what would happen if you performed the check.
R	Checks all file systems except the `root` directory (which is usually mounted).
V	Displays verbose output.
a	Repairs the file system automatically without prompting for user intervention, so it should be used with caution.

Activity 15-1: Performing a File System Check

Time Required: 20 minutes

Objective: Check the status of your file system with the `fsck` command.

Description: In this activity, you use the fsck utility. Next, you write down your mounted directories and determine which file system is mounted in the /home directory. You then boot your Linux machine into single-user mode, unmount the /home directory, and use the `fsck` command again to compare the results.

1. Start VMware Player and start an openSUSE virtual machine.

2. Open a terminal window. Switch to the root user by typing **su** and pressing **Enter**, and then enter the correct root password.

3. Perform a file system check by typing **fsck** and pressing **Enter**. What type of warning message did you get, and why? Cancel the check on each file system by typing **n**.

   _____

4. Display disk space use on the file system by typing **df -T** and pressing **Enter**. This command shows you which file systems are mounted. Find the file system that's mounted on /home. It should be similar to /dev/sda3 or /dev/hda3.

5. Unmount the /home directory by typing **umount /home** and pressing **Enter**. Were you able to unmount this directory? Why or why not?

   _____

6. Bring your Linux computer down to single-user mode by typing **init 1** and pressing **Enter**. (Entering single-user mode is necessary to kill other processes using the device.) Type the root user's password when prompted and press **Enter**.

7. Unmount the /home directory by typing **umount /home** and pressing **Enter**. How can you tell whether you were able to unmount the /home directory?

   _____

8. While still in single-user mode, use the `fsck` command on all file systems except /root by typing **fsck -R** and pressing **Enter**. What results do you get?

   _____

15

9. Mount the /home directory by typing **mount /home** and pressing **Enter**. To make sure this directory is mounted, type **df** and press **Enter**.

10. Restart your Linux machine by typing **reboot** and pressing **Enter**.

11. Power off the virtual machine.

Administering File Systems in Linux

A hard drive contains three components: cylinders, heads, and sectors. The system BIOS detects information for these components and passes it to the OS. The first sector, called the Master Boot Record (MBR), contains the boot loader and partition table. To create a partition table, add a partition, and create a file system on a disk, you can use partition utilities, such as fdisk. This command-line tool can create and modify the partition table provided by Linux. It can be run only as root and can access only IDE and SCSI hard drives. Table 15-2 describes the options you can use with this utility.

Table 15-2 Options for the `fdisk` command

Option	Description
-a	Toggles the bootable flag, which indicates whether a partition is bootable
-d	Deletes a partition
-l	Lists all partition types and their corresponding IDs
-m	Displays a menu of all options you can use with `fdisk`
-n	Adds a partition
-p	Displays a partition table
-q	Exits fdisk without saving changes
-t	Changes a partition's system ID (done to switch to a swap partition, for example)
-u	Toggles displaying entry units to sectors or cylinders
-v	Verifies a partition table
-w	Exits fdisk and saves changes

Creating a File System with the `mkfs` Command

You use the `mkfs` command to create a Linux file system on a device (usually a hard drive but can also be used on a USB thumb drive). To create a file system, the device must exist and be formatted with the fdisk utility. The following example shows the syntax of the `mkfs` command, and Table 15-3 describes the options used with it:

```
mkfs -V -t ext4 /dev/sda3
```

Table 15-3 Options for the `mkfs` command

Option	Description
-V	Displays verbose output and file system–specific commands
-t	Creates a specific file system type, such as ext3 or ext4
-c device	Checks the specified device for corrupted blocks before creating the file system
-v	Displays verbose output

Activity 15-2: Adding an Ext4 Partition with Fdisk

Time Required: 45 minutes

Objective: Add a partition table and create an ext4 file system.

Description: In this activity, you create a virtual machine, install openSUSE Linux on it, and customize the partitions. You then manipulate the partition table with the fdisk utility. Finally, you create an ext4 file system with the `mkfs` command.

1. Use the information you learned in Chapter 2 to create a virtual machine and name it **Activity 15-2**. Begin the openSUSE installation, accept the default settings, select the GNOME desktop environment, and then click **Next**.

2. In the Suggested Partitioning window, click the **Create Partition Setup** button.

3. Click the **Custom Partitioning (for experts)** option button, and then click **Next**.

4. Create a swap file system by clicking **Hard Disks** on the left under System View, and then click **Add Partition**.

5. In the Add Partition on /dev/sda window, make sure the **Primary Partition** option button is selected, and then click **Next**.

6. In the next window, make sure the **Custom Size** option button is selected, type **1 GB** in the Size text box, and then click **Next**.

7. In the next window, click the **File system** list arrow, click **Swap** in the list, make sure **Mount partition** is selected under Mounting Options, and then click **Finish**.

8. Now create a second primary partition by clicking **Add Partition**. This time, enter **10 GB** for the custom size, click **Next**, and click **Ext4** for the file system type. Click **Finish**, and then click **Accept**. Finish the openSUSE installation, and make sure you remember the password you set for your user account.

9. After the installation is finished, open a terminal window and switch to the root user.

10. Display the devices you have mounted by typing **df -T** and pressing **Enter**. What type of hard disk drive do you have? For instance, is it /dev/hda or /dev/sda?

11. To work with your partition table, type **fdisk /dev/sda** and press **Enter**. If the results of the `df` command in Step 10 listed your device as /dev/hda, use **fdisk /dev/hda** instead.

12. Display your partition table by typing **p** and pressing **Enter**. What are the IDs for the first primary partition and the second partition?

15

13. Display a list of each partition type and its corresponding ID by typing l and pressing **Enter**. What are the 82 and 83 file systems?

_____

14. Add a third partition by typing **n** and pressing **Enter**. Next, type **p** and press **Enter** for a primary partition, and then type **3** and press **Enter** for the third primary partition.

15. When you're asked for the first cylinder, accept the default by clicking **Enter**. For the last cylinder, you can enter the size you want for this partition in the format +10G; however, for this activity, just accept the defaults by pressing **Enter**.

16. Display your partition table again by typing **p** and pressing **Enter**. You should see your new partition. Exit the fdisk utility and save your changes by typing **w** and pressing **Enter**. Now restart your Linux machine by using the **reboot** command as the root user.

17. After your computer restarts, open a terminal window and switch to the root user.

18. Create an ext4 file system on the new partition and display verbose output by typing **mkfs -V -t ext4 /dev/sda3** (replacing sda with hda, if necessary) and pressing **Enter**.

19. Power off the virtual machine, and leave VMware Player running for the next activity.

Mounting and Unmounting File Systems

File systems can be mounted with the `mount` command. During installation, Linux stores information about where and how partitions should be mounted in the `/etc/fstab` table. Linux refers to this table and mounts file systems on devices according to preferences the user has set. The syntax for this command is as follows:

```
mount -t type device_to_mount mount_point
```

The argument following the `-t` option, `type`, indicates the file system to mount, such as ext3, ext4, and FAT. `device_to_mount` is the name of the device to be mounted, such as `/dev/sda` or `/dev/hda`. `mount_point` is the location (directory) where the file system should be mounted. This directory must already exist on the computer. If it contains any files, they can't be accessed until the file system is mounted. For example, if the computer is started before the `/var` directory is mounted, a `/var/tmp` directory in the `/root` file system is used in its place. When the `/var` directory is mounted, it makes the `/var/tmp` directory on the `/root` file system remote (inaccessible). In other words, if you mount a file system over an existing directory, the original directory can't be accessed. You can use the `-r` option to perform a read-only mount operation, which stops the kernel from writing to the file system and updating file access times in inodes. Read-only mounts are necessary for unwriteable media, such as CD-ROMs.

Table 15-4 describes devices that can be mounted with the `mount` command.

Table 15-4 Devices that can be mounted with the `mount` command

Device	Command
CD-ROM	`mount -t iso9660 /dev/cdrom /mnt/cdrom`
Remote host	`mount -t nfs remote_host:/dir /mnt`
Linux partition	`mount -t ext4 /dev/sda3 /mnt`

In Table 15-4, the mount point is /mnt in all examples, but you can create an empty directory with the mkdir command and use it as a mount point.

The umount command is used to disconnect (unmount) directories manually from the Linux file structure, but you can't unmount a file or directory that's open. If you attempt to do this, you get a "device is busy" error. When you shut down a Linux machine, all directories are unmounted automatically. The only directories that are mounted automatically are the ones listed in the /etc/fstab table.

Usually, you use the umount command without options. You just specify a directory, as shown in the following example. However, Table 15-5 describes options you can use with the umount command.

umount /mnt

Table 15-5 Options for the umount **command**

Option	Description
-V	Displays the umount version.
-h	Displays options you can use with the umount command.
-v	Displays verbose output.
-r	If the umount command fails, it tries to remount the directory as read-only.
-a	Unmounts all files in the /etc/mtab file.
-n	Unmounts a file system without writing information to the /etc/mtab file.
-t	Issues the umount command on a specified file system; multiple file system types can be separated with commas.

The /etc/mtab file manages mounted devices, which are updated automatically with the mount and umount commands.

15

Automatic Mounting and Unmounting

The /etc/fstab configuration file contains options and preset mount points so that file systems can be mounted or unmounted automatically. The fdisk, mount, and umount commands refer to this file while operating. The /etc/fstab file maintains a table of all file systems with preferences users set during installation. Only the root user can configure this file. Here's an example of an entry in this table:

/dev/hda3   swap   swap   defaults   0   0

Each entry in this file consists of six fields:

- The block device or remote file system that needs to be mounted
- The mount point on the local system
- The type of file system to mount
- The list of mount options delimited by commas
- Used by the dump command to determine whether the file system needs to be backed up; a 1 indicates it should be backed up, and a 0 means it shouldn't
- Specifies in what order the file system should be checked (with 0 indicating that file checking is disabled)

File System Management Tasks

Say an administrator needs to back up system data regularly to a local hard drive. Backups are stored in different partitions on the hard drive based on the type of project. The number of projects has increased, so more partitions and storage space are needed. For this reason, the administrator needs to repartition the local hard drive periodically, which is a cumbersome process and exposes the file system and data on the hard drive to damage and corruption. She needs to manage the Linux file system to ensure smooth backups without damaging files or losing data.

In this section, you learn about using logical volume management and the dumpe2fs utility to manage repartitioning and other file system tasks. File system management includes effective use of space on partitions and checking the file system structure periodically to prevent data corruption.

Logical Volume Management

Logical volume management (LVM) is a technique for collecting information on free space from all disk partitions and storage devices into one logical volume. The tool for this task, Logical Volume Manager, uses an abstraction layer that hides details about the type of hardware and the location of stored data from the OS. It also separates hardware and software management. LVM maintains a table with information on which volume and volume group data has been written to. (A volume group is a collection of logical and physical volumes contained in a single unit.) This table makes it possible to add and change drives without applications or users being aware of these changes.

A logical volume is divided into logical groups that are assigned mount points, such as /home and /, and have a file system, such as ext4. With the LVM tool, you can do the following:

- Make snapshots of a changing logical volume during a backup. These snapshots can then be mounted and backed up to prevent loss of data.
- Resize storage space and transfer free space from one volume to another during runtime.
- Remove physical disks at runtime without any loss of data. The data is transferred to existing disks that form part of the logical volume.

A Linux partition, such as /dev/sda2, is an example of a PV that can be used to create a VG.

Activity 15-3 walks you through using the LVM module.

Activity 15-3: Creating a Logical Volume with the YaST LVM Module

Time Required: 45 minutes

Objective: Create a logical volume in YaST.

Description: In this activity, you create a Linux virtual machine and customize the partitions. You then use the YaST LVM module to configure the physical volume, create and configure the volume group, and create and configure the logical volume.

1. Start VMware Player, if necessary. Create a new virtual machine and name it **Logical Volume Activity**. Use the information you learned in Chapter 2 to install the latest version of openSUSE on this virtual machine. Make sure you accept all the defaults until you get to the Desktop Selection window, where you should choose **GNOME Desktop**.

2. In the Suggested Partitioning window, you delete one of your partitions so that you can configure the physical volume for LVM. First, click **Edit Partition Setup**.

3. At the left under System View, click **Hard Disks**, and then click the last partition on the right under Hard Disks. This partition should be listed as something like **/dev/sda3**.

4. Next, click **Delete**, and then click **Yes** to confirm. Finally, accept your changes by clicking **Accept** and then finish the rest of the installation.

5. After the installation is finished, open a terminal window and switch to the root user.

6. Follow the steps you learned in Activity 15-2 to use the fdisk utility and display the partition table. Notice that it doesn't contain the partition you removed in Step 4.

7. Open the YaST LVM module by using the **yast2** command as the root user. Type **LVM** in the Filter text box and press **Enter**. Continue through all warnings by clicking **Yes**.

8. The first step is to configure your physical volume, which is the third primary partition in this case (for example, /dev/sda3). Click **Hard Disks** on the left under System View (see Figure 15-1).

15

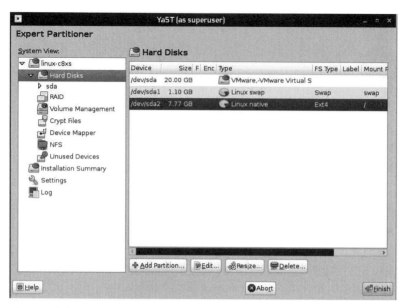

Figure 15-1 The Expert Partitioner window
Source: openSUSE

9. Click the **Add Partition** button. Make sure the **Primary Partition** option button is selected, and then click **Next**.

10. Click **Maximum Size,** and then click **Next.** Click the **Do not format partition** option button, and then change the file system ID to **0x8E Linux LVM.** Make sure the **Do not mount partition** option button is selected, and then click **Finish.** Figure 15-2 shows the new LVM Linux partition listed.

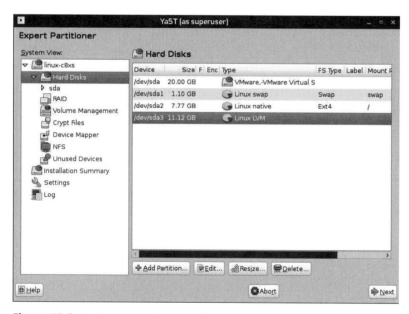

Figure 15-2 Adding a new Linux partition
Source: openSUSE

11. Click **Volume Management** in the left pane. Click the **Add** button, and then click **Volume Group**.

12. In the Add Volume Group window, type **system** in the Volume Group Name text box, and make sure the default **4 MB** is entered in the Physical Extent Size text box (see Figure 15-3).

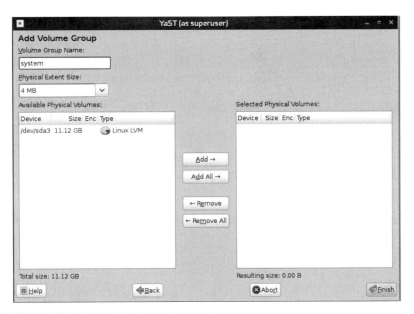

Figure 15-3 The Add Volume Group window
Source: openSUSE

13. In the Available Physical Volumes list box, click **Linux LVM**, click the **Add** button, and then click **Finish**.

14. In the Expert Partitioner window, click **Next**, and then click **Finish** in the Summary window.

15. Check the partition table with the fdisk utility to ensure that the LVM partition has been added.

16. Power off the virtual machine.

Using the `dumpe2fs` Command

You can also use the `dumpe2fs` command to find file system information. For example, if the system reports an error when you're creating a partition, you can use this command to display file system details, such as superblock and block information. Table 15-6 lists many of the options used with the `dumpe2fs` command, which has the following syntax:

```
#dumpe2fs [-bfhixV] [-ob superblock] [-oB blocksize] device
```

Table 15-6 Options for the `dumpe2fs` command

Option	Description
-b	Displays bad blocks
-ob superblock	Forces use of a superblock while checking the file system
-oB blocksize	Forces use of blocksize in bytes while checking the file system
-f	Forces display of the entire file system
-h	Displays only superblock information
-i	Displays file system data from an image file created by e2image, using device as the pathname to the image file
-x	Displays detailed group information on block numbers in hexadecimal format
-V	Displays the dumpe2fs version and then exits

Chapter Summary

- The OS uses a file system to manage available disk space and keep track of how files are organized on a disk.

- The Linux file system is a hierarchical directory structure with the highest level (root directory) at the top.

- The two types of file systems that Linux supports are Network File System (NFS) and disk file systems.

- You can mount a disk file system, such as ext2, ext3, or ext4, on your local computer.

- The major difference between ext2 and ext3 is journaling, a key feature of ext3 that enables administrators to retrieve deleted data.

- The default file system in openSUSE is ext4, an improvement over ext3. It allows much larger files and a larger file structure. It also provides better compatibility, unlimited subdirectories, the use of extents to cut down on fragmentation, multiblock allocation, faster performance of the `fsck` command, and journal checksumming.

- To prevent loss of data, journaling caches data in a hidden file until the kernel has finished writing the data to a drive. It supports three modes: writeback, ordered, and data.

- The Linux file system writes metadata changes on the hard drive. The `fsck` command can be used to check these changes and repair the Linux file system.

- The first sector on a hard drive, called the Master Boot Record, contains the boot loader and partition table.

- You can create partition tables, add partitions, or create a file system on a hard drive with the fdisk utility.

- The `mkfs` command is used to create a Linux file system on a device.

- The `mount` command is used to connect file systems to the Linux file structure manually. The `umount` command is used to disconnect (unmount) file systems manually from the Linux file structure.

- During installation, Linux stores all information about where and how partitions should be mounted in a configuration file called `/etc/fstab`. You can automate the mounting process with this file.

- Logical volume management (LVM) can be used to create one logical partition from multiple storage devices. LVM uses an abstraction layer that hides details about the type of hardware and the location of data stored on the hardware.

- The three steps in configuring LVM are configuring physical volumes, creating and configuring a volume group, and creating and configuring a logical volume.

- You can investigate a file system for possible errors by using the `dumpe2fs` command, which displays block and superblock information, for example.

Key Terms

data mode   One of three journaling modes first introduced in ext3. It's the slowest mode because it requires the file system to write every change twice: first to the journal and then to the file system.

extents   In ext4, a set of contiguous physical blocks used to reduce fragmentation and improve performance.

Fourth Extended (ext4) File System   A journaling file system included with openSUSE Linux that offers better performance and increased reliability along with several new features, including unlimited subdirectories, extents, and multiblock allocation. *See also* extents.

journaling   A Linux file system feature that caches data in a hidden file until the kernel writes it to the hard drive.

logical volume management (LVM)   A technique for collecting information on free space from all disk partitions and storage devices into one logical volume.

ordered mode   The default journaling mode, first introduced in ext3. It stores metadata, but it writes data first, which is important to prevent data corruption.

Second Extended (ext2) File System   A replacement for the extended file system that doesn't support journaling. Features include support for standard UNIX file types, larger partition sizes, variable-length filenames up to 255 characters, and reservation of blocks for root.

Third Extended (ext3) File System   A Linux file system that supports journaling and a maximum file size of 2 TB.

writeback mode   One of three journaling modes first introduced in ext3 that writes only metadata.

15

Review Questions

1. In Linux, what's the maximum number of primary partitions a hard drive can have?

   a. 2

   b. 4

   c. 6

   d. Unlimited

2. Which of the following features is new in ext4? (Choose all that apply.)

   a. Journaling

   b. Extents

   c. Up to 32,000 subdirectories

   d. Multiblock allocation

3. Which of the following ext4 features reduces data fragmentation and improves performance?

   a. Multiblock allocation

   b. Larger file sizes

   c. Journaling

   d. Extents

4. Which Linux command is used to check file system integrity?

   a. `fsck`

   b. `fdisk`

   c. `mount`

   d. `mkfs`

5. Ext3 supports file sizes up to 2 TB. True or False?

6. Which journaling mode requires writing every file system change twice?

   a. Ordered

   b. Data

   c. Writeback

   d. Metadata

7. Which journaling mode stores metadata? (Choose all that apply.)

   a. Ordered

   b. Data

   c. Writeback

   d. Metadata

8. Which command should you use to check the consistency of all file systems except /root?

   a. fsck -a

   b. fsck -r

   c. fsck -R

   d. fsck -A

9. Which Linux command is used to create and modify partition tables?

   a. fsck

   b. fdisk

   c. mount

   d. mkfs

10. Which Linux command is used to create a Linux file system on a device?

    a. fsck

    b. fdisk

    c. mount

    d. mkfs

11. You can use the YaST LVM module to do which of the following? (Choose all that apply.)

    a. Make snapshots of volumes during backups.

    b. Mount and unmount volumes automatically.

    c. Transfer free space between volumes during runtime.

    d. Remove physical disks at runtime without data loss.

12. Using the fsck command on the /root directory is a good idea to ensure its integrity. True or False?

13. Which Linux file contains information about where and how partitions should be mounted?

14. Which of the following commands can be used to find file system information?

    a. mkfs

    b. fsck

    c. dumpe2fs

    d. mount

15

Case Projects

Case Project 15-1: Finding File System Information from the Command Line

In this chapter, you learned some Linux command-line utilities for managing a Linux file system. List the command you should use to find the following information:

- Your company has decided to upgrade all Linux servers to ext4. You aren't sure which file system is used on one Linux server. Which command should you use to determine its file system?

- Every time your Linux machine boots, the file system you added isn't mounted automatically. What can you do to make sure it's mounted automatically each time your computer starts?

- A customer calls to complain that she can't view the contents of a directory she mounted. What command should you use to view all mounted file systems on her computer?

Case Project 15-2: Benefits of Upgrading to Ext4

Your company still uses the ext3 file system. Everything seems to work as expected, and no employees have complained about problems accessing files. Your manager has asked you to research whether upgrading to ext4 would be beneficial. Write a one-page memo to your manager, explaining your recommendation to upgrade or not upgrade.

## chapter 16

Managing Resources in Linux

After reading this chapter and completing the exercises, you will be able to:

- Identify common X Window versions and configure X Window with Linux utilities
- Explain how to use a display manager in KDE and GNOME
- Manage the root user account as well as disk quotas

In this chapter, you learn how to manage resources in openSUSE, particularly display managers and disk quotas. First, you learn about the X Window System for managing the graphical user interface and input devices and how to start it from the command line. Then you move on to learning about display managers in the most common Linux desktop environments: GNOME and KDE. Finally, you learn commands for managing the root account and techniques for working with disk quotas to limit users' use of disk space.

Overview of the X Window System

The **X Window System** provides a method for writing device-independent graphics and windowing software that can be transferred from one computer to another easily. Because the average user can't fully appreciate the power of Linux from working just at the command line, developing a more user-friendly environment was important. X Window was developed to unleash the graphical capability of Linux and set a protocol for creating and manipulating graphical elements (such as windows, buttons, icons, and so on) on a computer screen. With this system, you can run multiple graphics applications simultaneously. This section gives you an overview of X Window's development, its configuration file, and using X Window with XF86 client and XFREE 86.

X Window Background

In the mid-1980s, the Massachusetts Institute of Technology (MIT) developed the X Window System as a way to use computers with a graphical environment. X Window includes libraries for building frames, buttons, menus, and other components that constitute a window in an application. It's based on the client/server architecture that allows users to access local and remote applications. For instance, X Window clients request graphics from the X Server to be displayed on a monitor. X Window is popular with Linux users because it operates with any hardware-based graphics system, so it can be used on high-end workstations. X Window also provides portable and multiplatform programming standards. Many organizations, including small office/home office (SOHO) companies and large corporations, run Linux distributions and X Window.

X Window consists of the following components:

- *Client*—Includes the applications running on a computer; also known as a window manager
- *Display server*—The software that controls hardware components (such as screen, monitor, and keyboard) and gives client applications access to hardware

The display server listens to both local and remote network sockets for clients. The client communicates with the display server and sends input requests, such as keyboard or mouse input. The server then processes these requests and sends the output to the client by displaying the information onscreen or sending it to a client application. There are two open-source X Window versions: XFree86 (originally written for the Intel x86 platform) and X.Org, the default version in openSUSE.

You can find more information on the XFree86 Project at *www.xfree86.org* and on the X.Org Foundation at *www.x.org*.

Configuring X Window

X Window interfaces with video hardware to display graphics on a monitor. To do this, it needs information about specific hardware components, such as the type of keyboard and mouse being used, how much RAM the video card has, and the type of video card adapter. This information is stored in configuration files, described in the following sections.

The XFree86 Project's goal was to develop a free version of X Window. XFree86 is an X Window server used with Red Hat Linux. If you want to use Linux as a desktop OS, you can install and configure XFree86 to use hardware devices graphically, such as the monitor, mouse, and keyboard. (Other Linux distributions have their own tools to run X Window.) When you install a Linux distribution, such as Red Hat Linux, the /usr/X11R6 directory is also installed and contains the majority of XFree86 software. Table 16-1 describes some important subdirectories of this directory.

Table 16-1 Subdirectories of /usr/X11R6

Subdirectory	Description
/usr/X11R6/bin	Defines the location of the X Window server and clients
/usr/X11R6/include	Defines the path to files for developing X Window clients and graphics, such as icons
/usr/X11R6/lib	Contains software libraries to support the X Window server and clients

The configuration file needed to run XFree86 is XF86Config. It's created during a Linux installation (as long as that distribution uses the XFree86 version of X Window) in the /etc/X11 directory. This file contains file location paths, hardware descriptions, and specifications. The XFree86 server needs this information to work with the graphics card and display monitor. Table 16-2 describes the sections of this file used for different operations, such as specifying the X session or server layout.

Table 16-2 Sections of the XFree86 configuration file

Section	Description
ServerLayout	Defines display and screen layouts and lists input devices, such as mouse and keyboard
Files	Lists available colors for a session in the rgb.txt file and lists the port number to the X font server, which functions when the OS starts and doesn't require an active X session
Module	Specifies drivers for loading an X session and contains modules (in the /usr/X11R6/lib/modules directory) ranging from special video card support to font rasterizers
InputDevice	Used for configuring an input device, such as a mouse or a keyboard; the XF86Config file might contain multiple Input Device sections if there are multiple input devices
Monitor	Used for configuring the display device declared in the ServerLayout section
Device	Lists details about the video graphics chipset and contains a Driver entry that prompts the XFree86 server to load the available module from the drivers subdirectory of the /usr/X11R6/lib/modules directory
Screen	Combines information from other sections, such as Device and Monitor; also specifies color depths and screen resolutions for the X Window session

16

The latest version of openSUSE includes the X.Org version of X Window. Its configuration file is `xorg.conf.d`, located in the `/etc/X11` directory. Table 16-3 describes the sections in this file.

The sections in a configuration file don't have to be in any particular order, and not all must be present.

Table 16-3 Sections of the X.Org configuration file

Section	Description
Files	An optional section for specifying pathnames required by the server.
ServerFlags	An optional section for specifying global X.Org server options.
Module	An optional section for specifying X.Org server modules to load; typically includes X.Org server extension modules and font rasterizer modules.
InputDevice	A mandatory section including an identifier entry (defines a unique name for an input device) and a driver entry (defines the driver name for an input device). The keyboard and mouse are the most common input drivers.
Device	A mandatory section that must have at least one section for the video card; also includes identifier and driver entries.
Monitor	Typically at least one monitor section is included; the only mandatory entry in this section is the identifier entry.
Modes	An optional section for specifying video modes independently of the Monitor section.
Screen	A mandatory section that includes the screen identifier, video card, monitor, and default color depth.
ServerLayout	Represents the server layout, which consists of entries in the Screen and InputDevice sections.
DRI	Contains information for the direct rendering infrastructure (DRI).
Vendor	An optional section containing vendor-specific configuration information.

Most configuration files in Linux can make your system inoperable if you make a mistake when editing the file. The same is true for the `/etc/X11/xorg.conf.d` and `/etc/X11/XF86Config` files. For instance, a mistake made in editing these files could prevent the GUI from working. Therefore, using a GUI program to configure X Window is best.

Mouse Configuration To configure a mouse in openSUSE Linux, you use the YaST Mouse configuration module. As mentioned, you need to supply some hardware information about your mouse, such as whether it's a USB or two-button serial mouse. In a terminal window, switch to the root user and issue the `yast2 mouse` command to open this module (see Figure 16-1).

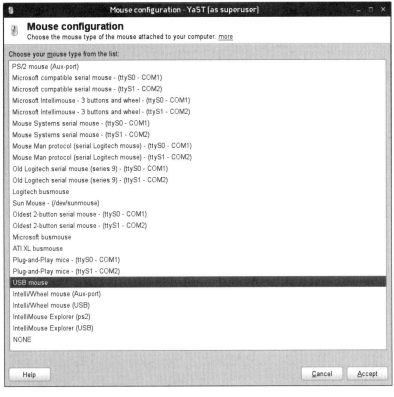

Figure 16-1 The Mouse configuration window
Source: openSUSE

Use the arrow keys to select the type of mouse you have, and then click Accept. As with any configuration change in X Window, you must restart X Window for the change to take effect. To do this, you issue the /etc/init.d/xdm restart command as the root user. It displays a login prompt where you enter your username and password. Then you use the startx command to start an X Window session (explained in more detail later in "Using X Window from the Command Line").

Keyboard Configuration Configuring the keyboard works in much the same way as configuring a mouse. To open the YaST System Keyboard Configuration module (shown in Figure 16-2), use the yast2 keyboard command. In this window, you select the keyboard layout to use for your system. Click the Expert Settings button to change options such as repeat rate or delay and to disable caps lock.

Monitor and Display Configuration To configure the monitor and display settings, you use the YaST Display module. Any changes you make in this module update the X Window configuration file automatically. Depending on your hardware (graphics card, monitor type, dual-monitor setup, and so forth), you have different options; the Display module detects your video and monitor hardware automatically. To start this module, click the Computer icon at the lower left, click Control Center, and type "display" in the Filter text box (see Figure 16-3).

16

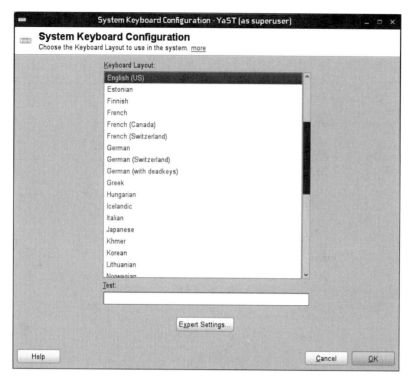

Figure 16-2 The System Keyboard Configuration window
Source: openSUSE

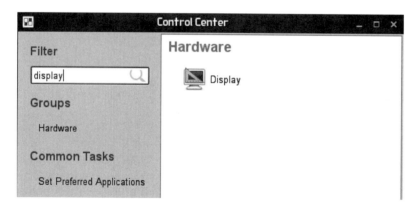

Figure 16-3 Starting the Display module
Source: openSUSE

You can configure the following settings in the Display module:

- *Resolution*—Select a screen resolution in this drop-down list. The options depend on the type of monitor you have.

- *Refresh rate*—The **refresh rate** is the number of times the display is refreshed per second. OpenSUSE detects the refresh rate automatically. Depending on your video card, you can change this setting; however, if you change it to an unsupported setting, your monitor might stop working.

- *Rotation*—If you use a nonstandard monitor, such as a widescreen monitor, you can select a rotation mode (landscape or portrait). Switching to portrait mode is convenient when you want to edit long documents or work with portrait images.

- *Panel icon*—Select this check box if you want to show the Display module in the panel at the lower right.

You use the xdpyinfo command to display information about the X server. The output is typically larger than the screen, so you might want to pipe the command's results with the more or less commands. For instance, you can type xdpyinfo | less to view results one page at a time. If you're looking for specific values, you can pipe the command to grep. This command enables you to pull specific information from a file by searching for keywords. For instance, if you want to view the screen resolution setting, use the xdpyinfo | grep resolution command.

To adjust video modes, you can use the Xvidtune utility (see Figure 16-4), which is started with the xvidtune command. Most monitors now support a wide range of display values (such as resolution and refresh rate), but you should still be cautious when using this utility because selecting values that are too high can damage your monitor. For example, if you set the refresh rate values (HSync and VSync) higher than what the monitor supports, you run the risk of causing permanent damage to the hardware, rendering the monitor unusable. In fact, this utility shows a warning message if you attempt to use an incorrect setting.

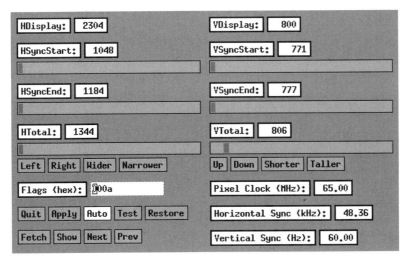

Figure 16-4 The Xvidtune utility
Source: openSUSE

16

Using X Window from the Command Line

You can start the X Window session from the command line with the startx utility. It simplifies the process of starting an X Window session by setting a user's display environment variable to identify the X Window server to X Window clients. Table 16-4 lists options for the `startx` command, which follows this syntax:

```
startx -- -option
```

The two hyphens after the `startx` command represent the end of client arguments and the beginning of server arguments.

Table 16-4 Common options for the `startx` command

Options	Description
-depth ##	Makes an X Window session start with a specified color depth.
-dpi ###	The `DisplaySize` setting in the X Window configuration file is typically used to set the dots per inch, but you can change it with this option.
-layout Multihead	Forces X Window to start as a multiheaded session, meaning more than one monitor can be used.

The startx utility first looks for a hidden file called `.xinitrc`, which should be in the user's home directory. This file is a shell script that the user can configure to run programs in the background. If this file isn't found, startx searches for the systemwide `.xinitrc` file, located in the `/etc/X11/xinit` directory. Using one of the options in Table 16-4 overrides startx's default operation. Table 16-5 describes files associated with the `startx` command, and Table 16-6 describes variables used with this command.

Table 16-5 Files associated with the `startx` command

Files	Description
$HOME/.xinitrc	A script that defines the client to run and programs to run in the background.
$HOME/.xserverrc	A script that defines the server to run (default is the X Server).
/etc/X11/xinit/xinitrc	If the user doesn't have an `.xinitrc` file in his or her home directory, this file is used to define the client and programs to run in the background.
/etc/X11/xinit/xserverrc	If the user doesn't have an `.xserverrc` file in his or her home directory, this file is used to define the server.

Table 16-6 Variables associated with the `startx` command

Files	Description
DISPLAY	Specifies the name of the display device to which clients connect
XAUTHORITY	Typically defined as $HOME/.Xauthority and is a security measure to prevent the X Window server from automatically setting up host-based authentication (which isn't secure) for the local host

You can view the value of variables in Table 16-6 by using the `echo` command. For example, you can type `echo $DISPLAY` to view the value of the `DISPLAY` variable.

Activity 16-1: Using the Startx Utility

Time Required: 20 minutes

Objective: Start an X Window session with the `startx` command.

Description: In this activity, you stop and start an X Window session and edit the screen resolution from the command line.

1. Start VMware Player and log in to an openSUSE virtual machine.

2. Open a terminal window and switch to the root user.

3. Start X Window by typing **startx** and pressing **Enter**. Did the command work? Why or why not?

_____

4. You're currently in runlevel 5 (required if you're using KDE or GNOME). Bring your openSUSE virtual machine down to runlevel 3 by typing **init 3** and pressing **Enter**. Log in with the root username and password.

5. Start X Window by typing **startx** and pressing **Enter**.

6. When X Window starts, make sure the virtual machine window is maximized, open a command prompt window, if necessary, and then check the screen resolution (dpi) by typing **xdpyinfo | grep resolution** and pressing **Enter**. Write down your screen resolution:

_____

7. Make the virtual machine window smaller by clicking the double square at the upper-right corner. Now check the dpi setting again. Did the number change? (If you aren't using a virtual machine, you can't change the monitor size. This step just shows you that Linux can determine the screen resolution automatically.)

_____

8. To change the dpi setting manually, first restart your Linux computer with the **reboot** command, and then bring your computer down to runlevel 3 (as in Step 4). Log in with the root username and password.

9. Type **startx -- -dpi 100** and press **Enter**.

16

10. After X Window starts, use the **xdpyinfo** command again (see Step 6) and check to see whether the screen resolution changed. If Linux is capable of determining the resolution automatically, why do you think you were able to change it manually?

11. Restart your Linux computer. Leave the virtual machine running and the terminal window open for the next activity.

Using a Display Manager

An X display manager presents a graphical login that prompts for a username and password before allowing access to the openSUSE Linux desktop. GDM is the display manager for GNOME, and the KDE desktop uses KDM as the display manager. In addition, the display manager enables you to select a different desktop for an X Window session. The way the X Window display manager is shown after you start your Linux system depends on the runlevel. Runlevels are defined as a system state entry in the `/etc/inittab` file. Table 16-7 describes these runlevels.

Table 16-7 Runlevels for controlling the X Window display manager

Runlevel	Description
0	Also known as system halt; shuts down Linux and powers off the computer
1	Also known as single-user mode; comparable with safe mode on a Windows machine and used by administrators for repairs and maintenance
2	Also known as multiuser mode; gives you access to most services except the network
3	Also known as full-user mode; gives you access to all services except X Window (meaning no access to the GUI, including GNOME and KDE)
4	A custom runlevel that's typically not used
5	Also known as X11; gives you access to all services, including the GUI

To set the display manager, you edit the `/etc/sysconfig/displaymanager` file or use the /etc/sysconfig Editor, which is a YaST module (see Figure 16-5). You can access this editor by issuing the `yast2 sysconfig` command as the root user. Expand the Desktop node and then the Display manager node, and then select the `DISPLAYMANAGER` variable to change its settings.

Configuring GNOME

The main GUI configuration tool for GNOME is the GNOME Control Center. You don't have to be the root user to use this tool. To start it, use the `gnome-control-center` command. Table 16-8 describes the modules you can access in the GNOME Control Center.

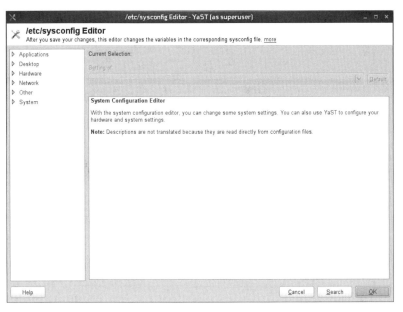

Figure 16-5 The /etc/sysconfig Editor
Source: openSUSE

Table 16-8 GNOME configuration modules

Module	Command	Description
GNOME Display Properties	gnome-display-properties	Configure monitor preferences, such as resolution, refresh rate, and rotation. Can also display a panel icon for fast access.
GNOME Window Properties	gnome-window-properties	Customize window preferences for the GNOME desktop, such as selecting a window when the mouse moves over it.
Keyboard Properties	gnome-keyboard-properties	Customize keyboard preferences, such as repeating keys that are held down.
Desktop Keybinding Properties	gnome-keybinding-properties	Configure shortcut keys, such as Ctrl+Alt+Delete for the logout process.
Mouse Properties	gnome-mouse-properties	Customize mouse preferences, such as a right-hand or left-hand orientation.
Volume Control	gnome-volume-control	Configure sound preferences, such as enabling window and button sounds.
Audio Profiles	gnome-audio-profiles-properties	Modify the parameters of an audio profile.
Desktop Options and Application Configuration	gconf-editor	GConf is a central location for storing preferences and system configuration data. Should be used only by experienced users.

16

Table 16-8 GNOME configuration modules (*continued*)

Module	Command	Description
Desktop Properties Configuration	`gnome-session-properties`	Select programs that start automatically (such as a Web site) when a user logs in to the system.
Default Application Configuration	`gnome-default-applications-properties`	Specify preferred applications, such as which Web browser opens when a link in a document or e-mail is clicked.
Help	`gnome-help`	Starts the GNOME Help Browser, a collection of Web-based instruction guides.
About	`gnome-about`	Opens a welcome screen with the GNOME version number and Linux distribution.

Configuring KDE

The KDM display manager, part of the KDE X Window desktop suite, also provides a graphical logon prompt. To start the KDE Control Center (shown in Figure 16-6) for configuring this display manager, you use the `kcontrol` command.

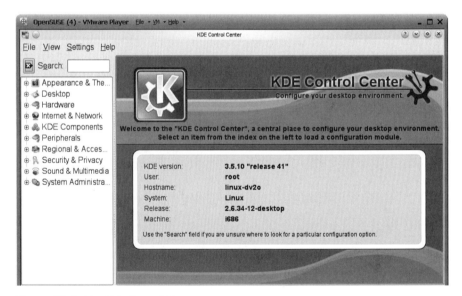

Figure 16-6 The KDE Control Center
Source: openSUSE

This window includes options for configuring the KDE environment of an X Window session. You can control the login display, prompts, and user icons, for example. Table 16-9 describes the modules you can access in the KDE Control Center.

Table 16-9 KDE Control Center modules

KDE module	Description
Appearance & Themes	Used to customize the desktop's appearance, including setting colors and fonts and customizing KDE icons
Desktop	Used to configure the desktop, including customizing window behavior, creating virtual desktops, and configuring the taskbar
Hardware	Used to configure hardware, such as the monitor, keyboard, mouse, printers, and so forth
Internet & Network	Used to configure network preferences, such as proxy settings, and Web browser settings
KDE Components	Used to access KDE components, such as Service Manager and KDE Performance
Peripherals	Contains the same settings as in the Hardware module
Regional & Accessibility	Used to configure keyboard layout and shortcuts
Security & Privacy	Used to access security features, such as password and user account information
Sound & Multimedia	Used to configure sound hardware and system notifications
System Administration	Used to configure the system date and time

ACTIVITY

Activity 16-2: Configuring Desktop Environments

Time Required: 45 minutes

Objective: Use GUI modules to configure the GNOME and KDE desktop environments.

Description: In this activity, you install the KDE4 Desktop Environment and Base System patterns so that you can switch between GNOME and KDE. Then you investigate the configuration modules available in the KDE and GNOME Control Centers.

1. If necessary, start VMware Player, open a terminal window, and switch to the root user.

2. Use the skills you learned in previous chapters to install the KDE4 Desktop Environment and Base System patterns.

3. Next, log out of the current session by clicking the **Computer** button at the lower left, clicking **Logout**, and then clicking **Log Out**.

4. Click your username in the openSUSE login window. At the bottom, click the **GNOME** list arrow and click **KDE** in the list of options. Type your password and click the **Log In** button to log in to KDE.

5. Open a terminal window, if necessary. Type **kcontrol** and press **Enter** to open the KDE Control Center. If you get an error, you need to install kdebase3 by typing **zypper install kdebase3** as root and pressing **Enter**. Log out of the current session and then log back in for the changes to take effect.

16

6. Sometimes when you click an icon, it's difficult to tell whether your system is responding. You can edit the Launch Feedback module to let you know the system is working in the background to process your request. To do this, click **Appearance & Themes** on the left, and then click the **Launch Feedback** module. If necessary, click **Enable taskbar notification** and then change the time to **10** seconds. Click **Apply** at the lower right.

7. Spend the next few minutes exploring the modules you can configure with the KDE Control Center. When you're finished, close the application.

8. Log out of the current session, and then repeat Steps 4 to 7, but this time click **GNOME** instead of KDE in the login window.

9. In the GNOME desktop environment, open a terminal window, if necessary. Start the Keyboard Shortcuts module by typing **gnome-keybinding-properties** and pressing **Enter**.

10. Navigate down to the Accessibility section, click to select **Run a terminal**, and then click the **Disabled** option. This should change the setting to "New shortcut." Press **Ctrl+T** and then click **Close**. Try your new keyboard shortcut by pressing **Ctrl+T**.

11. Leave the virtual machine running for the next activity.

Managing Resources

To manage an organization's network resources, Linux system administrators often have to fine-tune users' access privileges and restrict users' use of hard disk space. Several Linux commands, such as su, kdesu, and sudo, are available for managing the root user account to improve security. This section explains how to use these commands and describes the steps for setting and managing disk quotas.

Managing the Root User Account

Occasionally, "regular" users need to use commands that require root privileges. When installing software packages, for example, you need administrative privileges, so you can use the su command to switch to the root user account before performing the installation. The following sections explain commands for managing root accounts.

Using the su Command
At times, you need to issue a command as another user. Instead of logging out and logging in again as a different user, you can use the su ("substitute user" or "switch user") command as long as you have the password for the user account you're switching to. The syntax for the su command is as follows:

su *option username arguments*

The su command changes user credentials to those of the root user or the user specified by *username* and then starts a new session. Table 16-10 describes options used with the su command.

Table 16-10 Options for the `su` command

Option	Description
`-l`	Instead of carrying over environment variables from your current shell, you're logged in as though you're the root user.
`-m`	Preserves environment variables in Linux.
`--help`	Displays information about options or arguments for the `su` command and returns to the command prompt.
`--version`	Displays the command version and returns to the command prompt.

Using the `kdesu` Command The `kdesu` command is a GUI utility used in KDE that enables you to run applications with root privileges. The syntax for this command is as follows:

```
kdesu -c command
```

Although the `kdesu` command is designed for the KDE environment, you can use it in GNOME as long as you have the KDE package installed.

NOTE

The `kdesu` command is similar to the `su` command, but it allows you to remember passwords (see Figure 16-7).

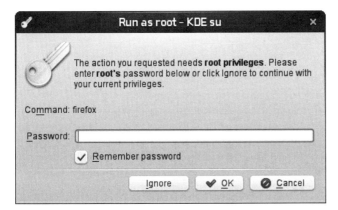

Figure 16-7 The option for remembering a password
Source: openSUSE

In the following example, this command enables the user to run the Nautilus file manager with root privileges, which allows access to all directories and files on the system:

```
kdesu -c nautilus
```

Using the `sudo` Command With the `sudo` (superuser do) command, system administrators can allow a group of users to run certain commands as root or another user and log the commands and arguments this group uses. In this way, administrators can restrict the type of commands a user issues on a per-host basis. The /etc/sudoers file contains a list of users authorized to use the sudo command (see Figure 16-8); only the root users can access this file.

```
# In the default (unconfigured) configuration, sudo asks for the root password.
# This allows use of an ordinary user account for administration of a freshly
# installed system. When configuring sudo, delete the two
# following lines:
Defaults targetpw  # ask for the password of the target user i.e. root
ALL     ALL=(ALL) ALL   # WARNING! Only use this together with 'Defaults targetpw'!

# Runas alias specification

# User privilege specification
root    ALL=(ALL) ALL
# Uncomment to allow people in group wheel to run all commands
# %wheel        ALL=(ALL) ALL

# Same thing without a password
# %wheel        ALL=(ALL) NOPASSWD: ALL

# Samples
# %users  ALL=/sbin/mount /cdrom,/sbin/umount /cdrom
  %users  localhost=/sbin/shutdown -h now
~
~
~
                                                50,1          Bot
```

Figure 16-8 List of authorized users in the /etc/sudoers file
Source: openSUSE

If a user attempts to use the sudo command without authorization, the event is logged and a warning message is displayed. Therefore, it's critical that users authorized to use the sudo command be assigned secure passwords.

You can edit the sudoers file with the visudo command. Under normal conditions, the sudo command prompts the user for a password and then checks it in the sudoers file to confirm that it's valid. This command then issues permissions that last for only a short time (15 minutes) so that repeated use of the sudo command can be controlled to prevent security problems.

You can configure the sudoers file so that the sudo command doesn't prompt users for the root password.

Managing Disk Quotas

Disk quotas are used to specify the maximum disk space allocated to each user. There are two types: hard limits and soft limits. **Hard limits** are inflexible, in that users can't go past a specified limit. **Soft limits**, on the other hand, are flexible and allow users to go past the specified limit for a certain amount of time (one week, by default). Soft limits are set to encourage users to be economical with disk space and warn them when they're approaching their hard limit. For example, a user might be allocated 10 GB of space as the hard limit and 8 GB as the soft limit. If the user exceeds the 8 GB soft limit, the grace period clock starts. After a specified time limit expires, if the user hasn't dropped back under 8 GB, he or she is blocked from using any additional disk space.

If a quota has been set in the /etc/fstab file, disk quotas are enabled when your Linux system starts; however, the administrator can use the quotaon command to enable quotas or the quotaoff command to disable quotas on a specified file system. The following sections explain the steps for enabling disk quotas.

Modifying the /etc/fstab File   The /etc/fstab file is used to control mounting file systems. To enable disk quotas, you need to add the usrquota and grpquota options to this file. The usrquota option is for user disk quotas, and the grpquota option is for group disk quotas. For example, to enable disk quotas for both users and groups for the /dev/sda1 file system, the entry in the /etc/fstab file is as follows:

```
/dev/sda1 / ext4  acl,user_xattr,usrquota,grpquota  1 1
```

Remounting the Affected File Systems   After editing /etc/fstab, you need to unmount the file system and then remount it with the mount and umount commands. If the file system is in use, you get a "device is busy" error. In this case, bring your system down to single-user mode (described in Table 16-7) before using the umount command, and then restart your system for remounting to take effect.

Creating Quota Files   After remounting the file system, the computer can work with disk quotas, but the file system still doesn't support them. To do this, use the quotacheck command, which scans the file systems that are quota enabled and builds a table of current disk use for each file system. This table updates the OS's copy of disk use. The quotacheck command isn't included with openSUSE, however. You can install it by using the zypper install quota command, which has this syntax:

```
quotacheck -b [-c] [-v] [-u] [-g] /dev/sda2
```

Table 16-11 describes the options used with the quotacheck command.

Table 16-11 Options for the quotacheck command

Option	Description
-b	Stands for "backup"; forces the quotacheck utility to make a backup of the quota file before saving new data
-c	Stands for "create"; performs a new scan and saves the file to the hard disk
-v	Stands for "verbose"; displays the quotacheck utility's operations as it runs
-u	Stands for "user"; specifies only user quotas
-g	Stands for "group"; specifies only group quotas

16

Assigning and Verifying Disk Quotas The last step is assigning a disk quota to a user with the edquota command, which has the following syntax:

edquota *username*

For example, say you've used the edquota Isaiah command to set a disk quota for Isaiah in the /etc/fstab file for the /home partition. Figure 16-9 shows the /etc/fstab entry for this user.

```
Disk quotas for user isaiah (uid 1000):
  Filesystem                    blocks       soft       hard     inodes       soft       hard
  /dev/sda2                      68472          0          0       1309          0          0

  ~
  ~
  -- INSERT --                                                                   3,89        All
```

Figure 16-9 Disk quotas for the user Isaiah
Source: openSUSE

The first column represents the file system that has quotas enabled. The second column lists the number of storage blocks in use. (One block equals 1 KB.) The next two columns show soft and hard block limits for the user. A zero means no limits have been set. The inodes column displays the number of inodes in use. (Recall that inodes contain information about files, so limiting them controls the number of files that can be created.) The last two columns set soft and hard inode limits for the user.

The edquota command can also be used to set time limits on soft quotas. For instance, you can use the following command to set a grace period (seven days, by default) before enforcing a disk quota:

```
edquota -t
Grace period before enforcing soft limits for users:
Time units may be: days, hours, minutes, or seconds
   Filesystem                Block grace period      Inode grace period
   /dev/sda2                       7 days                  7 days
```

To verify that the user's quota has been set, use the quota *username* command.

Maintaining Disk Quotas

To make sure quota limits are accurate and haven't been exceeded, you use the repquota command, which displays a summary of hard disk use and quotas for the specified file system. The syntax of this command is as follows:

```
repquota [-avtsug] [-t | -n] [-F frmt]
```

Table 16-12 describes the options used with this command.

Table 16-12 Options for the `repquota` command

Option	Description
-a	Shows disk use information on all file systems specified in the `/etc/fstab` file
-v	Lists information on all disk quotas
-t	Truncates usernames and group names that are longer than nine characters
-n	Skips resolving user and group IDs to usernames and group names to speed up display
-s	Displays disk use information in a more readable format
-u	Reports only user-based disk quotas
-g	Reports only group-based disk quotas
-F frmt	Shows disk use information in a specified format, including vfsold (version 1), vfsv0 (version 2), rpc (NFS format), and xfs (XFS format)

Activity 16-3: Setting Disk Quotas

Time Required: 60 minutes

Objective: Set and manage disk quotas.

Description: In this activity, you create a test user account that you use to edit the `/etc/fstab` file and enable disk quotas. Next, you bring your Linux computer down to single-user mode and remount the root (/) directory. Then you create a quota file, assign limits to user1, and verify disk quota settings.

1. If necessary, start VMware Player, open a terminal window, and switch to the root user.

2. Before you can use disk quotas, you must modify the `/etc/fstab` file. To simulate a real-world situation of setting disk quotas for users, create a new user, user1, with the skills you've learned in previous chapters.

3. Edit the `/etc/fstab` file by typing **vim /etc/fstab** and pressing **Enter**. Use the vim navigational commands you learned in previous chapters to edit the root (/) file system. It should look like the following when you're finished:

   ```
   /dev/sda2   /   ext4 acl,user_xattr,usrquota,grpquota   1 1
   ```

   Keep in mind that the `sda2` might look different depending on your hardware.

4. Save and close the file.

5. Now you need to remount the root file system. To do this, take your Linux computer down to single-user mode by typing **init 1** and pressing **Enter**.

6. Next, type the root password and press **Enter**.

7. Unmount the `/dev/sda2` file system by typing **umount /dev/sda2** and pressing **Enter**.

8. Restart your Linux computer by typing **reboot** and pressing **Enter**.

16

9. To create a quota file, open a terminal window and switch to the root user, if necessary. Install the quotacheck utility by typing **zypper install quota** and pressing **Enter**.

10. Before using the `quotacheck` command, you must turn off disk quotas by typing **quotaoff -f /dev/sda2** and pressing **Enter**. (*Note*: If you get an error message, restart your machine and try again.) Then type **quotacheck -mavug** and press **Enter**. It might take a few minutes.

11. Now that you have created the quota file, you can assign quota limits to user1. Switch to the root user, if necessary. Type **edquota user1** and press **Enter** to open the disk quota file for user1 in the vim editor. Use the skills you've learned in working with the vim editor and set a hard disk limit of 20 MB and 1000 inodes. (20 MB equals 20480 KB.) Don't change any other values. Your entry should look like the following:

```
Disk quotas for user user1 (uid 1001):
  Filesystem    blocks    soft    hard    inodes    soft    hard
  /dev/sda2       52        0     20480      0        0     1000
```

12. Save the file and exit the vim editor.

13. Verify the disk quota for user1 by typing **quota -v user1** and pressing **Enter**. When you're finished, power off the virtual machine.

As mentioned in Chapter 7, you can also manage disk quotas in YaST with the User and Group Management utility. Select the user in the User and Group Administration window, click the Edit button, and then click the Plug-Ins tab. Select Manage User Quota under Plug-In Description, click Manage User Quotas, and then click the Launch button. Figure 16-10 shows the settings you used in Step 11 of Activity 16-3.

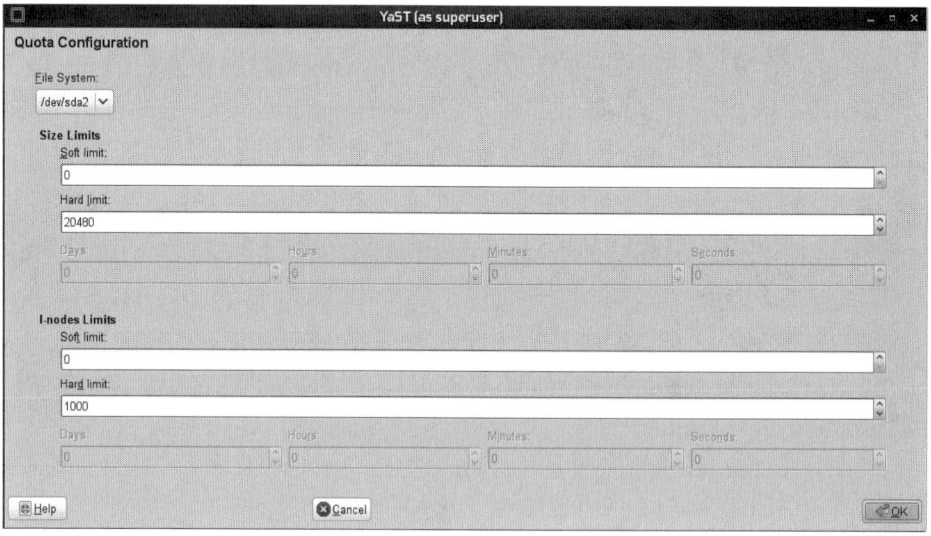

Figure 16-10 The Quota Configuration plug-in
Source: openSUSE

Chapter Summary

- The X Window System provides a method for writing device-independent graphics and windowing software that can be transferred from one computer to another easily. It was developed to unleash the graphical capability of Linux and set a protocol for creating and manipulating graphical elements onscreen. With this system, you can run multiple graphics applications simultaneously.

- The most common open-source X Window versions are XFree86 and X.Org (included with openSUSE). OpenSUSE offers GUI modules for configuring X Window. You need to restart X Window after making configuration changes.

- To display information about the X server, use the `xdpyinfo` command. You use the `startx` command to start an X Window session from the command line.

- An X display manager presents a graphical login that prompts for your username and password before allowing access to the openSUSE Linux desktop. In addition, it enables you to select a different desktop for an X Window session.

- The way the X Window display manager is shown after you start your Linux system depends on the runlevel. Runlevels are defined as a system state entry in the `/etc/inittab` file.

- The `su`, `kdesu`, and `sudo` commands are used to help manage root accounts. The `su` command changes user credentials to those of the root user or to the user specified by the *username* argument. The `kdesu` command is the GUI program in KDE that enables you to run applications with root privileges. System administrators can use the `sudo` command to allow a group of users to run certain commands as root or another user while logging the commands and arguments.

- Disk quotas are used to specify the maximum disk space allocated to each user. The two types of disk quotas are hard limits and soft limits. Hard limits are inflexible and used to set a specific limit that can't be passed; soft limits are flexible and allow users to pass the limit for a specified time.

- The `usrquota` and `grpquota` options in the `/etc/fstab` file are used to enable disk quotas for users and groups. The `quotacheck` command is used to scan the file system and build a table of current disk use for each file system that's quota enabled. The `edquota` command is used to edit user quotas. The `repquota` command displays a summary of hard disk use and quotas for the specified file system.

Key Terms

16

disk quotas   A Linux feature used to specify the maximum disk space allocated to each user.

hard limits   Inflexible disk quota settings that don't allow users to go past a specified limit.

refresh rate   Number of times the display is refreshed per second.

soft limits   Flexible disk quota settings that warn users when they're approaching the hard limit. *See also* hard limits.

X Window System   A system that provides a method for writing device-independent graphics and windowing software that can be transferred from one computer to another easily.

Review Questions

1. Which Linux command is used to set a quota for each user on the system?

   a. edquota

   b. quotacheck

   c. repquota

   d. quotaon

2. Which Linux command is used to enable disk quotas?

   a. edquota

   b. quotacheck

   c. repquota

   d. quotaon

3. You have just modified the /etc/fstab file to add the usrquota option and need to create a quota file for users. What Linux command do you use to scan the quota-enabled file system so that it builds a table of current disk use?

   a. edquota

   b. quotacheck

   c. repquota

   d. quotaon

4. Which Linux command is used to display a summary of hard disk use as well as quotas for a specified file system?

   a. edquota

   b. quotacheck

   c. repquota

   d. quotaon

5. If you're using KDE and need temporary root privileges while using a GUI application, which command do you use?

   a. su

   b. kdesu

   c. sudo

   d. sudo -user

6. Which Linux command do you use to change your user credentials to those of the root user?

   a. su

   b. kdesu

   c. sudo

   d. sudo -user

7. You're a Linux administrator and need to allow a group of users to run certain commands as a root user. What command do you use?

    a. su

    b. kdesu

    c. sudo

    d. sudo -user

8. Which command do you use to start an X Window session from a terminal window?

    a. xvidtune

    b. xdpyinfo

    c. startx

    d. quotaon

9. If you have an X Window session open and need to view display information, which command do you use?

    a. xvidtune

    b. xdpyinfo

    c. startx

    d. quotaon

10. If you have an X Window session open and need to adjust video settings, which command do you use?

    a. xvidtune

    b. xdpyinfo

    c. startx

    d. quotaon

11. Which runlevel, also known as halt, shuts down a Linux machine?

    a. 5

    b. 3

    c. 1

    d. 0

12. Which runlevel, also known as single-user mode, is comparable with safe mode in Windows?

    a. 5

    b. 3

    c. 1

    d. 0

16

13. Which runlevel, also known as X11, gives you access to all services, including the GUI?

    a. 5

    b. 3

    c. 1

    d. 0

14. Which of the following is a widely used version of X Window? (Choose all that apply.)

    a. GNOME

    b. XFree86

    c. KDE

    d. X.Org

15. Given the following contents of the `/etc/fstab` file, which file system is enabled for disk quotas? (Choose all that apply.)

```
/dev/sda1       swap        swap      defaults                                    0 0
/dev/sda2       /           ext4      acl,user_xattr,usrquota,grpquota            1 1
/dev/sda3       /home       ext4      acl,user_xattr,usrquota, grpquota           1 1
proc            /proc       proc      defaults                                    0 0
sysfs           /sys        sysfs     noauto                                      0 0
```

    a. `/dev/sda2`

    b. `/dev/sda1`

    c. `/dev/sda3`

    d. `/sys`

16. Which of the following statements about quotas is true? (Choose all that apply.)

    a. Hard limits can be exceeded for a specified amount of time.

    b. By default, a user can exceed a hard limit by seven days.

    c. By default, a user can exceed a soft limit by seven days.

    d. Administrators can use quotas to limit disk space as well as the number of files a user can own.

    e. Quotas limit only the amount of disk space a user can have.

    f. You can't set both soft and hard limits at the same time.

Case Projects

Case Project 16-1: Comparing Desktop Environments and Window Managers

In addition to desktop environments such as KDE and GNOME, there are window managers. For example, openSUSE includes IceWM and TWM. Conduct Internet research to learn more about desktop environments and window managers, and write a one- to two-page paper explaining the major differences between the two.

Case Project 16-2: Using Disk Quotas

You're the system administrator for a small department in your company that's responsible for an important database. You prefer having servers with more disk space, but your company can't afford to increase the budget for IT equipment. You have noticed that some users are storing old files on the server that are most likely obsolete. You don't want to delete any user files, so you decide to set up disk quotas for users. You have 20 users, and department servers are capable of holding 200 GB of data. What commands should you use to create disk quotas? Do you plan to use hard limits, soft limits, or both? Will all users have the same limits? Prepare a plan to submit to your manager for approval. Your plan should justify the need for disk quotas and the hard and soft limits you plan to set. If some users' quotas will be higher, explain why.

16

## chapter 17

Networking in a Linux Environment

After reading this chapter and completing the exercises, you will be able to:

- Describe key functions of the Network Information Service
- Install and configure an NIS server and client
- Configure a local printer queue
- Install and configure a DHCP server

In Chapter 13, you learned about the Network File System and how to connect different file systems across the network for file sharing. In this chapter, you delve into networking concepts further by learning about the Network Information Service, which allows one user to log in to his or her account from multiple locations on the network. Next, you install and configure an NIS server in YaST. You learn about other network services, such as the Common UNIX Printing System (CUPS), and configure printer queues in YaST. Finally, you learn how to install and configure a DHCP server to assign IP addresses on a network automatically, which reduces the administrative load.

Network Information Service

Users' environments should be the same regardless of which Linux machine they're logged in to, but managing user accounts and environments can be an administrative headache. Administrators must manage all local accounts and make sure they have the correct permissions and are assigned to the correct groups. **Network Information Service (NIS)** is a client/server protocol that centralizes user and group IDs by providing database access so that network computers can share configuration information, such as the contents of the /etc/passwd, /etc/shadow, and /etc/group files.

Databases that store shared configuration information related to NIS networks are called **maps**. The NIS setup consists of three types of host servers: master, slave, and client. The **NIS master server**, at the center of the NIS network, contains the NIS maps and makes them available over the network. It should be able to propagate NIS updates with little effect on network performance. You can also create **NIS slave servers** to distribute the NIS master server's load more evenly. If the NIS master server fails or stops functioning temporarily, the NIS slave server stores copies of the NIS maps and responds to requests from other host computers on the network. All hosts in an NIS-based network, including the master and slave servers, are called **NIS clients**. When a process on an NIS client requests configuration information, the NIS client broadcasts the request to the NIS server that serves the client's domain. A domain is a set of NIS maps shared by the NIS master and slave servers. Any NIS server, whether master or slave, containing the maps corresponding to the client domain can respond to the client request. The NIS domain determines which NIS server should process the client request.

A host can't be the master server for more than one domain, but it can be a slave server for multiple domains. A client belongs to only one domain.

NIS uses Remote Procedure Calls (RPC) technology, which enables clients to retrieve information from the central host running the NIS server. RPC is the standard method of allocating and managing shared resources between NIS clients and servers. In the NIS setup, clients and servers don't need to use separate networking code; they can communicate by using common RPC methods to access the NIS database. Figure 17-1 shows this process.

For NIS to operate correctly, the RPC portmapper must run on both the NIS client and server. When the NIS server starts, it communicates with the listening port and the RPC program number it's intended to serve. The RPC program number uniquely identifies an RPC service

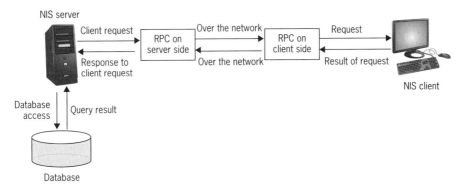

Figure 17-1 NIS communication with RPC
© Cengage Learning 2013

(portmapper, in this case). The NIS client trying to access an RPC service contacts the port-mapper first, which returns the port number where the RPC service can be reached.

Installing and Configuring NIS Servers

To install NIS, you need to have both the NIS server and client. Before installing NIS, decide whether the computer will be used as a master server, a slave server, or a client. If an NIS server (master or slave) is already installed on the Linux network, you need to install only the NIS client. On the other hand, if there are no NIS servers on the network, you need to install the server as well as the client. Before you configure your system for use as an NIS server or client, you must provide a domain name for the computer to ensure that a client and server in the same domain can communicate with each other. A client can't access a server in a different domain.

Creating an NIS Domain To create an NIS domain, determine which Linux computers will be part of the domain, and then specify the NIS domain name for them by using the domainname command, which must be issued from the root user account when setting a domain name. (Regular user accounts can use this command without arguments to display the domain name.) For instance, the domainname example command sets the domain name to example. This command doesn't save a Linux computer's domain name permanently, however. The domain name is lost when you restart the computer. To save the NIS domain name permanently, edit the runlevel script /etc/init.d/network, and specify the NIS domain name in the script, as shown in this line added to the script:

```
# Set the NIS domain name
domainname example
```

The nisdomainname and ypdomainname commands are interchangeable with the domainname command. NIS was formerly known as Yellow Pages, which is where the "yp" in some commands comes from.

17

Installing an NIS Master Server An NIS master server contains the source files for all NIS maps in a domain. If you want to make any changes in NIS maps, you have to make them on the NIS master server. This server gives clients the information they request and gives slave servers up-to-date copies of maps. OpenSUSE provides an NIS client by default; however, you need to install an NIS server. From the root user account, use the `yast2 -i yast2-nis-server` command to download and install the nis-server RPM package and dependencies.

Configuring an NIS Master Server in YaST To start the YaST NIS Server module, use the `yast2 nis-server` command. Figure 17-2 shows the opening window.

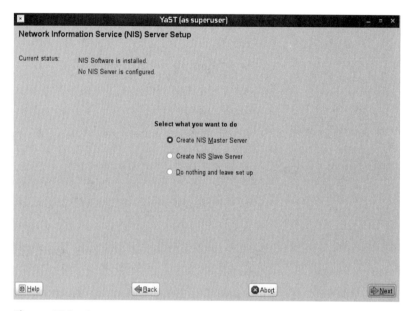

Figure 17-2 The Network Information Service (NIS) Server Setup window
Source: openSUSE

This window shows the current status of the NIS server. As you can see, the NIS software has been installed, but the server hasn't been configured yet. Select the Create NIS Master Server option, and then click Next to move to the window shown in Figure 17-3.

You can configure the following settings in this window:

- Set the NIS domain name, if you haven't done so already.
- Configure the NIS server to double as an NIS client so that users have access to data from the NIS server.
- Select the "Active Slave NIS server exists" option so that the NIS master server can cooperate with NIS slave servers in the network.
- Selecting the "Fast Map distribution" option speeds up map transfers from the master server to slave servers.

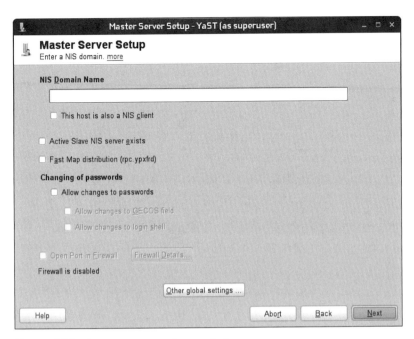

Figure 17-3 The Master server Setup window
Source: openSUSE

- The "Allow changes to passwords" option enables users to change their passwords with the `yppasswd` command. After selecting this option, the Allow changes to GECOS field and Allow changes to login shell options are enabled. The GECOS field option allows users to change their name and address settings with the `ypchfn` command, and the login shell option allows them to change their default shell with the `ypchsh` command.

- Select the Open Port in Firewall check box to configure firewall settings.

- Clicking the "Other global settings" button enables you to change the NIS server's source directory and define the lowest user and group IDs available. (UIDs and GIDs are set to 500 by default.) In most Linux distributions, UIDs and GIDs of 500 and higher are assigned to user accounts; those below 500 are reserved for system accounts. The option to merge passwords is enabled by default and should stay enabled. This setting creates the user database from the `/etc/passwd`, `/etc/shadow`, and `/etc/group` authentication files.

 If a user wants to switch to another shell, the shell must be in the `/etc/shells` configuration file.

17

If you selected the "Active Slave NIS server exists" option, the next window you see is NIS Master Server Slaves Setup (see Figure 17-4). Simply add the names of hosts to configure NIS slave servers.

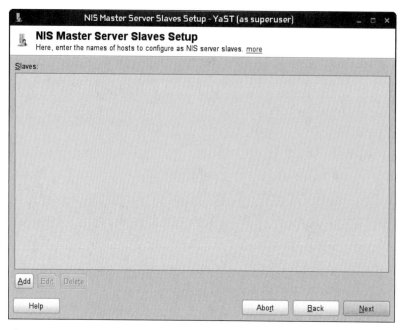

Figure 17-4 The NIS Master Server Slaves Setup window
Source: openSUSE

If you didn't select the slave server option, the next window you see is NIS Server Maps Setup (see Figure 17-5). The maps selected by default are usually adequate for most networks. If you want to add any, simply click the corresponding check box, and then click Next.

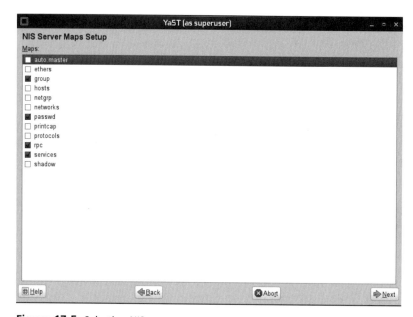

Figure 17-5 Selecting NIS maps
Source: openSUSE

The next window is NIS Server Query Hosts Setup, shown in Figure 17-6. You use this window to define which hosts on your network can query the NIS server. Notice that the first entry is 255.0.0.0 for the netmask and 127.0.0.0 for the network. This entry is required to allow connections from the local host. The second entry is 0.0.0.0 for both the netmask and network, which gives access to the NIS server to all the hosts in the network.

Figure 17-6 The NIS Server Query Hosts Setup window
Source: openSUSE

Configuring NIS slave servers follows the same procedure, but in the opening window, you select the Create NIS Slave Server option (refer back to Figure 17-2).

Configuring an NIS Master Server Manually
Configuring an NIS server is easy with the YaST NIS Server module, but as a Linux administrator, you should know more details about how this module changes configuration files. After the NIS server and client are installed, the /var/yp/ directory is created on the same computer to store all the NIS maps. NIS maps are multicolumn database files storing key/value pairs (for example, a user's login name and encrypted password) that provide fast database access and, therefore, speed up responses to client requests for configuration information. Each NIS map consists of two files:

- *Index*—Contains the key values (also called "indices") of an NIS map arranged in hash order. This file has a .dir extension.
- *Data*—Contains the actual data related to a key value. This file has a .pag extension.

OpenSUSE has several default NIS maps. Table 17-1 describes some commonly used maps.

17

Table 17-1 Common NIS maps

NIS maps	Description
/etc/group	Contains group-related information, such as group ID and name
/etc/passwd	Contains user attributes, such as user ID and password
/etc/shadow	Contains encrypted passwords for users whose attributes are in the /etc/passwd file
/etc/aliases	Contains names of aliases; used with the mail service
/etc/hosts	Contains hostnames and IP addresses of computers connected over a TCP/IP network
/etc/networks	Contains NIS network names
/etc/protocols	Identifies the names and numbers assigned to network protocols, such as TCP/IP and UDP

After the NIS Server module has been started, NIS exports data to the /var/yp directory. A directory with the NIS domain name is also created under the /var/yp directory. For instance, in an NIS domain named example.com, there's a directory called /var/yp/example.com containing databases for NIS maps. System administrators should examine the following NIS configuration files in this directory:

- /var/yp/Makefile—You can run this file with the make file command, which can be issued only from the /var/yp directory. It's used to push updated maps to the NIS slave server. Like most Linux configuration files, it includes extensive documentation and can be modified easily with the vim editor.

- /var/yp/securenets—This file specifies NIS clients' access rights to the NIS server. You can enter only IP addresses in this file; you can't enter hostnames, for example. The data in this file is populated during the final phase of the YaST NIS Server module (shown previously in Figure 17-6).

Activity 17-1: Installing and Configuring an NIS Server

Time Required: 30 minutes

Objective: Install and configure an NIS server in YaST.

Requirements: An openSUSE virtual machine (GNOME or KDE) and an Internet connection

Description: In this activity, you install the YaST NIS Server module and then use it to configure an NIS server.

1. Start VMware Player, and log in to an openSUSE virtual machine.

2. Open a terminal window, and switch to the root user.

3. Install the YaST NIS Server module by typing **yast2 -i yast2-nis-server** and pressing **Enter**. Make sure you click **I Agree** to confirm all package licenses.

4. Before starting the YaST NIS Server module, list the contents of the /var/yp directory and take note of which files are in this directory. Then start the YaST NIS Server module by typing **yast2 nis-server** and pressing **Enter**.

5. Click the **Install and set up an NIS Master Server** option button, and then click **Next**.

6. Set the NIS domain name by typing **example** in the NIS Domain Name text box. Configure the NIS server to also be an NIS client by clicking the **This host is also a NIS client** check box.

7. There will be no NIS slave servers, so make sure the **Active Slave NIS server exists** and **Fast Map distribution (rpc.ypxfrd)** check boxes are cleared.

8. To let users change their passwords, click the **Allow changes to passwords** check box. Then click the **Allow changes to GECOS field** and **Allow changes to login shell** check boxes.

9. Open the NIS port in your firewall by clicking the **Open Port in Firewall** check box, and then click **Next**.

10. In the NIS Server Maps Setup window, make sure the **group**, **passwd**, **rpc**, and **services** check boxes are selected, and then click **Next**.

11. Leave the default netmask (255.0.0.0) and network (127.0.0.0) settings, and then click **Finish**.

12. Now that you have installed and configured the NIS server, list the contents of the /var/yp directory to see the new files and directories added by NIS.

13. Leave the terminal window open and the virtual machine running for Activity 17-2.

Installing and Configuring NIS Clients

The YaST NIS Client module is packaged with the latest version of openSUSE. To start the NIS Client module, you use the yast2 nis-client command. Figure 17-7 shows the opening window.

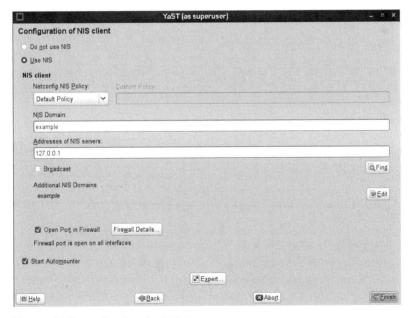

Figure 17-7 Configuring the NIS client
Source: openSUSE

17

The first task is to activate NIS by clicking the Use NIS option button. Next, you need to define the NIS policy to specify how the NIS configuration will be modified. By default, it's handled by the netconfig script. This method is suitable for most networks, but you can change it by selecting one of these options:

- *Only Manual Changes*—This selection ensures that the netconfig script can't modify the NIS configurations.

- *Custom Policy*—You use this option to customize the NIS policy by adding values separated by spaces. Entries in the netconfig script consist of fields specifying, for example, network ID and protocols, as shown in the following example. To learn more about the possible values, review the netconfig man pages.

```
# The <device> and <nametoaddr_libs> fields are always empty in this
# implementation.
#
udp        tpi_clts        v    inet       udp    -    -
tcp        tpi_cots_ord    v    inet       tcp    -    -
udp6       tpi_clts        v    inet6      udp    -    -
tcp6       tpi_cots_ord    v    inet6      tcp    -    -
rawip      tpi_raw         -    inet       -      -    -
local      tpi_cots_ord    -    loopback   -      -    -
unix       tpi_cots_ord    -    loopback   -      -    -
```

Netconfig is a modular tool for managing network configuration settings. Each netconfig module is called by different auto configuration mechanisms, such as the NIS client polices, and is responsible for applying these changes.

After setting the NIS policy, you need to specify the NIS domain, which is set during the NIS server configuration. Next, you enter the NIS server IP address. If there's more than one NIS server, separate the IP addresses with spaces. If you aren't sure what the NIS server's IP address is, you can have NIS search for it by clicking the Find button.

You select the Broadcast check box to keep the NIS client connected even if the specified NIS server fails. With this option, the NIS client searches the local network for another available NIS server. However, this option is considered a security risk because an intruder could bring down the NIS server and set up a fake one that the NIS client connects to. You can also select the Start Automounter check box to have the automounter daemon mount directories, such as users' home directories, automatically.

As in most YaST modules, you can open the firewall port by selecting the Open Port in Firewall check box. Finally, you can use the Expert button to open the Expert settings window shown in Figure 17-8.

By default, the Answer Remote Hosts setting is enabled. It allows any host on the network to query which server a client is using. You can also enable the Broken server setting, which allows clients to receive replies from the server through unprivileged ports. Privileged ports are under 1024, and unprivileged ports are 1024 and higher. Access to privileged ports is restricted to the root account, so a client accessing a server on a privileged port can be assured that the system administrator configured it.

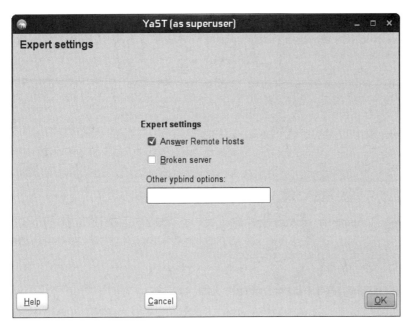

Figure 17-8 The Expert settings window
Source: openSUSE

   The Broken server setting is considered a security risk and in most cases shouldn't be enabled; however, according to the man pages for the `ypbind` command, it's required for compatibility with some NIS Server versions.

After configuring the NIS client, click Finish. If you have automatic login enabled, NIS asks whether you want to disable this feature now that you're using NIS. For security reasons, automatic login should be disabled when using NIS.

Activity 17-2: Configuring an NIS Client

Time Required: 15 minutes

Objective: Configure an NIS client in YaST.

Requirements: An openSUSE virtual machine (GNOME or KDE)

Description: In this activity, you configure an NIS client in YaST.

1. If necessary, start VMware Player, open a terminal window, and switch to the root user.

2. Start the YaST NIS Client module by typing **yast2 nis-client** and pressing **Enter**.

3. Enable NIS by clicking the **Use NIS** option button, and make sure the NIS policy is set to **Default Policy**.

4. If necessary, type **example** in the NIS Domain text box.

5. Click the **Open Port in Firewall** check box, and then click **Finish**.

6. To make sure the NIS server is running, type **ypwhich** and press **Enter**. What's displayed?

_____

7. To test client access to the NIS server, type **ypcat passwd** and press **Enter**. The output should list values from the `passwd` map file on the NIS server.

8. Close the terminal window, and power off the virtual machine.

Managing Other Network Services

In addition to NIS, Linux provides network services for managing other important administrative tasks. The following sections introduce two more essential network services: one to manage print queues and one to manage IP addresses on a network.

Network Printing in Linux

YaST has a module for configuring local and remote printers without installing additional drivers or editing configuration files manually. You can also use this tool to maintain the printer configuration file, printing spool directories, and filters, among other tasks. This tool uses printer daemons, such as the CUPS daemon in `/etc/cups` for setting up a local or network printer. The **Common UNIX Printing System (CUPS)** provides a printing interface on a local network. The CUPS software converts many different types of files into data a printer can understand and process. This software is referred to as a filter, which enables CUPS to print to a wide variety of printers.

Each time CUPS receives a print job, it determines the correct filters, printer drivers, and port monitors to handle device- and channel-specific data and back-ends that send data to the printer (such as USB and serial ports). The print job is then placed in a print queue for printing. Print queues point to printer devices and monitor the printer status and print jobs assigned to them. After a job has finished printing, it's removed from the queue so that the next one can be processed.

Before you set up a printer, you should be familiar with some common printing terms. A **printer device** is the physical printer that transfers a print job from a computer to actual hard copy. A **printer driver** is software used to manage the printer device. You don't access a printer device directly; instead, you access it through a **print queue**, which is a directory file where the printer daemon can store print jobs so that multiple users can use the same printer device. If more than one print job is submitted at the same time, these jobs are placed in the print queue and delivered to the printer device one at a time.

The YaST Printer Configurations module is used to set up local or remote printer queues. A **remote printer queue** is located on another host in the network, not on your local computer. You can access and use remote printer queues, but you can't modify them from your local computer. To start this module, you use the `yast2 printer` command. Figure 17-9 shows the opening window of this module. It lists local and remote printers. To set up a queue for your printer device, click the Add button.

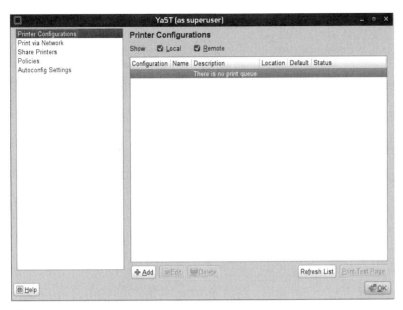

Figure 17-9 The Printer Configurations window
Source: openSUSE

Figure 17-10 shows the next window in this module. Typically, CUPS is used to print with remote print queues, so the Accept Printer Information from the Following Servers option under Use CUPS to Print Via Network is selected by default. It enables you to print with multiple CUPS servers. To print from one CUPS server that all clients can access, select Do All Your Printing Directly via One Remote CUPS Server.

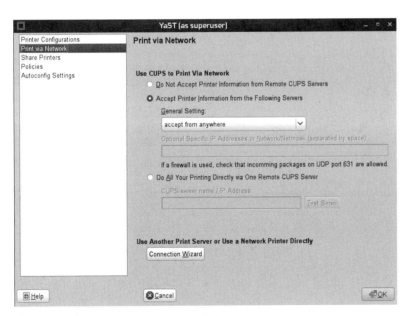

Figure 17-10 The Print via Network window
Source: openSUSE

17

The next window, Share Printers, is used to share your printer device with remote users (see Figure 17-11). You can even specify sharing a printer only with certain IP addresses. You use the next window, Policies, to configure policies for CUPS operation and errors. CUPS operation policies are rules used when CUPS can't send a print job to the printer device. The final configuration window is Autoconfig Settings, where you specify how USB printers are configured automatically. For instance, you can plug in a USB printer and have it enabled automatically, and then have it disabled automatically when you unplug it.

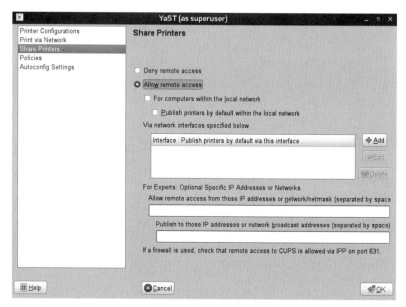

Figure 17-11 The Share Printers window
Source: openSUSE

Overview of DHCP in Linux

DHCP is used to assign IP addresses automatically for each network host, which saves time because you don't have to configure each host separately. You can also use DHCP to configure other network client settings, such as setting up name server entries in the /etc/resolv.conf file and configuring host gateway information. Table 17-2 describes some identifying information that DHCP provides.

Table 17-2 Information set by DHCP

Information	Description
Network subnet/host address	Used for connecting to the network
Subnet/hostname	Used for allowing a specified host to connect to a subnet
Subnet/hardware address	Enables a client to connect to the network after receiving a hostname from DHCP

A DHCP server leases IP addresses for a period you specify and assigns them to client computers dynamically. DHCP is useful when not all computers in a network stay connected permanently. In this type of network, the DHCP server has to provide only the maximum number of IP addresses that are active on the network at any time. This allows a system administrator to save IP addresses and reuse them after they're unallocated.

For example, IT Systems, Inc., is a multinational corporation with headquarters in New York and branches throughout North America that develops software for large manufacturing companies. To distribute the software, the company's marketing executives travel between the headquarters and branch offices often and carry their laptops with them to demonstrate the software to customers. Joe Matthews, the system administrator at IT Systems, Inc., has to reassign IP address details on these laptops each time executives travel, which is a time-consuming task. He wants to use DHCP to reduce his administrative load. With a DHCP server set up, client computers can retrieve IP address information from it without Joe having to assign addresses manually. He can also change IP addresses for several network computers at once simply by editing the DHCP configuration file on the server. If the DNS server for an organization changes, the changes are reflected on the DHCP server automatically.

Configuring a DHCP Server The YaST DHCP module isn't included with openSUSE. To use it, you have to install the DNS/DHCP pattern (which you did in Chapter 11 with the DNS Server). To start the DHCP module, you use the `yast2 dhcp-server` command.

The following list summarizes the settings you can make in each window:

- *Card Selection*—You use this window to select the NICs for the DHCP server. You can also open the firewall to allow access to the DHCP server from remote computers.

- *Global Settings*—In this window, you configure settings such as the domain name, primary and secondary name servers' IP addresses, default gateway, and WINS server IP address.

- *Dynamic DHCP*—In this window (shown in Figure 17-12), you review subnet information, such as network and netmask addresses. You can also configure the IP address range and lease time.

- *Start-up*—In this window, you can specify that the DHCP server starts automatically when your Linux machine boots.

After finishing this wizard, you have access to expert configuration mode, if you want to fine-tune the preceding settings for the DHCP server. You can tweak other settings in this mode, too, such as configuring the DHCP server to run in a chroot environment (which would prevent attackers from compromising the rest of the network if they gain access to the server). You can also access the Host Management window to configure static allocation, in which a host can be assigned the same IP address every time it connects to the network.

17

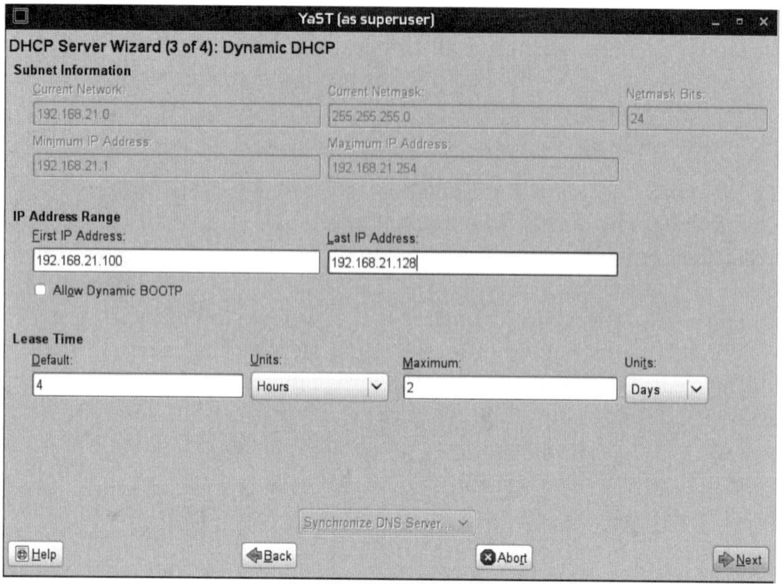

Figure 17-12 Configuring dynamic DHCP settings
Source: openSUSE

Chapter Summary

- Network Information Service is a client/server protocol that centralizes user and group IDs by providing database access so that network computers can share configuration information, such as the contents of the /etc/passwd, /etc/shadow, and /etc/group files.

- The NIS master server contains the source files for all NIS maps in a domain and makes them available over the network. Installing the NIS server also installs the NIS client. NIS slave servers are used to distribute the master server's load more evenly.

- All hosts in an NIS network, including master and slave servers, are called NIS clients. NIS clients broadcast requests for information to the NIS server for the domain. The NIS domain determines which NIS server should process client requests.

- The domainname command is used to display or temporarily specify the NIS domain name. To set the domain permanently, you need to edit the /etc/init.d/network file.

- You use the yast2 -i yast2-nis-server command to install the YaST NIS Server module. After this module is installed, you can start it with the yast2 nis-server command.

- NIS maps are multicolumn database files storing key/value pairs that provide fast database access and, therefore, speed up responses to client requests for configuration information. Each map consists of an index file (.dir extension) and a data file (.pag extension) and is stored in the /var/yp directory.

- The YaST Printer Configurations module uses printer daemons, such as CUPS, for setting up a local or network printer. You use the `yast2 printer` command to start this module.

- CUPS provides a printing interface on a local network that's used to convert files into data a printer can process.

- A printer device is the physical printer that transfers a print job from a computer to actual hard copy. A printer driver is the software used to manage a printer device. A print queue is a directory file where the printer daemon can store print jobs so that multiple users can use the same printer device.

- DHCP is used to assign IP addresses automatically for each network host. The YaST DHCP module isn't included with openSUSE; to use it, the DNS/DHCP pattern must be installed. To start the DHCP module, you use the `yast2 dhcp-server` command.

Key Terms

Common UNIX Printing System (CUPS)   A system that provides a printing interface on a local network; used to convert files into data a printer can process.

maps   Multicolumn NIS database files storing key/value pairs that provide fast database access and speed up responses to client requests for configuration information.

Network Information Service (NIS)   A client/server protocol that centralizes user and group IDS by providing database access so that network computers can share configuration information.

NIS clients   All hosts in an NIS-based network, including the master and slave servers.

NIS master server   The center of the NIS network; contains the authoritative or primary copy of host configuration information (NIS maps) and makes it available over the network.

NIS slave servers   Servers that maintain a copy of the host configuration information stored on the master server for redundancy; also used to distribute the load evenly between NIS servers.

print queue   A directory file where the printer daemon can store print jobs so that multiple users can use the same printer device.

printer device   The physical printer that transfers a print job from a computer to actual hard copy.

printer driver   The software used to manage a printer device. *See also* printer device.

remote printer queue   A printer queue located on a different host in the local network.

Review Questions

1. Which of the following can respond to network client requests? (Choose all that apply.)

    a. NIS domain

    b. NIS master server

    c. NIS client

    d. NIS slave server

17

2. Write the command for setting example.com as the NIS domain name.

3. NIS uses which of the following technologies for communication?
   a. TCP/IP
   b. RPC
   c. NFS
   d. DNS

4. Which of the following commands returns the NIS server's hostname?
   a. ypwhich
   b. nisbind
   c. domainname
   d. ypconfig

5. An NIS map consists of which files? (Choose all that apply.)
   a. Index
   b. Hash
   c. Data
   d. Page

6. Which of the following directories does NIS export data to?
   a. /etc/nis
   b. /bin
   c. /var/yp
   d. /nis

7. Which of the following configuration files specifies an NIS client's access rights to the NIS server?
   a. /etc/hosts
   b. /var/yp/securenets
   c. /var/yp/makefile
   d. /etc/protocols

8. The YaST NIS Server module must be downloaded from the openSUSE Web site. True or False?

9. Which of the following terms is used for a physical printer?
   a. Printer
   b. Printer device
   c. Printer driver
   d. Print queue

10. Which of the following terms defines software used to manage the physical printer?
    a. Printer
    b. Printer device
    c. Printer driver
    d. Print queue

11. Which of the following is a directory file where the printer daemon can store print jobs?
    a. Printer
    b. Printer device
    c. Printer driver
    d. Print queue

12. The subdirectory named after the NIS domain contains which of the following?
    a. The /etc/passwd, /etc/shadow, and /etc/group files
    b. The portmapper utility
    c. Databases for NIS maps
    d. Encrypted passwords for network users

13. Which of the following is the default policy for modifying the NIS configuration?
    a. Using the YaST NIS Modification module
    b. Modifying key/value pairs
    c. Using the vim editor to modify NIS maps
    d. Using the netconfig script

14. Which of the following information is provided by a DHCP server?
    (Choose all that apply.)
    a. Network subnet/host address
    b. Usernames/passwords
    c. Subnet/hostname
    d. Subnet/hardware address

Case Projects

CASE PROJECTS

Case Project 17-1: Researching DHCP

Of the Linux network services introduced in this chapter, DHCP is probably one of the most important because it manages hosts on a network. Use the Internet to research DHCP, and write a one-page paper describing its importance in a network and summarizing different aspects of DHCP, particularly methods for allocating IP addresses over a network.

17

## chapter 18

Using Samba for Interoperating Linux and Windows

After reading this chapter and completing the exercises, you will be able to:

- Install and configure a Samba server manually
- Use a Web-based utility to configure Samba

In this chapter, you learn how to operate in a multi-OS environment with Samba, a tool for accessing Linux shares on a Windows PC and Windows shares on a Linux machine. You also learn how to edit the Samba configuration file and use the YaST Samba module. Finally, you see how to use the Samba Web Administration Tool, a Web-based utility for configuring the Samba server.

Using Samba

Samba, an open-source tool developed under the GNU General Public License, is available free at *http://samba.org*. It serves as an interface between two OSs, such as Linux and Windows, by using the protocols Server Message Block and Common Internet File System, which allow sharing information and resources between different OSs. In addition, Samba has several services, described in Table 18-1, that add useful features.

Table 18-1 Samba services

Service	Description
File sharing	Samba can work as a central file server by providing access to directories.
Printer sharing	Samba can provide access to printers, which can be attached to a Linux system or a Windows client.
Authentication and authorization of users	Samba handles authentication and authorization of users in both Linux and Windows by using passwords and domains.
Name resolution	Browsing is the capability to view the contents of other systems in the same network after authorization. Remote users can access resources and share data between computers in the same way as local users. Name resolution is an integral part of browsing, used to find computer names in a network. Windows Internet Name Service (WINS) allows centralized mapping of NetBIOS names to IP addresses.

The Samba Configuration File

Samba uses the /etc/samba/smb.conf configuration file to provide the services listed in Table 18-1. Linux clients access shares via this file, and Windows clients access shares through the Network window. A standard Samba configuration file is divided into three sections enclosed by brackets: [global], [homes], and [printers]. Most sections in the Samba configuration file are optional, but the [global] section is mandatory, used to define authentication settings and workgroup/domain information. These sections contain parameters that can be grouped as global settings and share definitions, explained in the following sections.

Global Settings Global settings include the values all users and clients on a network use to set parameters for a Samba server. You find these parameters in the [global] section. Table 18-2 lists some important parameters and their default values.

Table 18-2 Global settings in the Samba configuration file

Parameter	Description	Default value
workgroup	Defines the workgroup the server appears to be in when queried by clients.	WORKGROUP
passdb backend	Defines which backend database is used for storing user and group information. This parameter is divided into two parts separated by a colon. The first part is the backend's name, and the second part is the location string, as in passdb backend = tdbsam:/etc/samba/passdb.tdb.	tdbsam
printing	The printing styles BSD, AIX, LPRNG, PLP, SYSV, HPUX, QNX, SOFTQ, and CUPS define how printer status information is interpreted.	cups
printcap name	Used to override the printcap name, which is usually /etc/printcap. For example, to use the CUPS interface, you use the parameter printcap name = cups.	cups
printcap cache time	Defines the number of seconds before you're prompted for known printers. Setting this value to 0 disables rescanning for new or removed printers.	750
cups options	This parameter is valid only if the printing parameter is set to cups. The default, raw, sends unfiltered printer data that allows you to use drivers on the Windows client.	raw
map to guest	Specifies what smbd (the Samba server daemon) does with user login requests that don't match a valid UNIX user in some way.	Bad User
include	This parameter is used to include one configuration file inside another, which enables you to customize settings for machines.	/etc/samba/dhcp.conf
logon path	Defines the directory where roaming profiles are stored. Doesn't work with Win 9x roaming profiles.	\\%L\profiles\.msprofile
logon home	Defines the home directory location for Windows 95/98 or NT Workstation users logging in to a Samba primary domain controller.	\\%L\%U\.9xprofile
logon drive	If a Samba server is set up as a login server, this parameter becomes valid. Used only by NT workstations and defines the local path the home directory is connected to.	P
usershare allow guests	Specifies whether user-defined shares can be accessed by unauthenticated users.	No

18

Share Definitions The share definitions part of the `smb.conf` file includes directories available for clients to share. Figure 18-1 shows part of a Samba configuration file containing share definitions, and Table 18-3 lists the share definition parameters in the Samba configuration file. Unless stated otherwise, a `yes` value enables the parameter, and a `no` value disables it.

```
[global]
        workgroup = WORKGROUP
        passdb backend = tdbsam
        printing = cups
        printcap name = cups
        printcap cache time = 750
        cups options = raw
        map to guest = Bad User
        include = /etc/samba/dhcp.conf
        logon path = \\%L\profiles\.msprofile
        logon home = \\%L\%U\.9xprofile
        logon drive = P:
        usershare allow guests = Yes
[homes]
        comment = Home Directories
        valid users = %S, %D%w%S
        browseable = No
        read only = No
        inherit acls = Yes

        inherit acls = Yes
[printers]
        comment = All Printers
        path = /var/tmp
        printable = Yes
        create mask = 0600
        browseable = No
```

Figure 18-1 Share definitions in the Samba configuration file
Source: openSUSE

Table 18-3 Share definition parameters in the Samba configuration file

Parameter	Description	Default value
comment	A description of a share displayed when a client queries the server, as in `comment = Data drive`.	`#  No comment`
valid users	Specifies a list of users, separated by commas, who are allowed to log in to this service. By default, this parameter is empty, which means any user can log in. To specify users, you could add an entry such as `valid users = Jane, Fred, Steve`.	`# No valid users list` `(anyone can login)`
browseable	Specifies whether a share is included in a browse list of available shares returned from the `net view` command. (In Windows, a browse list shows domains, computers, resources, and all available Samba servers.)	`yes`
read only	Prevents users of a service from modifying files in the service's directory.	`yes`
inherit acls	Guarantees that if default ACLs exist on parent directories, they're always followed when creating a new file or subdirectory.	`no`
printable	Allows clients to open, write to, and submit printer spool files on the directory specified for the service.	`no`

To see the full list of global settings and share definitions, review the
`smb.conf` man pages.

Configuring and Using a Samba Client

Server Message Block (SMB), originally developed by IBM and later modified by Microsoft, is a protocol that gives client computers read and write access to a network server. It provides a means of sharing files on a server. SMB is typically used in Windows environments; however, if you want to share information from a Linux machine to a Windows machine, you use Samba, which emulates the SMB protocol. OpenSUSE is configured to give Linux machines access to Windows shares. For instance, if you have a Windows machine on your network named `windows01` containing a share called `documents`, you can mount this share with the following command:

```
mount -t cifs //windows01/documents /mnt -o username=tracy
```

You must include the space after `documents` and before `/mnt`
for the command to function correctly.

The preceding command is used to access the Windows share. (Refer back to Chapter 13 for a review of the `mount` command.) The `-t` option specifies the type of file system to be mounted; in this example, it's **Common Internet File System (CIFS)**, which is the successor to the SMB protocol that allows users running different OSs to share resources across the network.

This example assumes the Linux computer can resolve the computer
name by using DNS or the `/etc/hosts` file.

The `smbclient` command is a Samba utility used to communicate with the Samba server for downloading or uploading files. You can also use this command to gather information from the server. Figure 18-2 shows how to view shares available on the host, and Table 18-4 describes some options used with the `smbclient` command.

```
linux-3w7l:/home/test # smbclient -L Serge-PC
Enter test's password:
Domain=[SERGE-PC] OS=[Windows 7 Ultimate 7600] Server=[Windows 7 Ultimate 6.1]

        Sharename       Type      Comment
        ---------       ----      -------
        activity18-1    Disk
        ADMIN$          Disk      Remote Admin
        C$              Disk      Default share
        HP Deskjet F300 Series Printer   HP Deskjet F300 Series
        HP Photosmart B110 series Printer   HP Photosmart B110 series
        HP Photosmart C3100 series Printer   HP Photosmart C3100 series
        IPC$            IPC       Remote IPC
        print$          Disk      Printer Drivers
        Users           Disk
```

Figure 18-2 Output of the `smbclient` command
Source: openSUSE

18

If you're using Windows 7, you might have to uninstall Windows Live Sign-In Assistant if your attempts to log in fail.

Table 18-4 Options for the `smbclient` command

Options	Description	Example
`-T`	Used to make tar-compatible backups of files on a Windows share. Follow it with another option to specify whether you're creating (c) or extracting (x) files with this option.	`smbclient //windows01/documents -N -Tc backup.tar`
`-L`	Used to list available shares on a specified host.	`smbclient -L windows01`
`-N`	Short for "no password"; by default, `smbclient` prompts for a password, but this option bypasses that requirement (which is useful for accessing services that don't require passwords).	`smbclient -N -L windows01`
`//server/service`	The *server* is the NetBIOS name, and *service* specifies the service. This option opens an FTP-like interface for transferring files to or from the share.	`smbclient //windows01/documents -N`
`-h`	Displays a summary of valid options for the command.	`smbclient -h`

The `smbtree` command is a Samba utility that's similar to what's displayed in the Network window in Windows. It shows a tree of all known workgroups/domains, servers in the workgroup/domain, and shares on these servers. Table 18-5 describes some common options used with this command, and the following example shows its output:

```
smbtree
Enter justin's password:
WORKGROUP
\\SERVER                  Samba 3.4.2-1.1.3.1-2229-SUSE-SL11.2
\\SERVER\IPC$ IPC Service (Samba3.4.2-1.1.3.1-2229-SUSE-SL11.2)
\\SERVER\netlogon         Network Logon Service
\\SERVER\activity18-2     Created in Activity 18-2
\\SERVER\print$           Printer Drivers
\\SERVER\groups           All groups
\\SERVER\users            All users
\\SERVER\profiles         Network Profiles Service
\\SERVER\homes            Home Directories
```

Table 18-5 Options for the `smbtree` command

Options	Description
-b	Used to query the network by sending a request as a broadcast. Typically, you query the local master browser.
-D	Displays a list of only domains.
-S	Displays a list of only servers.
-N	Same as this option with the `smbclient` command; used to bypass the requirement to prompt for a password.

ACTIVITY

Activity 18-1: Mounting a Windows Share

Time Required: 15 minutes

Objective: Mount a Windows share from an openSUSE Linux machine.

Description: In this activity, you need to know your Windows computer name and IP address. You create a share on a Windows machine, log in to a Linux machine, and mount the Windows share.

1. Start VMware Player and log in to an openSUSE virtual machine.

2. Open a terminal window and switch to the root user.

3. Switch to your Windows machine and create a folder named **activity18-1** on the C drive.

4. Open the `activity18-1` folder and create a file named **file1.txt**.

5. Share the `activity18-1` folder and name the share **activity**. To share the folder in Windows 7, simply right-click the folder and click **Properties**. Click the **Sharing** tab, and then click the **Advanced Sharing** button. The share name should be listed as "activity18-1." Click the **Permissions** button, add the **Everyone** group, and click **Allow** for the Full Control permission. Click **OK** twice. Then click the **Security** tab and add the **Full Control** permission to the Everyone group. Click **OK**, and close the Properties dialog box.

6. Switch to your Linux machine. Use the skills you've learned in previous chapters to edit the `/etc/hosts` file so that your Linux machine can resolve the Windows computer name to its IP address. To do this, enter **vim /etc/hosts** at the command prompt and press **Enter**. At the end of the `hosts` file, enter your Windows IP address on the left, press **Tab**, and enter your Windows computer name. Save the file, and exit the vim editor.

7. Mount the Windows share by typing **mount -t cifs //*pcNAME*/activity /mnt** (replacing *pcNAME* with the name of your Windows computer) and pressing **Enter**. Depending on how you shared the Windows share and which Windows version you're using, you might get a password prompt. Because you've set up the share to give access to everyone on the network, a username and password aren't required. If you're prompted for a password, press **Enter** to proceed with the mount.

18

8. Change to the mount point by typing **cd /mnt** and pressing **Enter**. View the contents of this directory. You should be able to see the `file1.txt` file you created in Step 4.

9. Leave the terminal window open and the virtual machine running for the next activity.

Configuring the Samba Server with YaST

The YaST Samba Server module is installed in openSUSE Linux automatically, but if you don't have the module for some reason, you can install it by starting YaST and opening the Software Management tool. Select Filter from the menu, point to Patterns, and click File Server. You can also start the module with the `yast2 samba-server` command. The first time you start this module, you're prompted to enter the workgroup or domain name. After entering this information, click Next to move to the window shown in Figure 18-3, where you specify the Samba server type.

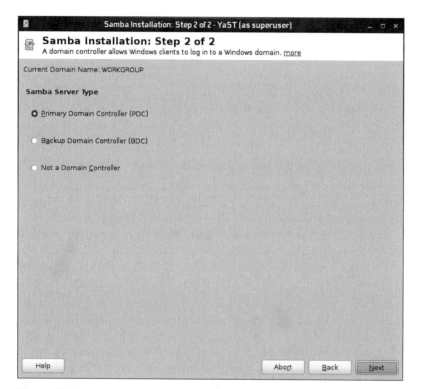

Figure 18-3 Specifying the Samba server type
Source: openSUSE

You can select a primary domain controller (PDC) or backup domain controller (BDC) or choose not to make the server any type of domain controller. A domain controller is a server role or function that handles authentication on a Windows domain. If the PDC goes down, a BDC allows Windows clients to log on to a Windows domain but uses information from another domain controller for authentication; therefore, if the PDC is unavailable, authentication can still take place.

The next window is for advanced Samba configuration. The following list describes the tabs in this window:

- *Start-Up*—You use this tab (see Figure 18-4) to configure how the Samba service starts (automatically when your system starts or manually). You can also open the corresponding port in the firewall.

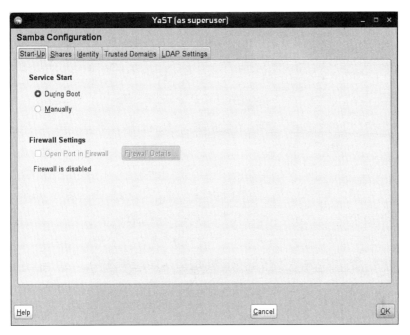

Figure 18-4 The Start-Up tab
Source: openSUSE

- *Shares*—You use this tab (see Figure 18-5) to add, edit, and remove Samba shares. You can also view basic information about a share, such as whether it's enabled or disabled and its status, such as read-only.

- *Identity*—You use this tab (see Figure 18-6) to define the server and its primary role in the network. For instance, you can specify the server as a primary domain controller in the Base Settings section. You can also specify that the Samba server use Windows Internet Name Service (WINS) for hostname resolution. WINS is an alternative to using DNS and is available only with older versions of Windows.

18

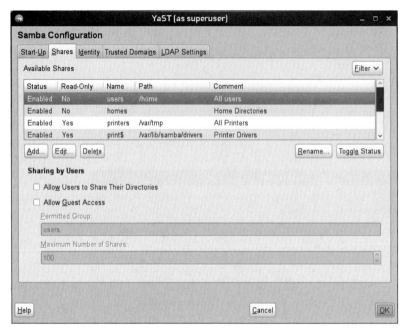

Figure 18-5 The Shares tab
Source: openSUSE

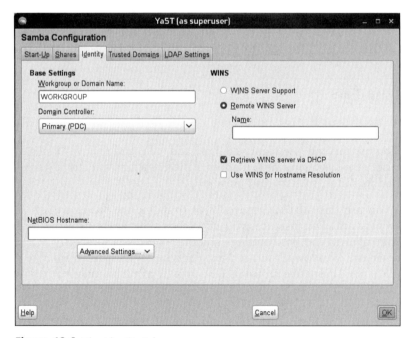

Figure 18-6 The Identity tab
Source: openSUSE

You can also edit global settings by clicking Advanced Settings and then selecting Expert Global Settings to open the window shown in Figure 18-7. The smb.conf parameters described previously are listed here, and you can add, edit, or delete these parameters.

- *Trusted Domains*—You use this tab to add a trusted relationship between a local network domain and a remote domain, which allows users from other domains to access your domain. You need the remote domain's password to add the relationship.

- *LDAP Settings*—You use this tab to specify the LDAP server to use for account information and authentication.

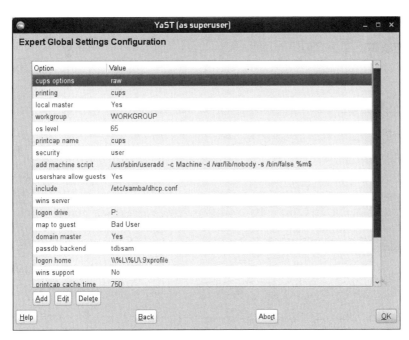

Figure 18-7 The Expert Global Settings Configuration window
Source: openSUSE

Creating Samba Users

The Samba password file (smbpasswd) in the /etc/samba directory contains usernames, UNIX IDs, and SMB hashed passwords. You use the smbpasswd command to add or modify users in this file. The following example shows how to add a Samba user:

```
smbpasswd -a user1
New SMB password:
Retype new SMB password:
Added user user1.
```

This file is the default password backend for older versions of Samba; however, it isn't typically used because it stores password information in plain text. This particular backend was suitable for interoperability with Windows 95 when encryption wasn't required

18

to share files. To use it with newer Windows versions, you have to enable encrypted passwords by modifying the `smb.conf` file to include the global parameter `encrypt passwords = yes`. Using `smbpasswd` with Windows isn't recommended because it doesn't scale well or hold Windows information, such as home directory, password expiration time, and relative identifiers (RIDs). The `smbpasswd` file uses a plaintext ASCII layout and requires carrying out password lookups sequentially, which can cause bottlenecks on networks with a large number of users. Later, an indexed database format was determined to be a much better option. The preferred `passdb` backend introduced in Samba 3.4.0 is `tdbsam`. It's the default `passwd` backend with the Samba version (3.4.2) included with openSUSE 11.2.

To access the Samba server from a Windows machine, you must have a Samba user account that matches a regular Linux user account. Steps 10 and 11 in Activity 18-2 explain how to create matching accounts.

Activity 18-2: Mounting a Linux Samba Share

Time Required: 15 minutes

Objective: Use YaST to configure a Samba server, which allows a Windows user to access a Linux share.

Description: In this activity, you use the Samba Server module to create a Linux share. After creating Linux and Samba user accounts, you switch to a Windows machine and map the Linux Samba share. Finally, you view the Samba configuration file to see how it changed after configuring Samba with YaST.

1. If necessary, start VMware Player, log in to an openSUSE virtual machine, open a terminal window, and switch to the root user.

2. View the Samba configuration file by typing **less /etc/samba/smb.conf** and pressing **Enter.**

3. To edit the Samba configuration file, start the YaST Samba Server module by typing **yast2 samba-server** and pressing **Enter.**

4. If it's the first time you have started the YaST Samba Server module, enter the workgroup or domain name, and click **Next.** In the Step 2 window, make sure the **Primary Domain Controller** (PDC) option button is selected, and then click **Next.**

5. In the Samba Configuration window, click the **Start-Up** tab, if necessary. Make sure the Samba service starts when the computer starts by clicking the **During Boot** option button. Open the corresponding port in the firewall by clicking the **Open Port in Firewall** check box.

6. Click the **Shares** tab, and then click **Add** to create a Linux share. Type **activity18-2** in the Share Name text box and **Created in Activity 18-2** in the Share Description text box.

7. Make sure the Share Type is **Directory**, type **/activity18-2** in the Share Path text box, and click **OK.** When prompted to create the directory, click **Yes** and then **OK.** When prompted to enter a root password, type **password** twice, and then click **OK.**

8. In the terminal window, switch to the **/activity18-2** folder and create a file named **file2.**

9. Switch to your Windows machine and try to map to the Linux share. In Windows 7, open Windows Explorer, and click **Tools, Map network drive** from the menu. Type **\\\\Linux\\activity18-2** in the Folder text box (replacing *Linux* with the name of your Linux machine). In the window that opens, try to access the Linux share by entering your Linux username and password. Did it work? Why or why not?

———————————————————————————————

10. Switch to the terminal window on your Linux machine, and create a user by typing **useradd user1** and pressing **Enter**. Change the user1 password by typing **passwd user1** and pressing **Enter**. Type **P@$$w0rd** for the password.

11. Create a Samba user by typing **smbpasswd -a user1** and pressing **Enter**. Type **P@$$w0rd** for the new SMB password, and then retype the password when prompted.

12. Switch to your Windows machine and try to map to the Linux drive. This time, use **user1** for the username and **P@$$w0rd** for the password.

13. Switch to the Samba server and view the Samba configuration file again. How has it changed?

———————————————————————————————

14. Leave the virtual machine running for the next activity.

Using the Samba Web Administration Tool

Samba can be configured with the Web-based Samba Web Administration Tool (SWAT), which is bundled with the standard Linux package. SWAT is compatible with all Linux distributions and makes it easy to administer and configure Samba from a browser on any platform, including Windows, Linux, and Macintosh.

SWAT is controlled by the xinetd daemon, but the daemon doesn't need to be dedicated (meaning it starts the SWAT service only when needed). The SWAT configuration file is /etc/xinetd.d/swat. SWAT is disabled by default, so you need to edit this file to enable it. To edit this file and start SWAT, follow this general procedure:

1. Start the computer where you're configuring Samba, and open a terminal window.

2. Open the /etc/xinetd.d/swat file in the vim editor.

3. Change the disable variable's value from yes to no. Save the changes and close the file.

4. Restart the xinetd daemon with the service xinetd restart command.

5. Start a Web browser.

6. Start SWAT by typing the hostname or IP address in the browser's address bar with port number 901, in this format: http://hostname or IP address:901.

If you're using SWAT on the Samba server, you can use localhost as the hostname, as in *http://localhost:901*.

TIP

18

7. When you're prompted for the username and password, enter this information, and click OK. Figure 18-8 shows the opening window.

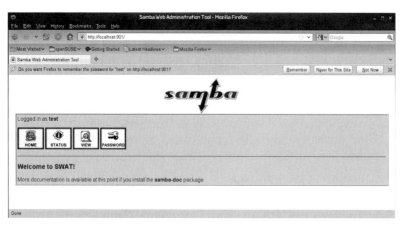

Figure 18-8 The opening window in SWAT
Source: openSUSE

You can configure many settings in SWAT, such as share name and path, permissions, comments, and valid users. SWAT makes Samba configuration easy and reliable because making errors is less likely than when editing the `smb.conf` file.

Activity 18-3: Using SWAT

Time Required: 15 minutes

Objective: Use SWAT to view the Samba configuration file and edit shares.

Description: In this activity, you enable SWAT and view the Samba configuration file and share you created in Activity 18-2.

1. If necessary, start VMware Player, log in to an openSUSE virtual machine, open a terminal window, and switch to the root user.

2. To enable SWAT, you edit the Samba configuration file. First, type **vim /etc/xinetd.d/swat** and press **Enter** to open the file in vim.

3. Find the `disable` variable, and change its value from yes to **no**. Save and close the file.

4. Next, restart the xinetd daemon by typing **service xinetd restart** and pressing **Enter**.

5. Start a Web browser, enter the URL **http://localhost:901**, and press **Enter**. When prompted for a username and password, enter the ones you created in Step 11 of Activity 18-2.

6. Click the **VIEW** icon and scroll all the way down to the bottom. You should see the [activity18-2] parameter you created in Activity 18-2.

7. Enter the URL **http://localhost:901/shares**.

8. Click the **Choose Share** drop-down list and click **activity18-2** (see Figure 18-9). You can now use SWAT to edit the same parameters available in the `smb.conf` file.

9. When you're finished, power off the virtual machine, and close all open windows.

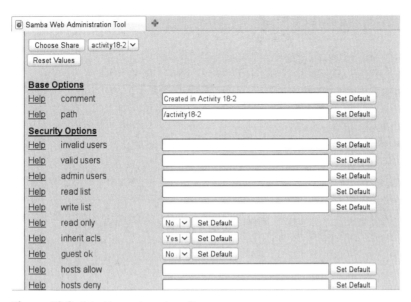

Figure 18-9 Selecting a share to edit
Source: openSUSE

Chapter Summary

- Samba makes interoperating Linux and Windows possible with the SMB/CIFS protocol. Samba works in a client/server architecture and provides services such as file sharing, printer sharing, and authentication.

- The Samba configuration file is `/etc/samba/smb.conf`. This file is typically divided into sections called `[global]`, `[homes]`, and `[printers]`.

- The sections of `smb.conf` contain parameters that can be grouped as global settings and share definitions. Global settings include values all users and clients on a network use to set parameters for a Samba server. These settings in the `[global]` section of `smb.conf` are mandatory. Share definitions include directories available for clients to share.

- You can use the following protocols to configure and use a Samba client: Server Message Block (SMB), which gives client computers read and write access to a server on the network, or Common Internet File System (CIFS), which allows users running different OSs to share resources across the network.

- You can configure the Samba server in the YaST Samba Server module, which is started with the `yast2 samba-server` command.

- You can create and modify Samba users with the `smbpasswd` command.

- The Web-based Samba Web Administration Tool (SWAT) enables you to configure Samba from a browser on any platform, including Windows, Linux, and Macintosh.

18

Key Terms

Common Internet File System (CIFS)   The successor to SMB that allows users on different OSs to share resources across the network.

Samba   An open-source tool that provides an interface between two OSs, such as Linux and Windows, by using SMB/CIFS. *See also* Common Internet File System (CIFS) *and* Server Message Block (SMB).

Server Message Block (SMB)   A protocol that gives client computers read and write access to a server on the network.

Review Questions

1. Samba uses which of the following to authenticate users? (Choose all that apply.)

    a. Passwords

    b. ACLs

    c. Domains

    d. Log entries

2. Which of the following is the Samba configuration file?

    a. `/etc/samba/dhcp.conf`

    b. `/etc/samba/smb.conf`

    c. `/etc/hosts.conf`

    d. `/etc/samba/smbpasswd`

3. Write the command for mounting a share named `project` in the `/projects` directory on a Windows server named `server1`.

4. Write the command for viewing available shares on the `server1` host.

5. Which of the following commands do you use to connect to a Windows share in an interactive mode? The Windows server is `mainoffice`, and the share name is `documents`. Make sure you aren't prompted for a password.

    a. `smbclient -L mainoffice -N`

    b. `smbclient -N -L mainoffice/documents`

    c. `smbclient //mainoffice/documents -N`

    d. `smbclient //mainoffice/documents`

6. Which of the following commands is used to create and modify users in Samba?

    a. `useradd`

    b. `createsmbuser`

    c. `smbpasswd`

    d. `smbcreate`

7. What is the URL if you're accessing SWAT on the Samba server?

   a. *http://sambahost:901*

   b. *http://localhost:901*

   c. *http://localhost:903*

   d. *http://swat:901*

8. Which of the following daemons controls SWAT?

   a. Smbd

   b. Nmbd

   c. Xinetd

   d. Winbindd

9. Parameters in the Samba configuration file are grouped in which of the following categories? (Choose all that apply.)

   a. Global settings

   b. Permissions

   c. Security logs

   d. Share definitions

10. A domain controller handles which of the following in a Windows domain?

    a. Logging

    b. File transfers

    c. Authentication

    d. Web sites

11. Which of the following protocols allows file sharing over a network? (Choose all that apply.)

    a. SMB

    b. DNS

    c. CIFS

    d. DHCP

Case Projects

CASE PROJECTS

Case Project 18-1: Using the Samba Client Module

OpenSUSE includes the Samba Client module. Conduct research on this module and write a one-page summary of its features. Explain the pros and cons of using it as well as any other software required to start the module.

18

## chapter 19

Securing Linux

After reading this chapter and completing the exercises, you will be able to:

- Describe attacks on servers
- Summarize system security measures
- Secure Web servers
- Explain how to use Linux-based firewalls
- Secure data from the command line

In this chapter, you learn how to secure Linux systems. First, you learn about types of server attacks. You then review a variety of system security measures, including shutting down nonessential services, to prevent vulnerabilities. Next, you learn how to secure Web servers and configure Linux-based firewalls. Finally, you see how to secure data from the command line.

System Security

System security is the task of configuring network computers to prevent unauthorized users from accessing them. The growth of the Internet makes remote and local computers increasingly vulnerable to attacks from intruders. In addition, data transfers over a network are susceptible to attacks and unauthorized access.

Types of Server Attacks

Linux, like any OS, is susceptible to attacks from intruders and unauthorized users. However, when security vulnerabilities are detected, it's up to development and user communities to find a solution. The Linux source code is under constant scrutiny to check for and repair vulnerabilities, which makes this OS an excellent choice for developing a secure network. This section describes some common attacks against Linux servers.

A Web server is highly susceptible to attacks because its configuration parameters increase its vulnerability on the network level and the file system level. On the network level, intruders can take advantage of unnecessary or incorrectly configured services listening on unsecured open ports. On the file system level, attackers can use common directories (such as /, /tmp, and /var) to stage denial-of-service attacks (explained later in this section). Attacks on Linux Web servers are usually of two types:

- *Common Gateway Interface (CGI) script intrusions*—The cgi-bin directory contains executable scripts that the server calls on behalf of a remote user. **CGI scripts** are used to generate a dynamic Web page's contents and can be written in a number of programming languages, such as Java, C, and Perl. If the Web server isn't configured correctly, a remote user can run CGI scripts as a root user. As mentioned, the file system is a major vulnerability, so a remote user might be able to install and run a CGI script from a poorly secured /tmp directory and gain unauthorized access to the server. Configuring the Web server to run CGI scripts only from specified locations prevents CGI script intrusions.

- *Buffer overflows*—In a **buffer overflow**, data that has exceeded a buffer's storage capacity overflows into another buffer. This attack has become more prevalent with the growth of the Internet. Attackers replace the part of memory containing the Web server's instructions with random instructions that they embed in the URL, enabling them to overwrite permissions so that they can gain access to the Web server and run malicious code.

Attacks on other types of servers are common, too. Intruders use root compromises, for example, to gain root user privileges to a server. They might use one or more of these methods to find the root password: network sniffing, guessing via brute-force attack tools, and browsing system logs. Intruders might also stage a buffer overflow attack on a vulnerable application to gain root access.

19

Denial-of-service (DoS) attacks involve overloading a server with an overwhelming amount of network traffic so that it can't handle legitimate requests for network services. The goal of this attack isn't to steal or modify data; it's done to disable the server. Table 19-1 describes some types of DoS attacks.

Table 19-1 Examples of DoS attacks

Type of attack	Description
Teardrop	The attacker floods a server with a large number of fragmented IP packets that overlap each other during assembly, which causes the server to crash when it tries to reassemble these packets.
SYN flood	To establish a TCP connection, a SYN (synchronize) message is sent to the server, and the server responds with a SYN-ACK (acknowledgement message). The attacker exploits this vulnerability by opening a large number of TCP connections halfway by sending multiple SYN requests until the victim's network buffers, waiting for the connection to finish, become unavailable.
Ping flood	A simple attack in which ICMP Echo Request (also known as ping) packets are sent to a victim, who continues to send packets in response, effectively choking available bandwidth. This attack is usually more successful if the attacker has more bandwidth than the victim, thus consuming all incoming and outgoing bandwidth on the network.

A computer can't be completely safeguarded from DoS attacks, but incidents can be reduced by tightening the Linux Web server's security. A variation of a DoS attack is a **distributed denial-of-service (DDoS) attack**, in which many sources are used to generate bogus packets (SYN requests, ICMP Echo Requests, and so forth) sent to a single system. For example, instead of one computer carrying out a teardrop attack in a typical DoS attack, in a DDoS attack, multiple computers carry out their own teardrop attacks against a single victim's computer.

Address spoofing is most often used on packet-filter firewalls, which are configured to allow only known addresses to initiate connections. Internal attackers can easily forge their source IP addresses and cause damage just by sending packets randomly. Forged source IP addresses conceal the intruder's identity and can't receive responses from a destination computer. The most common type of address spoofing is a DoS attack in which traffic is sent, but no response from the destination computer is needed for the attack to be successful.

Trojan programs are hidden scripts embedded in seemingly legitimate programs that are authorized by the unsuspecting victims. When the authorized program runs, the Trojan program opens a backdoor, which is a vulnerability an intruder can use to infiltrate the computer, often with root privileges. The Trojan presents itself as a useful tool and is often partially functional. However, it can cripple or destroy a server and even an entire network. Trojan programs are extremely difficult to detect.

Session hijacking is a specialized form of address spoofing in which a hijacker gets unauthorized control of a network session. A TCP hijacker observes the sequence of numbers sent in a TCP conversation, and then uses an expected sequence number to impersonate one of the session participants. To prevent the impersonated party from continuing to take part in the conversation, the hijacker stages a DoS attack on the network session. Using an authentication method that isn't based only on IP addresses is one solution for preventing session hijacking.

Similar to phone wiretapping, attackers use network eavesdropping to collect confidential information, using security vulnerabilities in network services running on a Linux computer. To do this, they use packet sniffers, which are tools that "listen" to network packets so that attackers can discover password information and subsequently gain access to an unsuspecting victim's server. To help prevent eavesdropping attacks, administrators should ensure that unencrypted root passwords never traverse the network.

The goal of cryptographic algorithms is to ensure an adequate level of confidentiality, integrity, and authentication, but some have been found vulnerable to attacks or mathematical exploits. Mathematical exploitation takes advantage of flaws in the functions algorithm designers use to derive prime numbers or generate keys.

Brute-force attacks take place by guessing passwords and keys. Potential intruders use a brute-force approach to guess encryption keys—that is, using every possible combination of characters until the correct one is found. This type of attack can crack any key, given the time to do so. By contrast, a dictionary attack uses a dictionary file to try to guess a user's password. This type of attack is limited to words supplied in the dictionary file, so the password might never be discovered. A brute-force attack, on the other hand, uses all combinations of characters until a key is found, although doing so might take considerable time.

Shutting Down Nonessential Services

Linux includes many network services that aren't essential. Cleartext protocols, such as FTP and Telnet, are known for having security weaknesses, such as transmitting unencrypted usernames and passwords, that could give intruders unauthorized access. A first step is examining configuration files in the /etc/xinetd.d directory to determine which network services are running. This directory contains a configuration file for each network service running on a computer. For example, here's the configuration file for the services service:

```
cat /etc/xinetd.d/services
service services
{
    type            = INTERNAL UNLISTED
    port            = 9098
    socket_type     = stream
    protocol        = tcp
    wait            = no
    disable         = yes
    only_from       = 127.0.0.1
    FLAGS           = IPv6 IPv4
}
```

The service line specifies the name of the service (services, in this case). The only_from line specifies the remote host the service is available to, and the FLAGS line sets the service to an IPv4 service and IPv6, if available.

The simplest approach to reducing Linux systems' vulnerability is disabling unnecessary network services, particularly those that send sensitive information, such as usernames and passwords, across the network without being encrypted. Table 19-2 lists some network services that are candidates for disabling. Some are disabled by default, but network administrators should check to make sure they've been disabled.

Table 19-2 Disabling network services

Network service	Description	When to disable
ftp	Allows users to transfer files across a network with FTP.	Should be disabled when there's a risk of information being accessed by intruders using advanced methods, such as packet sniffing.
telnet	Allows users to log in to remote computers and interact with them via a terminal window.	Should always be disabled because Telnet transmits data (including usernames and passwords) over a network in a plaintext format. You should use the Secure Shell (SSH) service instead to log in to remote computers.
rsh and rlogin	Allows users to access a remote computer's command shell without entering a login password.	Should always be disabled because of weak security features; they're a common avenue of exploits.
lpd	Allows users to print jobs on a print server.	Should be disabled when the Linux system doesn't need to share printers over a network.
finger	Gives information about local computers or users to remote computers.	Should always be disabled because it can reveal information about users, such as usernames and passwords, in plaintext format.
nfs	Allows users to share file system or directory structures over a network.	Should be disabled when the file system contains sensitive data.
sshd	Allows users to log in to remote computers and interact with them over a secure network connection. It was designed as a replacement for Telnet.	Should be disabled when access to a remote computer's command shell isn't required.
smb	Allows Windows systems to share files and printers with Linux systems.	Should be disabled when the file system to share contains sensitive data.
echo	Sends identical received characters back to the sender. For example, if you enter "echo test" on the command line, "test" is returned to the sender. It was originally used to measure round-trip times.	Should always be disabled unless you need to debug remote terminal problems.

To enable or disable services, you can use the YaST System Services (Runlevel) module. For example, if you don't want to share files stored on the server, you might decide to disable the smb and sshd services. Activity 19-1 walks you through disabling these services.

Activity 19-1: Disabling System Services

Time Required: 10 minutes

Objective: Enable and disable network services in YaST.

Description: In this activity, you learn how to use the YaST System Services (Runlevel) module to disable network services.

1. Start VMware Player and log in to an openSUSE virtual machine.

2. Open a terminal window and switch to the root user.

3. Open the YaST System Services (Runlevel) module by typing **yast2 runlevel** and pressing **Enter.**

Changing runlevels is an expert administrative task and should be done only with caution. If you enable a service in YaST, any dependent services are enabled, too, and start automatically when the system boots. Likewise, disabling a service also disables all dependent services and prevents them from running when the system boots.

4. Disable the smb service by clicking **smb** and then clicking **Disable.** In the message box stating that the command for disabling the smb service was successful, click **OK.**

5. Next, click **sshd** and click **Disable.** What message do you get?

_____

6. Click **OK** in the message box, and then click **OK** at the lower right to close the YaST System Services (Runlevel) module.

7. Leave the virtual machine running and the terminal window open for the next activity.

Securing Network Connections

Data transferred over a network connection, particularly a TCP/IP connection, is vulnerable to attackers who use advanced methods, such as packet sniffers, to intercept transmissions and perhaps alter or corrupt the data. Network connections must be secured to prevent unauthorized users from accessing data and other resources for malicious purposes.

TCP Wrappers, developed by Wietse Venema, is a widely used tool that logs connections and is used to allow or deny access to network services. The TCP Wrapper daemon (tcpd) monitors incoming requests for services, such as Telnet, finger, and FTP. TCP Wrappers support is integrated into the extended Internet services daemon (xinetd), which controls access to Internet-based services. TCP Wrappers consults the /etc/hosts.allow and /etc/hosts.deny files to determine when a connection should be allowed or denied. The /etc/hosts.allow file contains the names of hosts that are granted connection requests, and /etc/hosts.deny lists hosts that are denied connection requests. This tool scans the hosts.allow file first for the IP address of the requesting client. If the address is found in this file, the connection is allowed, even if it's been denied access to the service in the hosts.deny file. If the address isn't found in the hosts.allow file, the hosts.deny file is scanned. If the address is found in this file, the connection is denied. Finally, if TCP Wrappers doesn't find the IP address in either file, the connection is allowed.

For more information on TCP Wrappers, see *ftp://ftp.porcupine.org/pub/security/index.html.*

The following example shows the format of entries in the `/etc/hosts.allow` and `/etc/hosts.deny` files. The information between brackets is optional.

daemon_list:*client_list*[: *shell_command*]

Here's an example from the `hosts.allow` file:

```
Fire up a mail to the admin if a connection to the printer daemon has
been made from host foo.bar.com, but simply deny all others:
lpd : foo.bar.com : spawn /bin/echo "%h printer access" | \
                            mail -s "tcp_wrappers on %H" root
```

In this file's syntax, *daemon_list* is a comma-separated list of server names, *client_list* is a comma-separated list of patterns matching one or more clients, and *shell_command* is the action to carry out when a match is found. Table 19-3 describes wildcards that can be used in these fields.

For more information on patterns and wildcards, see the hosts_access(5) man page by entering man 5 hosts_access at the command prompt, or visit *http://linux.about.com/od/commands/l/blcmdl5_hostsal.htm.*

Table 19-3 TCP Wrappers wildcards

Keyword	Description
ALL	Matches any hostname or IP address
LOCAL	Matches the hostname, which doesn't contain the dot character
KNOWN	Matches hosts whose name and address can be resolved by DNS
UNKNOWN	Matches hosts whose name and address can't be resolved by DNS
PARANOID	Matches hosts whose names don't match the IP address

After the administrator configures the `hosts.allow` and `hosts.deny` files, the `tcpdchk` command is used to check the TCP Wrappers configuration to detect any potential problems, such as nonexistent pathnames and syntax errors. By default, this command looks for the `/etc/inetd.conf` configuration file; however, because the more secure xinetd daemon is used now, the `/etc/xinetd.conf` file has replaced it, which means you need to specify this file when using the `tcpdchk` command. Figure 19-1 shows a sample output of this command. In this example, in the first rule, all hosts except the local host are granted access to the telnet daemon; in the second rule, all hosts except the localhost are denied access to the http-rman service, which allows viewing man pages in a Web browser. Table 19-4 describes common options used with the `tcpdchk` command.

```
server:/usr/share/YaST2/include/inetd # tcpdchk -v -i /etc/xinetd.conf
Using network configuration file: /etc/xinetd.conf

>>> Rule /etc/hosts.allow line 62:
daemons:  in.telnetd
clients:  ALL EXCEPT LOCAL
access:   granted

>>> Rule /etc/hosts.deny line 5:
daemons:  http-rman
clients:  ALL EXCEPT LOCAL
access:   denied
server:/usr/share/YaST2/include/inetd # ▊
```

Figure 19-1 Sample output of the `tcpdchk` command
Source: openSUSE

Table 19-4 Common options for the `tcpdchk` command

Option	Description
d	Checks the `hosts.allow` and `hosts.deny` files in your current directory instead of their default directory.
i /etc/xinetd.conf	This option is used to specify the `xinetd.conf` file, which has replaced the `inetd.conf` file in openSUSE.
v	Displays detailed output for access control rules, which define who can access what service. Figure 19-1, for example, lists two access control rules: one to grant access to telnet and one to deny access to http-rman.

Activity 19-2: Configuring TCP Wrappers

Time Required: 20 minutes

Objective: Configure TCP Wrappers to allow and deny connection requests for network services.

Description: In this activity, you partner with another student or use two virtual machines. You start by configuring the firewall to allow SSH remote logins. Then you configure TCP Wrappers to allow and deny servers remote access to your machine.

1. Students 1 and 2: If necessary, start VMware Player and log in to an openSUSE virtual machine.

2. Students 1 and 2: If necessary, open a terminal window and switch to the root user.

3. Student 1: Configure the firewall so that Student 2 can use SSH to access your machine. To do this, type **yast2 firewall** and press **Enter**. When the Firewall module opens, click the **Allowed Services** option, and then click the **Service to Allow** list arrow. Click **Secure Shell Server** and then click **Add**. Finally, click **Next** and then **Finish**.

4. Student 1: Start the ssh daemon by typing **/etc/rc.d/sshd start** and pressing **Enter**.

5. Student 1: Display the TCP Wrappers configuration file by typing **tcpdchk -v -i /etc/xinetd.conf** and pressing **Enter**. What's displayed onscreen? Do you think Student 2 will be able to use SSH to access your machine?

6. Student 2: Request the IP address and password of the remote machine from your partner. Use SSH to access Student 1's machine by typing **ssh *xxx.xxx.xxx.xxx*** and pressing **Enter**. (You need to know Student 1's IP address and root password.) Were you successful?

7. Student 1: Edit the `/etc/hosts.deny` file by typing **vim /etc/hosts.deny** and pressing **Enter**. Add the following line to the end of this file: **sshd : ALL**. Save the file and exit the editor. Restart the xinetd daemon by typing **/etc/rc.d/xinetd restart** and pressing **Enter**.

8. Student 1: Check the TCP Wrappers configuration file by issuing the same command used in Step 5. Does the result look different than it did in Step 5?

9. Student 2: Try to use SSH to access Student 1's machine by issuing the same command used in Step 6. Were you able to? Why or why not?

10. Student 1: Edit the `/etc/hosts.allow` file by typing **vim /etc/hosts.allow**. Add the following entry: **sshd : ALL**. Save the file and exit the editor. Restart the ssh daemon.

11. Student 2: Try one more time to use SSH to access Student 1's machine. Were you able to? If there are entries in both the `/etc/hosts.allow` and `/etc/hosts.deny` files, which one takes precedence?

Securing Linux on a Network

A **packet sniffer** is a program that captures and views packets as they're transmitted over a network. Every computer contains a network interface card (NIC) to send and receive data from other computers over a network. A NIC normally operates with a filter that ignores traffic that isn't intended for it. When put in promiscuous mode, a NIC receives all packets on a network, including packets destined for other computers. Only the root user can put a NIC in promiscuous mode. A packet sniffer is able to "listen" in on network transmissions because the NIC on the packet analyzer's machine is put in promiscuous mode. To put a NIC in promiscuous mode, you use the `ifconfig ethx promisc` command (replacing *x* with the number of the Ethernet adapter).

Packet sniffers can be used for both good and bad. Unauthorized users can use them to access sensitive data, such as usernames and passwords, that might be transmitted in plaintext form over a network. Packet sniffers have several beneficial uses, however. Network administrators often use them to analyze network problems, monitor bandwidth use, detect and prevent network intrusions, and more. The following sections describe methods for detecting sniffers and preventing them from intercepting network traffic.

Monitoring Processes All processes running on a computer must be monitored periodically with the ps command to check for rogue or malfunctioning processes. A process using an usually high amount of CPU time might be an indication of a frozen or crashed program, for example. If you suspect this is the case, terminate the process with the kill -9 command. For example, to kill a process with the process ID (PID) 5125, you use kill -9 5125.

Packet sniffers are passive and don't generate much traffic, so they can be difficult to detect simply by using the ps command; however, you can use the ps -aux command to list all running processes on your machine, who's running them, and the percentage of CPU time they're using to help determine whether an unauthorized user is running a questionable process.

Using Secure Shell Secure Shell (SSH) is a protocol used to ensure that data transmitted to and from a remote computer is encrypted and secure. The original SSH is proprietary software; however, the open-source community realized the importance of SSH being available in the public domain. As a result, a free derivative called OpenSSH was created to replace unsecured services, such as rsh and rlogin, and ensure a secure, encrypted network connection. OpenSSH can be configured to tighten network security; it allows all users to access it by default, but you can customize it to restrict user access to SSH, for example.

To configure the OpenSSH server, you use the /etc/ssh/sshd_config file. Entries in this file are in the following form:

server_option value

For example, the default entry for the Kerberos option is as follows:

KerberosAuthentication no

Table 19-5 lists common server options in the /etc/ssh/sshd_config file.

Table 19-5 Options for the /etc/ssh/sshd_config file

Option	Description	Value
AllowTcpForwarding	Specifies whether TCP forwarding is permissible.	Possible values: yes or no; default: yes.
AllowUsers usr1 usr2 . . .	Specifies users allowed to access SSH. The arguments list users by username.	By default, all users are allowed to access SSH.
DenyUsers usr1 usr2 . . .	Specifies users who are denied access to SSH. The arguments list users by username.	By default, no users are denied from accessing SSH.
Ciphers	Specifies the encryption cipher to use.	aes128-cbc, 3des-cbc, blowfish-cbc, arcfour, cast128-cbc.
DSAAuthentication	Specifies whether DSA authentication is allowed.	The default value is allowed.
IgnoreRhosts	Specifies whether .rhosts and .shosts should be ignored. These files contain lists of remote users who aren't required to enter a password.	Possible values: yes or no; default: yes.

19

Table 19-5 Options for the `/etc/ssh/sshd_config` file (*continued*)

Option	Description	Value
KerberosAuthentication	Specifies whether Kerberos authentication is allowed.	Possible values: yes or no; default: no.
PasswordAuthentication	Specifies whether password authentication is allowed.	Possible values: yes or no; default: yes.
RhostsAuthentication	Indicates whether clients should be authenticated by using .rhosts authentication.	Possible values: yes or no; default: no.
PermitEmptyPasswords	States whether empty passwords are allowed for authentication to the OpenSSH server.	Possible values: yes or no; default: no.
PermitRootLogin	Specifies whether root logins should be allowed over an OpenSSH connection.	Possible values: yes or no; default: yes.
StrictModes	Indicates whether OpenSSH should verify the ownership of user files or home directories. This option verifies a user's home directory and .rhosts file permissions before allowing access. This check is important in case a user's world-writeable permission is enabled, which could allow another user to assume his or her identity.	Possible values: yes or no; default: yes.

As mentioned, you use the `/etc/ssh/ssh_config` file to configure the OpenSSH client. Entries in this file are in the following form:

```
client_option value
```

Here's an example showing the entry for the batch mode option in this file:

```
BatchMode no
```

Table 19-6 lists common client options in this configuration file.

Table 19-6 Options for the `/etc/ssh/ssh_config` file

Option	Description	Value
BatchMode	Disables username and password prompting for accessing OpenSSH	Possible values: yes or no; default: no.
Ciphers	Specifies the encryption cipher to use	aes128-cbc, 3des-cbc, blowfish-cbc, arcfour, cast128-cbc.
RSAAuthentication	Specifies whether RSA authentication is allowed	Possible values: yes or no; default: yes.
PasswordAuthentication	Specifies whether password authentication is allowed	Possible values: yes or no; default: yes.

Table 19-6 Options for the `/etc/ssh/ssh_config` file (*continued*)

Option	Description	Value
CompressionLevel	Specifies the gzip compression level	Ranges from 1 to 9; the default value is 6.
StrictHostKeyChecking	Specifies whether the client adds host keys to the `$HOME/.ssh/known_hosts` file automatically	Possible values: yes, no, or ask; default: ask. The value yes means the host key is never added automatically to the `$HOME/.ssh/known_hosts` file. The value no means the host key is always added automatically to the `$HOME/.ssh/known_hosts` file. The value ask asks Linux users whether to add the host key to the `$HOME/.ssh/known_hosts` file.

You can also add an authentication tool to use with OpenSSH. **Pluggable Authentication Module (PAM)** provides a centralized mechanism for authenticating services. It's configured in OpenSSH with the `/etc/pam.d/sshd` file. Table 19-7 lists common options in this file.

Table 19-7 Options for the `/etc/pam.d/sshd` file

Option	Description	Values
auth	Prompts the user for identification, such as a password	required, requisite, optional, and sufficient
account	Checks aspects of user accounts, such as password age and limiting computer access to certain time periods	required, requisite, optional, and sufficient
password	Updates the user authentication password	required, requisite, optional, and sufficient
session	Provides functions before and after establishing a session	required, requisite, optional, and sufficient

The following list explains the values used in the `/etc/pam.d/sshd` file:

- required—This value causes the entire stack to fail if the module's demands aren't met, but only after the entire stack has been processed.
- requisite—Similar to the required value, except that when the module fails, control is returned to the application. This value is used as an extra measure of security.
- sufficient—Success of the module is enough to satisfy the requirements of the stack of modules, after which no other modules are processed. If it fails, the process moves on to the next rule.
- optional—The success or failure of this module is important only if it's the only one in the stack.

The OpenSSH daemon is sshd. Typically, it's started automatically during the boot process from the `/etc/rc.d` directory. After you configure the OpenSSH configuration files, you start the sshd daemon with the `/etc/rc.d/sshd start` command. After sshd runs on the server, a client can connect to it with the `ssh` command, a command-line utility that replaces rlogin and rsh for logging in to remote machines. Here's an example of the `ssh` command, with the argument *server_name* indicating the Linux server on which the sshd daemon is running:

```
ssh server_name
```

For example, if the sshd daemon is running on the server `myserver`, you use the following command to connect the client computer with this server:

```
ssh myserver
```

If the client is connecting for the first time, the `ssh` command prompts for confirmation of a connection to a server. Type yes and press Enter to confirm the connection. The `ssh` command then prompts for a username and password to connect to the server.

Increasing NFS Security There are two steps for an NFS client to access files on a remote NFS server:

1. The client attempts to connect to a server by using the `/etc/exports` file (a process called "mount access"). The `/etc/exports` file contains the name or IP address of computers allowed to share files or a directory in a local file system. A client computer with an IP address matching one specified in the `/etc/exports` file is permitted to access the shared directory on the server.

2. The client gains access to a shared file or directory with the permission specified for the shared file or directory.

Although NFS is an excellent way of sharing files over a network, its use does involve some security concerns. After gaining access to a shared drive or directory, the client is allowed access to all other files in it. In addition, a user on the client computer can become a superuser and gain access to other shared drives and directories because NFS has no security measures against this possibility. As a result, an NFS server can become vulnerable to attacks from unauthorized users. So when you're configuring an NFS server, you must apply some critical security measures to prevent unauthorized users from accessing it. NFS can be secured with one of these methods:

- *Using the* `root_squash` *option in the* `/etc/exports` *file*—A client can log in to the NFS server as root by using the `su` command, thus becoming the "superuser" and having the same privileges as the root user. The `/etc/exports` file on the server is configured to have the `root_squash` option, which prevents the superuser from modifying the contents of files owned by the root user. For example, you want to reject a client's (named `myclient`) requests for accessing and modifying the contents of all files in a server's home directory when `myclient` is logged in as a superuser. To do this, you add the following entry in the `/etc/exports` file:

```
/home myclient(rw,root_squash)
```

- *Using the* nosuid *mount option*—The nosuid option is used on the client with the mount command to restrict SUID-root programs on the server from accessing NFS files and directories on the client. SUID stands for "set user ID." When the SUID bit is set, the program changes the ID of the user running the file to the file owner. For example, passwd is an SUID program. An SUID-root program is owned by a root user. By using an SUID-root program, a user on the server can log in to the client and become a root user on the client. By setting the nosuid option, you prevent potentially dangerous attacks, such as buffer overflows, from running malicious code on the client.

Securing a Web Server

Network security helps secure data transmitted over a network, but some network services open a number of ports for Internet connections. For example, httpd is the daemon for running Apache Web Server. It opens several ports, which makes a Web server more vulnerable to external attacks. Through the Web server, an intruder can gain control of a network. As a result, you need to include security measures, such as authentication and access control, for Apache Web Server. You also need to make sure the Web server itself has been secured. The following sections explain methods for securing Apache Web Server.

Using Access Control Methods

In Linux, http daemon security is carried out by configuring the Apache server with certain access control methods. Two methods are available to secure access: authentication and authorization. Authentication includes requiring usernames and passwords or checking a client's IP address or hostname against a list of users or groups. Apache uses Allow and Deny directives to restrict users. Both directives take an IP address as a parameter. Some parameters used with Allow and Deny directives are as follows:

- all (used when it needs to affect all addresses)
- A domain name, such as test.linux.com
- An IP address, such as 255.100.10.10
- A network/netmask pair, such as 255.100.10.0/255.255.255.0
- A network address specified in Classless Interdomain Routing (CIDR) format, such as 255.100.10.1/20

Basing access control on IP addresses rather than hostnames makes authentication faster because you don't have to resolve hostnames.

The default method of authentication in Apache Web Server is to check for the Deny from all statement first and then check the Allow directives. You can set authentication directives in the Apache Web Server configuration file, httpd.conf, as discussed in Chapter 10. The Order statement controls the default access state and the order of authentication (the order in which Allow and Deny directives are evaluated). You can change the order of authentication by using the Order statement as follows:

- Order Deny Allow—This is the default order. The Deny directive is checked before the Allow directive. If an address isn't found in the Deny directive, the host is allowed to access the server's resources.

- Order Allow Deny—In this order, the Allow directive is checked before the Deny directive. If an address isn't found in the Allow directive, the host is denied access to the server's resources.

- Order Mutual-failure—Hosts or addresses specified in the Allow directive but not the Deny directive are allowed access.

For example, if server administrators want to view the Web server status for *www.gnu-linux.org*, they can add the following lines to the httpd.conf file:

```
<Location /server-status>
   SetHandler server-status
   Order Deny Allow
Deny from all
Allow from www.gnu-linux.org
</Location>
```

Another authentication method in Apache Web Server is verifying a user's identity by requesting a username and password to access restricted resources. Usernames and passwords for Apache users are stored in a text file called the "user authentication file." To create this file, you use the htpasswd -c command, which is included in the Apache package. For example, to create a user authentication file called linuxers for the user wsb, use the following command:

```
htpasswd -c linuxers wsb
```

 The htpasswd command isn't installed by default. You must install the Web and LAMP Server pattern before you can use it.

This command prompts for a password. After it's entered, the user authentication file is created. Now the AuthUserFile directive can be used to point to the file. This directive specifies the name of the file containing usernames and passwords used for authentication and needs an absolute path supplied as a parameter. For example, if the preceding authentication file is created in the user's home directory, the absolute path is as follows:

```
AuthUserFile /home/wsb/linuxers
```

You also use the AuthType directive to set the type of authentication (basic or digest) for a resource. With basic authentication, passwords are sent in plaintext. In digest authentication, passwords are encrypted with the MD5 algorithm.

Authorization After you set up measures for authenticating users, you need to specify the users who are authorized to use the server's resource. You do this with the Require directive, which is also added to the server configuration file. It can be used to specify a single user, a list of users, or a list of groups in the user authentication file who are allowed to access the resource.

The following directives must accompany the Require directive for it to function correctly: AuthType, AuthName, AuthUserFile, and AuthGroupFile. Take a look at this example:

```
AuthType Basic
AuthName "Restricted Resources"
AuthUserFile /www/users
AuthGroupFile /www/groups
Require group administrators
```

As explained earlier, two methods of securing access are authorization and authentication. If there's a mix of both methods, you use the Satisfy directive to allow access to server resources. This directive can be set to one of these values:

- all—If set, all access control methods must be satisfied.

- any—If set, at least one access control method must be satisfied.

For example, you want to allow all client computers in the *www.mylinux.com* domain to view server status information, and all client computers outside the domain must be authorized before being allowed to view server status information. In this case, you'd use the following entry:

```
Require valid-user
Allow from www.mylinux.com
Satisfy any
```

Using Linux-Based Firewalls

In addition to using the Internet to transmit data and information, organizations use intranets, which are private local area networks (LANs) for transmitting data only inside the internal network. To ensure security, organizations need to protect intranets from being accessed from the Internet, so a firewall is used to keep intranet and Internet connections separate. A firewall analyzes network packets passing through it and decides whether to allow them to pass through. Figure 19-2 shows how a firewall protects a network.

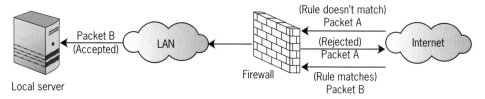

Figure 19-2 Using a firewall to protect a LAN
© Cengage Learning 2013

OpenSUSE includes the Firewall module for configuring a firewall. You can start the YaST Firewall module, shown in Figure 19-3, with the yast2 firewall command.

19

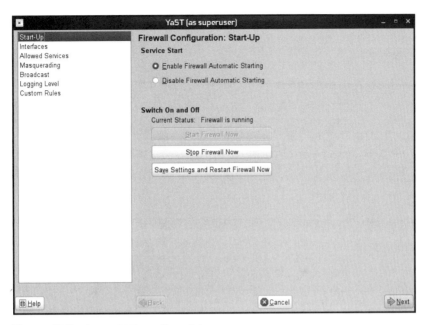

Figure 19-3 The YaST Firewall module
Source: openSUSE

The Firewall module consists of seven sections:

- *Start-Up*—You use this section to enable the firewall service to start automatically when the computer is booted. You can also start or stop the firewall service immediately by clicking the corresponding button. Finally, you can save your changes and restart the service by clicking the Save Settings and Restart Firewall Now button.

- *Interfaces*—You use this section to assign your network device to a firewall zone, such as the internal zone, demilitarized zone, or external zone. Every network device should be assigned to a firewall zone so that traffic through any unassigned interface is blocked. For example, if the NIC is connected directly to the Internet or another unsecured network, it should be assigned to the external zone. The internal zone is for private networks, such as LANs. The demilitarized zone is mostly for large networks that need an extra line of defense in front of the internal network.

- *Allowed Services*—Used to specify services or ports that should be allowed on the network after you've selected a zone. For instance, if you want to allow the NFS Client service, first click External Zone in the Allowed Services for Selected Zone list box, and then select NFS Client in the Service to Allow list box (see Figure 19-4).

- *Masquerading*—Used to hide an internal network behind the firewall. With masquerading, the internal network can access the external network (such as the Internet) automatically. Any requests from the Internet to the internal network are blocked, however.

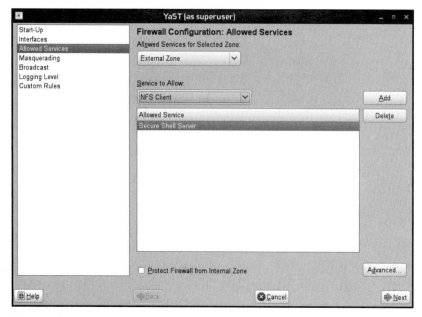

Figure 19-4 Specifying allowed services
Source: openSUSE

- *Broadcast*—Use this section to specify which broadcast packets (UDP packets sent to every computer on a network) are allowed to pass through the firewall.

- *Logging Level*—Logging levels are categorized into two groups: Accepted Packets and Not Accepted Packets. You can specify the amount of logging in each level, too: Log All, Log Only Critical, and Do Not Log Any. OpenSUSE recommends logging at least critical packets.

- *Custom Rules*—Used to set special firewall rules for network connections; you can specify source network, protocol, destination port, and source port, for example. You might use a custom rule to allow communication with a new server added to your network.

Securing Data from the Command Line

In addition to securing a Linux system, security measures should be used to protect the data stored in the computer. These measures protect data from internal and external unauthorized users. To ensure protection of data, you can set permissions on files and directories. In this section, you learn how to set file permissions with the umask command.

Files and file system security are the most important aspects of data security. The following measures are undertaken to protect data stored in the file system. Closely monitor SUID and SGID programs, which grant special privileges to users. To find all SUID/SGID programs running on a computer, use the following command:

```
find / -type f \( -perm 04000 -o -perm 02000 \)
```

This command searches for all files in the computer with the permissions 04000 or 02000. The octal value 04000 represents SUID programs, and the octal value 02000 represents SGID programs. If any suspicious SUID or SGID program is found, the computer could be under attack from intruders. Many factors might signal an attack; the presence of new or unfamiliar files and programs could be an indication of an intruder. Other factors you might consider are unexplained changes in file size, changes in file permissions, and missing files. SGID or SUID permissions should be removed from the suspicious programs with the chmod command.

Using the umask Command

You use the umask command to specify default file and directory permissions, which can have a major impact on a server's security when files are created. Users who create world-writeable files (files that can be modified by any user) can pose a risk to server security. For example, a vulnerable file, such as .rhosts, could allow an attacker to take over a user's account remotely.

Permission modes make it possible to control users' and groups' access rights to view or make changes to files and directories. The umask command displays current access settings and acts as a permission mode filter for files and directories. If you use it with no arguments, a three-digit number is displayed, as shown in this example:

```
umask
022
```

This command displays the default umask settings for the shell. In this example, file permissions are set to allow the owner to create and write data to files, and everyone else is granted only read permission. Each digit represents a permission mode. The first digit represents the owner permissions, the second digit represents the group permissions, and the third digit represents the other permissions.

For example, to give yourself, the owner, full access (read, write, and execute) and deny all others access when creating files, you enter the following:

```
umask 077
```

Then enter the following command to see your changes:

```
umask -S
u=rwx,g=,o=
```

You can see that the user (u) is granted full access (rwx), and group (g) and other (o) have no permissions set.

If you create a new file called student.txt, you can see that the default permissions have been set accordingly:

```
touch studentfile.txt
ls -l
-rw------  1 root     root      0 2012-03-06 11:56 studentfile.txt
```

Table 19-8 defines the possible umask values. In this table, r means read, w means write, and x means execute.

Table 19-8 Umask values

Option	Description
0 (rwx)	Allows all default permissions (read, write, and execute)
1 (rw-)	Allows read and write permissions only
2 (r-x)	Allows read and execute permissions only
3 (r--)	Allows read permission only
4 (-wx)	Allows write and execute permissions only
5 (-w-)	Allows write permission only
6 (--x)	Allows execute permission only
7 (---)	No permissions allowed

Setting File Permissions

Linux treats most resources, such as directories and disks, as files, so file permissions affect system security. Being lax about controlling file permissions can result in unauthorized use of files and other computer resources. Permissions are granted or removed based on three types of users, as you learned in Chapter 5:

- *User*—The file owner
- *Groups*—The file owner's group
- *Other*—Any other user who's not the file owner and doesn't belong to the file owner's group

The permission mask determines which users have a certain level of file access, if any. As you've learned, each user is assigned one of three permissions: r for read, w for write, and x for execute. File permission settings for each type of user are represented by three bits of information in the permission mask in addition to three special-purpose high-order bits (setuid, setgid, or sticky bit), for a total of 12 bits. As shown in the following example, each letter in a permission mask represents an octal number:

AAABBBCCCDDD

These bits have the following meanings:

- AAA—Represents the setuid (set user ID), setgid (set group ID), or sticky bit. The setuid and setgid flags allow a user to run an executable file with the owner's permission. The sticky bit prevents users from deleting or renaming files. The octal value 4 represents setuid, the octal value 2 represents setgid, and the octal value 1 represents the sticky bit.
- BBB—Represents read, write, and execute permissions for the file's owner. The octal value 4 represents read permission, the octal value 2 represents write permission, and the octal value 1 represents execute permission.
- CCC—Represents read, write, and execute permissions for a group, with the same octal values as for user permissions.
- DDD—Represents read, write, and execute permissions for all others, with the same octal values as for user permissions.

For example, you have an executable file named `student`, and you want read, write, and execute permissions for the file's owner but read and execute permission for everybody else. Set the file's permissions with the following command:

```
chmod u=rwx g=rx o=rx student
```

You can also use octal numbers to represent file permissions, as shown:

```
chmod 755 student
```

This command translates to the following:

```
4 (read) + 2 (write) + 1 (execute) = 7
4 (read) + 1 (execute)             = 5
4 (read) + 1 (execute)             = 5
```

It produces the following results:

chmod 755 student
ls -l
```
-rwxr-xr-x  1 root      root      0 2012-03-06 09:54 student
```

If you set the sticky bit along with the preceding permissions, the command looks like the following:

chmod 1755 student
ls -l
```
-rwxr-xr-t  1 root      root      0 2012-03-06 10:14 student
```

In the permission mask, the first character denotes the file type (- for a regular file, d for a directory, and so on). In the next three groups, the r means readable, the w means writeable, and the x means executable. The high-order bits s or t are for executable and the setuid/setgid/sticky bit, or you can use S or T for nonexecutable and the setuid/setgid/sticky bit.

Activity 19-3: Using File Permissions

Time Required: 15 minutes

Objective: Use the `umask` command to set default file permissions.

Description: In this activity, you use the `umask` command to set the default file permissions from the command line.

1. Start VMware Player and log in to an openSUSE virtual machine.

2. Open a terminal window and switch to the root user.

3. Check the `umask` setting by typing **umask** and pressing **Enter**. What's the `umask` setting?

_____

4. Create a file in your home directory called **file1**. Check its file permissions by typing **ll file1** and pressing **Enter**. What are the file permissions?

_____

5. For now, you want all files you create to have read and write permissions for everybody (owner, group, and other). To do this, change the umask setting to 000 by typing **umask 000** and pressing **Enter.**

6. Create a file called **file2**, and then check the file permissions by typing **ll file2** and pressing **Enter.** Does file2 have read and write permissions for each permission level (owner, group, and other)? If 0 is the number that allows all default permissions, why doesn't the file have execute permission?

    _____

    _____

7. Change the umask setting back to **022.**

8. Create a new directory called **dir1**. Check its file permissions by typing **ll** and pressing **Enter.** Scroll until you find the dir1 directory. What are its permissions?

9. Change the umask setting back to **000** and create a new directory called **dir2**. Check the file permissions on this directory. Why are the permissions on dir2 different from those on file2? Both were created with the umask setting 000.

    _____

Chapter Summary

- Like any OS, Linux is susceptible to attacks from intruders and unauthorized users. Therefore, system security measures are important to help prevent unauthorized access.

- Web server attacks are of two types: CGI scripts and buffer overflows.

- Intruders use methods such as packet sniffing, guessing the root password, browsing system logs, and staging buffer overflows to gain root access.

- Linux computers connected to a network by TCP/IP are vulnerable to outside attacks, and TCP Wrappers is used to help prevent these attacks. TCP Wrappers logs connections and is used to grant or deny access to network services.

- Intruders can gain unauthorized access by exploiting the weakness of network services that are running. Disable unnecessary network services, particularly those that send sensitive information, such as usernames and passwords, across the network without being encrypted.

- Processes running on a computer must be monitored periodically to check for rogue or malfunctioning processes.

- OpenSSH is used to ensure that data transmitted to and from a remote computer is encrypted and secure.

- NFS is an excellent way to share files over a network, but it should be secured by using the root_squash option and the nosuid mount option.

- Security measures in Apache Web Server include authentication, access control, and securing the physical server.

- The Linux firewall analyzes network traffic that passes through it and decides what to do with it.
- The umask command is used to display current umask settings or act as a permission mode filter for files and directories.
- Setting file permissions is critical for system security. Permissions are granted or removed based on these user types: user, group, and other.

Key Terms

address spoofing An attack most often used on packet-filter firewalls, which are configured to allow only known addresses to initiate connections; attackers forge their source IP addresses and cause damage just by sending packets randomly.

brute-force attacks In these attacks, potential intruders use every possible combination of characters to guess passwords or encryption keys until the correct one is found.

buffer overflow A condition in which data that has exceeded a buffer's storage capacity overflows into another buffer.

CGI scripts An executable script used to generate a dynamic Web page's contents.

denial-of-service (DoS) attacks Attacks that overload a server with an overwhelming amount of network traffic so that it can't handle legitimate requests for network services.

distributed denial-of-service (DDoS) attack An attack in which a large number of traffic sources are used to generate bogus traffic to a single system.

packet sniffer A program that captures and views packets as they're transmitted over a network.

Pluggable Authentication Module (PAM) A system that provides a centralized mechanism for authenticating all services.

session hijacking A specialized form of address spoofing in which a hijacker assumes unauthorized control of a network session.

TCP Wrappers A widely used tool for logging connections and controlling access to network services.

Trojan programs Hidden scripts embedded in authorized programs.

Review Questions

1. Which of the following is a common attack on Web servers? (Choose all that apply.)

    a. CGI script intrusion

    b. Buffer overflow

    c. Session hijacking

    d. Brute-force attack

2. A Web server is highly susceptible to attacks because its configuration parameters increase its vulnerability on which of the following levels? (Choose all that apply.)

    a. Network level

    b. User access level

    c. Logging level

    d. File system level

3. List three approaches an attacker might use to gain the root password.

4. Which of the following is a type of DoS attack? (Choose all that apply.)

    a. Teardrop attack

    b. CGI script

    c. SYN flood

    d. Buffer overflow

5. Explain the difference between a brute-force attack and a dictionary attack.

6. Which of the following describes a hidden program or script embedded in an authorized program or script?

    a. DoS

    b. Session hijacking

    c. DDoS

    d. Trojan program

7. Which of the following is a specialized form of address spoofing in which a hijacker assumes unauthorized control of a network session?

    a. DoS

    b. Session hijacking

    c. DDoS

    d. Trojan program

8. Which of the following is a good first step in deciding which nonessential services to shut down in Linux?

    a. Disabling the ssh service

    b. Issuing the ps command

    c. Examining configuration files in the /etc/xinetd.d directory

    d. Examining the Firewall Allowed Services log

9. Which of the following involves overloading a Linux server with large amounts of network traffic, which prevents the server from handling legitimate requests for network services? (Choose all that apply.)

    a. DoS

    b. Session hijacking

    c. DDoS

    d. Trojan program

10. Which of the following services should you consider disabling because it sends unencrypted password information over the network? (Choose all that apply.)

    a. smb

    b. ftp

    c. telnet

    d. ssh

11. TCP Wrappers uses which of the following files to grant access to a client?

    a. /etc/hosts

    b. /etc/allow.hosts

    c. /etc/hosts.deny

    d. /etc/hosts.allow

12. Which of the following Linux commands is used to check the TCP Wrappers configuration?

    a. tcpdchk

    b. umask

    c. ssh

    d. tcpd

13. Which of the following Linux commands replaces the rlogin and rsk services for remote logins?

    a. tcpdchk

    b. umask

    c. ssh

    d. tcpd

14. Both attackers and network administrators use packet sniffers. True or False?

15. Which of the following methods can be used to secure NFS? (Choose all that apply.)

    a. Set PasswordAuthentication to yes in the /etc/ssh/sshd_config file.

    b. Use the root_squash option in the /etc/exports file.

    c. Use the nosuid mount option.

    d. Set StrictModes to yes in the /etc/ssh/sshd_config file.

16. Which of the following commands gives full access to the owner but only read and execute permissions to all others?

    a. umask 011

    b. umask 044

    c. umask 022

    d. umask 077

17. In the Interfaces section of the YaST Firewall module, which of the following is a valid zone? (Choose all that apply.)

    a. Internal zone

    b. Secure zone

    c. Demilitarized zone

    d. External zone

18. Which of the following commands is used to alter file permissions after they have been set?

    a. umask

    b. passwd

    c. chmod

    d. ps

Case Projects

CASE PROJECTS

Case Project 1: Researching SELinux

You're a systems administrator for a small parts manufacturing company; its network includes Linux servers and workstations. The company is about to begin contract negotiations with the government and plans to bid to supply the government with specialized parts for the Defense Department. Your network manager has heard about SELinux and has assigned you to research it. She wants you to write a report summarizing its features and explaining how SELinux could be useful in meeting the government's strict security requirements for defense contractors. Research SELinux and write a one- to two-page report on your findings.

## chapter 20

Advanced Linux Administration

After reading this chapter and completing the exercises, you will be able to:

- Manage kernel modules and load and configure the kernel
- Explain how to monitor system resources and use system-monitoring tools
- Use commands to fine-tune a file system
- Describe emergency recovery procedures
- Summarize common troubleshooting measures in Linux

This chapter covers advanced administration in Linux. First, you learn about the Linux kernel, which is the most important OS component because it manages system resources and facilitates interaction between hardware components and applications. Then you focus on system monitoring and performance tuning, including how to use basic system-monitoring commands, the GNOME and KDE system-monitoring tools, and other Linux utilities to fine-tune hard drives and file systems. Finally, you get an overview of problem solving, including emergency recovery procedures, and how to troubleshoot a Linux network.

Working with the Linux Kernel

Amber Standridge, a marketing manager, wants to create a printout while working on a marketing brochure, which requires handling two kinds of processes simultaneously on her Linux computer. The Linux kernel makes this task possible. The innermost layer of the Linux OS, also called the core, acts as an interface to hardware attached to the computer and manages communication between processes. Each Linux distribution includes a precompiled kernel that gives you control over the OS. In this section, you learn the basics of the kernel and where you can download kernel source code. In addition, you learn about managing kernel modules as well as patching, compiling, and installing the kernel.

Basics of the Linux Kernel

In the early years of Linux, you had to understand how the kernel worked and how to configure it. Having this knowledge isn't as important now because Linux distributions provide a kernel that includes everything you need. Typically, you can set up and manage a Linux network without ever needing to compile or reconfigure the kernel. However, there are some reasons you might want to compile the kernel, such as needing special drivers for hardware that isn't supported by the kernel or wanting to file a report because you discovered a bug in the kernel. You might also need to recompile the Linux kernel if you're a kernel developer or just want a better understanding of how it works.

The **kernel**, the central module of the Linux OS, performs two main tasks: acting as an interface to hardware attached to the computer and managing communication between processes. When a Linux computer starts, the boot loader transfers control to the kernel. The kernel then identifies the type of hardware installed with the computer, initiates the boot scripts, and starts the network and terminal daemons. The Linux kernel can function in one or more modes, such as user mode and kernel mode. Program execution takes place in user mode, without any direct access to the kernel's data structures or hardware devices.

The latest release of Linux kernel 3.3 contains more than 15 million lines of source code.

The difference between the Linux kernel and the OS can be confusing. The kernel is an essential part of the OS's overall functioning, and neither can work without the other. Richard Stallman, founder of GNU/Linux, explains the difference between the two at *www.gnu.org/gnu/linux-and-gnu.html*.

The source code for the Linux kernel is stored in a group of directories called the kernel source tree. The source tree's structure helps automate the process of compiling the kernel. Scripts called `makefiles` control this automation process.

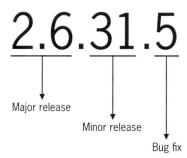

20

Installing the kernel source code on your computer isn't necessary for the Linux OS to run or perform certain tasks, such as e-mail or word processing. You can download the latest stable kernel version from *www.kernel.org*.

The Linux kernel is generally one of two types:

- *Monolithic*—This type of kernel is designed for a single architecture and interacts directly with hardware. It's compiled as a single block of code.

- *Modular*—This type of kernel compiles the kernel source code, where code for device drivers is stored as a module. All other parts of the kernel are compiled but aren't linked to the kernel. When you require certain services of a module, the module loader loads the module into the reserved slot and runs it. With this approach, you don't have to load all kernel services into memory immediately. It helps you save memory space and increase portability because you just need to replace a module, without having to rewrite any code.

Linux differentiates types of kernels with a numbering scheme. From version 1.0 to 2.6.0, each kernel version is specified as three numbers separated by periods. The first number indicates major changes (only three major versions since Linux was created), and the second number indicates the release, such as an experimental or a production release. If the second number is an even number, it denotes a stable kernel; if the second number is an odd number, it denotes a development kernel. The third number indicates minor revisions. The version numbering scheme then changed with Linux 2.6.x; the first two numbers stayed the same, and the third number was incremented with each new release. In this new scheme, a fourth number is sometimes added to indicate patches and bug fixes (see Figure 20-1). On May 29, 2011, to commemorate the 20th anniversary of Linux, the version number jumped from 2.6.39 to 3.0. With this latest numbering scheme, the second number will be used for new releases and the third for bug fixes. To display the kernel version you're running, use the `uname -r` command.

openSUSE 11.2 kernel release:

2.6.31.5

Major release

Minor release

Bug fix

Figure 20-1 Numbering of Linux kernel versions
© Cengage Learning 2013

To see a detailed display of the kernel's version number, use the uname -a command. It displays all information, including the kernel name, hostname, kernel release, kernel version, machine hardware name, processor, hardware platform, and OS, such as Linux linux-c8xs 2.6.31.5-0.1-desktop #1 SMP PREEMPT 2009-10-26 15:49:03 +0100 i686 i686 i386 GNU/Linux.

You need to build the kernel to select the devices and services you need on your Linux computer. You might also need to discard certain services that don't apply to your needs. You can load and unload components from the kernel, depending on your requirements, during runtime. For this purpose, you have the modules included in the kernel (saved in the /lib/modules directory) and removed from memory by the system when they aren't required. These modules might include support for file systems or network protocols that are needed only for certain applications. Modules automatically configure any new hardware installed on the system and load the drivers. To manage modules, you use special commands. For example, to view a partial list of all kernel modules, use the lsmod | less command, which lists all modules that can be viewed and verifies that a particular module is loaded. Table 20-1 describes some of these commands.

Table 20-1 Commands for managing kernel modules

Command	Description
lsmod	Lists modules in the system.
insmod	Loads a specific module into the kernel. If you don't specify a module's full path, the system automatically searches the default path, /lib/modules/*/.
rmmod	Removes a specified module from the kernel.
depmod	Creates a dependency file for kernel modules.
modprobe	Uses the dependency file created by depmod and automatically loads or unloads modules with the -r option.

Kernel Configuration

In openSUSE, you must install the Linux Kernel Development pattern to have access to important packages, such as the gcc and make utilities. To build the Linux kernel, you must be in the /usr/src/linux directory because kernel-building commands refer to the makefile in this directory. It's a symbolic link to the /usr/src/linux-*VersionNumber* directory (replacing *VersionNumber* with the kernel version you're running). The .config file is the configuration build file for the kernel, so create it with the touch command before you try to build the kernel. If the file already exists, back it up before trying to build the kernel. After the .config file is in the /usr/src/linux directory, you can issue the make config command. Editing the .config file directly isn't recommended; instead, you should use configuration tools to edit this file. The following list describes some tools for this purpose:

- make oldconfig—Used to update the current kernel configuration based on the .config file

- make menuconfig—Used to update the current kernel configuration with a menu-based program (see Figure 20-2)

- make config—Used to update the current kernel configuration with a line-oriented program (see Figure 20-3)

20

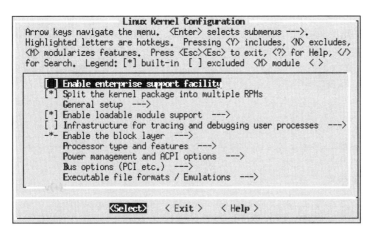

Figure 20-2 The menuconfig option for kernel configuration
Source: openSUSE

```
linux-cvo4:/usr/src/linux # clear

linux-cvo4:/usr/src/linux # make config
scripts/kconfig/conf arch/x86/Kconfig
*
* Linux Kernel Configuration
*
Enable enterprise support facility (ENTERPRISE_SUPPORT) [N/y/?] y
Split the kernel package into multiple RPMs (SPLIT_PACKAGE) [Y/n/?] y
Kernel to suit desktop workloads (KERNEL_DESKTOP) [Y/n/?] y
*
* General setup
*
Prompt for development and/or incomplete code/drivers (EXPERIMENTAL) [Y/n/?] y
Local version - append to kernel release (LOCALVERSION) [-12-desktop] y
Automatically append version information to the version string (LOCALVERSION_AUT
O) [N/y/?] y
Kernel compression mode
> 1. Gzip (KERNEL_GZIP)
  2. Bzip2 (KERNEL_BZIP2)
  3. LZMA (KERNEL_LZMA)
  4. LZO (KERNEL_LZO)
choice[1-4?]:
```

Figure 20-3 The line-oriented config option for kernel configuration
Source: openSUSE

Compiling the Kernel

To update the kernel from the Linux source tree you download, you need to compile and install the new kernel so that you can use the source code. Compiling the kernel involves translating its contents into a binary format the computer can understand. This process is automated by using the make utility. You can use the zcat command to view the gzipped kernel configuration, which is running in real time in the /proc/config.gz virtual file. The following example shows how to view the config.gz virtual file's contents:

```
zcat /proc/config.gz | less
#
# Automatically generated make config: don' t edit
#
# CONFIG_64BIT is not set
CONFIG_X86_32=y
# CONFIG_X86_64 is not set
CONFIG_X86=y
CONFIG_OUTPUT_FORMAT="elf32-i386"
CONFIG_ARCH_DEFCONFIG="arch/x86/configs/i386_defconfig"
CONFIG_GENERIC_TIME=y
```

Scroll through this file to view available options and hardware supported by the kernel. Table 20-2 describes some options you might find.

Table 20-2 Options in the `config.gz` virtual file

Option	Description
=y	Indicates what's compiled in the kernel. For example, in the preceding output, CONFIG_X86_32=y means the 32-bit version of the kernel is compiled.
is not set	Indicates what isn't compiled in the kernel. In the preceding output, CONFIG_X86_64 is not set means the 64-bit version of the kernel isn't compiled.
=m	Indicates what's supported but not compiled in the kernel.

After you have finished configuring the Linux kernel, you can build it by using the make command with no arguments. Activity 20-1 walks you through the steps.

Before you begin this activity, install the Linux Kernel Development pattern in YaST.

Activity 20-1: Configuring and Building the Linux Kernel

Time Required: 30 minutes

Objective: Configure and build the Linux kernel.

20

Description: In this activity, you view your kernel version number with the `/proc/config.gz` virtual file. Next, you use different methods to create a new kernel configuration, and then build a new kernel from this configuration.

1. Start VMware Player and start an openSUSE virtual machine.

2. Open a terminal window. Display your Linux kernel version number by typing **uname -r** and pressing **Enter**.

3. The kernel components or modules are installed in the `/lib/modules/*` directory (with `*` representing the kernel version number). Change to the `/lib/modules/*-default` directory. To display a long listing of files and subdirectories in this directory, type **ls -l** command and press **Enter**.

4. To check the kernel configuration, type **zcat /proc/config.gz | less** and press **Enter**. Press q to exit the `less` command.

5. Change the current directory by typing **cd /usr/src/linux** and pressing **Enter**, and then display a long listing of all files and directories. In openSUSE 11.2, the directory is `/usr/src/linux-2.6.31.14-0.8`.

6. If you already have the `.config` file, make a backup of it by typing **cp .config .config.bak** and pressing **Enter**. If you don't have this file, switch to root and create one by typing **touch .config** command and pressing **Enter**. When you're finished, switch back to the standard user.

7. There are a few ways you can create a new kernel configuration. One way is to use the line-oriented program, make config. This program prompts you with a series of yes or no questions. Type **make config** and press **Enter**, and then answer y to all questions.

8. Another way to create a new kernel configuration is to use the menu-based program. Type **make menuconfig** and press **Enter**. Scroll through the menu options, and then click the **Exit** option at the bottom.

9. After you have the new kernel configuration, you can use the make command to build the new kernel. If you use this command with no arguments, it builds the new kernel based on your new configuration, which could take several hours. Ask your instructor before building the new kernel.

10. Close the terminal window, and power off the virtual machine.

System Monitoring

Monitoring a server or a workstation for CPU and memory use is an important task because it helps identify possible performance problems. System monitoring is required whether you're working on a critical application or performing transactions over the Internet. In this section, you learn about system-monitoring concepts and commands. In addition, you learn about administering system log files. A Linux system administrator should usually monitor a system's performance only if something seems amiss; continuous performance monitoring and logging use a lot of resources and shouldn't be done indiscriminately. OpenSUSE has several commands for monitoring system performance, such as `free` and `top`. Monitoring system performance helps determine possible system errors or performance bottlenecks. These errors can be diagnosed with the help of system log files.

Monitoring System Resources

System monitoring is the process of observing portions of a system for problems or anomalies. It includes monitoring CPU utilization, network bandwidth, storage space use, and memory use.

Monitoring CPU Utilization

CPU utilization should be monitored periodically to determine the maximum processing power being consumed. The following are important CPU utilization statistics:

- *Context switching*—**Context switching** specifies when the CPU stops the currently running process and starts a new process. Excessive context switching results in a heavy workload on the CPU because the OS has to manage each context switch, which increases CPU utilization.

- *Interrupts*—An interrupt occurs when the CPU suspends its current execution, saves the current work status, and transfers control to an interrupt handler. An **interrupt handler** is a special routine containing instructions for handling interrupts. The OS handles all interrupts, so a large number of interrupts causes an increase in system-level CPU utilization.

- *Load percentage*—This statistic specifies the percentage of time a user-level or a system-level process spends on a CPU. It helps determine whether the current workload on the CPU is caused primarily by OS overhead or running software applications.

Monitoring Network Bandwidth

Monitoring a network connection's bandwidth helps determine possible performance bottlenecks. Two important statistics are associated with this monitoring:

- *Number of bytes received or sent*—Specifies the number of bytes that can be sent or received over a network connection. These statistics are used to determine network bandwidth utilization and help indicate excessive collisions in a network connection, particularly if the number of bytes sent or received is very high.

- *Data transfer speed*—Specifies the maximum number of I/O operations that a network connection can perform per second. This statistic helps determine whether a device's maximum bandwidth has been reached. If the number of I/O operations exceeds the specified data transfer speed, network connection performance decreases.

Monitoring Storage Space

Monitoring storage space helps determine the amount of available space as well as performance bottlenecks in a storage device. The important statistics are as follows:

- *Free space*—Specifies the amount of available space on a disk device. A disk device that has little free space available hinders system performance. Insufficient disk space can be a result of users or applications using a hard drive excessively.

- *Data transfer speed*—Specifies the maximum number of I/O operations that a hard drive can perform per second. If the number of I/O operations exceeds the data transfer speed limit, the storage device's performance is reduced.

- *File system–based information*—Specifies statistics such as maximum number of files in a directory and average file size. A Linux system administrator can configure these settings to improve system performance. For example, a very large file takes more time to perform I/O operations than a small file, so splitting a very large file into smaller files improves system performance.

- *Seek time*—Specifies the time hard disk heads take to reach their position on the track to perform read and write operations.

- *Latency*—Specifies the maximum time for a sector on a disk platter to arrive under a disk head for writing.

Monitoring Memory Use Track the following statistics to monitor how memory is used and managed:

- *Memory pages*—Gives detailed information about memory-resident pages, which can be active or inactive, and how the system uses memory pages. Active pages have been accessed recently and are mapped to an application. Inactive pages haven't been accessed recently and aren't associated with any application. A high number of active pages indicates a shortage of physical memory in a system.

- *Swapping statistic*—Specifies a system's swapping behavior. **Swapping** is the technique of moving data pages from memory to a swap space on a hard drive. Excessive swapping also indicates a shortage of physical memory.

Using Basic System-Monitoring Commands

You can use Linux command-line utilities to monitor system resources and processes. The basic commands are top, vmstat, free, du, and df. The top command gives you an active view of a running system and can display system summary information, such as CPU use, swap space use, and load averages. It refreshes the display periodically because a system's resource consumption fluctuates rapidly. Table 20-3 describes options used with the top command.

Table 20-3 Common options used with the top command

Option	Description
-b	For batch mode operations; batch mode doesn't accept input until the process is killed or the iteration number has been reached (which is set with the -n option).
-U	Monitors processes matching a specific UID or username.
-d	Specifies the delay between display updates.
-h	Displays the current library version and the usage prompt.
-i	Toggles between displaying and not displaying idle processes.

The `vmstat` command displays virtual memory statistics and information about processes, CPU activity, and disk space use. Its syntax is as follows:

```
vmstat -n delay cnt
```

In this syntax, `-n` displays the heading only once instead of repeating it. The `delay` parameter specifies the elapsed time in seconds between updates, and `cnt` specifies the number of times the screen should be updated. For example, the following command displays virtual memory statistic information with a delay of seven seconds between screen updates:

```
vmstat -n 7
```

The `free` command shows in column format the total amount of free, physical, and swap memory in the system as well as buffers used by the kernel. Table 20-4 describes options used with this command.

At the time of this writing, the shared column is displayed; however, it should be ignored because it's no longer valid.

Table 20-4 Common options used with the `free` command

Option	Description
-b	Displays memory-related information in bytes
-k	The default option, used to display memory-related information in kilobytes
-m	Displays memory-related information in megabytes
-o	Disables addition or subtraction of buffer memory to or from the free/used memory report
-s *delay*	Repeats output after the number of seconds specified by *delay*
-t	Displays a summary of total physical memory use with swap space use

The `df` command displays the amount of available disk space on the file system. You can use arguments to show available space on a specific mounted file system. Table 20-5 describes options used with this command.

Table 20-5 Common options used with the `df` command

Option	Description
--total	Adds an extra line at the bottom of the output that shows the totals of each column.
-h	Displays output in a human-readable format. For instance, instead of displaying 12474168, it displays 12G (meaning 12 gigabytes). Examples of human-readable formats are K (kilobytes), M (megabytes), and G (gigabytes).
-i	Changes columns to show inodes instead of block use.
--help	Displays a list of options that can be used with the `df` command.

The du command shows disk use information for all files in a specified directory and its subdirectories. Table 20-6 describes common options used with this command.

Table 20-6 Common options used with the du command

Option	Description
-a	By default, du displays disk use information for directories. The -a option also displays disk use information for files.
-k	Displays disk use information in kilobytes.
-c	Displays a specified directory's total disk use.
-s	Similar to the -c option but displays only the total disk use. The "s" is short for summarize.
-h	The same as the -h option for the df command; displays output in human-readable format.

ACTIVITY

Activity 20-2: Using System-Monitoring Commands

Time Required: 10 minutes

Objective: Work with Linux system-monitoring commands.

Description: In this activity, you use system-monitoring commands with options to modify the display.

1. Start VMware Player and log in to an openSUSE virtual machine.

2. Open a terminal window and switch to the root user.

3. Display an active view of your system as well as system summary information, such as CPU use, swap space use, and load averages, by typing **top** and pressing **Enter**. Press **Ctrl+C** to stop running the top command.

4. Type **vmstat** and press **Enter** to display virtual memory statistics.

5. Type **free** and press **Enter** to display the total amount of free, physical, and swap memory in a column format. Record the total memory used versus the total available memory:

    _____

6. Use the **df** command with no options to display available disk space on your file system. Then use the **df -h** command. How do the results differ with this option?

    _____

7. The du command displays disk use information for files in your current directory. First, use the **du** command with no options, and then use the **du -s** command. How does the -s option change the output?

    _____

8. Leave your virtual machine running for the next activity.

Administering System Logs

System log files give you an idea of what's going on in your system. As a Linux administrator, you need to know how to review these files to determine anomalies and other possible problems. Most programs list errors in standard logs in their own directory or in another predetermined location or save error messages in the system log file. The messages generated in /var/log should be kept at a minimum, however; otherwise, log files grow rapidly and occupy a lot of disk space. If the system log's size isn't controlled, no new system-related messages can be stored after the log file exceeds its maximum capacity. OpenSUSE includes the logrotate utility that administrators can use to manage large numbers of log files; it offers automatic rotation, compression, removal, and mailing of log files. Typically, you don't use the logrotate command manually; instead, you run the utility as a daily cron job. This utility has its own configuration file in the /etc directory called logrotate.conf. The /etc/logrotate.conf file is well documented with comments that can be viewed with the less /etc/logrotate.conf command. The following is an example of a simple logrotate configuration file with line numbers added for readability:

```
1. compress
2.      /var/log/messages {
3.          rotate 5
4.          weekly
5.          postrotate
6.              /usr/bin/killall -HUP syslogd
7.          endscript
       }
```

In this example, line 1 sets the global compress option so that logs are compressed after they're rotated. Line 2 defines the log file (/var/log/messages) to be managed. Lines 3 and 4 force the log to go through five weekly rotations before being removed. Line 6 issues the killall -HUP syslogd command after the log file has been rotated. Most rotation information on log files is stored in the /etc/logrotate.d directory. The following example shows configuration files in this directory:

```
ls -l /etc/logrotate.d
total 52
-rw-r--r-- 1 root root  196 2012-07-05 07:34 mcelog
-rw-r--r-- 1 root root 1052 2012-07-05 11:45 mysql
-rw-r--r-- 1 root root  187 2012-07-05 10:03 ntp
-rw-r--r-- 1 root root  141 2012-07-05 16:00 rsync
-rw-r--r-- 1 root root  289 2012-07-05 10:16 samba
-rw-r--r-- 1 root root 1337 2012-07-05 07:23 syslog
-rw-r--r-- 1 root root  148 2012-07-05 13:07 wpa_supplicant
-rw-r--r-- 1 root root  134 2012-07-05 07:15 wtmp
-rw-r--r-- 1 root root  140 2010-07-22 22:01 xdm
-rw-r--r-- 1 root root  200 2012-07-05 07:43 xinetd
-rw-r--r-- 1 root root  134 2012-06-11 06:41 zypper.lr
-rw-r--r-- 1 root root  137 2012-06-29 11:51 zypp-history.lr
-rw-r--r-- 1 root root  139 2012-06-11 06:41 zypp-refresh.lr
```

The `logrotate` utility generates files (and copies of files) in the `/var/log` directory. The most recent log file doesn't have a numbered extension. For example, `boot.log` is the most recent log file, followed by `boot.log.1`, `boot.log.2`, and so on.

Using GUI System-Monitoring Tools

In addition to the basic system-monitoring commands, Linux offers sophisticated system-monitoring tools, such as the `sysstat` package. Graphical tools in the GNOME and KDE desktop environments are also included for monitoring system resources and processes.

The GNOME System-Monitoring Tool GNOME System Monitor, shown in Figure 20-4, displays information on CPU, memory, and swap utilization in tabular form. To start this tool, use the `gnome-system-monitor` command.

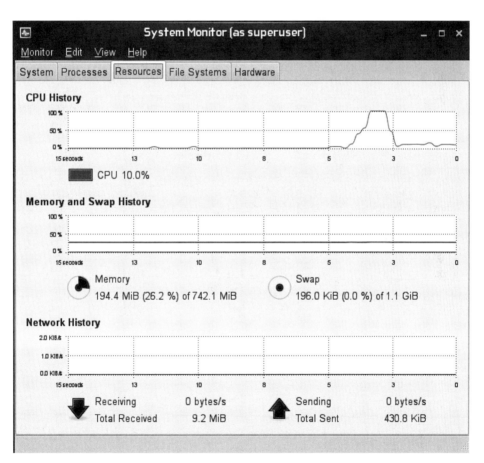

Figure 20-4 The GNOME System Monitor interface
Source: openSUSE

System Monitor contains five tabs: System, Processes, Resources, File Systems, and Hardware. Table 20-7 lists the information in each tab.

Table 20-7 GNOME System Monitor tabs

Tab	Description
System	Displays information about the system's hardware and software, such as the computer's hostname, current SUSE and kernel version, amount of memory, and processor type and speed
Processes	Displays detailed information about active processes and can be used to control these processes
Resources	Displays a live feed of system resources, such as CPU, memory and swap space, and network use
File Systems	Displays all mounted file systems as well as information on each file system (such as type of file system and available free space)
Hardware	Displays a list of devices and their associated types (for example, an Intel processor might be listed under Device, and "CPU" would be listed under Type)

The KDE System-Monitoring Tool You can also use KDE System Monitor to monitor processes (see Figure 20-5). To start this tool, use the `ksysguard` command.

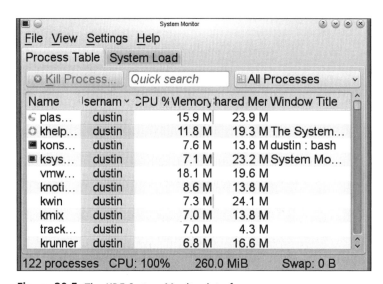

Figure 20-5 The KDE System Monitor interface
Source: openSUSE

You don't need to be logged on as the root user to issue the `ksysguard` command. Keep in mind that if you switch to root, you need to use the dash option (`su  -`) to make the shell a login shell.

TIP

KDE System Monitor contains two tabs: Process Table and System Load. Table 20-8 describes the information in these tabs.

20

Table 20-8 KDE System Monitor tabs

Tab	Description
Process Table	Displays all running processes and allows you to control them. You can control multiple processes at once by selecting them.
System Load	Displays three graphs of system utilization: CPU History, Memory and Swap History, and Network History.

Using the `sysstat` Package for Resource Monitoring

You can use the `top`, `vmstat`, and `free` commands for monitoring the system performance over a short period. However, to display detailed information on system performance, you need more sophisticated tools, such as the `sysstat` package. You can install this package in YaST.

The `sysstat` package consists of the `iostat` and `mpstat` commands. The `iostat` command is used to report CPU utilization and I/O statistics for devices, partitions, and network file systems. Table 20-9 describes common options used with this command.

Table 20-9 Common options used with the `iostat` command

Option	Description
-c	Displays a report on CPU utilization.
-d	Displays a report on device utilization.
-k	By default, `iostat` displays statistics in blocks per second. The -k option changes statistics to kilobytes per second.
-m	This option is similar to the -k option but displays statistics in megabytes per second.
-t	Displays a report with a timestamp at the top.

The following examples show how to use the `iostat` command. In the first one, it's used without options to display a single report for all CPUs and devices:

```
iostat
Linux 2.6.31.5-0.1-desktop (linux-cvo4)  02/05/2012 _x86_64_ (1 CPU)

avg-cpu:  %user   %nice %system %iowait  %steal   %idle
           2.14    0.04    0.90    0.15    0.00   96.76

Device:         tps   Blk_read/s   Blk_wrtn/s   Blk_read   Blk_wrtn
sda            0.92      76.79         7.27      1557578     147368
fd0            0.00       0.00         0.00           16          0
```

The next example displays a continuous device report at 4-second intervals. To exit the report, press Ctrl+C.

```
iostat -d 4
Linux 2.6.31.5-0.1-desktop (linux-cvo4) 02/05/2012 _x86_64_ (1 CPU)
```

Device:	tps	Blk_read/s	Blk_wrtn/s	Blk_read	Blk_wrtn
sda	1.01	79.58	7.51	1652322	156008
fd0	0.00	0.00	0.00	16	0

Device:	tps	Blk_read/s	Blk_wrtn/s	Blk_read	Blk_wrtn
sda	6.50	0.00	242.00	0	968
fd0	0.00	0.00	0.00	0	0

The mpstat command is used to display information for each processor, starting with processor0. Table 20-10 describes common options used with this command.

Table 20-10 Common options used with the mpstat command

Option	Description
-A	Same as using the -I All -u -P ALL option.
-I	Displays interrupt statistics in the report. You can use three keywords with this option. SUM reports the total number of interrupts per processor, CPU displays each interrupt received per second by the CPU, and ALL displays all interrupt statistics (equivalent to using all three keywords).
-u	Displays CPU utilization.
-P	Specifies the processor number. You can enter the CPU number or use the ALL keyword to show statistics for all processors.

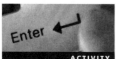

Activity 20-3: Using Tools to Monitor System Performance

Time Required: 20 minutes

Objective: Display detailed information on system performance with the sysstat package and GUI system-monitoring tools.

Description: In this activity, you install the sysstat package and use its commands. You also use the GUI system-monitoring tools included with KDE and GNOME.

1. If necessary, start VMware Player and log in to an openSUSE virtual machine. Open a terminal window and switch to the root user.

2. The sysstat package isn't installed by default, which means you need to download and install it by using the Software Management module in YaST.

3. After installing the sysstat package, issue both the **iostat** and **mpstat** commands and notice the differences in the output.

4. If you aren't using KDE, log in to an openSUSE virtual machine running KDE. Type **ksysguard** and press **Enter**. Spend a few minutes examining the tabs, paying attention to the amount of memory each process uses. Power off this virtual machine.

5. Log in to an openSUSE Linux machine running GNOME. Type **gnome-system-monitor** and press **Enter**. Spend a few minutes examining the tabs, paying attention to the amount of memory each process uses.

6. Close the terminal window and power off the virtual machine.

Performance Tuning

After you determine resource use with system-monitoring tools, you should fine-tune system resources to improve performance. Two frequently used resources that require tuning are the hard drive and file system. This section describes how to tune these resources in openSUSE.

Performance Tuning a Disk

A system's benchmark performance largely depends on the disk I/O performance, which can be improved by fine-tuning the hard drive. For example, you can tune the hard drive to increase the disk transfer speed, which improves system performance.

Using the `hdparm` Command You use the `hdparm` command to tune an IDE hard drive. You must be logged in as root to use this command, which has the following syntax:

```
hdparm option device
```

In this format, *option* specifies flags that can be used to improve drive performance, and *device* specifies the hard drive to be tuned. Table 20-11 describes common options used with this command.

Table 20-11 Common options used with the `hdparm` command

Option	Description
`-cn`	Enables or disables 32-bit IDE I/O operations. The argument n can have the value 0 (disables 32-bit I/O support), 1 (enables 32-bit I/O support), or 3 (enables 32-bit IDE I/O operations with a special synch sequence supported by almost all 32-bit IDE chipsets).
`-dn`	Enables or disables direct memory access (DMA) mode for a specified IDE drive. The argument n can have the values 0 (DMA mode disabled) or 1 (DMA mode enabled).
`-g`	Displays the drive geometry, drive size in sectors, and starting offset position of a specified IDE drive.
`-Kn`	Saves settings of a specified IDE drive during a soft reset that's performed during error recovery. The argument n can have the value 0 (specifies that IDE drive settings aren't saved during a soft reset) or 1 (specifies that IDE drive settings are saved during a soft reset).
`-t`	Tests the performance of a specified IDE drive for benchmark and comparison purposes.
`-X`	Sets the data transfer speed of a specified IDE drive.

The hdparm command also works with some SCSI drives, such as a CD-ROM drive.

Fine-Tuning a File System

The file system has a major effect on system performance. For example, if the file system size is very large, response time for performing I/O operations increases, which results in reduced system performance. To improve system performance, you need to tune the file system. The following sections describe openSUSE commands for this purpose.

Using the mke2fs Command The mke2fs command is used to create a Linux ext2, ext3, or ext4 file system on a specified device, which is usually a hard drive partition. The general format of this command is as follows:

mke2fs *options device*

In this format, *options* specifies options to use with the mke2fs command, and *device* specifies a Linux device name where the new file system will be created. Table 20-12 describes common options used with this command.

Table 20-12 Common options used with the mke2fs command

Option	Description
-b *block size*	Specifies the block size in bytes for the new ext2, ext3, or ext4 file system.
-c	Verifies a device for bad blocks before creating a file system on the device.
-f *fragment size*	Specifies the fragment size in bytes for the new ext2 file system.
-i *bytes per inode*	Specifies the bytes/inode ratio for a specified device. The value should be more than the block size; otherwise, many inodes are created, which reduces system performance.
-j	Creates the file system with an ext3 journal.
-l *filename*	Reads the bad block from the specified file.
-L	Specifies the volume label for the new file system.
-M	Sets the last mounted directory for the new file system.
-T *file system type*	Specifies how the file system should be used for optimized performance. The valid values are news (single inode per 4 KB data block), largefile (single inode per 1 MB data block), and largefile4 (single inode per 4 MB data block).
-V	Displays the version number of the mke2fs command and terminates this command.

For example, to create an ext2 file system on the hard drive partition /dev/hda2 with a block size of 2048 bytes and the file system type largefile, here's the command:

```
mke2fs -b 2048 -T largefile -c /dev/hda2
```

This command checks the /dev/hda2 device for bad blocks before creating the new file system. In addition to creating a file system, you can use the mke2fs command for tuning a file system with the -T and -b options. The -T option specifies the optimized performance for a file system, and the -b option sets the block size, which affects a file system's performance. A large block size results in less overhead for a file system because few data blocks are allocated to it. As a result, large amounts of data can be retrieved with a single file access. However, if a file isn't a multiple of the block size, allocating a large block size can waste a lot of storage space.

Figure 20-6 shows the results of allocating 1024-byte data blocks to a file with a 2.2 KB capacity. Because the file size isn't a multiple of the block size, storage space is wasted. If the file size is large (2.2 MB, for example) and you specify the block size as 10520576 bytes (1 MB), you waste 819 KB of storage space.

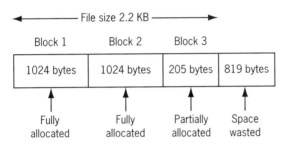

Figure 20-6 Allocating 1024-byte data blocks to a file capacity of 2.2 KB
© Cengage Learning 2013

On the other hand, a small block size increases overhead for the file system because a large number of data blocks are allocated to the file system, which increases the number of file accesses. However, if a file to be accessed isn't a multiple of the block size, allocating a small block size wastes less storage space.

The best practice is to use a large block size for large files, but if the file size isn't a multiple of the block size, you should specify the block size as a factor of the file size. For small files, you should use small block sizes for optimized performance. For example, a file system containing a lot of executable programs or a database that has to perform a lot of I/O operations performs better if it has a large block size. Allocating large blocks for a partition containing a lot of small files is a waste of resources, however.

Using the tune2fs Command You use the tune2fs command to tune file system parameters on a Linux ext2, ext3, or ext4 file system. The general format of this command is as follows:

```
tune2fs options device
```

In this format, *options* specifies options to use with the tune2fs command, and *device* specifies the device containing the file system to be tuned. Table 20-13 describes common options used with this command.

Table 20-13 Common options used with the `tune2fs` command

Option	Description
`-c max count`	Specifies the maximum number of mounts between two file system checks.
`-f`	Forces completion of the tune2fs command even in an error condition.
`-i interval between checks [d|m|w]`	Specifies the maximum time interval between two consecutive file system checks in days (d), months (m), or weeks (w).
`-j`	Adds an ext3 journal to the file system to be tuned.
`-l`	Displays contents of the file system's superblock. A superblock is part of a partition containing partition information used by the Linux OS for internal purposes.
`-e error behavior`	Modifies the kernel's behavior on error detection. The valid values are continue (continue normal execution of the tune2fs command), remount-ro (remount a file system as read-only), and panic (causes a kernel panic—an action taken as a result of a system error the OS fails to recover from).
`-L volume label`	Specifies the volume label for a file system; it shouldn't exceed 16 characters.
`-U UUID`	Specifies the universally unique identifier (UUID) for a file system in a series of hexadecimal digits separated by hyphens.

For example, to change the number of maximum mounts on the /dev/hda4 partition to 60, you use this command:

```
tune2fs -c 60 -L mypartiton1 /dev/hda4
```

This command creates the volume label mypartition1 for the file system in the /dev/hda4 partition.

Using the `e2fsck` Command You use the e2fsck command to check an ext2, ext3, or ext4 file system for bad data blocks. The syntax of this command is as follows, and Table 20-14 lists common options used with e2fsck:

```
e2fsck options device
```

Table 20-14 Common options used with the `e2fsck` command

Option	Description
`-c`	Checks a file system for bad blocks and marks them as bad.
`-f`	Forces checking on a file system regardless of whether the file system is clean.
`-l filename`	Adds the block numbers listed in the specified file to the list of bad blocks.
`-L filename`	Sets the block numbers in the specified file to the list of bad blocks. However, before adding blocks from the file, the bad blocks list is cleared.
`-n`	Opens a file system as read-only.
`-V`	Displays the e2fsck version number and terminates the e2fsck command.

For example, to force a file system check on the /dev/hda2 device, you use this command:

```
e2fsck -f /dev/hda2
```

Using the badblocks Command The badblocks command is used to check a device for bad data blocks. The general syntax of this command is as follows, and Table 20-15 lists common options used with it:

```
badblocks options device
```

Table 20-15 Common options used with the badblocks command

Option	Description
-b block size	Specifies the block size in bytes.
-c number of blocks	Specifies the number of blocks to be tested at a time. The default value is 64.
-i input file	Reads a list of existing bad blocks from the specified file.
-o output file	Writes a list of bad blocks to the specified file.
-s	Displays the progress of scanning a device for bad data blocks.

For example, to check the /dev/hda1 device for bad data blocks and write all bad blocks to the badblockdata file, use this command, which tests 20 blocks at a time:

```
badblocks -c 20 -o badblockdata /dev/hda1
```

Using the noatime Option The noatime option is a special mount option for a file system, stored in the /etc/fstab configuration file. When the noatime option is used, Linux eliminates the need to update the access time of an inode in the referenced file system. Eliminating this update speeds up file access if files on the referenced file system are accessed frequently. Otherwise, there's little difference in file access speed. The following example shows using the noatime option with the /etc/fstab file in the file system /usr:

```
/dev/hda5 /usr ext2 defaults,noatime 1 2
```

Problem Solving in Linux

A network's security must be updated judiciously from time to time. As an administrator of a Linux network, you should be equipped to face any critical situation and have a thorough knowledge of troubleshooting techniques. In this chapter, you learn about critical situations that can affect systems and how to recover systems after a disaster. You also learn disaster recovery techniques to minimize network downtime.

Preventive Measures

If you have an overall view of a problem, you can usually troubleshoot it regardless of its severity. Critical situations that can cause major losses to an organization can occur in many ways and at any time. Applying preventive measures can minimize the effect of these situations, so you should be familiar with these measures. They include backups, configuration notes, and rescue disks.

Backups The most important way to minimize the effect of an emergency is to back up data regularly and store it on CDs, tapes, and other removable media. Software bundled with openSUSE Linux can also be used for backing up data. To start YaST System Backup, use the `yast2 backup` command. This tool (see Figure 20-7) is an easy-to-use backup program that searches files on a Linux system to create a backup archive.

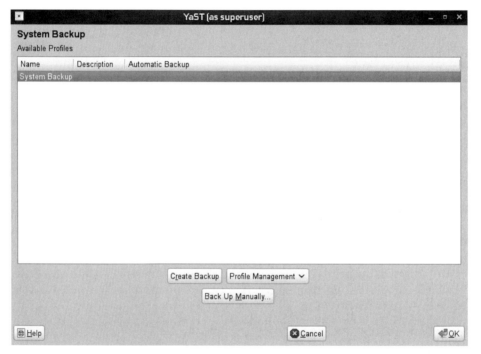

Figure 20-7 The YaST System Backup tool
Source: openSUSE

Another backup utility is pax, a POSIX utility that can read and write a wide variety of archive formats. It's a command-line utility included with openSUSE Linux, and it has several options. For example, -r is used for read, -w is used for write, and -f specifies the archive filename. Table 20-16 shows some important options used with the pax utility.

Table 20-16 Common options used with the pax utility

Option	Description
-r	Read files from an archive
-w	Write files to an archive
-f archive	Specify the archive name
-a	Append files to an existing archive
-d	Match filename wildcards
-t	Preserve the access times of archived files
-U user	Select a file based on a specified user's input
-L	Follow symbolic links

NOTE Pax supports using wildcards, such as ? and *, to avoid having to use long or similar filenames in commands. A single command can be used instead of a separate command for each file. For example, the names of files with the .png extension can be supplied as *.png for archiving.

Table 20-17 gives examples of the pax command.

Table 20-17 Examples of the pax command

Example	Description
pax -f testfiles	Lists the contents of an archive named testfiles
pax -r -f testfiles	Extracts the contents of the archive named testfiles
pax -w -f testfiles /usr	Creates an archive named testfiles containing everything in the /usr directory
pax -w -f trailfiles *.txt	Archives all files in the current directory with the .txt extension
pax -r -U jack -f arkiv	Extracts all files owned by the user jack from the archive named arkiv

The KDE archiving tool is Ark (see Figure 20-8). This GUI tool is used for managing a variety of archiving formats, such as tar, gzip, bzip2, zip, rar, and lha. To start Ark, log in to KDE. On the Utilities menu, click Archiving Tool.

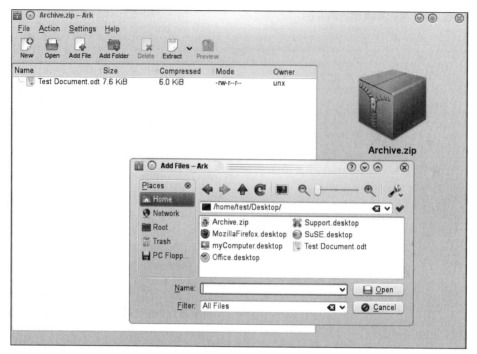

Figure 20-8 The Ark interface
Source: openSUSE

Configuration Notes Another method of minimizing an emergency's effects is keeping notes on the system configuration. These notes should contain data about partition table entries and other important information, such as the partition number and size, mount points, user details, and network card details. Maintaining records of these details seems unimportant in normal situations, but they play a vital role in recovering from a system crash or other disaster because they're useful in retrieving information that helps you save data after reconfiguration.

Rescue Disks Rescue disks are emergency disks you create ahead of time to save critical data. To use the openSUSE bootable CD as a rescue disk, select Rescue System from the boot menu (see Figure 20-9).

Recovering from a Disaster

You can't prevent all disasters, of course, but you should try to identify the root cause and find a solution to recover from the problem. To identify the cause, do the following:

- *Observe and read*—Read the INSTALL and README files or any other document files the vendor has supplied. With installation problems, reading the error log files can be helpful.

- *Monitor the system log file*—Error messages generated by the system are stored in the system log file, which can be helpful in solving problems. Open the `/var/log/messages` file and analyze the information. Using options such as `tail` or `less` makes the information easier to read.

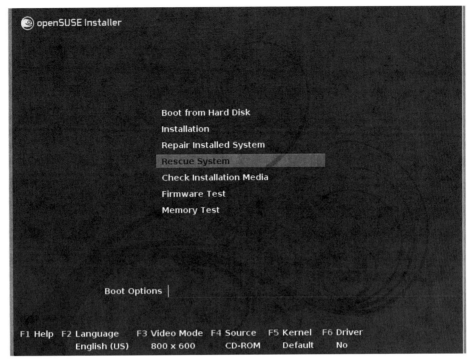

Figure 20-9 The option for creating a rescue disk
Source: openSUSE

- *Refer to Linux user groups*—Subscribe to Linux user groups, also known as LUG, to discuss problems and find others who might have solutions.

OpenSUSE has a Web forum at *http://forums.opensuse.org* where you can register and post queries.

TIP

A disaster can also result from server downtime caused by a system crash. You can use some of the methods discussed previously, but other techniques, discussed in the following sections, are more useful in this situation.

Single-User Mode Single-user mode, also known as maintenance mode, is an OS mode in which only the root partition is active and mounted, and Linux runs in runlevel 1. This mode is useful in repairing file systems corrupted by users or system activity. To boot your computer into single-user mode, use the `init 1` command. It displays a command prompt (see Figure 20-10) where only the root user can log in and perform system maintenance tasks.

```
Welcome to openSUSE 11.2 "Emerald" - Kernel 2.6.31.5-0.1-desktop (tty1).


INIT: Going single user
INIT: Sending processes the TERM signal
Give root password for login:
```

Figure 20-10 Single-user mode
Source: openSUSE

Rescue Mode In Linux **rescue mode**, you can boot a small Linux environment from some type of medium, such as a CD-ROM. (This medium is called a rescue disk, as explained earlier.) This mode is helpful if you can't recover from a system crash or are having hardware or software problems. Rescue mode enables you to access files on the system's hard drive, even if you're having trouble running Linux from it.

Troubleshooting Linux

Two widely used Linux boot loaders are LILO and GRUB. The **boot loader** is a small program stored on the Master Boot Record (MBR) that can load one or more OSs by reading file system information through a pointer from the disk partition containing OS files. Linux Loader (LILO), one of the original boot loaders, is no longer supported by openSUSE.

Using GRUB

Grand Unified Boot Loader (GRUB) is a more flexible boot loader than LILO and has become the boot loader of choice for current Linux distributions. It's packaged with the latest version of openSUSE. In openSUSE, the GRUB configuration file is controlled by the /boot/grub/menu.1st file, shown in Figure 20-11. Table 20-18 describes some common default entries in this file.

```
# Modified by YaST2. Last modification on Thu Jan 19 12:52:33 EST 2012
# THIS FILE WILL BE PARTIALLY OVERWRITTEN by perl-Bootloader
# Configure custom boot parameters for updated kernels in /etc/sysconfig/bootloa
der

default 0
timeout 8
##YaST - generic_mbr
gfxmenu (hd0,1)/boot/message
##YaST - activate

###Don't change this comment - YaST2 identifier: Original name: linux###
title Desktop -- openSUSE 11.2 - 2.6.31.5-0.1
    root (hd0,1)
    kernel /boot/vmlinuz-2.6.31.5-0.1-desktop root=/dev/sda2 resume=/dev/sda1 sp
lash=silent quiet showopts vga=0x314
    initrd /boot/initrd-2.6.31.5-0.1-desktop

###Don't change this comment - YaST2 identifier: Original name: failsafe###
title Failsafe -- openSUSE 11.2 - 2.6.31.5-0.1
    root (hd0,1)
    kernel /boot/vmlinuz-2.6.31.5-0.1-desktop root=/dev/sda2 showopts apm=off no
resume nosmp maxcpus=0 edd=off powersaved=off nohz=off highres=off processor.max
menu.1st lines 1-20/26 81%
```

Figure 20-11 The /boot/grub/menu.1st configuration file
Source: openSUSE

Table 20-18 Settings in the `/boot/grub/menu.lst` file

Setting	Description
default	This setting is the default menu entry. The numbering starts from 0, meaning the second entry is 1, the third entry is 2, and so on.
timeout	This setting specifies the number of seconds before the default entry is booted. If it's set to 0, the default entry is booted instantly. If it's set to -1, the default entry waits until a key is pressed before it's booted.
gfxmenu	This setting defines the file that provides the graphical GRUB display.
title	This setting specifies the boot entry title, which is displayed on the boot screen.

When using the LILO boot loader, you must issue the `lilo` command after making configuration changes; however, you don't have to use a similar command when working with GRUB. You see configuration changes after you reboot the Linux system. You might find that your system doesn't boot because of a problem with the `/boot/grub/menu.lst` file, but you should have a fail-safe entry that allows you to boot your Linux system. If you don't have a fail-safe option or this option isn't working, you can press the Esc key in the GRUB menu screen to display the splash screen shown in Figure 20-12. Click OK to edit raw GRUB boot entries (see Figure 20-13).

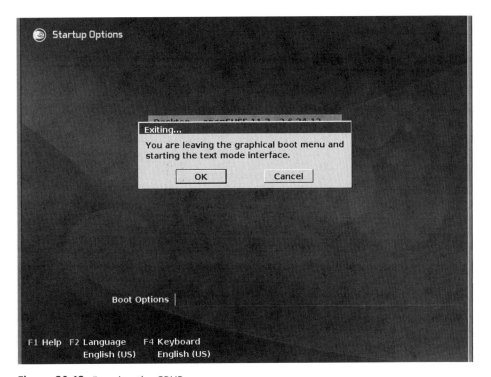

Figure 20-12 Escaping the GRUB menu
Source: openSUSE

```
   GNU GRUB  version 0.97  (638K lower / 784320K upper memory)

 ┌──────────────────────────────────────────────────────────────────────┐
 │Desktop -- openSUSE 11.2 - 2.6.31.5-0.1                                  │
 │Failsafe -- openSUSE 11.2 - 2.6.31.5-0.1                                 │
 │Floppy                                                                   │
 │                                                                        │
 │                                                                        │
 │                                                                        │
 │                                                                        │
 │                                                                        │
 │                                                                        │
 │                                                                        │
 └──────────────────────────────────────────────────────────────────────┘
     Use the ↑ and ↓ keys to select which entry is highlighted.
     Press enter to boot the selected OS, 'e' to edit the
     commands before booting, or 'c' for a command-line.
```

Figure 20-13 Editing GRUB entries
Source: openSUSE

Login Problems

The first stage of starting a system is booting, followed by login. This stage requires a username and password for validation. After validation, the system displays a prompt to continue working. A login, like any other process, occurs after passing through a series of steps, such as entering a username and password. Sometimes root users forget their passwords, but fortunately, you can change this password by editing the kernel entry in the GRUB menu screen, which tells the system to boot to a specific shell. The following activity walks you through changing a root password.

Activity 20-4: Changing a Root Password

Time Required: 10 minutes

Objective: Change a root password.

Description: In this activity, you escape the graphical boot menu and edit a kernel command before booting your system. You force your Linux system to boot directly to the BASH shell, where you use the `passwd` command to change your root password.

1. Start VMware Player and log in to an openSUSE virtual machine. If VMware Player is configured so that it doesn't power down the virtual machine when you turn it off, open a terminal window and reboot the virtual machine by typing **reboot** and pressing **Enter**. If the virtual machine was already powered off, make sure you press **Esc** when you get to the GRUB boot menu.

2. In the warning screen, press **Enter**.

3. In the GRUB boot menu, use the arrow keys to highlight **Desktop**, and press **e** to edit the commands before booting your system.

4. Use the arrow keys to select **kernel** and press **e** to edit the selected command in the boot sequence.

5. Press the **spacebar**, and then type **init=/bin/bash** and press **Enter** to force your system to boot directly to the BASH shell.

6. When you return to the GRUB boot menu, press **b** to boot your system and display a root prompt. Type **passwd** and press **Enter**.

7. A message is displayed stating that you're changing the root password. Type a password you can remember easily and press **Enter**. Enter your password and press **Enter** again. Finally, type **reboot** and press **Enter** to restart your system.

8. Leave the virtual machine running for the next activity.

File System Problems

During booting, the system usually mounts all file systems (partitions) according to information in the /etc/fstab file and unmounts the file system at system shutdown or reboot. The problem occurs when a system fails to unmount the file system because it's been powered off by a hard reboot or power failure. In this situation, the system might need to run a file system check (by using the `fsck` command) to fix problems in the file system. Note that journaling file systems don't use `fsck`; instead, they use a log to recover from problems. To use the `fsck` command, you need to know partition details. To view this information, use the `fdisk -l` command as shown to list the partition table, where you can determine the partitions that need a file system check:

```
fdisk -l


Disk /dev/sda: 21.5 GB, 21474836480 bytes
255 heads, 63 sectors/track, 2610 cylinders
Units = cylinders of 16065 * 512 = 8225280 bytes
Disk identifier: 0x000a4a82

Device     Boot   Start    End    Blocks      Id    System
/dev/sda1             1    144    1156648+    82    Linux swap/Solaris
/dev/sda2    *      145    1158    8144955    83    Linux
/dev/sda3         1159    2610    11663190    83    Linux LVM
```

Network Troubleshooting

Two commands that are useful for diagnosing networks are `ping` and `traceroute`. The `ping` command is used to send Internet Control Message Protocol (ICMP) packets to a remote host in an attempt to get the remote host to send back an Echo packet. By design, the `ping` command tests the connection between two computers, whether they're in the same room or across the world. To send an ICMP packet to a remote host, you use the `ping` command as shown in the following example (with line numbers added for readability):

```
1.  ping server1
2.  PING server1 (204.21.112.100) 56(84) bytes of data.
3.  64 bytes from 204.21.112.100: icmp_seq=1 ttl=128 time=108 ms
```

```
4.   64 bytes from 204.21.112.100: icmp_seq=2 ttl=128 time=106 ms
5.   64 bytes from 204.21.112.100: icmp_seq=3 ttl=128 time=94.9 ms
6.   ^C
7.   --- server1 ping statistics ---
8.   3 packets transmitted, 3 received, 0% packet loss, time 2003ms
9.   rtt min/avg/max/mdev = 94.941/103.174/108.212/5.882 ms
```

In this example, an ICMP Echo Request is sent to a remote host named `server1`. After `server1` receives it, it sends a reply. ICMP packets continue to be sent and received until you press Ctrl+C (see line 6). After you interrupt the `ping` process, `ping` statistics are displayed, as shown in lines 7 to 9. In this example, three packets were transmitted and three packets were received, which means no packets were lost. Line 9 gives you round-trip information. For instance, you can see the minimum, average, and maximum time for one packet to go from the host computer to the remote computer. Table 20-19 describes some common options used with the `ping` command.

Table 20-19 Common `ping` options

Option	Description
-b	Sends ICMP packets to a broadcast address.
-c	Short for "count"; used to send a specific number of ICMP packets.
-f	Short for "flood"; used to give a picture of how many packets are being dropped. For instance, if you use this option, packets sent display a . (period), and packets received simply show a backspace.
-i	Short for "interval"; used to set the amount of time between each sent packet.

When you're using the `ping` command to determine where the problem is in a network, you should ping your local host machine's NIC address first to make sure the network interface is configured correctly. Next, you should ping local host machines in the network as well as the default gateway and continue until you determine where the connection is broken. Keep in mind that an IP header is at least 20 bytes, and ICMP packets add another 8 bytes, which means you don't want to use the `ping` command repeatedly during normal business hours. Notice the time to live (TTL) value 128 on lines 3, 4, and 5; it sets the maximum number of IP routers a packet hits before being dropped.

The `traceroute` command is slightly different from the `ping` command because it tracks the route packets take through a network and displays the routers used along the way. Then it notifies you after the TTL has reached 0. For instance, the TTL is set to 1, and the packet is destroyed after it hits the first router. To find the next router, the TTL value is set to 2 and decreased by 1 after reaching each router. After it reaches 0, the packet is destroyed. This process continues until the packet reaches the target host. The `traceroute` command helps you determine where the connectivity problem is. The following example shows this command:

```
1.  traceroute -I 192.168.1.36
2.  traceroute to 192.168.1.36 (192.168.1.36), 30 hops max, 40 byte
packets using ICMP
```

```
3.  1  192.168.46.2 (192.168.46.2)   0.078 ms   0.009 ms   0.006 ms
4.  2  192.168.1.36 (192.168.1.36)   1.581 ms   2.990 ms   1.329 ms
```

Table 20-20 describes common options used with the `traceroute` command.

Table 20-20 Common `traceroute` options

Options	Description
-6 or -4	Forces `traceroute` to use IPv6 or IPv4
-F	Sets the "Don't Fragment" bit, which means the large packets aren't fragmented
-f #	Replaces # with a number to define the TTL value (set to 1 by default)
-I	Forces `traceroute` to use ICMP Echo packets instead of the default UDP packets
-m #	Replaces # with a number to define the maximum number of hops `traceroute` takes (set to 30 by default)
-T	Forces `traceroute` to use TCP packets instead of the default UDP packets

ACTIVITY

Activity 20-5: Using the `ping` and `traceroute` Commands

Time Required: 10 minutes

Objective: Use the `ping` and `traceroute` commands to check network connectivity.

Description: In this activity, you use the `ping` command on your host machine's IP address to determine that your TCP/IP settings are configured correctly. Then you use the `traceroute` command to ping your host machine's IP address.

1. If necessary, start VMware Player, start your openSUSE virtual machine, open a terminal window, and switch to the root user.

2. Use the **ping** command with your host machine's IP address. The host machine is the actual physical machine where VMware Player is installed. After three or four replies, press **Ctrl+C** to exit the process. If you aren't sure what the machine's hostname is, use the **ifconfig** command.

3. Were you able to ping your host machine's IP address? What was displayed onscreen?

   _____

   _____

4. Use the **traceroute** command to try to reach your host machine. For instance, if your host machine's IP address is 192.168.46.2, the command looks like this: **traceroute -I 192.168.46.2**. What's displayed onscreen? What's the purpose of the -I option?

   _____

   _____

5. Power off the virtual machine, and close all open windows.

Chapter Summary

- The Linux kernel performs two main tasks: servicing low-level hardware programming requirements and providing an environment for different processes in the computer.

- An OS can function in different modes, such as user mode or kernel mode.

- The Linux kernel's source code is stored under a group of directories known as the kernel source tree.

- A monolithic kernel is designed for a single architecture and interacts directly with hardware. In a modular kernel, all other parts of the kernel are compiled but not linked into the kernel, which helps save memory and increase portability.

- You can use the lsmod and insmod commands to manage Linux kernel modules. The zcat command is used to view the kernel configuration while it's running in real time.

- System monitoring is used to determine possible performance bottlenecks and errors.

- Monitoring CPU utilization determines where the majority of processing power is being consumed. Monitoring a network connection's bandwidth helps determine possible performance bottlenecks. Monitoring storage space, as on a hard drive, determines the amount of available storage space and pinpoints performance bottlenecks. System monitoring should also track memory use.

- The basic system-monitoring commands in Linux are top, vmstat, free, du, and df.

- The logrotate utility enables administrators to manage large numbers of log files by allowing automatic rotation, compression, removal, and mailing of log files.

- Linux includes GUI tools in GNOME and KDE for monitoring system resources and processes. Linux also has sophisticated system-monitoring tools, such as the sysstat package, consisting of the iostat and mpstat commands.

- Two frequently used resources that require tuning are hard drives and file systems.

- Preventive measures, such as making backups and maintaining configuration notes, can minimize the effect of critical situations. YaST System Restore, bundled with openSUSE Linux, can be used to back up data.

- In single-user mode, also known as maintenance mode, only the root partition is active and mounted.

- Grand Unified Boot Loader (GRUB) is a small program stored on the Master Boot Record (MBR) that can load one or more OSs.

- If you forget your root password, you can change it by editing the kernel entry in the GRUB menu screen.

- A useful command for fixing file system problems is fsck.

- Two commands that are useful for diagnosing networks are ping and traceroute. The ping command, which tests the connection between two computers, is used to send ICMP packets to a remote host in an attempt to get the remote host to send back an Echo packet. The traceroute command tracks the route packets take through a network and lists the routers a packet uses along the way.

Key Terms

boot loader   A small program stored on the Master Boot Record (MBR) that can load one or more OSs by reading file system information through a pointer from the disk partition containing OS files.

context switching   The CPU stops the currently running process and starts a new process.

Grand Unified Boot Loader (GRUB)   A flexible boot loader included in most current Linux distributions. *See also* boot loader.

interrupt handler   A special routine containing instructions for processing interrupts, which occur when the CPU suspends its current execution, saves the current work status, and transfers control to the interrupt handler.

kernel   The core part of the Linux OS that acts as an interface to hardware attached to the computer and manages communication between processes.

rescue mode   An OS mode booted from a repair disk that enables you to access files on the system's hard drive, even if you can't run Linux from it.

single-user mode   An OS mode in which only the root partition is active and mounted; also known as maintenance mode.

swapping   The technique of moving data pages from memory to a swap space on a hard drive.

system monitoring   The process of observing portions of a system for problems or anomalies; includes monitoring CPU utilization, network bandwidth, storage space use, and memory use.

Review Questions

1. Which of the following is a function the kernel performs? (Choose all that apply.)

    a. Acting as an interface to hardware attached to the computer

    b. Maintaining the system clock

    c. Managing communication between processes

    d. Storing running programs in RAM

2. Why might you want to recompile the Linux kernel?

3. Which of the following kernel types is compiled as a single block of code?

    a. Modular

    b. Core

    c. Production

    d. Monolithic

4. When loading a module with the `insmod` command, what default path does the system search in the kernel?

    a. `/modules/*/`

    b. `/src/linux/*/`

    c. `/lib/modules/*/`

    d. `/src/lib/*/`

5. What's the role of the `modprobe` command in managing kernel modules?

6. Which of the following tools is used to edit the `.config` file? (Choose all that apply.)

    a. `make oldconfig`

    b. `make config`

    c. `make menuconfig`

    d. `make .config`

7. Which of the following options indicates that the corresponding information isn't compiled in the kernel?

    a. `=n`

    b. `is not set`

    c. `=false`

    d. `=m`

8. The Linux `top` command displays which of the following? (Choose all that apply.)

    a. CPU use

    b. Swap space use

    c. The host machine's IP address

    d. The system's load averages

9. What command should you use to display disk use information for all files in the `/var/log` directory in kilobytes?

10. Which of the following is an important statistic to monitor with CPU utilization? (Choose all that apply.)

    a. Context switching

    b. Data transfer speed

    c. Interrupts

    d. Load percentages

11. When monitoring connection bandwidth, you know that if the number of I/O operations exceeds the specified data transfer speed, network connection performance increases. True or False?

12. Which command is used to report CPU utilization and I/O statistics for devices, partitions, and network file systems?

   a. mpstat

   b. iostat

   c. sysstat

   d. vmstat

13. You should monitor seek time and latency for which of the following system resources?

   a. CPU utilization

   b. Storage space

   c. Memory use

   d. Network bandwidth

14. Write the command that checks a file system for bad blocks and marks them as bad.

15. How does using the noatime option affect system performance?

   a. File access time speeds up.

   b. File access time slows down.

   c. File updates are faster.

   d. File modification times are faster.

16. Which of the following describes what the traceroute command does?

   a. Verifies network connectivity

   b. Determines response times of hosts

   c. Tracks IP addresses

   d. Displays the path packets take through a network

17. Which of the following commands extracts the backup_files archive's contents?

   a. pax -a -f backup_files

   b. pax -f backup_files

   c. pax -r -f backup_files

   d. pax -w -f backup_files

18. You use the fsck command to fix problems in a journaling file system. True or False?

Case Projects

Case Project 20-1: Researching the Linux Kernel

Because understanding the Linux kernel's architecture is important for system administrators, your manager has asked you to write a two- to three-page report, to be included in training manuals for new IT personnel, that explains how the kernel works and describes its major subsystems. Conduct research and write this report; include a description of new features in the latest Linux kernel, version 3.3.

Glossary

absolute path The full directory pathname starting from root (/).

address spoofing An attack most often used on packet-filter firewalls, which are configured to allow only known addresses to initiate connections; attackers forge their source IP addresses and cause damage just by sending packets randomly.

archive A file containing many other files called members; members are identified by their filename, owner, permissions, and modification time.

arithmetic logic unit (ALU) A component of the CPU responsible for mathematical and logical operations.

authentication The process of verifying a user's identity by checking for his or her username and password in a system database.

AutoYaST profile An ASCII XML configuration file used to configure an automatic openSUSE installation.

Berkeley Internet Name Daemon (BIND) Open-source software that contains all DNS protocols needed to resolve hostnames to IP addresses.

binary numbering system A numbering system consisting of only 1s and 0s; it's the language computers use.

bit Also known as a binary digit; a single binary value.

bookmarks A feature in KWrite for placing markers on lines of text to help navigate the file.

boot loader A small program stored on the Master Boot Record (MBR) that can load one or more OSs by reading file system information through a pointer from the disk partition containing OS files.

brute-force attacks In these attacks, potential intruders use every possible combination of characters to guess passwords or encryption keys until the correct one is found.

buffer An area of RAM used for temporary storage.

buffer overflow A condition in which data that has exceeded a buffer's storage capacity overflows into another buffer.

bus A channel that allows you to connect components such as a video card to your computer's processor.

cache A place where the CPU can store frequently accessed data and instructions.

caching A DNS feature that stores DNS queries on the local site for fast hostname–to–IP address resolution.

CGI scripts An executable script used to generate a dynamic Web page's contents.

clock speed The number of pulses per second generated by the oscillator on the motherboard.

command completion A BASH shell feature that finishes a command for you after you enter the first few characters; it's enabled by pressing the Tab key.

command mode A vim mode in which key combinations instead of text are used to enter commands.

command-line argument Information entered after a command to include specific instructions.

command-line prompt An interface that enables users to interact with the OS by typing commands, options, and arguments.

comment A piece of information added as documentation to scripts to explain their purpose.

Common Internet File System (CIFS) The successor to SMB that allows users on different OSs to share resources across the network.

Common UNIX Printing System (CUPS) A system that provides a printing interface on a local network; used to convert files into data a printer can process.

compiled program A program that converts source code to machine code and stores it in a binary file before the user runs the script. *See also* machine code.

compression The process of reducing the size of data to store information in less space.

configuration phase An openSUSE installation phase in which the network, Internet access, and hardware components are configured.

context switching The CPU stops the currently running process and starts a new process.

control unit (CU) A component of the CPU that regulates instructions.

copy-in mode The cpio mode in which files are extracted from an archive.

copy-out mode The cpio mode in which archives are created from the output of the `ls` or `find` command.

copy-pass mode The cpio mode in which files from one directory tree are copied to another without creating an archive.

cron daemon (crond) A system daemon that uses a configuration file called a cron table to schedule commands to run at set intervals. *See also* cron table.

cron table A configuration file that specifies tasks for the cron daemon to run at specific times.

current directory The directory a user is working in.

Cyrus A type of IMAP server designed to handle increased mail demands. *See also* Internet Message Access Protocol (IMAP).

daemons Programs that run in the background independently of the user. Typically, a daemon waits for specific system activity and then acts accordingly.

data mode One of three journaling modes first introduced in ext3. It's the slowest mode because it requires the file system to write every change twice: first to the journal and then to the file system.

default host The first declared virtual host in the Apache configuration file. *See also* virtual host.

demand paging A feature that makes it possible to load only the needed sections of a program into RAM. *See also* random access memory (RAM).

denial-of-service (DoS) attacks Attacks that overload a server with an overwhelming amount of network traffic so that it can't handle legitimate requests for network services.

device file A file in the /dev directory that represents a hardware device.

direct assignment A method used to assign a value to a variable by entering it explicitly in the command.

directives Instructions embedded in Apache configuration files that tell Apache how to run.

directory file A file that can contain regular files and other directory files.

disk quotas A Linux feature used to specify the maximum disk space allocated to each user.

distributed denial-of-service (DDoS) attack An attack in which a large number of traffic sources are used to generate bogus traffic to a single system.

DocumentRoot directive An Apache instruction that defines the directory path Apache uses to serve files for the host.

domain name The name of the network a host belongs to.

Domain Name System (DNS) A distributed and hierarchical database that allows controlling DNS management on the local site and is used to translate hostnames to IP addresses.

Dynamic Host Configuration Protocol (DHCP) A networking protocol used to assign IP addresses and other network configuration information to hosts automatically.

dynamic RAM (DRAM) The most common type of memory used in computers; stores information by refreshing the capacitors thousands of times per second.

environment variable A placeholder for data that can change; typically gets its value automatically at OS startup or from the shell the user is using.

execute A Linux file permission that allows users to run files (scripts or programs) or work in a directory.

exit status code A numeric code indicating success or failure that a program or command sends to the shell when it ends.

extended mode A vim mode in which advanced commands, such as saving files and searching and replacing, are available.

extended partition A primary partition that contains a logical partition.

extents In ext4, a set of contiguous physical blocks used to reduce fragmentation and improve performance.

extraction The process of unpacking an archive.

file server A network system where users can store and share files.

file system The way files and directories are stored and organized to make access to data easier.

Filesystem Hierarchy Standard (FHS) A standard specifying requirements and guidelines for file and directory placement in UNIX-like operating systems.

forwarder A type of DNS server that forwards unknown DNS requests generated on the local site to an off-site DNS server.

Fourth Extended (ext4) File System A journaling file system included with openSUSE Linux that offers better performance and increased reliability along with several new features, including unlimited subdirectories, extents, and multiblock allocation. *See also* extents.

fragmentation The process of packets being broken down into small packets to transmit them through different networks.

full backup Also known as a level 0 backup; it's an archive of all files in the file system.

GNOME applets Small programs available on the GNOME Panel for providing quick access to useful applications.

Grand Unified Boot Loader (GRUB) A flexible boot loader included in most current Linux distributions. *See also* boot loader.

group A category of file permissions given to the group of users assigned to a file.

group identifier (GID) A unique number corresponding to a group.

guest A virtual machine that uses the host's physical hardware resources.

hard disk drive (HDD) The main storage device; typically holds the largest amount of data in your computer.

hard limits Inflexible disk quota settings that don't allow users to go past a specified limit.

hard links Files that point to data on the hard disk and share the same inode number.

home directory A user's default directory on the file system.

host The physical computer where a virtual machine is installed.

host ID The second part of an IP address; identifies the computer or device on the network.

hostname A computer's machine name in the network.

hypertext Text with references or links embedded that take users to other files or text.

incremental backup An archive that contains only files modified since the last backup.

inode A data structure that stores information about a file, such as the inode number, file permissions, file owner, and so on; the file's actual data and name aren't stored in the inode.

inode number A unique identification for an inode that references an entry in the inode table. *See also* inode.

inode table A list of inodes for all files on a Linux partition; entries in this table point to where files' actual data is stored. *See also* inode.

insert mode A vim mode in which text that's typed is displayed onscreen.

installation phase An openSUSE noninteractive installation phase in which software is installed with the settings configured during the preparation phase.

Integrated Drive Electronics (IDE) A type of interface that connects up to four hard drives via a flat 40-wire parallel cable or a seven-pin connector.

Internet Control Message Protocol (ICMP) A protocol in the Internet layer of the TCP/IP model that generates IP error messages.

Internet Message Access Protocol (IMAP) An advanced client/server protocol for receiving e-mail from a server; includes options for storing and organizing e-mails on the server.

Internet Protocol (IP) The main protocol in the TCP/IP suite; contains addressing information that enables packets to be routed.

interpreted program A program that converts source code to machine code as it's running. *See also* machine code.

interrupt handler A special routine containing instructions for processing interrupts, which occur when the CPU suspends its current execution, saves the current work status, and transfers control to the interrupt handler.

IP address A unique number that identifies a computer or device on a TCP/IP network.

IP-based virtual hosts Multiple IP addresses for a single machine.

ISO image A virtual copy of a CD or DVD.

journaling A Linux file system feature that caches data in a hidden file until the kernel writes it to the hard drive.

kernel The core part of the Linux OS that acts as an interface to hardware attached to the computer and manages communication between processes.

level 1 (L1) cache The small RAM chip built into the CPU.

level 2 (L2) cache A small RAM chip that's connected directly to the CPU or incorporated into processors. It's larger and slower than an L1 cache and is capable of reading larger quantities of data from RAM.

level 3 (L3) cache A small RAM chip that's connected directly to the CPU when an L2 cache is used and is incorporated directly into the CPU in multicore processors. Similar functionality as an L2 cache but is even larger and slower.

log files Text files that gather information about a system continuously.

logical partition A partition that's created in one of the four primary partitions; begins with the drive number 5.

logical volume management (LVM) A technique for collecting information on free space from all disk partitions and storage devices into one logical volume.

looping Performing a set of commands repeatedly.

machine code A language consisting of binary 1s and 0s that a computer's CPU understands.

mail transfer agent (MTA) A program for sending and receiving messages between systems via SMTP. *See also* Simple Mail Transfer Protocol (SMTP).

mail user agent (MUA) An e-mail application that users run to access their mailboxes and send and receive e-mail.

man (manual) pages Documentation files that describe Linux shell commands, executable programs, system calls, special files, and so forth.

maps Multicolumn NIS database files storing key/value pairs that provide fast database access and speed up responses to client requests for configuration information.

markup language Consists of instructions called tags that define how text is displayed.

master name server An authoritative name server that stores primary copies of zone records.

members Files stored in an archive. *See also* archive.

metadata The contents of a label containing descriptive information about a software package.

mount Making a file system appear as though it's on a local machine.

mount point Typically an empty directory on the local file system that's used as a logical space to mount another file system.

multiboot A configuration that allows you to install more than one OS on a computer.

multiplier A number hard-wired into the CPU for determining processor speed.

multitasking A feature that allows running multiple processes at the same time.

multiuser A feature that enables multiple users to log on to a computer at the same time.

name server A central database that translates hostnames to IP addresses (or IP addresses to hostnames).

name-based virtual hosts Multiple Web sites sharing the same IP address.

NameVirtualHost directive An Apache instruction that specifies the IP address to use for name-based virtual hosts.

Network File System (NFS) A distributed file system protocol that allows remote access to shared resources across networks.

network ID The first part of an IP address; identifies the network on which the host is located.

Network Information Service (NIS) A client/server protocol that centralizes user and group IDS by providing database access so that network computers can share configuration information.

NFS server A Linux machine on the network that exports directories to all network hosts that have access to it.

NIS clients All hosts in an NIS-based network, including the master and slave servers.

NIS master server The center of the NIS network; contains the authoritative or primary copy of host configuration information (NIS maps) and makes it available over the network.

NIS slave servers Servers that maintain a copy of the host configuration information stored on the master server for redundancy; also used to distribute the load evenly between NIS servers.

octet An 8-bit binary number making up each of the four sets of numbers in an IPv4 address.

open source A licensing agreement term describing software that's distributed free with its source code so that users can view or modify it.

operating system (OS) Software designed to control computer hardware so that users and applications can make use of it.

options Information entered after a command to modify the way it's carried out.

Order, Allow, and Deny directives Apache instructions that define which hosts can and can't access the files in a particular directory.

ordered mode The default journaling mode, first introduced in ext3. It stores metadata, but it writes data first, which is important to prevent data corruption.

other A category of file permissions given to all users on a Linux system, as long as they aren't the file owner or don't belong to the group assigned to the file.

packet sniffer A program that captures and views packets as they're transmitted over a network.

packets Packages of data that are routed through the network.

partitioning The process of dividing a hard drive into logical sections; each one is a contiguous section of blocks treated as a separate physical drive.

patterns Collections of software packages that relate to a specific function, such as server software.

Pluggable Authentication Module (PAM) A system that provides a centralized mechanism for authenticating all services.

port An interface for connecting a hardware device, such as a disk drive or printer; in networking, a data connection established for communication between hosts.

positional parameter A method used to assign a value to a variable according to the order of arguments in the command.

Post Office Protocol 3 (POP3) A standard client/server protocol for receiving e-mail.

preemptive multitasking A method of multitasking in which the scheduler decides when a process stops and another process starts. *See also* multitasking.

preparation phase An openSUSE installation phase in which users can configure settings for language, time zone, desktop environment, hard disk setup, and user account and password.

primary group The group owner for all new files a user creates (specified in the /etc/passwd file).

primary partitions Partitions installed as part of the Linux boot sector. Linux supports only four primary partitions, which can be subdivided further. *See also* logical partition.

print queue A directory file where the printer daemon can store print jobs so that multiple users can use the same printer device.

printer device The physical printer that transfers a print job from a computer to actual hard copy.

printer driver The software used to manage a printer device. *See also* printer device.

process A program the kernel launches into memory for the purpose of performing specific tasks. *See also* kernel.

procmail A Linux utility used for filtering and sorting incoming e-mail.

programming language A set of rules for instructing a computer how to perform a task.

prompt method A method used to assign a value to a variable, in which the user is asked to enter data.

random access memory (RAM) The volatile storage space where a computer can read and write data.

read A Linux file permission that allows users to view the contents of files or directories.

read-only memory (ROM) Nonvolatile computer memory used to store data permanently.

refresh rate Number of times the display is refreshed per second.

relative path The directory pathname starting from the current directory.

remote printer queue A printer queue located on a different host in the local network.

Remote Procedure Calls (RPC) A protocol that allows one computer on a network to request a service from a program on another computer on the network.

repository A storage location that's usually a remote Web server; however, it can also be local (CD or DVD).

rescue mode An OS mode booted from a repair disk that enables you to access files on the system's hard drive, even if you can't run Linux from it.

resolution The number of horizontal and vertical pixels a monitor is capable of displaying.

resource record A file containing resource information or characteristics about a zone or domain.

root A special user account with full access to all system resources.

root DNS servers DNS servers that control the top-level domains (TLDs) of the Internet.

RPM dependencies A feature of the RPM utility that determines whether a software package requires the capabilities of another application to run and then displays this information.

RPM Package Manager (RPM) A utility for installing and managing software packages.

runlevel The operating state of the Linux OS.

Samba An open-source tool that provides an interface between two OSs, such as Linux and Windows, by using SMB/CIFS. *See also* Common Internet File System (CIFS) *and* Server Message Block (SMB).

Second Extended (ext2) File System A replacement for the extended file system that doesn't support journaling. Features include support for standard UNIX file types, larger partition sizes, variable-length filenames up to 255 characters, and reservation of blocks for root.

secondary groups Additional groups the root user assigns to other users on the system.

Secure Shell (SSH) A remote login program designed to provide a secure encrypted connection to a host on the network.

Serial Advanced Technology Attachment (SATA) An advanced IDE interface for high performance and better reliability; it uses a much thinner cable, which simplifies cabling and improves airflow in the system.

server farms A group of servers networked together in a single location.

Server Message Block (SMB) A protocol that gives client computers read and write access to a server on the network.

ServerAdmin directive An Apache instruction that specifies the Apache administrator's e-mail account.

ServerAlias directive An Apache instruction that associates multiple names with a virtual host.

ServerName directive An Apache instruction that defines the server name and tells Apache which virtual host to display.

session hijacking A specialized form of address spoofing in which a hijacker assumes unauthorized control of a network session.

shareable file A file that can be stored on one machine and used by multiple users on other machines.

shell A command-line interface between users and the kernel. *See also* kernel.

shell script A text file containing a sequence of commands.

shell variable A placeholder for data that can change; typically gets its value from the user or shell script.

Simple Mail Transfer Protocol (SMTP) The TCP/IP protocol that defines how e-mail is sent across a network.

single-user mode An OS mode in which only the root partition is active and mounted; also known as maintenance mode.

skeleton directory A directory containing files copied to every new user's home directory by default.

slave name server An authoritative name server that receives its zone information from the master name server. *See also* master name server.

small computer systems interface (SCSI) An interface typically used to connect hard drives in a server rather than a home desktop; it's faster and more expensive and creates more noise and heat than other types of hard disk interfaces.

smart update An RPM feature that retains the previous version's configuration file.

snapshot file A file specified as an argument to the `--listed-incremental` option, which is designed to tell the tar utility which files have been changed, added, or deleted since the last backup.

soft limits Flexible disk quota settings that warn users when they're approaching the hard limit. *See also* hard limits.

software package An archive of related files, such as configuration, data, and documentation files, constituting a software application.

source code A set of instructions defining how a program works.

standard input A source of input, usually the keyboard.

standard output A source of output, usually the screen.

Start of Authority (SOA) A mandatory resource record in a zone file that contains basic information about the zone. *See also* resource record.

static files Files that don't change on their own.

static RAM (SRAM) Memory capable of storing information without the need to refresh its capacitors, as long as there is power to the computer.

subnet mask A method for determining which part of an IP address is used for the network ID and which part is used for the host ID.

subtree checking A process the NFS server uses to check whether a requested file is in the exported subdirectory.

swap partitions Partitions on the HDD that the Linux kernel uses for storing pages from RAM.

swapping The technique of moving data pages from memory to a swap space on a hard drive.

symbolic links Special types of files that point to other files (even on separate partitions or different computers) instead of pointing to data on the hard drive; they don't share the same inode number. *See also* hard links.

syntax highlighting A text editor feature for displaying text in different colors and fonts for programming languages.

system backup The process of copying files and directories to an archive for the purpose of retrieval in the event of a system failure.

system monitoring The process of observing portions of a system for problems or anomalies; includes monitoring CPU utilization, network bandwidth, storage space use, and memory use.

tags Instructions for formatting text in HTML. They come in pairs to indicate the start and end of text formatted with these instructions.

TCP Wrappers A widely used tool for logging connections and controlling access to network services.

text editor A program that enables users to create or edit plain text files.

Third Extended (ext3) File System A Linux file system that supports journaling and a maximum file size of 2 TB.

time to live (TTL) The amount of time a DNS server caches a resource record. *See also* resource record.

Transmission Control Protocol (TCP) A connection-oriented protocol responsible for keeping track of packets and reassembling them into a single file after they've arrived.

Transmission Control Protocol/Internet Protocol (TCP/IP) Also known as the Internet Protocol suite, it's an internationally accepted set of rules for connecting computers to the Internet and most other networks.

Trojan programs Hidden scripts embedded in authorized programs.

Uniform Resource Locator (URL) An address to a resource on the Internet.

unshareable file A file that can be used only on the local machine.

user A category of file permissions given to the owner of a file.

User Datagram Protocol (UDP) A connectionless protocol that uses IP to get packets from one computer to another; used when a faster transfer rate is more important than the accuracy of the data being sent.

user identifier (UID) A unique number representing the username.

variable files Files that can change on their own.

video adapter cards Expansion devices that plug into a bus on the motherboard; used to send graphical information to the monitor.

virtual host An Apache feature that makes it possible to run multiple domains on one physical machine.

virtual machine (VM) A software container with its own OS, IP address, and applications.

Web server A computer on the network with the primary role of serving Web pages to clients on request.

wildcard A character used in searches to specify certain conditions.

workspace An area of the desktop that can contain different windows and processes.

write A Linux file permission that allows users to edit the contents of files or add files to a directory.

writeback mode One of three journaling modes first introduced in ext3 that writes only metadata.

X Window System A system that provides a method for writing device-independent graphics and windowing software that can be transferred from one computer to another easily.

zone file A text file that stores DNS zone data.

zones Portions of the domain namespace.

Index